STRONGER THAN EVER

Psychography by
ELIANA MACHADO COELHO

By the Spirit
SCHELLIDA

English Translation:
Olenka Muñoz Dávila
Lima, Peru, May 2021

Original title in Portuguese:
"Mais Forte do que Nunca"
© Eliana Machado Coelho

Revision:
Claudia Fernanda Tasayco Morón

World Spiritist Institute
Houston, Texas, USA
E–mail, contact@worldspiritistinstitute.org

About the medium

Eliana Machado was born in Sao Paulo, the capital city, on october 9th. Since her childhood, she was in touch with the Spiritism, and the continuous presence of the spirit Schellida in her life, who until now, appeared as a beautiful, delicate, sweet smile and always lovely young woman that had already heralded a solid partnership between Eliana and the beloved mentor for the work they would do together.

The time passed by. Protected by her lovely parents, her grandfathers, and later, by her husband and a daughter, Eliana, always with Schellida by her side, she was working. After years of studies and training in psychographics, in July, 1997, wrote her first book called: *"Despertar para la Vida"*, a book that Schellida wrote barely in twenty days. Later, other books were written, among them, *Corazones sin Destino*.

This work is about natural curiosities about this duo (medium and spirit) that is amazed by the beauty of the received love stories. One of them is about the origin of the name Schellida. Where did this name come from and who is Schellida? Eliana answered us that this name, Schellida, came from a real story between them and, by the ethic, she will leave the revelation on behalf of the mentor herself, since Schellida warned her that she will write a book recounting the main part of her terrestrial trajectory and the love affair with the medium. For that reason,

Schellida once stated that, if she had to write books using another medium, she would sign with a different name, so as to preserve the suitability of the worker without making her go through dubious, questioning, embarrassing and dispensable situations, since the name of a spirit matters little. What prevails is the moral content and the high teachings transmitted through the reliable works.

Eliana and the spirit of Schellida have many published books (among them, the best ones, *The Right to be Happy, No Rules to Love, A Reason to live, Awakening to life and A Diary through Time*). Other unpublished ones will go into production soon, in addition to the old works to be reissued. In this way, the Schellida spirit guarantees that the task is large and there is a long road to be hackneyed by them, who will always continue together to bring teachings about love on the spiritual plane, the concrete consequences of the Law of Harmonization, the happiness and achievements of each one of us, because good always wins when there is faith.

Table of Contents

1.– THE SHADOW OF DREAMS

THE SHADOW of the great building under construction lay in the bright, intense light of that sunny morning.

Wearing a safety helmet, holding a clipboard in one hand and a pen in the other, the architect spoke to the foreman and gave him precise instructions to follow.

"That's right Dr. Abner. I'll do it well. You can rest assured."

"Thanks, Mr. Antonio." Said the architect politely.

Almost interrupting them, the engineer, who was visiting the construction site with his colleague, called him:

"Abner! Did you see the foundations of the garages that will be under the pools." Asked a nervous voice.

"Not yet. What about them." He asked calmly as always.

"We'll have to dismantle two columns that were miscalculated. Goddamn! I swear I'm going to fire Zé. This is the second time something like this has happened."

"What's the height of the columns?"

"It's more than a meter!" He replied, still nervous "The measurements are wrong. It was very clear. He was supposed to calculate the rafters from the foundation beams, but he didn't. I hate stupid people!"

"Calm down. I will go and check it out. Maybe there is a solution."

"There is not, Abner!"

Calmly, the architect went to the place the other was talking about and began to make new calculations while carefully examining the plans in his hands. Meanwhile, his colleague kept complaining, until Abner agreed:

"In fact, Ivan… you are right. The measurement is wrong. However…"

"However?! The kid is stupid!"

"But someone should have accompanied him when he was installing the frame and placing the braces. He is neither an engineer nor an architect. He just obeys orders. He did not study for that."

"But he miscalculated! Look at the damage!" Ivan was nervous.

"Do not demand something from those who shall not do it. The obligation to accompany him when he made the iron frame was yours."

"Do not tell me that…"

"Calm down, please…" He asked in a calm tone while extending his hand in his colleague's direction. "Give me one day. Do you see that area where the ramp to the garages will be?" The other nodded and Abner continued. "Since that part was not done, I think I have an idea. I'm going to work on it today and we will take a look at it tomorrow. I think we will even have more natural light coming from there." He pointed out.

Abner's colleague seemed disdainful, hesitant. But he said nothing. At that moment, Abner's cell phone rang and walking away he asked.

"Excuse me." Then he answered in a cheerful tone. "Hey, Rúbia! Is everything alright?"

"Almost everything. Did you talk with the people in the company?" Asked the sister.

"Not yet. I'm at work. From here I will go to the office and call an acquaintance of mine."

"Oh, Abner... I can't stand being at home anymore. One thing about dad...!"

"Calm down, little sister..." He laughed. "I'll find a solution. What am I not doing for you?" He laughed again.

"I just can't take it anymore. You said you were going to talk to your acquaintance today."

Looking at his watch, the young man expressed himself in a funny way:

"Today is until midnight. It's still ten in the morning. I think I have plenty of time, right?"

"You know how I feel. I'm anxious, nervous... I don't know how to run out of work."

"Just relax. Give the resume another review, go online... get distracted a bit."

"I'm sorry I bothered you."

"You never bother me, Rúbia. Now I'm going to the office. Later, if I have news, I will give you a call. Okay?"

"That's ok. I'll wait. Thanks… Kisses."

"Kisses. Bye."

After hanging up, the young man saw that the foreman seemed to be waiting for the call to end.

"¿Mr. Abner?"

"Yes, Mr. Antonio."

"Look... I think Mr. Ivan was a bit wrong." He said as they walked side by side.

"Why do you think that?"

"I even saw him when he told Zé to drill right there for the frames."

"Are you sure, Mr. Antonio?"

"Yes, I'm sure. And the poor Zé is not here, otherwise he would confirm it." Faced with the architect's silence, the man said; "I don't want to cause problems, but I think it's unfair to fire Zé for something he did not do."

Approaching where his car was parked, Abner put his hand over Antonio's shoulder and reassured him;

"Nothing will happen to Zé. Be sure about that. It is just that Ivan is nervous."

"Yes... he is always nervous. Right, Mr. Abner?"

The other man smiled, patted him on the back and said;

"Leave it, we will fix this. Don't worry. See you tomorrow Mr. Antonio."

"See you tomorrow…"

After getting into his vehicle, placing the clipboard and plans on the seat next to him, the young man headed for the office where he worked and was a partner.

✳ ✳ ✳

In the late afternoon, Abner called Rúbia, who was euphoric:

"Wow! I don't believe it! You made it!"

"I did not do a thing! I just scheduled an interview for you tomorrow morning. You must be able to present yourself properly to take up the job."

"Leave it to me!"

"Look, Rúbia!"

"Tell me."

9

"The company, as far as I know, is a familiar, conservative type. I know you dress properly. Don't get me wrong, but... I'm just going to reinforce it so that you can attend without showing your legs above your knees, your shoulders, your lap..." He laughed. "Do you understand?"

"Of course! You did not even need to say it. Still, thanks for the reminder. I won't even wear perfume." He laughed too.

"And... well remembered. A very mild cologne works well. We must not disturb others with our smell. Use a little and whoever likes it will come closer to smell it better."

The sister laughed out loud and said;

"You can be at ease. I know how to do it right"

"I know. I'm sure you can do it"

"Thanks Abner. I don't know how I'm going to pay you for this"

"I know! I know just how you are going to pay me!" He said jokingly and with a bratty voice.

They continued talking animatedly for a while. She was cheerful with the opportunity and started asking more questions about the company.

✳ ✳ ✳

Rúbia, who was well qualified, got the job she wanted. Recently, she was feeling fulfilled and very happy.

She was a smart woman, in her twenty-nine years. Beautiful, tall, tanned, a kind of smooth skin whose color was naturally tanned. She had long, curly hair, but she preferred to wear it straight, because she liked it that way. Her big brown eyes were very expressive. She had beautiful fleshy lips, where she always wore a striking lipstick that further emphasized her beauty.

Since the beginning of her new job, she came home with a lively expression of joy and cheerfulness.

That day, when she walked into the kitchen, she saw Abner making his food by the stove, full of pots and pans.

"Hello disappeared!" She greeted him, giving him a kiss on the cheek.

"Hello! You are the missing one!"

"I got back to the gym, so I won't be coming home early for a few days."

"What about the company? Everything ok?"

Excited, she replied.

"If it gets better, it will be spoiled. I'm loving it. There is too much to do. I lead a team of twenty employees. The other manager, who left the job, abandoned it in the biggest disaster. The staff was lost." She laughed.

At that moment, Rúbia took the pot and grabbed a small piece of chicken. She was about to put it in her mouth when her mother, walking in without being seen, slapped her and complained.

"Take your dirty hand out of my pots!"

"Oh! You scared me mom!" She exclaimed and laughed when she saw the piece of chicken fall to the ground, after picking it up and throwing it away, she requested. "The blessing, mother."

"God bless you. But don't be crazy, Rúbia. You come from the street, your hands are dirty and you want to eat like that? Have mercy! Go wash yourself, take a shower... then you will eat."

"It's just that the smell is killing me, mommy. I can't resist it." She expressed herself in a pampered tone.

"Then, at least go and wash your hands. The news that your dad is watching on the TV is ending and he's coming to dinner.

11

Let's eat together. We haven't been together for dinner in a long time."

"I will be right back." Her mother agreed, so she left, coming back without delay. "I'm starving. I'll take a shower later."

Mr. Salvador, already seated at the head of the table, waited for Mrs. Celeste to finish preparing his plate and complained;

"Rogue and scoundrel politicians. They promise this and that, but then they spend the town's money on an entourage of more than five hundred people to travel abroad. While the leaders of other countries, who also attended the same convention, took an entourage of fifty people or less! Look how ridiculous!"

"After retiring, you only know how to watch the news and complain about politics and people... Keep calm, and check if you can eat in peace." Argued his wife, serving him the steaming plate.

"The food is delicious, mom! I will even repeat it." Said Abner, standing up.

Mrs. Celeste was filled with pride when, trying to be humble, she answered;

"Why, son... What's that? Mom did what she always does."

When he walked by his mother's side, Abner kissed her on the cheek and waited for his sister to finish preparing her own plate.

They were all seated when the young man asked:

"And there, Rúbia? What is it like to work with Jefferson?"

"Very well. He is a very quiet director."

"I have known him for a short time. He seems to be a nice person." Said her brother.

"Everyone is nice to you, Abner. Everyone." Said the father in a critical tone.

"It's just that he does not see people as bad as you do, Salvador." His wife replied.

"People who do not see the evil in others end up being trampled on. They get their faces broken." Replied the man.

"Dad, let us eat in peace. Don't start..." Softly asked Rúbia.

"That's right, let's change the subject." Suggested Mrs. Celeste cheerfully.

"I agree." Said Mr. Salvador with his mouth full of food. "And in this new job, you'll earn more than in that bank, right?"

"Pretty much the same, dad. I can't complain or demand anything yet. I've been working for a short time. I have to thank God for getting such a good job. I was unemployed for four months. It was not easy for me."

"It's a great advertising and marketing company. Very well respected in the market." Said Abner in turn.

"You would earn more if you had not withheld taxes. It is absurd how much we pay in taxes in this country." Said the father, complaining again with his mouth full.

"If you stopped smoking and drinking, Salvador, we would pay even less taxes." Mrs. Celeste replied.

"Do not bother me, woman. Do not bother me." He murmured, looking at his wife with dissatisfaction.

"Daughter, you have to come to church with me to pay for a promise I made to Our Lady. If you got a good job, we would both bring flowers to the altar for her." Rúbia did not speak.

A few minutes passed and, seeing her son get up and take the plate to the sink, the lady asked affectionately;

"Do you want milk pudding, Abner? I thought of you, son."

"Ok! Yes, of course." He answered with a smile.

13

"It's only for Abner that she does things. She just thinks about him." Her husband complained.

"It is just that when I make a cake, a dessert or any meal thinking of him, he does not go away. They say that when we do things thinking of someone and it works, the person we think of has a good heart."

"So, why did you not think of me?" Said the husband.

"Because if I make a cake thinking of you, it won't rise. It turns into a stone."

"Jeez..! You are the one full of things." Seeing his son fill himself with the sweet. "Come on... give me a piece."

Mrs. Celeste smiled impishly and served him a piece of the desert. It was then that Rúbia asked;

"Mom, what about Simone? Did she call?"

"I called her. Your sister said she will go to see the doctor tomorrow. They're very happy."

"Have you thought about it, mom? When you have your first grandchild, how will it be? Then you will not bake a cake thinking of me, you will only think of him." Said Abner emphatically and laughed.

"And you? When will you marry and give us grandchildren? You are the only one who will give continuity to my name and that of your grandfather." Interrupted Mr. Salvador in a rude way.

In silence, the young man stared at him and replied;

"I'm not getting married, dad. That is not in my plans." Saying that, he placed his dessert plate on the sink. He was leaving the kitchen when he heard his father say;

"I thought I had a man, but I do not."

"Salvador! Stop it! Are you going to start?" Shouted Mrs. Celeste.

"What do you want me to say to you?! He is thirty-five years old, he doesn't want to get married, and he lives here at my expense...!"

"I may live in your house, but I don't live at your expense, father." Replied the young man strongly and immediately. "I work and earn very well. If this house depended only on your pension..." He did not finish his speech. However, after a brief pause, he finished. "If my presence bothers you, you should know that I'm preparing everything to get out of here."

Affirming this, he turned and left while Mr. Salvador still complained:

"Where are you going? Living with whom? You think life is easy, right?"

"Salvador!"

"Dad!"

Mother and daughter exclaimed at the same time.

It didn't take long for Rubia to go to her brother's room and knock on the door.

"Come in." Said the young man, lying on the bed, face up, with his hands folded behind his neck.

Settling down on the edge of the bed beside him, face down, he rested his elbows on the bed and held his chin in his hands. Seeing him thoughtful, she asked;

"When you said you were going to get out of here, you were not serious, were you?"

"I was. I'm looking for an apartment. Something small, just for me. I intend to live there until the one I bought at the plant is ready."

"If you are leaving, I want to go with you. I cannot get along with dad. Did you see how he was today? And look, he didn't drink. When he drinks, no one can stand him."

"He is right, Rúbia. I'm thirty-five years old. I'm too old. I can support myself very well. There is no reason for me to stay here. In fact, I did not leave before because of mom. I feel sorry for her. However... the time has come."

The sister approached, pressed her face to his chest and hugged him around the waist, saying softly;

"Will you have a place for me in your apartment?"

"A permanent place, no. You can even go to sleep there from time to time." Despite the playful tone in his voice, he was sincere.

"Oh Abner! How selfish!" She complained in a spoiled way.

"I definitely want independence, little sister."

"You will continue helping here at home financially, right?" She wanted to know, curious.

"I will, of course. Even if you help them, I know it will not be enough. What dad contributes out of his pension is not enough. I don't want to see you with any difficulty. I will not abandon you. I just need my place, a space, you know?"

"To be honest... sometimes I think about finding a place for myself too. The idea of independence appeals to me a lot. However, I'm afraid of some financial instability. Look, I was fired in that personnel cut and I was unemployed for four months. I rent an apartment, fix it up, and suddenly I lose my job. It's different with you. A partner of an architecture and engineering firm that worked so well! My God!" She laughed. "Instead of administration, I should have studied engineering or architecture. I see you earn so well and, from now on, you will only prosper."

After a moment she said.

"Oh... I admire you so much... We are so different. You are so peaceful, confident, you know what you want in your life... Everything you do works."

"It's funny how others see me. Nobody really knows what is going on inside of me. They think that I'm calm, that I do not suffer, that I do not feel sad, that I do not have intimate conflicts... You see me as if I were not made of flesh and blood."

Moving away from the embrace, the sister sat up, stared at him and said:

"You will agree with me that you are the most peaceful creature in this family. No..." She corrected himself. "You are the most peaceful and balanced person we know."

Abner's cell phone rang at that moment. He quickly sat down to pick it up, but his sister reached for the device first, looked at the screen, and informed when she handed it to him.

"David."

The young man took his cell phone, verified the name, but did not answer, and hung up.

"You are not going to answer?"

"No. I will speak to him tomorrow."

"I think David is the only friend you have and we don't know him. Talking of friends... Ricardo is lost, right?"

"Due to those personal problems, he buried himself in work. But he is doing well, he has recovered a lot. As for David... someday you will meet him. You will love his mother, Mrs. Janaina. She is a loving person."

Rúbia got closer, kissed his cheek and said:

"Thank you. I do not think I have thanked you enough for getting me that job yet."

17

"You would do the same for me" He smiled as generously as always.

"I'm going to take a shower and go to sleep. I have to get up early tomorrow." Looking him straight in his eyes, she said tenderly. "Thank you for everything. For being the elder brother that you are." She smiled. "God could not have given me a better brother."

"Stop it." Reaching her hair, he tousled them as he played.

She kissed him again, got up, and left. Minutes later, Rúbia went to the bathroom and went through the door of her brother's room, which was half open, and heard him say:

"It's me. Hi, when you called my sister was with me. I could not answer." There was a brief pause. "And I wanted to know; was he there to sign the papers?" Another pause. "That's true. The staff is still strange. An apartment in the name of two men is not common. Everything must be done in the name of both. Is better this way. It's more secure. Did you tell your mother?"

As he asked the question, Abner approached the door to close it and Rúbia moved quickly away so as not to be seen. But she was intrigued. His brother may perhaps be talking to David. He was the only one who called while they were together. Why would the documentation for the apartment be done in someone else's name? Who was this friend that she did not even know? Was it the apartment that he was about to rent or the one he bought and was being built?

Pondering these and other questions, she planned to discuss the matter with her brother. She would need to find an opportunity. Perhaps would even tell him that she overheard the conversation.

✳ ✳ ✳

Simone's pregnancy made everyone very happy. She was the second daughter of Mrs. Celeste. She was thirty-two years old, married to Samuel for five years.

"Do you know what it is, daughter?"

"Not yet. It is too soon. I can't wait to confirm the sex to make the baby's bassinet, decorate the room... Ahhh... I saw every little thing in a baby clothing store!" She expressed herself in a kind and gentle way. "You have to see it, mom."

"These modern things about knowing the sex of the baby just get in the way. They take the surprise away. In the past, when you did not have any of this, it was much better." Said Mr. Salvador.

"Oh, dad, it will be good to make the trousseau in the right color, decorate the room, buy toys..."

"It's true. There is one type of toy for a girl and another for a boy. The other day I saw wallpapers for a boy's room that were so beautiful. There was one with strollers and parachutes with teddy bears for boys, and others with strawberries, little houses and dolls for girls. There was one that was just a strip, it was not placed on the entire wall. It was so beautiful!" Mrs. Celeste cheered up.

"I have also seen it. That is why I want to know if it's a boy or a girl." Said Simone.

"If the baby is a girl, I'd give her the earrings." Said the lady as her daughter laughed and commented;

"Nowadays earrings are not just for girls, Mom."

Mr. Salvador took the opportunity and gave a rude opinion, as always.

"It is true. There's a lot of shamelessness in someone who says he's a man and has an earring. So disgusting! A man who is a man does not use these indecencies. If I find my son using an earring, I will rip his ears off. He will know me!"

"Salvador, stop being a beast! How can you criticize everything you see? You can't say anything near this man, because he always has something bad to add."

"It's just that I'm telling the truth. That's why you guys don't like it. For me, a man with long hair and earrings is not a man. He only needs to wear a skirt."

"Dad, Jesus had long hair and used to wear a dress." The man was silent. He seemed to have been taken by surprise. "Mom is right. You have to think that people cannot be the same. They have the right to be different. And being different is to be normal. Everyone should be happy in their own way, as long as they do not disturb others."

"It is not like that. If I had a business, I would fire an employee if he wore earrings or got a tattoo. This is something criminal, a jailhouse thing, a convict thing."

"Dad, I agree that the tattoos of yesteryear, the ones done in prisons, were things of that type of people, as you say. But nowadays, there are tattoos that are works of art and there are people who want to express or expose art on their body. I would not like to have one on me. So far, I do not think about getting one. There is nothing I would want to express on my skin for the rest of my life. Anyone who does something like this on their body should remember that it is for the rest of their lives. I do not criticize anyone who wants to show, on their skin, what they feel, in their mind, in their heart. The tattoo is like a work of art where each artist shows his inner self, his ideas, his desires, his will, his way of seeing life. But in tattooing, the person chooses an image and tells the tattoo artist to do what he wants to show."

"The other day I saw a young woman with such beautiful butterflies on her back." Said the lady.

"There are people, mom, who want to show their joy for life and get tattoos of butterflies, stars, angels, flowers, fairies, enigmatic or philosophical things like dragons, Buddha or meaningful symbols. Others need to express tribal things, because they are part of a group of friends, for example. Now, there are people who want to show their revolt for life and tattoo things that we consider ugly like skulls, horrible animals, desperate human bodies in the middle of flames? Others even put horns implanted under the skin of the forehead and other things that are aggressive to human nature. Each one shows, on his body, through the tattoo or whatever, what is in his heart. Undoubtedly, everyone will be responsible for what they do. Just as we are responsible for what we say and think, we are responsible for what we show on our bodies. We have the power to enliven, sadden or attack the life around us."

"It does not matter to me. A tattoo is a tattoo, period." The man protested.

"Come on, Simone. Let's go to the kitchen. Leave your father here watching TV and the news. This is how this man doesn't complain or criticize others."

Mother and daughter went to the kitchen and, sitting at the table, Simone commented:

"Every day dad gets more and more intolerant!"

"I'm going to brew some coffee for us."

"Dad was not like this, was he, mother?"

"He was always a complainer. He complained about everyone. But in the last few years, he started criticizing, complaining a lot... As you said, every day is worse."

"He does not care. He hardly goes out, he has no friends, he does not walk outside, does not go to church..."

"No, daughter. He does not do any of that. He only knows how to sit in front of the TV all day watching the news, tragedies, crime... And when he's not watching that, he watches violent movies. I already told him that's bad. But your father is hopeless."

"Watching a newscast to catch up is good. But the obsessive way he does it... is wrong. The pleasure in following news of crimes, violence, kidnappings, and more tragedies? Wow! This is harmful to the mind and will certainly be reflected in the body. We are impregnating ourselves with negative energies. Few people know that when we see or hear something violent or aggressive, our brain interprets it as being near us or with us, even if it is something fictitious like a simulation, a fabrication. And our body reacts with violent and unnecessary hormonal charges that cause great physical stress. With that, we get exhausted. Then, when a real situation that makes us nervous arises, we can feel extremely irritated, depressed and exhausted, because we have already stressed ourselves unnecessarily with simulated things and situations."

"Your father does not understand that. I wish an angel of kindness would appear in front of him to make this man understand and change his attitude. After retirement, he never stops smoking, he drinks almost every day. Did you see the curtains behind the couch where he sits to watch TV?" Before the daughter answered, she continued; "They are yellow, horrible. The worst thing is that the dirty cigarette smoke doesn't even come out when I wash them."

"I think it is because of the fabric type."

"Imagine how your father's lungs are. The worst thing is that I end up smoking without being a smoker. There must be a law against smoking at home when another person that lives there does not smoke."

"Ask him to go smoke outside."

"Do you think I have not asked him? I can't deal with your father. If I tell him anything, he starts a fight."

"If only he was busy…"

"He could help me with the housework. Dry the dishes, pick up the clothes, take out the garbage, sweep the yard... But nothing! He is only retired. I will never retire. There is the cleaning lady to help, but you know a maid does not do everything."

"Have you asked him to dry a plate, for example? Maybe dad will help."

"I have already asked him. He replied that he is retired. That he has already worked what he needed to work."

After a brief pause Mrs. Celeste offered her daughter a cup of coffee, saying;

"It's delicious."

"Thanks, mom." She took a sip of coffee and then confirmed. "It is delicious."

"So, tell me, Simone." Asked her, smiling, seated in front of her daughter. "Samuel is excited about your pregnancy?"

"Oh! Yes, he is! You have to see him. He told everyone in college." She laughed as she said. "He doesn't want me to go upstairs, carry weight... He acts like a fool." She smiled. "Every night, before going to sleep, he talks to the baby."

"You have a good husband. I think it took you both a long time to get you pregnant."

"Not at all. It was all at the right time. I'm happier as I have never been in my life." Simone said with a bright smile. Then she asked. "Mom, Abner told me that he got an apartment for rent and is leaving home. I have laughed, I did not believe it. Is it true?"

"That is right. You know your brother. He helps everyone and everything, but he is a very reserved young man. Nobody really knows what he is thinking."

"Abner has always been very calm, quiet. That is all."

"No, my daughter. It is not just that. I think your brother is too quiet."

"It's just the way he is. I just think it's weird that he leaves home."

"We will see if you want to have his little life without satisfying anybody. Isn't it the same?" Said the mother, trying to find a justification for the situation.

In that moment, Mr. Salvador walked into the kitchen and complained;

"I could smell the coffee from the living room. I was waiting for someone to bring me a cup, but nothing. Everyone forgets about me."

"It's impossible to forget about you. I was going to bring it to you. It only took me a while." Answered Mrs. Celeste, taking a cup to pour the coffee.

"I heard you talk about your brother. That young man worries me a lot."

"Don't complain about him, dad." Said Simone, firmly. "To this day, Abner has never caused you any trouble. He always worked, studied, did not get involved with bad companies…"

"I don't know… I feel like he is still up to something. Everything is going very well for him. He studied, met with friends and created a construction company or whatever... He works, he earns well... But I just don't know. He needs to get married and have children. He would have something important to worry about. Until then, with no occupation in my personal life, he will still give me a headache."

Mrs. Celeste, used to her husband's comments, paid him no attention. She poured coffee and tried to change the subject.

2.– THE TRUTH ALWAYS EMERGES

IT HAD PASSED SOME TIME since Rúbia started working at her new job. She was satisfied with the service and with the new colleagues. Everything was going well. She had become close friends with Talita, a manager from another area, and they were always together.

That day, at lunch time, Talita asked:

"Today Silvana will deliver the cosmetics we bought, right?"

"It's today. Ah! I can't wait to wear that lipstick. It is so beautiful, is it?

"In a mouth like yours, Rúbia, everything looks fine." Her friend laughed.

"Let me ask you something…" The conversation changed. "What do you think about Jefferson?"

"The manager?"

"Yes."

"I'm not sure... I don't know him very well. He is a reserved man. We don't know much about him. What I know about him is…"

She was interrupted.

"I think he is a handsome man in his forties." She laughed amused.

"Yes, he is handsome. I think his wife must be very jealous." Smiling Talita concluded.

"Is Jefferson married?!" Asked Rúbia, surprised.

"I think he is."

"He does not wear a ring or talk about his family, his wife…"

"Rúbia, why do you think every man has to wear a ring? Be realistic!"

"Do you think he is…"

"What? Married?"

"Yes"

"Why the tension, Rúbia? Did he hit on you?" She joked.

"No… I'm just curious."

The friends continued talking, but that topic came up again in Rúbia's mind.

On the early Friday night, Jefferson had his car parked on a street near the company where he worked. Rúbia, hurriedly, fleeing the rain, opened the door of the vehicle and sat down.

"I thought you would not come because of the weather." He says.

"Hi, everything alright?"

"Yes." He answered, kissing her quickly. Then he asked: "Do you want to go to a special place?"

"I need to talk to you first." She said, staring at him. Rúbia had been thinking about the same thing all afternoon and wanted to ask him about it so that he would answer truthfully. Then she ventured. "I heard from someone in the company that you are married."

Jefferson seemed to expect that finding at some point. He smiled for a moment and answered with a calmed voice.

"I'm getting divorced." There was a brief pause in which he lowered his sad gaze, took Rúbia's wet hands and expressed himself ashamed. "Just today, I was going to talk to you about this."

"It is true that you are married! I can't believe it!" She exclaimed, letting go of the hands he was holding and rubbing them across her face in a sorrowful gesture.

"I'm going to get divorced, Rúbia. The situation is very complicated. I should have left the house by now, but…"

"I'm leaving."

When she got out of the car, Jefferson took her arm and asked generously.

"Please, stay. Listen to me first."

"I won't be the other woman! I will not be the reason for your break up."

"It is not because of you that I'm ending my marriage. Believe me. Besides, you are not the other one. Despite living with her in the same house, we already sleep in separate rooms for a long time."

"So why haven't you gotten divorced yet?"

"Due to family problems. One of the reasons is my mother… she… she is an elderly person, very conservative and lives with us. She has serious health problems. Her heart, mainly… I… I…" He stuttered, showing himself touched, victimized. "I tried talking to her, but it did not work. I had to help her every time. Recently, my mother was hospitalized for two weeks. She had kidney problems, had to undergo dialysis… I cannot take the blame for serious consequences for her, because of my divorce. You can't imagine how difficult it is."

"I can't believe this, Jefferson. Moreover…"

"Rúbia, I love you! I adore you! I did not expect to experience such a strong feeling for a person and… You were the

27

best thing that ever happened to me!" He expressed himself as asking for understanding. He touched her face affectionately, and made her look into his eyes and said sincerely. "If I had dreamed that I would find a person like you, I would have divorced before, even with my mother suffering so much. This badly resolved situation of mine will be for a short time."

"So, first get divorced and leave your house. Then…"

Interrupting her, he became sentimental.

"I thought you loved and trusted me, Rúbia."

"I love you so much, but…"

"I'm asking you to trust me and give me time. Give me some time in the name of this love!" He implored again, caressing her face with the back of his hands.

Rubia was confused, shaking and speechless. Her aching heart sank. Staying together with a man she had just found out was married, was contrary to her principles. Her moral values demanded that she stayed away from Jefferson, but on the other hand, she enjoyed his company and felt very lonely. She did not want to be alone. She was afraid that life would reserve loneliness for her.

Anguish clenched in his chest as she said.

"I have always disliked being the other one, the mistress… That is a detestable status."

"That is not your status. You are not the other woman." He declared with conviction. "I have nothing else to do with my wife, except an unresolved situation on paper." After a few moments he asked in a touching manner. "Please, Rúbia, believe me. Trust me. That is all I'm asking for." Without delay, he straightened on his seat, reached inside the pocket of his jacket and pulled out a box, declaring. "I love you." He handed it over and inquired. "Open it. It is proof of my love."

"For me?!" She asked, with a slight smile as she took the small box. Opening it, she saw a beautiful ring sparkle. After a few seconds, Jefferson gently lifted the jewel, took her thin, smooth hand, and slid the ring onto her finger. It was then that she murmured. "It's beautiful!"

"It is the symbol of what we feel." Saying that, he approached her gently and kissed her lips tenderly. Then he suggested. "We can have dinner in a very special place, extend the night and…"

Rúbia, despite being happy with the gift, felt her chest tighten again. Still, she smiled and said nothing. Satisfied, he turned on the car and they drove off.

✻ ✻ ✻

The next morning, Abner knocked on his sister's door and she answered loudly, through the sound of the hair dryer;

"Come in! It's open!"

"Good morning! Jezz!" He marveled, laughing and fanning the air to dissipate the heat and the little steam around. "You are the one causing global warming with this hair dryer and straightener."

"Ah! Do not bother me!" She answered, laughing and turning off the device. "If I do not do all of this, my hair gets horrible."

"Your natural hair is beautiful. Do not exaggerate."

"Everyone may think so, but not me. I prefer it when it's straight."

"You will end up ruining it up with that straightener."

"Do not bother, Abner! Did you come here to talk about my hair?" She laughed, running the hot straightener through her hair.

Without waiting for her brother to respond, she explained. "I could not find an appointment at the salon where I usually go. That is why I'm doing everything at home."

"Mom was mad the other day because you burned the bedspread and upholstery on the chair."

"I did. I forgot it was hot."

"Rúbia…" He waited for his sister to look at him and say; "I'm moving today. The apartment is almost ready. I just need to bring the latest clothes and books."

"Today?" She was surprised. "I thought you were staying here another week."

"I thought so too, but no. Everything is ready. All that remains is for the technician to start the piped gas. I will be without a stove for a few days, but that is not a problem. Do you want to go with me to see what it looks like?"

"Yes, I want to!" She was excited. However, thinking a bit more about it, she hesitated. "It is just… I'm waiting for a call…"

"So…? I already know that falling in love is complicated." He just laughed.

"How is that? Why do you say falling in love is complicated?" She became interested, stopping what she was doing.

"When a relationship is not complicated, usually both are free on weekends and one does not need to depend on the other to confirm whether they are going out or not."

Rúbia was thoughtful with a very serious face. That comment from her brother made her feel very uncomfortable.

"Sometimes a person is free, but there are things to do and…" She tried to argue, but she did not know what to say.

While Abner, simply touching what was on the furniture, took the small box with the ring and opened it, admired.

"Jeez! Is it real?"

"No. It's virtual. There is nothing in your hand. Didn't you notice?" She laughed.

"Meaningful!" He answered.

"I got it yesterday."

"I know… yesterday you came late and said that you were hanging out with your friends to celebrate someone's birthday. Were there any gifts left over?" Smiling, he asked suspiciously.

"No… It's just that…" Rúbia did not know what to say. The brother smiled relaxed and asked.

"Keep calm. You do not have to answer anything. I have nothing to do with your life. I just noticed that it is a very beautiful and expensive jewel."

More relaxed, she sighed deeply and say;

"I'm seeing someone. We celebrated three months of dating and he gave me this ring."

"If you have been dating for three months and this is the gift… I wonder what the gift will be when you have a year dating!" He joked, looking at her. When he saw that his sister seemed to force a smile, he asked. "You are not happy?"

"Yes, I'm. It's just that… I feel insecure."

"Safety is sometimes the responsibility of knocking your door."

"I do not get it?" She wanted to know.

"When we are going to do… or when we are doing something important and we have many problems involved, certain duties must be observed and obligations must be answered for the very acts of those who accompany us. And we experience a feeling of insecurity, of doubt. Insecurity also occurs when we run away from our principles."

31

"It all happened so fast…"

"Why do you say it was fast? You are just dating. You don't have serious commitments along the way… or do you?

"No."

"Then there was nothing fast. We don't know the man. You don't bring him home. You aren't planning a wedding… There is nothing fast in this story."

"It's hard to explain."

"Is he from your workplace?"

"Yes." She simply answered.

"I can only advise you this, little sister: when you are unsure or doubtful about something, you should not go any further if it bothers you too much. Go slowly, get to know him well. Then you won't regret anything you do." For a moment he looked at her thoughtfully and then asked; "So? Are we going to my apartment?"

"Yes, wait until I finish combing my hair…" She smiled.

"Alright. I'm going to finish loading my last things into the car."

✳ ✳ ✳

Abner carried his boxes of books and clothes to the car, but his sister hadn't gotten ready yet. Then he went into the kitchen and had a cup of coffee while talking with his mother.

"Do it this way: you come here for lunch and dinner until the gas is installed on the stove." Said Mrs. Celeste, trying to help.

"We will do the following, mother: when I go to lunch here, I will call, as usual. As for dinner… The microwave is working. I eat just a snack. Don't worry about it. Besides, it will be for two or three days.

"As for your dirty clothes…"

"Mom...! Don't worry. I can handle it by myself. If I need it, I'll ask for help, alright?" There was a brief pause and he said; "By the way! Where is Simone? She has disappeared. I've barely seen her in the last few weeks."

"The doctor ordered more specific tests for the baby. He said it's just to clear up some doubts. Nothing serious. However, they are worried. They think the doctor saw something wrong with the baby's health and doesn't want to scare them."

"Jeez... That expectation is worse than a quick result. Didn't the doctor say what he suspected?"

"No. That's what is killing them. Your sister had been crying, she wasn't teaching at the university either."

"If I didn't have to finish getting my stuff done in the apartment, I'd go talk to her. Maybe tomorrow I'll have time to do it."

"That damn apartment is taking up all your time." Interrupted Mr. Salvador, walking in the kitchen.

"That's the way it is, dad. Until I put everything in order..." Abner explained patiently.

"You barely have time for your family. Your mother had to shop at the market and had to take a taxi to return."

"And why didn't you go to pick her up? Is your car damaged?" Asked the son.

"No." Answered the mother instead of the father. "He was watching the news on the TV and he forgot to pick me up."

"It was not like that" He tried to defend himself. "You didn't say the right time for me to pick you up. And I was looking at an interesting case and..."

"More interesting than me, of course!" The wife shouted. "That is why you didn't remember to pick me up."

"The story was interesting, yes. When it comes to my money, when it comes to what I pay in taxes for this thieving government, which spends all that is mine without me having a benefit, it's really interesting! Bunch of shameless bastards. I worked hard all my life and to raise you so that nothing is missing at home. I had to pay for health insurance because public care is terrible. I paid a dentist because if I were to rely on the government, you wouldn't have any teeth. Despite that, I still had to pay taxes and I'm not even rich! That's why your mother and I decided to have just you, or rather... It was supposed to be just you and Simone, but Rubia ended up coming by mistake. Then your mother decided that I was the one who was going to have the operation. I had the operation. Reluctantly, but I had the operation. It was the best thing we did. You can have three children to eat, but if you have four or five, they will all go hungry and needy. It is not possible to provide good living conditions for everyone. Today we see on TV that even with everything so advanced, those women appear like rats with five, six, seven and even ten children! Could it be that after the second one, she did not learn how not to have more children? Or rather, what do you have to stop doing in order not to have more children?"

"Salvador! You have nothing to do with that!" Scolded his wife.

"Ah! Of course I have! The shameless woman complains that she can't pay for a daycare, nor a school for the kids, she's hungry, and that the government doesn't give her anything. Did she go ask the government if she could have children, one after another, so that the government and taxpayers will support them? Yes, because those who support her and her children are the ones who pay taxes. Where does she think the money they receive from the scholarship comes from? Family, gas coupons, milk coupons, school supplies offered in public schools, school uniforms, construction of daycare centers...? The money for all this comes from my pocket and the taxpayers' pockets! I'm sure she doesn't pay taxes! Then, she screams, wanting the government to give her a house, a place to live. When I wanted to, I bought this land and I built it with my effort! No government helped me! I have to pay taxes, until today, for what I built! That people want everything to be easy. They don't think, they just give expenses to the government." Without offering a breath, he continued. "Your grandfather and I build the walls of this house on weekends. He towed everything and his mother was a mason's helper, she carried a lot of brick and sand. She would even turn the mix. We all went to a lot of effort to have everything we have. Today, if I need someone to fix the sidewalk, which is cracked, I can't find a good, responsible mason who wants to work. Paying, I don't think so! But people are asking for things at the door.... Ah...! There are those!" The wife and his son did not speak. They knew him well. They knew that, if they did, the matter would never end. "Do you know what the government should do?" Without waiting for an answer, he said; "Put contraceptives in the water treatment network and give these people water to drink. No one would have a child they couldn't support. Then everyone would be immunized."

"You are not immunizing, dad. You are sterilizing. They would all be sterile to have no more children... But... What am I talking about?" He laughed at himself. "How absurd!"

"What's absurd is that these people complain that the government does not provide a home, a nursery... So,, they build shacks in inappropriate places and when it fills with water or catches fire, they stop an avenue or road, setting fire to tires, disturbing others who work and pay taxes. Lots of scoundrels! Rascals! And they still stay in the city hall shelters complaining about the conditions. Where does the money that supports these shelters come from? The taxes that I and the others pay!"

"Ready!" Rúbia said when she got to the kitchen. "Am I late?"

35

"Well, well!" Exclaimed Abner, getting up. "We will be back later."

"I still don't know your department, Abner. When will you take me there?" The father complained.

"The day I called you, you didn't want to go. Today you can't. The back seats of the car are full of boxes. Another day I will take you, okay?"

"It's because I'm old, retired... But if it were a few years ago…"

Mr. Salvador found another reason to complain, while Abner and Rúbia quickly said goodbye and left the house.

✳ ✳ ✳

Already in her brother's new apartment, she noticed:

"What a beautiful table! I loved it." Looking forward, she commented. "Wow! What a great TV!"

"It was delivered yesterday." He said, placing the box he was carrying on the floor. "Do you like it?"

"I love it. I'd like an apartment like this one."

"In less than a year, I'll get the other apartment I bought. Who knows, couldn't you rent this one? If so, I can leave a lot of stuff here."

"Who knows." She smiled, looking dreaming. Then she asked. "Let me look at the view from your room. The day we came here, I couldn't get in there. The painter was putting the finishing touches." Looking around, she joked. "What a big bed! Did it have to be a double bed?"

"You look like Little Red Riding Hood from the children's story when you ask: what a great TV! What a beautiful table! What a big bed!" He said. "You just have to ask what it's for." He laughed.

The sister found the comparison amusing and smiled. As she approached the window, she opened it and stood admiring the view.

"Very nice view. Not many buildings in the front. You don't need to close the curtains to avoid looking at other people's living room or bedroom."

"I think that's very important. When buying an apartment, it's important to check in details like this. Some people don't care at first. Only over time will they see how unpleasant it is to look over and see a neighbor from another building looking into your home. That's awful. I think about it a lot when designing an apartment." At that moment, the phone rang and Abner was rejoicing. "The telephone line is active! Finally! It hasn't rung since it was installed." Rúbia admired the wide view of the downtown panorama as her brother went to answer the phone.

It wasn't long before the young man came back saying;

"It was Ricardo. He is on his way and..." Seeing her sister thoughtful, he asked. "Would you mind coming to the office with me? I want to put the books I bought in order."

"Let's go, if I can help..."

"Ah...! Of course you can! Let's go."

While installing a bookcase, they were talking.

"Dad is terrible. With each passing day he criticizes more and more. However, some of his observations are well founded, though harsh. When I got there in the kitchen, I heard what he said." Rúbia laughed, amused.

"Ah...! Was it the story about putting contraceptives in water?" The brother laughed too.

"Yes, that one." The sister chuckled. "His imagination is too wild. It was fun, but I didn't say anything as he was going to go on and on."

"You can't say that about people in difficult conditions. We don't know the reason to go through situations like these."

"I don't know... Come on! Sometimes I think... They don't know how to prevent unwanted pregnancy? Because I think that, with more than one child and with needs, no one would want to have more children, don't you think?"

"You know, Rúbia, I think people like that need guidance and not criticism. They learned differently."

"I don't agree with you. The media is vast. We all know the difficulties. Nowadays there are people who get together first. After getting pregnant, they stay at a relative's house. After a few fights or even due to hostile natural conditions, they move into a cottage. Only then, they decide to find a job. No one wants to work, but they all want to be employed, receive their salary and have their rights to, at the first opportunity, put the company *on the stick*, as they say. They then discover that the job is difficult and that they have no specialization or qualification. And there they are; unemployed, depending on subsidies, government vouchers and everything. And one day their cottage fills with water, they have nowhere to go, there is no nursery to leave their kids for to work. When they get a nursery, she gets pregnant again and now, here comes the maternity leave, the sick leave, this and that leave. That is why many people think a lot before hiring a woman."

"Rúbia, don't be so demanding. It is not like that. You have this point of view because we come from a family that, despite having a father without culture and a bit rude, is a man who planned the future, he tried to do everything right and taught us that way. But those individuals, who live in such precarious conditions, did not learn this from their parents... if they had parents to teach them something. So, unfortunately, it will be life that will have to teach them, often through bitter experiences. Do not think that they like it, that they enjoy living in those conditions."

"You... Always in defense of the poor and oppressed."

The bell rang and Abner went to answer it. Rúbia heard a voice saying.

"I forgot my keys here yesterday."

There was a murmur she couldn't hear, and then his brother returned to the office and introduced them;

"This is my sister, Rúbia and... This is my friend, David."

"Nice to meet you, David. We finally met. Everything okay?"

"The pleasure is mine. Really... It took us a while to meet, but anyway..." He was a handsome young man, thirty-two years old, of medium height, one meter and seventy-five tall. Normal body, no protruding muscles. White skin, straight black hair. Light honey-colored eyes, almost greenish, a very rare type of color. His face was angelic, very soft. Thin, clean-shaven beard. He had a confident, cheerful and loving expression. He conveyed affection and happiness in his eyes. His voice was generous and very polite. His smile, with extremely white and impeccable teeth, was beautiful.

"It's a pleasure to meet you."

"Thank you. I'm glad to hear that." Looking at her, he joked. "You are beautiful! Congrats. Just... you lied, Abner! Rúbia is beautiful!"

"My brother is a... a..." She looked for words that matched the provocation of the joke, but could not find it.

"It's a lie, Rúbia. He told me that you are very beautiful. Now I know that you are not a liar."

"What did you bring, David?" The sister wanted to know him.

39

"I stopped at a bakery and bought a cake, I mean, a brownie and some cookies to keep the balance." He laughed. "I think you can make coffee here, right?"

"Yes, I brought the coffee machine yesterday." said Abner.

Rúbia's thoughts flew. So, this was David. The friend her brother didn't want to talk to on the phone near her. But then he called him and they talked about putting the apartment in his name. What was Abner's interest in putting the apartment in David's name too? Would he do it in the one he was renting or the other one he bought? No, the one he bought could not be. Maybe this one. Maybe he and David would share the apartment, but she only saw one room installed. After a moment she remembered: David said he forgot the keys. Why would he have the keys here? It was strange to whisper so she wouldn't hear. There was a lot of mystery in the appearance of that friend. Why?

A slight thought passed through her head; however, she found it impossible, absurd, and immediately chased it away, returning her attention to their conversation.

"If I had to depend on the stove…" Said Abner.

"The gas has not been connected yet?" Asked the friend.

"No. I left the key with the concierge, but he said the technician didn't come."

"Relying on the service provider is a problem. They never deliver what they promise."

"Don't even tell me." Said Abner, walking in the kitchen to make coffee while David followed him.

Rúbia smiled and stayed in the office arranging some books. It didn't take long until they called her. Sitting at the dining table, she remarked.

"Wow! How fragrant these lilies are. They are cute!"

"My mother said that white lilies bring joy, love and luck. So, we were in the market and she decided to buy them for Abner. To bring prosperity to the new home."

"And how is Mrs. Janaina? Why didn't she come?" Abner asks.

"She is fine. He stayed with my brother. He complained about you for not going home last Sunday. You promised."

"It didn't work out. You know. In fact, I have two of her books and I found them today when I was bringing mine here. I have read them. When you leave, don't forget to take them with you, please. I put them on the office desk."

"Don't worry about it. I'm sure she's in no hurry."

"*Lending is a pleasure. Giving back is a must*, the popular saying goes. I like to have an open path when it comes to borrowing, so I don't fail to return books or let anything I borrow go to waste. By the way, the books are very good."

"Books about what?" Asked Rúbia.

"Spiritist romances." David replied. "My mother is a Spiritist and Abner was interested in the subject. I took him to my house. He and my mother spent hours talking about everything. It is logical that the conversation has been watered with coffee and rain cake" They laughed. "Now, they do not stop talking."

"I know a little about Spiritism, but not much. Are you a Spiritist?" She wanted to know.

"The Spiritist is said to be a frequent visitor to a Spiritist home, taking doctrinal courses and doing volunteer work at the center. If you ask me if I'm a frequent visitor to the Spiritist center and if I'm currently taking courses, the answer is no. Now, if you ask me if I'm a spiritist in heart, soul and in my daily practices, the answer is yes."

"I have read countless romances, tales and Spiritist stories. The first one I read was *Nuestro Hogar*, by Chico Xavier, from the spirit of André Luiz. It was my sister who lent it to me. She attended the Spiritist center for a long time."

"This book is a classic of Spiritist literature."

"I loved it." Rúbia took a sip from the coffee cup and asked. "What do you do for a living, David?"

"I'm an odontologist, popularly known as a dentist." He smiled.

"Hey! I'm talking to the right person. I have a tooth that shows no signs of life." She laughed.

"That can become a problem if you don't fix it soon."

"Where is your dental office?"

"It's nearby. I'll give you a card." He said getting up and going to the sofa to take a folder that he had left there. When he came back, he handed it to Rúbia.

"Thank you. I'll call and schedule an appointment."

"Do it. Tell the secretary that you are Abner's sister and you will quickly have an appointment."

At the time, Abner commented;

"Ricardo was supposed to bring me some projects, but he's taking too long."

"I hope he arrives soon. I'm waiting for a call and may have to go."

As soon as Rúbia said that, the intercom rang and Abner went to answer. It didn't take long and the doorbell rang. The young man went to open the door and returned with Ricardo and a boy who seemed to be about ten years old. Upon reaching the room, Abner's partner greeted and then introduced them.

"This is my son, Renán."

Courteous, the boy greeted everyone and sat on the sofa at his father's suggestion. He carried a small electronic gaming device in his hands and was watching it.

Ricardo gave Abner what he needed, accepted the offered cup of coffee, and then commented.

"We haven't seen each other in a long time, have we, Rúbia?"

"It is true. I haven't been in your company in a few months. Neither have you been in our house."

"What good have you done?" He asked.

"I have a new job."

"Great news. That is great. Congratulations!"

"How horrible it was to be unemployed. You can't imagine."

"I have an idea. You haven't been unemployed for a long time though, have you?"

"For those who are used to working, it was too long." Ricardo, turning to the other man, asked. "David, tell your mother I haven't forgotten her book. I'm almost done reading it."

"As I understand it, David's mother is lending everyone a book." Rúbia jokes. "I also want to meet her."

"Anytime." David said willingly. "Mrs. Janaina loves meeting new people. Receiving visitors depends on herself."

"Let me know before you go there. She will prepare the best rain cake you have ever eaten."

"And she bakes a chocolate cake to eat while you pray! It seems to have been made by angels. Mrs. Janaina cooks very well." Abner said.

"You're going to miss mom's food when you come to live here, right, David?" Ricardo joked when asking.

David and Abner looked at each other without knowing how to answer, while Rúbia found the question strange. She frowned and looked suspiciously at her brother demanding an answer.

In that instant, Ricardo's eyes widened and he realized that he had made a mistake. There would be no way to delete what he said or even try to correct it. Silence reigned. He was very embarrassed and, since he had nothing to say, he decided to leave.

Abner accompanied him, leaving his sister and David in the room. In the hallway, while waiting for the elevator, he apologized.

"I'm sorry, Abner. I thought you already told your sister. I saw you both so excited and... You said when you introduced them, you were going to reveal everything."

"That was my idea at first." He smiled awkwardly. "After she and David talked for a bit, I thought about telling her, but it didn't work. I lacked courage. Then you came here..."

"I'm sorry man. Please." He said. "I'm really sorry."

"Don't worry. Don't worry. Maybe I'll go back there now and tell her everything at once."

"What I did was unforgivable. Try to understand it. I didn't do it on purpose."

"I told you, don't worry. Nothing is just by chance."

"Thank you then. I have to leave, Flora is waiting for me. She is going on a trip today."

"Take it easy." He said, shaking his friend's hand. "Have a good trip, Renán." He said to the boy, saying goodbye as well.

After watching them take the elevator, the young man took a deep breath. He knew he would have to face his sister. As he entered his apartment, he saw Rúbia and David standing, talking in an energetic, almost heated tone.

"Abner, for God's sake! What he's saying is a lie, right? Is it a joke? Am I right?!"

"Rúbia, sit down. Let's talk." Asked the brother softly.

"We have nothing to talk about!" She practically screamed. "It's stupid!" She took a few careless steps, ran her fingers through her hair, and rubbed her face. Incredulous, she asked, forcing a smile. "Are you kidding?"

Staring at her, seriously, the brother replied;

"No, Rúbia. It's not a joke. I'm gay. I've known David for about four years. A year and a half ago, almost two years ago, we dated and we have the intention to live together."

She felt frozen. It seemed to be a dream. She thought she was not hearing well. Her legs went weak and she reached for the couch, sitting down slowly. Lowering her head, she held it in her hands and rested her elbows on her knees. Her brother approached, sitting next to her.

David sat down at the table, where he looked at them, and was completely silent. With his sister, Abner stroked her back affectionately. Then he said;

"Try to understand…"

"I never thought… I could never imagine… I even feel dizzy, nauseous… I can't believe it!"

"I can't deny it anymore. The truth always emerges, Rúbia…"

She did not let him continue and interrupted him.

"I don't want to hear anything else. I'm leaving."

"Not like this. Let's talk." Insisted her brother.

"We don't have much to talk about. Do we?!" Asked seriously, looking at him with a hard expression in her face and an almost aggressive voice.

At the scene, David decided;

"Well... I'm leaving. I think you better be alone and talk. My presence may interfere. Goodbye."

After he said that, he left without saying goodbye. Rubia followed him with her eyes and measured him up and down until the man was gone. She didn't say anything for a long time.

3.– LIFE IS MUCH MORE

ABNER STAYED WITH HIS SISTER for long minutes. Nobody said anything. She seemed quite nervous, frantically flailing her foot and leaning on the tip to swing her leg in very short, quick movements. He decided to go to the kitchen and bring her a glass of sugar water. Offering it, the sister accepted, drinking it slowly.

Pulling out a chair and sitting in front of her, he could see the tears, which did not fall, tremble in her sad eyes.

"Why are you so surprised? I thought you were not prejudiced."

"Prejudiced...?! At this point I completely lost the trail. I'm stunned, with a bad feeling... It hurts, you know..." She stuttered, looking away from him as she lowered her head.

"Rúbia, you are talking as if homosexuality was a disease. But it is not."

"When did you become homosexual?" Abner smiled and calmly explained.

"Homosexuality is a normal condition for part of the world's population. In the past it was believed that homosexuality was caused by some childhood trauma or a problem with the family. Today we know that it's nothing like that. The person is born homosexual. Homosexuality is not, and never has been, an emotional and psychological disorder. In fact, it is good to remember that the Federal Council of Psychology prohibits any psychologist from attempting to cure a person of his homosexuality.

"Wasn't that your choice? I don't know... Suddenly you decided to be different..."

"Why did you... Please... No one chooses to have homosexual desires, feelings and emotions. No one can decide the hardest or the easiest. Life just happens. It is not easy to admit this in a world so hypocritical, ignorant and tyrannical."

"If so... Have you always been a homosexual?" She spoke calmly now.

"Yes always. Look, sister, homosexuality is not an option, it is a condition. I was born that way. I'm like this. I did not choose this as someone who chooses to get a tattoo and live tattooed for the rest of their life. It turns out that we are educated and raised to be heterosexual, that is, when a boy is born, all his clothes and toys are male. When a girl is born, parents and relatives choose clothes and toys for women. Even color is sex determination for someone. Blue for boys, pink for girls. They don't even know that blue is a feminine color, you know?" The sister was silent and Abner continued; "The family always expects that a boy is interested in the opposite sex. So it is with a girl. Even when they realize their orientation and desires are homosexual. Parents do not like or do not want to admit that their son or daughter is different from the majority. It is common to hear someone say that a man became homosexual. When, in fact, it's correct to say that the guy assumed he was gay."

"How come I never noticed?" She muttered.

"Maybe because I never felt like expressing myself with gestures. People can express themselves however they want, as long as they don't offend someone. Expressions are a right. Some gays need to show off with gestures, clothes, ways of speaking. Others don't have that desire. We must respect that. I, like David, do not want to expose myself with gestures, mannerisms, clothes…" Faced with Rúbia's silence, he continued. "You know… the gestures, the masculine gestures in a woman does not necessarily mean that she is homosexual. Still less, the delicate and feminine gestures don't indicate that a man is homosexual. I met women with rude gestures, some would say masculine, but they were heterosexual. Maybe they were like this because of the harshness of their lives, the difficulties, and the environment in which they were raised. Just as I met men with a very evident feminine side. They were kind, polite, delicate, and straight. They only liked women. In the same way that there are strong homosexuals, masculine appearance, martial arts practitioners, the type of "bad boy guy", that nobody would say that they are homosexual, but they are. As well as women with speech, style, gestures, and extremely feminine clothing. They like other women and interact with other women."

"What about transsexuals? Is being transsexual the next step after a homosexual comes out?"

"Don't be ignorant." He said patiently. "One thing has nothing to do with the other. The transsexual dresses, behaves and, mainly, feels like a person of the opposite sex to what his body presents. They go to great lengths for a name change and sex change surgery. Nowadays the government offers this type of surgery in public hospitals. It is difficult to achieve, but it is possible, as well as a name change on all documents. I understand that the male transsexual is a female soul trapped in a male physical body and the female transsexual is a male soul trapped in a female physical body. Everyone has a reason, an individual spiritual reason for being born that way. The transsexual is not homosexual. One is different from the other. The homosexual man knows that he is a man, he accepts himself as a man, he accepts his body as it is, but he likes people of the same sex as him. Despite not appreciating it, he can have sex with a woman. It is the same with a homosexual woman. A transsexual does not accept her male sexual organs. She strongly believes in being a woman and does not admit to having sex with a woman. Transsexuals are people who did not choose to be that way. That is not a wish. They were born that way." There was a brief pause and he said; "I said the example with male transsexual because most of them are men, they have the body of a man."

"Abner, this is not normal." She said, still angry.

"Rúbia, you and many other people are prejudiced because this topic is about sex and the unknown stuff. Look, talk about sex is delicate and, for some, complicated. Talking about the unknown causes fear, because we are going to deal with the mysteries of God. If we say that the person is born homosexual and not that the person decided to be homosexual, we are talking about the existence of something before birth, we are talking about reincarnation. This leads us to believe that God admits that a person is different because of their evolution and for innumerable reasons we cannot even imagine. This topic is extensive and leads us to philosophize a lot. We must admit that not everyone likes to think and rethink, as this leads to revisiting concepts and admitting mistakes."

"Not to mention past lives. Suddenly, I think God decided that someone must have been born gay to control himself and that's it. Wouldn't that be?"

"Within your belief, we have an unjust and tyrant God who offers a life considered normal, perfect. That person finds his soulmate, gets married, and has children." Ironically, he added; "Let's not forget that He offers this person health, long life, money, travels and lots of joy. On the other hand, the same God decides to create another person who is poor, ugly, with difficulty learning, with some disability, who suffers, is sick, depends on public health services, lives unemployed... Or this same God, in whom you believe, creates someone who lives in conflict with his sexuality by discovering his homosexuality, because the majority of the world's population is heterosexual and can relate to the opposite sex with what he doesn't want. Look please! We are different from each other because God allows us to be like that to improve ourselves, to learn from experiences. There is a reason for all this. That reason remains a mystery. We don't have an unjust and tyrant God, but a Father who allows us to learn through different life experiences."

"And why don't we know the mysteries of God? Why isn't it clear to everyone that there is reincarnation? Why don't we remember past lives? This would explain why someone is born homosexual, for example.

"About reincarnation... What I can say is that it's mentioned in many writings, by Socrates and Plato, even in the Bible. Many other non-Christian religions and philosophies also observe and teach about reincarnation, but many do not care. Perhaps because they are afraid that, in the future, in the next life, they will have to harmonize with everything they did wrong in this one." He smiled. "As for knowing the mysteries of God, I believe that we don't know them precisely to evolve, to develop our potential for good thoughts, justice, faith, love, kindness. We do not remember past lives so as not to go crazy with the memories of so many stupid things that we did and not suffering for it today, or worse yet, imagine what our future would be like if we had to pay the debts of the past. Or, it could also be that we do not remember our previous life so as not to be vain, bragging about something generous and correct that we have achieved in the past. God allows us not to remember past lives to do well, to do the right thing by our choice, by our will and not out of fear. No one should do a good thing by coercion, but from the heart."

"It is still difficult for me to understand this difference, your condition. You are not homosexual to me. You don't seem to be. I think you should review the concept."

"Little sister, this is not like that. Instead of talking about sex, let's talk about personal tastes to understand the differences. In the sixties, seventies, and mid-eighties, we had the hippies. It was a non-conformist group, characterized by a break with traditional and conservative society, especially with regard to personal appearance and life habits and an emphatic ideal of universal peace and love. They advocated for a free and more liberal way of life. Because they like it, and because of their will, they wore loose and colorful clothes, hair blowing in the wind, flowers... Many took drugs to reach another state of consciousness, as they said. Anyway, they liked to live like that. Hippies were free just because they looked at themselves that way. At the same time, and even today, there are people who like to be free, like or maybe approve of some of the hippie ideas, but not all, because these people don't stop bathing or wear their clothes. However, they certainly want peace, they defend love, freedom and ideas similar to their own."

"I understand what you mean, but I can't agree."

"Rúbia, the biggest problem when it comes to homosexuality is fear, ignorance, and the religious, political and false moral dogmas."

"You're just trying to justify yourself, to make excuses for your new way of life." She said rudely, standing up.

"Please sit. Let's talk better. You are a smart person. I did not know that you were so prejudiced."

"I was not prejudiced. You never are until you have a brother who suddenly decides to be gay. You went out, you had girlfriends, how come you haven't seen your homosexuality before?"

"You are upset. I don't like talking to people in that state. It's not good."

"How did you want me to be?" She asked heatedly. He did not answer, so she continued. "What if suddenly I come and tell you that I like another woman? How would you feel?"

"At first, I would listen to you. But you are not listening to me. You are so involved with your fears, prejudices and ignorance that you do not listen to me. You ignore me. You don't want to understand or even learn."

"Fear? Ignorance? Me?"

"Yes, fear. Fear of having to introduce myself as your brother and for other people to find out I'm gay. Ignorant because you do not want to learn about something new, different and unknown, because, for centuries and centuries, homosexuality, in some parts of the world, has been classified as a disease, psychological deviation, reason to go to stake or concentration camps. Homosexuality has always existed in a large part of the world's population, all around the planet. But many homosexuals did not reveal themselves for fear and shame of being different. They have always been a reason for discrimination, they have suffered rejection from family, friends and acquaintances, they have suffered violence of all kinds simply because they are not like the majority. Prejudice against gays is huge. And it has a name, it's called homophobia. Homophobia is the cause of much suffering for homosexuals because it is full of attacks of all kinds. Only those who have been discriminated against, rejected and humiliated know how great this pain is."

"Their suffering, like that of many who call themselves homosexuals, is not due to prejudice, but because, deep down, their conscience doesn't accept them."

"You are wrong, sister. I became happier when I recognized myself, when I understood myself and admitted being what I am. You can't imagine what it's like to have a girlfriend today and another just to satisfy the family and show it off to friends and society. It is difficult to be with someone incompatible, someone with whom you do not want intimacy. Enough. I mistreated myself too much by doing that. Today I can say that I'm a determined person. I know who I'm and what I want. If others do not accept or do not understand, it is their problem. I'm not attacking anyone, physically or morally. I have a clear conscience."

"I can't believe what I'm hearing" She said bitterly, in a low and angry voice. "What will your next speech be? The one that tells me you love David and that you're going to bring him to live here?"

"You said that for me. I don't need to repeat it." He answered firmly, looking at her calmly.

"What about your conscience? How do you justify yourself before God?"

"I don't need to justify myself. God is the creator, Father of all things. God is love and goodness. He knows who I am and what I am, because he created me. If He does not understand that I'm sincere, honest... If He does not understand that I'm good and fair with others and, mainly, with myself in being and living as I'm... If He, the Creator Father, doesn't understand, then He is not God. But I think He understands, because I exist."

Rúbia took a deep breath, incredulous at what she was hearing. She picked up her bag, turned around, and without saying anything else, closed the door.

Abner closed his eyes, brought his hands to his face and ran them through his hair, leaning back in the chair. He believed that the conversation with his sister would be much easier. He considered her less judgmental and ignorant. She was confused, insecure, and upset.

For an instant, he worried.

What would her sister do now? Would she tell their parents? Would she no longer talk to him?

He thought it was better to wait. There was nothing else to do. Maybe she needed to think about it. Maybe she would seek guidance and learn more about it.

At that moment the phone rang. Distraught, the young man replied;

"Hello!"

"Abner?"

"Tell me, Simone." She remained silent.

When he realized she was crying, he insisted.

"Tell me, Simone. What happened?" He asked, trying to keep his voice calm.

"I need to talk to you."

"Stay calm. Let's talk."

"Abner... Can I go there?"

"Now?"

"Yes... if you don't mind..."

"Can you drive here, or do you want me to pick you up?"

"I'm down here. In front of your building."

"Then come up! You don't even have to ask. I'm waiting."

The young man went to the kitchen and called the janitor, allowing his sister to enter the building. He waited a few minutes and Simone went up the stairs. When she saw him outside the apartment, she didn't even say hello and threw herself into his arms.

As soon as he could, he said generously.

"Come... Let's go inside." After leading her to the couch, he went into the kitchen and brought her a glass of water and gave it to her. He waited to see her calmer and asked her. "Have you calmed down?"

"I don't know... I'm desperate."

Abner sat in the chair across from her and asked:

"What happened to make you like this?"

"Samuel and I went to the doctor and the tests indicated a problem with the baby..." She cried. After composing herself, she explained. "I was distressed when I saw his face when doing an ultrasound..." She did not coordinate her ideas and was wrong with what she said. "He said he was already suspicious, but now he could guarantee..." Simone was crying compulsively. What she was saying was barely understood. "I did all the tests the obstetrician-gynecologist ordered and..."

Seeing her so nervous, the brother gently suggested.

"Calm down, Simone. Take a deep breath and tell me everything correctly. From the beginning."

"I did all the tests the doctor ordered. I went there to take them. Samuel accompanied me and... After seeing the laboratory tests, the doctor went to do the ultrasound and... My baby has Patau Syndrome."

Simone lost control as she wiped her tears away. Her brother sat next to her, hugged her and even without knowing what the syndrome was about, he understood that it was something serious for her to be like that.

As he patted her, he said.

"Try to calm yourself. Desperation won't help at this point." There was a brief pause and he asked lovingly. "Can you explain to me what Patau Syndrome is?"

"It is a very rare genetic defect. A genetic accident, so to speak. The doctor said it is an abnormality on chromosome 13, due to trisomy. Trisomy is a type of chromosomal disorder in which a chromosome has three copies instead of the usual two. So... this chromosomal alteration, or chromosomal abnormality, promotes, provides various... several malformations in the fetus. It will be born, if it is born..." She screamed. "If it is born, it will have many physical defects. It is a genetic problem so serious that it can totally deform a baby. It is very sad..."

The brother doesn't know what to say. He got up, took a box of tissues and offered it to her.

Simone wiped her face, took another sip of water, and then said.

"You know that before doing Economics, I did Nursing." She referred to the university courses she took. "I don't remember studying it, but... I researched it and..." She took out a folded paper from her bag, opened it, and said as she read. "Patau syndrome is also known as Bartholin-Patau syndrome. I understood that this syndrome is caused when there is no chromosomal disjunction during anaphase of meiosis, therefore gametes with 24 chromatids are generated. Therefore, the gamete has a pair of chromosomes 13, which together with chromosome 13 from the father, form an egg with trisomy."

"I did not understand well. Is it a hereditary problem?"

"Everything indicates that it is not hereditary. Is genetic. It is a coincidence, an accident. Like Down syndrome, or chromosome 21 trisomy, caused by one more chromosome 21. It is an accident, it happens by accident."

"So... It is not known if it was the man or the woman who produced the chromosome mutation?

"No, it's not known. Male gametes with chromosomal number changes are known to have less viability than normal gametes. Nothing is impossible. There is not much chance that an altered gamete in man will fertilize an egg. The woman, on the other hand, produces a single ovum, and if it has a change... It usually occurs with women older than thirty-five years, but it can

occur with a boy of eighteen years. I'm thirty-two years old…"
Careful, Abner asked kindly.

"And… What can we understand as… various malformations in the baby? What can happen to your son?"

"Serious abnormalities in the central nervous system, so… everything gets complicated. He has holoprosencephaly, arhinencephaly…" She read, crying. "…malformations of the cerebral, cranial or facial midline. The result is a deficiency in the embryo. These deformations are variable. Prosencephaly, read on paper, is the most serious form. The face is deformed, it can be very ugly. It can have extremely small eyes, or even have no eyes at all, or even have a kind of… a single hole where the two eyeballs are together…" She was still crying. "Altered eyelids, malformed and dislocated ears, nasal deformities of varying degrees, mild or absent facial deformities… Hands and feet may have a sixth finger or the fifth finger overlaps the third or fourth… Retardation… Mental illness can be moderate or severe. The baby usually has a cleft lip and palate or even without a palate, that is, the baby does not have the top of his mouth." She cried compulsively, and then she said; "On the ultrasound… We can see that my son has a cleft lip. In one hand… the fist is closed, as if the fingers are not well formed and in the other only two fingers can be seen. It's already seen that the head has an abnormal shape." Anguished, she continued; "This anomaly is incompatible with normal life. Patau syndrome occurs in one of 20,000 live births. When they are born, about eighty percent die in the first month of life. Others live up to six months. In rare cases they live up to ten years. They have congenital heart problems or heart malformation, kidney, mental, genital problems…" There was a brief pause and she added. "Only two and a half percent of fetuses with this syndrome are born alive." Digging again into her bag, she pulled out other papers and handed them to Abner, crying. "I printed these photos from the internet. Take a look."

The young man was surprised to see such sad images and was impressed. After carefully observing them, she folded them again and placed them in her sister's bag that was open on the sofa.

"I also investigated the possibility of having a second child with the same syndrome and... I understood that the possibility is the same as for a woman who has never had children. This is an accident, but..."

"Is the diagnosis about the baby definitive?" Ask worried her brother. "Like... No treatment?"

"No, there is no treatment. There is nothing we can do. I'm anguished. I can't work. I can't focus on anything else. I can only think about that. This is our first child! You understand? We didn't expect any of this." Abner don't answer and she continued. "We plan everything in our lives. We bought a house, after putting it in order we got married, we worked very hard... Only after being well stabilized did we decide to have a child. Now... he will come with serious problems and will not even have a long life, if he is born..." After a few minutes she asked sadly. "What do I do, brother?"

"If you can't do anything, if there's nothing that anyone can do, then let it happen according to God's will."

Simone looked at him, wiped her tears with her hands and commented.

"I didn't think about abortion. I wouldn't have the guts even if the doctor spoke about it. But... I don't know what I'm doing. I don't know if I will get attached to the baby, if I keep talking, playing and telling stories..." A sob drowned out her voice. "I'm afraid of suffering... The doctor said that boys with this problem don't have long to live and I can't stop thinking about it."

Abner took a deep breath, thought for a moment, and replied.

"This little creature here..." He said while passing his hand lovingly over her belly. "Is the fruit of your love for Samuel. It doesn't matter what difficulty you have or this baby has. I think it is a loved one. And I will say that because you have wanted to help him, give him shelter, affection, love and you have even wanted to learn from him. A baby does not come as a son or daughter if he is not to be loved. It doesn't matter if he is going to be born and live for only a few days, months or a few years. It doesn't matter how long it must be around you. This boy must be loved every day, every moment, every second, as if he were the only and the last."

"I wanted it to be perfect." She said, expressing himself sadly.

"Of course, yes. It's logical. And this is wonderful, because you wish the best for your son. But our Father, who is in heaven, knows what is best for him. Heavenly Father knows what his son needs to be a better creature, to evolve. Life is not just limited to the years we live here on Earth. Life is eternal. Life is much more than what we experience here. It may seem strange what I'm going to say, but it is the reality: this experience is for evolution, it is also for the spiritual growth of you, your son and Samuel."

"I know. I believe in that. Only when such a situation happens to others, it is easier to understand and find explanations. When it happens to us, it hurts." She reached out her hands and her brother took them, gently pulling her closer to him. Simone leaned against his chest and hugged him. As she felt the caress of long hair and a kiss on the top of her head, she said. "I'm very sad. Disappointed with myself. It's like I had the blame for his condition."

"Do not say that. You are an intelligent person. You know that isn't true."

"And I wish it were different."

"Of course. But you are strong enough to deal with this situation or God would not allow you and your child to pass this test. He's also strong and probably asked for that experience."

"Do you also believe that?" She asked, pulling away from the hug and staring at him.

"Definitely. I know you also know that challenges and difficulties exist just to show our faith and evolve." After a few moments, he asked. "And... Samuel, how is he dealing with this situation?"

"We haven't talked about it since we left the doctor's office. We couldn't talk about it. Sometimes he comes, he caresses me... That's all. He never spoke or played with the baby again." Tears rolled down her face. This time she seemed calmer, crying without despair.

"Did you tell mom?"

"No. I had no courage. I don't know how to tell her." After a moment she said. "I was making the basket... I bought every beautiful little thing... And now? Should I continue? What would you do in my place?"

"I would do everything that needs to be done, normally. I'm not exaggerating, but I would do everything naturally."

"But... we may not even use it."

"Just like that. You see, I think you need to do everything in a normal way, like you don't know anything. After all, if it weren't for the very modern clinical and laboratory tests, you wouldn't know anything, right?"

"Yes, but..."

"Simone, take care. Take care of your child normally. You both have to treat him with love, care, and kindness. Show him all your love."

"By doing so, I will suffer more when the baby is gone." She shouted.

"You will suffer anyway. But let your suffering not fill you with remorse, pain, and regret for not being a good mother in the

61

moments when your son needed it most. He understands that you have been his mother from conception, and he knows it. Your son feels that. Suffering you will, but not from regret for having refused to love him."

"The doctor said he doesn't know how well the pregnancy is going."

"That's because God, you and your child want it that way. Non-spiritual doctors can only tell what the limitations of science show them."

The sister had stopped crying and was much calmer than when she arrived.

Abner's spiritual achievement was the gift, the gift of diffusing calming energies, especially in recent times when he began to understand a little more about spirituality.

Simone took a deep breath and said;

"Let's go to the kitchen. I'll make tea for us." When he got up and extended his hand, he commented to change the subject and distract her. "The water must be heated in the microwave." He smiled.

"Didn't you get the gas from the stove?"

"Not yet."

In the kitchen, the sister sat on a stool and looked around. Even without emotion, she commented.

"The kitchen is beautiful"

"You need to see everything. So let's go inside."

"Your other apartment is about to be delivered. If you are going to live here for a short time, why did you decorate so well?"

"I know the owners of the planned furniture company. They offered me a good discount. They know that as an architect, I use the services they provide and recommend them too."

After a few seconds, she asked kindly.

"Abner, did you really need to get out of mom's house?"

He was silent for a moment. He got the hot water out of the microwave and placed it with the tea bags in cups on the counter. He reflected, before replying.

"Yes, I do. The moment has come. I want to have my own life. Dad, as you know, is always teasing me with what I do and stop doing." He paused briefly, sweetened the tea, and asked. "Didn't you find Rúbia when you arrived?"

"No. Was she here?"

"She went out and you called. I don't know how you didn't meet."

"What a pity... I wanted to talk to her too, but away from mom. Maybe if she were with me when I went to tell her, I would have more strength."

"It was good not to find her. Our sister was very nervous."

"Why?"

"We argued."

"You and Rúbia argued?" She was alarmed. Before receiving an answer, she asked again. "Why? What happened?"

Abner stared at her and said;

"I know you have too many problems, but at any moment you will know and it will be better for me."

"Know what? What are you talking about?"

"Rúbia is upset because today I told her about my homosexuality." Simone stopped drinking, looked at him for a long time, then looked down and said almost in a whisper.

"It is not a surprise to me."

"How?!" He was intrigued, worried.

"I thought about that a long time ago." With a casualness that her brother did not expect, she added. "I did not notice anything in your way of being. I realized you were very laid back and a few years ago I ran into a girlfriend who didn't mean much to you and she said that for the most part you were alone."

"Are you not going to be angry or upset or will you argue with me?"

"Why would I do that, brother?"

He took a deep breath and offered a slight smile.

"I expected this behavior from Rúbia, not from you. How wrong I was." He smiled.

"To tell you the truth, when the idea that you were gay crossed my mind, I was scared. I didn't want it to be like this. Then I didn't care anymore. From then on, I began to reach out and be friends with other gay colleagues, professors at the university where I teach." Simone smiled as she admitted. "I realized how silly it was to distance myself from people so good, sensitive and with a heart capable of understanding our most intimate conflicts, however insignificant they may be. Then, I was able to have the pleasure of observing generally intelligent people, who are very dedicated to the subjects that interest them. They are caring, helpful, loving, understanding, with an incredible capacity for attention and affection. They are transparent. You know, one of them became a good friend. It is with him, Cláudio, that I have vented since I learned about the problem with the baby. He's so generous, he comforts me, he listens. He talks his head off." She smiled. "I feel better after our comforting and calming conversations. Cláudio is more reliable than many friends I had. Wow, how things change! I learned to look at homosexuals very differently."

"You learned to respect them."

"Respect them... I've always respected them. I think I learned to know what homosexuality is. I understood that the person is like that and that's it. I used to be very ignorant, you know. At the university there is a history professor who is homosexual. I didn't go near her because I thought she was going to make a pass at me or something. One day, at a meeting, we started talking. We became closer colleagues. I never noticed a different look or a strange conversation, you know?"

"People often make mistakes, just like you. It is not because I'm gay that I'm going to sing or want to go out with all my co-workers or partners just because they are men. This is a mistake. And, just think about it... Do all your heterosexual colleagues live flirting and asking you out, because they are interested in a more serious relationship?"

"No, of course not."

"So why the fear of a lesbian coming up and doing the same thing?"

"Pure prejudice, I know. And even if that happens, I must say no, as I would say to a man if I'm not interested."

"Exactly."

Simone offered a slight smile when she admitted.

"So it was: it was very difficult for someone to publicly reveal or assume their homosexuality. Only recently has it become a bit more common. Even so, people still ignore it and don't know how to act."

"It is simple, one must act as always. I know how strange it may seem, but once you know, it's simple." After a while he said; "I didn't expect Rúbia to have that reaction."

"Didn't you tell her in the same way you just told me?"

65

"I actually didn't tell her. It happened like this: Ricardo was here and…" Abner told her everything and finally said; "If she had stayed to talk things out… but she left."

"Rúbia loves you. We have never been as close as you two. I've always been jealous of that. I think she will reflect about this and then look for you, for sure."

"I think she will tell mom and dad. I'm glad I left home."

"I don't think she will say a word." She waited a few seconds, thought and wanted to know. "Are you going to tell them or let them find out? After all, as I understand it, David will live here, right?"

"Maybe I'll tell mom. As for dad… He better find out for himself. Right now, I don't even want to see him."

"Me neither." She admitted.

"You know, I'm very sad, hurt. I didn't expect Rúbia to react the way she did. In fact, I thought you were going to do what she did. Will mom react the way she did?"

"Mom feels things about this, Abner. Deep down she knows it."

"Sometimes I think so too. Mom understands me, accepts me…"

"When we both talked about you moving here, she expressed herself in a… different and supportive way. She said you needed to have your life, giving no one satisfaction. She spoke in her quiet way and we never know what she's thinking. So deep down, I think she knows."

"Me too, I think she knows." He said with some consternation.

"Abner, the shock, the surprise of a truth like that is only at the beginning. That's it. Time heals all." Simone simply smiled and said; "Look, I came here in pieces and look how I'm after we talk. I feel so sad, anguish... There is a moment when I cannot bear it and I have to cry. However, people who say things like what I said help me a lot. It seems that I'm beginning to understand and accept a little more."

"And Samuel, where is he?"

"At the university. Now that he has become the director of the History course, he is overwhelmed. The other director left a big mess. There are many students complaining. So, I was alone at home, that pain, that sadness hit me and... I called Cláudio, my friend, but he was not at home and the cell phone gave me a voice message. I think of you, I wanted to give more time before telling the family, but... I thought you would be the only person who could understand me." After a while, she commented. "I'm finding my husband very strange, distant."

"He must be in shock. As soon as possible, get closer to him. Talk about it. It will be good for both of you. He will give you a lot of strength, support. It's the time when you need each other." He said, patting her arm. "Know that you can count on me. No matter the day or the hour, you can find me. I'm in this with you"

Simone's eyes filled with tears. She took her brother's hand and pressed it against hers. He reached closer and hugged her tenderly.

4.– REJECTING A CHILD

EVEN AS THE DAYS PASSED, Rúbia couldn't accept the revelation about her brother's homosexuality.

It was always easy for her to accept homosexuality from friends and acquaintances, but when she faced Abner's sexual condition, she refused. She did not want to accept it.

Unable to bear it, she sought out her friend and told her everything.

"I'm not satisfied, Talita. He is my brother! How come I never notice it?"

"I'm just sorry he's a cat...! I was even hopeful."

"Do not joke!" She said angrily.

"I'm not kidding, Rúbia. I loved Abner from the first time I saw him. He is cute! I don't understand why you are like that, so resistant to accept. Look, girl, think of it this way: he continues and will continue to be your dear, loving, caring and dedicated brother. That will never change. As for his life... Well, he's happy, sexually speaking, in his own way. This is none of your business or mine. Nobody's business either."

"That's not good, Talita."

"¿What is not *good*? It's his life, it's his body. Your brother is responsible for everything he does or does not do."

"God says it's wrong."

"Where? Where did God say that it is wrong to love someone of the same sex? I want to know." The other did not

68

answer and Talita continued. "Look, I was an evangelical for more than twenty years. I got caught up with all those sermons that the pastors said were the word of God, the will of God. I read the entire Bible several times. I was blindly evangelical. Until one day I was in a bookstore and wanted to buy a Catholic Bible and have a look. It would have to be hidden, because the pastor said that taking a bible, which was not evangelical, was a sin."

"And do you have an evangelical and catholic bible?"

"I have both. So, I took it and read it. I noticed that the placement of the words gave a different meaning to the words, the teachings and consequently changed my way of thinking. I came to the conclusion that it was the men who wrote those manipulative words and their understanding. I stopped going to church. As I like to read, I started to consume all kinds of books that talked about Protestantism, Catholicism, Spiritism, Hinduism, Buddhism... I read everything I could find. I built superhuman courage and went to Catholic churches, Spiritist centers, Umbanda centers, Buddhist temples, synagogues and other places. Just that I was an observer, a researcher, you know?" Rúbia nodded positively and Talita continued. "Girl! There was so much evil in so many places that spoke in the name of God! You can't imagine. Well... In summary, today, when someone tells me that something is sin, that God does not allow it, that the Bible says otherwise... First, let's be careful with the interpretation of what is said in the Bible, because it was written by men who, perhaps, had an ulterior motive and could manipulate words when telling a story. Second, to say that a thing is a sin, that it is not right... I don't know. What do we mean by sin? The dictionary says that sin is a transgression, it is to contradict any order or commandment, rule or religious norm. I know that religions were created, or even invented, by men and I still say that men invented religions to help their personal and political interests... So, an order, a rule, a religious norm was invented by men and not by God. Third, to believe that God does not allow something that is absurd. God allows everything. God understands everything. But the person is and will be responsible for everything he does with his life and the lives of others."

"So, you don't believe in the Bible?"

"Yes I do, however, I reflect, I think about it a lot. I no longer have a religion. Jesus did not have an institute, did not create any religion. He, in a way, replaced the long Ten Commandments with the following: *Love the Lord your God, with all your heart and above all things and your neighbor as yourself.* Stop for a while every day and reflect on that phrase. Say it out loud and make it your lifestyle. Think about it when you need to make a decision. It's what I do daily. I believe that no matter how much a Bible translation has been tampered with, they can never undo or misinterpret the meaning of "Love God above all else and others as yourself."

"We are talking about homosexuality. God is against that."

"How do you know? Did you by any chance go there and talk to Him and He told you He was against it?"

"Don't joke, Talita!" She was angry.

"I'm not kidding." She smiled. "I have never been so serious." After a brief pause, she said; "If you cannot understand or accept someone's homosexuality, use the magic formula that Jesus taught: Love your neighbor as yourself. Do not offend, because you do not want to be offended. Jesus also said that with the same weight that you judge, you will be judged. And more: the light of the body is the eyes. If your eyes are good, your whole body will be light. If your eyes are evil, your whole body will be dark. Do not have bad eyes on homosexuality." She waited a few seconds for her friend to reflect. "I can't believe that God is against homosexuality."

"Why?"

"Because He created us. Homosexuality has always existed. It exists among rational animals, it means we, humans..." She

70

laughed kindly. "And it exists among irrational animals, you know?"

"No. Are you serious?"

"I am. There is homosexual behavior among various species of animals, such as giraffes, penguins, whales, chimpanzees, dolphins, and others. Some of these animals choose a partner of the same sex and the union lasts even for a lifetime, even though the females are available to mate in the same flock."

"I don't understand this well, Talita. What makes you believe that God is not against homosexuality?"

"Because it is not a disease. It is a condition of the person today, in this life."

"Do you also believe in other lives before and after this one?"

"Of course. After so much searching for the truth, I would be crazy not to believe it. Or else, I should believe in a cruel and evil God, capable of making us suffer without a reason. If I don't believe in reincarnation, I will believe that God is a Nazi or Middle Ages executioner, as He pleases, to cause so much pain, so much free suffering. But God is not like that. God is the source of energy, life and helps us when we need it. It is the Father who does not abandon, but supports, helps and even allows us to experience suffering in order to learn, evolve and walk on the evolutionary journey, towards true happiness."

"I don't think homosexuality is something to rejoice about. If homosexuality is a condition, isn't that condition a punishment?"

"No. In no way can it be a punishment. A homosexual is not unhappy because he is homosexual. Of course not. You may not be happy when you don't understand or accept your condition, your same-sex attraction. There is a lack of knowledge, a lack of self-acceptance. There is a poorly resolved person. This non-acceptance can occur in another condition of existence like…" She thought. "Be

71

short, tall, red-haired. Ah…!" She remembered. "I met a colleague who hated being a redhead. Also, poor one! People called him sausage water, match head, etc. Hurt and battered, he started coloring his hair, which helped a bit and tried everything to get rid of freckles, which didn't do much. This friend did not accept himself, he hated himself. It took a long time for him to accept himself and see that being a redhead didn't hamper his ability. The people who offended him were poor, and will certainly one day experience the offense to the same extent of pain that they caused. However, I did meet other redheaded people who loved being redheads. In fact, there are many people who dye their hair red because they want to be that way. The homosexual is no different. First, he needs to understand and accept his condition. Then decide what is best for him, what is best for his life. Under the vision of advancing towards evolution, the best thing would be for him not to be corrupt, not to prostitute himself, not to deviate, like any other creature. A rebellious life is not legal and this is for homosexuals and heterosexuals. The greatest difficulty for the homosexual is to assume his sexuality, his condition or, as they say, his sexual orientation. He faces family, relatives and acquaintances. This, if he discovered at a certain age his homosexuality, his preference for people of the same physical sex. The greatest difficulty for homosexual people is facing ignorant prejudices. Those unfortunates bother me. A prejudiced person is an unhappy person. These prejudices are the cause of sadness, pain, suffering, due to discrimination, crimes with malicious words, obscenities in the language when referring to homosexuals, physical, moral and psychological violence. It is difficult and sad to face rejection because it is different from most. Rejection is a major cause of suffering. The prejudice against homosexuality is called homophobia. Phobia means fear and homo means equal. It is a term used to determine aversion, prejudice, hatred, contempt for homosexuals and, obviously, against homosexuality. This aversion, hatred, discrimination, non-acceptance can be veiled, that is, silent, it can be expressed in a subtle, insidious, treacherous or strongly declared way."

"The term phobia means fear and is used as an aversion, isn't that strange?"

"The term homophobia was created using the Greek word *phobos*, which means phobia, with the radical *homo-*, also from the Greek, which means equal. *Phobos* means fear in general, an irrational or not, primal, instinctive fear, often without explanation. In this case, the term phobia is used not only to designate fear in general, but also repulsion, aversion for no reason. The most correct would be the word homophilophobic, which means fear of those who like the same thing. The term homophobia is the subject of much discussion. Some go so far as to say that homophobic people have a mental attitude of fear that they themselves are homosexual or that others think they are. There are also those who say that homophobic people are afraid of those who like the same thing, so they do not accept them. In any case, I believe that the homophobic, the person who does not accept homosexuals, is someone who does not yet have knowledge, is ignorant, has no control over his feelings and therefore despises or attacks in some way. Ignorance is the mother of many evils. Remember the time when left-handed people were forced to do things with their right hands?" She nodded and Talita continued. "This happened mainly due to the ignorance of parents, teachers and religion. The left-handed person was believed to have leftist tendencies, a connection to evil. So much so that, in the Middle Ages, they were sentenced to death. How much ignorance…" She lamented. "Today no one is forced with this type of condition and the world has been adapting to lefties. There are left-handed scissors, left-handed can openers, and other things for people with more left-handed skills. Forcing a boy to write with his right hand, if he is left-handed, can even lead people to legal proceedings. Pastors, priests, nuns, and many other religious people who viewed lefties as creatures who had a pact with the devil or something like that, lost their battles with science. The left-handed person was born with this condition. The person does not insist or force himself to use his left hand. It is estimated that around ten percent of the population is left-handed or sinister, as some call it. Science shows that in lefties, the right side of the brain is more active and this is said to be associated with great intelligence and genius, in addition to skill as an artist. Albert Einstein was left-handed. Being left-handed is not a punishment."

Rúbia was thoughtful and commented;

"So, what are God's punishments like?"

"God doesn't punish anyone. It is our conscience that imposes the punishments. If homosexuality is a punishment, being red-haired, too tall, too short, too fat, thin, black, white, ugly, is also a punishment. Punishment is our way of seeing things. The punishment is imposed by the person himself when he does not accept himself, when he does not understand himself, he does not accept being what he is. Of course, he causes a punishment imposed by himself, because he will live in an intimate conflict and saying in his thoughts: look, I was not accepted here or there because I'm black, because I'm fat, because I'm too white, because I'm gay, and so on. Not accepting you is a punishment."

"What if someone is not accepted for the same reason?"

"So, who is wrong is the group that does not accept someone. People who don't accept each other shouldn't be good company. You know, sometimes, we have to use that old saying: *what others think of me is none of my business*. What should matter is consciousness itself with God. We can lie to others, but we cannot lie to ourselves or to God." She pondered for a second, then added. "I believe that God is not against anyone's condition. Because the Father, good and fair, of whom Jesus spoke and made us believe, would not be prejudiced or cruel. You know, Rúbia, we have to be careful with our beliefs about what we read. I believe a lot in Jesus and we can see that there are no prejudices in the Gospel of Christ. With what I read in the Old Testament, in the Bible, I take great care. The Old Testament or the Hebrew Scriptures, as some call it, was written by Jews and for Jews. This means that they bring an ancient history and concept to an ancient people, written by themselves. Jews are not Christians, they do not believe in Jesus like we do, they do not accept the Master's teachings. Then we turn to what I said before: it was written by men according to the needs of a people. So much so that there are errors, contradictions in the Old Testament, exactly where they say the word of God is. Do you think that if it were written by God, God would be wrong?"

"Where? I've never heard of that."

"Let me see…" She thought. "In Exodus, chapter 20 verse 5 says; …*because I, the Lord your God, am a jealous God, who visits the wickedness of parents in their children until the third and fourth generation of those who hate me.* So, God is saying that whatever the parents do wrong, the children will pay or suffer until the third or fourth generation. In the same Bible, in Deuteronomy, chapter 24, verse 16, it says; *Parents will not die for their children nor children for their parents, each one will die for their sin.* This is an example that I remember." After a brief pause, she said. "You know, girl, the problem is not having a condition. The problem is that we use our condition in an abusive, reckless and irresponsible way. For example: think of a very beautiful girl. Nature has allowed her to have a beautiful condition, but she can use this beauty in the wrong way. She uses her condition to seduce, make conquests, take advantage of situations like going out with the director of a company to get a position or something like that. Use her beauty to win gifts, money… So, she is corrupting herself, prostituting herself. This is not legal for his conscience that he will one day accuse her."

"Shouldn't homosexuals abstain from sex?"

75

"If they are happy abstaining, voluntarily depriving themselves of sex, yes. If sexual abstinence brings him peace and happiness, it is the right thing to do for him. In terms of sex, in fact, in everything in life, the problem is imbalance, moral misconduct and abuse. What can and usually brings some psychological damage is that the heterosexual is involved with someone of the same sex and has a homosexual relationship, since their sexual identity is firmly established for the sexual act with someone of the opposite sex. He, the straight man, is not going to feel good about the experience. This can happen before, during or after the act. It will be very bad for your privacy, for your heterosexuality. You may experience significant psychological distress. This is common when the straight participates in situations involving drinks, drugs, questionable friendships. I believe that the practice of abusive, promiscuous, irresponsible and unsafe sex is harmful to heterosexuals and homosexuals, morally and spiritually speaking. Whether the person is straight or gay, they are the ones who will have to account to their conscience and to God for all that he has done wrong. As long as they don't hurt or offend us, we have nothing to do with their life. However, it is important to keep in mind that homosexuality is not, and never has been, a disease, an option, or a choice. The homosexual is not marginal, as some organizations, especially religious and educational ones, believe they are. The homosexual is born homosexual. This story that someone joined a certain religious organization, received psychological or psychiatric treatment and stopped being homosexual, is a lie. I even believe that the person was never homosexual and lived or experienced homosexual experiences and then decided not to want this practice anymore. So far, I think so. But to say that someone was cured of homosexuality, married someone heterosexual and of the other sex and changed their life because of religion or psychological treatment, ah! I do not think so. Whoever did this was not homosexual."

"It is difficult to accept it. He is my brother."

"This is because we were created and used to seeing men bond with women and women with men. We have no family orientation, education or knowledge about people's sexual identity. Perhaps older people did not comment on it because they considered it ugly, impolite. No one could talk about it. In recent times, people's minds are more open. Today we talk more about sex, menopause, menstruation, premenstrual syndrome, andropause, homosexuality, heterosexuality and, even so, some speak with some reserve, some shame. Let's think that sex, and everything related to it, is part of life and it is good to discuss it, discover it, know more so as not to be ignorant or prejudiced and not to live in error."

"I don't know what to say to Abner."

"Do you think you need to say something?" The other did not answer. "Maybe you should say something and alert him, if necessary, to avoid promiscuity, the practice of sex without a personal relationship, multiple partners, true feelings. Casual sex is not good for anyone, I think. Maybe you can say something about it, but remember that it's his life."

"Talita, don't you think that if we accept homosexuality, we will have to accept pedophilia in a moment?"

"One thing has nothing to do with the other. Pedophilia is a disease. Not homosexuality. Think about it, pedophilia involves having sex with children and these are creatures without guidance, with no sense of what they are doing. Exempt from responsibilities. Pedophilia is cruel, inhuman. Don't mix things up."

"I'm distraught, Talita. I thought I was going to see this only in the family of others, you know?"

"I get it. This anguish will pass when you understand that your brother is what he is. He does not force himself to anything. He just assumed, admitted his condition." In order not to see her so focused on the subject, Talita asked. "And your sister? How is the pregnancy going?"

"I haven't seen Simone in a long time. We talked a bit on the phone. She teaches at the university. Our schedules are incompatible."

"Your mother can't wait for her grandson to arrive, can she?"

"Yeah, it is true! We are all happy and very anxious." Talita looked at her watch and was alarmed.

"Oh! Our lunch break is over."

"It's true. Let's go."

Rúbia felt much better after the conversation with her friend. She came to understand his brother's condition.

* * *

In the evening, upon meeting her boyfriend, Rúbia couldn't resist the urge to talk about her brother and told Jefferson about him.

After listening carefully, he was surprised.

"Abner?! I don't believe it!"

"It is true. I didn't believe it at first. Now I'm getting used to the idea, but…"

"And his partners, do they know?"

"If everyone knows, I don't know. Ricardo knows it. I called him at the company."

"Ricardo?"

"Yes, we talked for a while. He apologized to me for talking about it. He thought I already knew."

"I'm very surprised. I have never imagined."

"Neither did I, being his sister, suspect that."

"What about your parents?"

"They can't imagine something like this. My dad is going to break down. I don't even want to see it. My father's dream is for Abner to marry and give him grandchildren. My brother is the only one who can carry on my grandfather's last name."

"Don't get involved. Let your brother lead his life."

"And not us?"

"Of course."

"Talking about it…"

"What is that?"

"You know, Jefferson. I don't like our situation."

"My love... it's for a while. I'm trying to resolve the situation with her. Although we have nothing else, Cícera is demanding. She is making it difficult to have an amicable divorce."

"Then get out of there. Get an apartment and stay away from her."

"And my mother, Rúbia? I can't do that. Mrs. Zenaide is sensible."

"Did you talk with her?"

"I'm on it. Little by little, of course. I show her that I no longer have a solid marriage, that we are both dissatisfied."

"And your children?"

"They are teenagers who do not care much about what is happening. They don't spend much time at home. Pedro Henrique studies in the morning, English in the afternoon and stays online at night. Juan Victor studies in the morning, in the afternoon and at night, when he does not go out with his friends, he stays at the computer like his brother. On weekends they go to the club and then spend the day sleeping. It is always like that."

"You should get an apartment, take your mother and move out."

"I'm working on it." Getting closer, he kissed her and said; "Let's talk about something good now. I like being with you like this... Just like this. With you I find tranquility, peace... Is so good to have peace…"

Jefferson changed the subject and Rúbia was distraught. Once again, he seemed to flee from what was most important.

* * *

It was the weekend when Abner decided to go to his parents' house. He really needed to talk to Rúbia. He just didn't think that his sister, Simone, would be there that day.

She had decided to tell her parents about the health problem of the baby she was expecting. Her husband, Samuel, still seemed very upset by the fact and was isolated. He didn't want to talk about it or tell his parents or in-laws. Still, she decided it was time.

Upon arrival, Simone found out that Abner was in Rúbia's room. She felt more secure, since her brother, so understanding and caring, was there. He would support her. Then she decided to wait. She knew that he and her sister needed to get it right. When they were done, she would gather them all together and tell them about the problem.

In the living room, with her parents, Simone waited as they talked. Mrs. Celeste, an observant mother, was concerned.

"You look sad, daughter. What happened?"

"Nothing, mom."

"Is it the maid again?" Said Mrs. Celeste.

Before the daughter answered, Mr. Salvador commented;

"These maids have no manners. First, they come saying they know how to do everything. They want the job anyway. After they start working, they get lazy, they don't clean anything properly. When we go to show them what they didn't do, they still look upset, they murmur and even respond with some malice. The one we have here at home lives hung up on the cell phone, talking or texting. It is true that she is the one who pays the bill or takes advantage of the operator's promotion. Except while she's on the phone she's not doing the job properly, stops working, keeps wandering around, and doesn't pay attention to anything. It's all done wrong. Then when she sits down to eat, she doesn't have a shred of courtesy. She's greedy, fills the mixing plate, attacks the fruit bowl, and finishes it all."

"Salvador! Is that something you should say?" She scolded her husband.

"Yes, it is. And it's my home, it's my food, it's my fruit! I doubt if in her house, when there is fruit and dessert, she offers it to everyone to be finished in a single day. Another hobby she has is complaining that she is sick. Every day she complains that a different part of her body hurts. That's because she doesn't want to work. She wants to justify the bad service. She always leaves early for any reason. Of course! Nobody discounts anything. But if one day she works a little more, she wants to earn extra. If she does a little work that is not hers, she wants to receive money for it. Now, what she earns from something that is not part of the salary, aaaah...! That she does not see or value. I see your mother shopping in the market and giving her fruits and vegetables, when not, even meat ready to take home."

"I see we can't talk here. Let's go to the kitchen, daughter. I'm going to brew the coffee." When he saw them stand up, the man growled.

"Do not forget about me!"

81

While Mrs. Celeste and Simone were in the kitchen, Abner scolded Rúbia. He spoke in a low voice and emphasized almost whispering.

"What are you getting involved in? Jefferson is married! He already has teenage children!"

"We are friends." She tried to lie.

"Talk! I saw you two kissing. So, is he the mystery boyfriend?"

"No! He's not!"

"So, why didn't you bring your boyfriend home? Why don't I know him? I've always known all the guys you have dated."

"You have nothing to do with my life." She was irritated and exclaimed in a whisper. "I'm all grown up and vaccinated!"

"Can't you see that a married man will never make a serious commitment? He just wants to hang out, take you to bed, have an affair. And when he goes to sleep every night, he will be on his wife's side. If this person was going to abandon his wife and children, he would have already done so. You shouldn't show up in his life."

"He does not live well with his wife. Their bodies are separate."

"Lies! It's engulfing you! Come back to reality, Rúbia! Do you feel good being the other one? Do you feel good being the lover? The destroyer of a home?"

"Who are you to talk to me like that? Take care of your own affairs! Go get a treatment! Where have you seen that! You left our home to establish a house with another man! That is abnormal, you are sick!"

"Watch your words!" He warned firmly.

"If I have someone in my life, it is another man. And you? Dating a man! You want to live maritally with a man! It's

82

disgusting! How are you going to say this to your father and mother? When will you have the courage to tell your parents that you like another man? That you are depraved and disgusting?"

At that moment, they both noticed a figure outside the room. When they looked, Mr. Salvador was standing still and silent, looking at his son.

The man was flushed and sweating.

Without saying anything, he went to Abner and grabbed him by the shirt. Only then did he scream out, at the top of his lungs.

"Dammit!!! You wretch!!! I knew!!! I knew... I suspected...!!!" As he yelled, he shook his son by his shirt. Abner, although much taller and stronger than his father, did not react. He simply balanced himself so as not to fall. Mr. Salvador struck him twice in the face and offended him with innumerable obscene words. "You're not my son!!! It can't be!!! I will kill you...!!!"

Rúbia tried to cling to her father, but in vain. The screams attracted the attention of Mrs. Celeste and Simone, who came to the room and, frightened, tried to hug Mr. Salvador who was tilting at his son, hitting him.

In the midst of the commotion, Abner released himself, looked at the deplorable scene for a moment, turned and left.

Mr. Salvador calmed down when he saw the nervous and fragile state of Simone, who was crying. When he remembered that she was pregnant, he held on himself, so as not to continue with his attacks and screams. He thought that his daughter did not deserve to be nervous like that.

Leaving everyone in the room, he went to the living room, but did not find his son.

Enraged, he looked at the wife who followed him and had a tantrum. He grabbed a dining room chair, lifted it over his head, and slammed it violently on the floor, breaking it.

"What did I do to deserve this?" He screamed, going mad. "That bastard can't be my son! I want him to die! To die!!!"

Mrs. Celeste, with tears on her face, said nothing. She believed that staying there would fuel her husband's anger. Especially if she tried to argue. She wisely left the room, leaving him alone. She went to the kitchen where she sat and cried.

Meanwhile, Simone and Rúbia remained in the room. Even nervous, Rúbia tried to explain to her sister.

"It was not my fault. We... I was telling Abner that he's not sure about what he does, what he is."

"Talk elsewhere! You have no right to offend our brother!"

"¡He is gay!"

"So what?"

"That's not true!"

"Rúbia, is his life. Gay or not, Abner is our brother. He was always a wonderful person, kind-hearted, caring, and helpful. He has countless qualities. I don't care about his sexual identity."

"I'd love to see you talk like that. You were always the right fit for the family."

"Because I grew up."

"Would you like your child to be gay?"

"I learned to respect God's will. Whatever my son is, he is what I need him to be. If God sends me a little creature with some difficulty, it is because both of us, my son and I, have the capacity and human evolution to face this test. And it was Abner who made me understand that." There was a brief pause and she finally said. "You have no right to offend him. Know that. In fact, no one does."

Visibly nervous and trembling, Simone left the room, looking for her mother. Finding her sitting in the kitchen, she stroked her back and, standing next to her, asked in a soft and gentle voice.

"Oh, mom... are you ok?"

"I am, daughter. Don't worry about me." She said, stroking her other arm and belly. "You shouldn't be here. You can't be this nervous... The baby senses everything."

"I'm sad, mother. I'm not nervous. I'm worried about you and dad." Seeing her in silence, she commented. "I wonder how you must feel. It is not easy for a mother to know that her son..." She stopped the words.

"He is my son." She said confidently, wiping her face with her hands. "No one is going to do or say anything that hurts Abner here in this house. No matter what it is. Abner is my son." She tapped her chest lightly with her right hand.

"I'm glad you think so. I thought..."

"You thought wrong, baby." Looking into her eyes, she confessed. "I knew it. I knew your brother was different."

"Did you see something in his behavior?"

"Not exactly. He didn't behave like a woman." She said simply; "I noticed something different in friendships, for a while now. A friend who always called him... They always leave... But it doesn't matter. He is my son. It was what God entrusted to me with care."

"What about dad?"

"He must have gone to the bar. When he comes back and the fire is over, I will talk to him." Mrs. Celeste got up and stroked her daughter's face. She gave a forced smile and said; "I'm going to make lemon balm tea. We need to calm down. In the meantime, call your brother. I want to talk to him and see how he is."

Simone tried to make the call several times, but Abner's apartment phone went unanswered and the phone dropped to voicemail.

Mrs. Celeste made tea and served it to her daughter. She called for Rúbia and the three of them remained at the kitchen table, sipping the steaming drink in total silence.

5.– A CRUEL HEART

A FINE, COLD NIGHT RAIN WAS FALLING when Mr. Salvador partially recovered from the effect of alcohol.

He was lucid, but he still felt dizzy and had a severe headache.

"Have that cup of tea." His wife offered him. "It will help improve your liver." He sat on the bed, took the cup and took a few sips.

"Drink it all." Demanded firmly the woman.

"It's bitter." he complained.

"It tastes better than brandy. Come on, drink it." She said energetically.

Holding the cup with both hands, he leaned over and looked at the floor of the room.

In the next moment, he spoke in dismay.

"I can't believe I have a faggot, cheeky, naughty, scoundrel child…" Interrupting him, Mrs. Celeste said harshly.

"I think I have an alcoholic husband. I live with it and I don't want to. This is something you can change and you don't. That's why I say yes, you are naughty and scoundrel. Something that you can stop doing."

"Shut your mouth! Look how you talk to me!"

"Look at you, how you talk to me! I've kept my mouth shut too many times!"

"Who do you think you are?"

"I'm your wife! Mother of your children. I'm the one who cleans up your vomit, washes your soaked clothes, makes tea and coffee to cure your hangovers! I'm tired of having to watch while you drink. Look at you now! Do you want to complain about your son? Look who you are and what you do. Beautiful example, beautiful father you were and are. What morals do you have to offend your son? By the example you set, he could have become an alcoholic and he didn't."

"But he became a faggot!"

Mrs. Celeste, taking advantage of the discomfort that she knew her husband was feeling, pushed him hard, imposing herself.

"Shut up! I won't admit that you curse him! You may have put food in the house, given him clothes and school, but you never give him attention, affection, love, understanding... Now, you have no right to complain about what is or what is not."

"He is not my son!"

This time, when she heard this, she pushed him so hard that the porcelain cup was released from her husband's hands and shattered on the floor. When he fell sideways on the bed, she screamed.

"Do not offend me! You clown! Abner is your son and if you want you have an exam that proves it. If you say that again, I'll break your face and get you out of this house! I'm tired! I'm tired of babysitting a scoundrel drunk, as naughty as you! Shut your mouth!" She yelled. "Otherwise, you will see what I do to you!"

The headache was severe and he was very ill. Mr. Salvador could not react. He was confused and even afraid of the reaction his wife had.

Later, on the phone, in his apartment, Abner spoke with Simone.

"I went there today to tell our parents about the baby."

"Oh God…" He lamented. "Sorry. I started the discussion with Rúbia. Wanting me to stop scolding her, she started talking about my life. In a way, she is right."

"Our sister has no right to offend you."

"And I have no right to interfere with her life."

"What did Rúbia do now?"

"Never mind. Is her life… those are her problems…"

"If she's doing something wrong, I think it's okay to scold her."

"Now, thinking it through, I don't think it's my business, Simone."

"Ah… it is. If she does something wrong and gets in trouble, who is she going to ask for help? To the family, of course! However, if she does something wrong, and you tell her about it, she says; *you have nothing to do with my life, in my life I'm in charge.* So, when she goes wrong, you don't have to help. You know, I think if she doesn't listen to my advice, don't ask for my help."

"And… But… we can't be like that. Rúbia is fooling, or rather she fools herself."

"Fooling herself at twenty-nine? Don't you think she's a bit mature for that? Rúbia is a big girl now. She knows how to separate right from wrong."

"Well… let her go. When the dust settles I'll talk to her." Changing the subject, he asked. "And Samuel, didn't he want to go with you to dad's house?"

"No. He seems very distant. He's moving away from this. He doesn't stay at home. He lives at the university… spends most of the morning on the computer or watching movies. I don't know what to do. He no longer accompanies me to the doctor, he does not want to know about me…" Her voice broke. She took a deep breath, calmed down, and added. "I'm alone with this. I haven't even told my in-laws yet."

"You are not alone. I'm with you, see? When will you go to the doctor again?"

"On Wednesday."

"What time?"

"At…" She thought. "Ten in the morning."

"Wednesday at half past nine I'll be there. I'm with you."

"No, Abner. You don't have to…"

"Hey! You don't have to tell me what to do or not to do" He said in a friendly tone. "I want to join my sister and my nephew. And you won't be the one to stop me, huh!"

"I appreciate it. I shudder a lot at each appointment, at each exam."

"Clearly yes. You are human, you have feelings. It couldn't be any different."

"Sorry if I call too much. When I talk to you or to Cláudio, I feel much better. Cláudio is my friend, I don't want to bother him too much. You…" She laughed. "You are my brother and I can be a little annoying... But if I'm bothering you, let me know."

"You never bother me." After a moment he asked. "Simone, how is mom? How did she react after everything she heard?"

"Mom said she already knew. She said she won't admit to anyone offending you. She reacted in a way that I did not imagine, did not expect."

"And Rúbia?" He wanted to know.

"She was completely silent. She didn't say anything else about it, near mom. Just what I told you. I think she regrets not being careful, for having talked too much."

"Like I said, I'm going to let the dust settle."

"You should call mom. She wants to talk to you."

He was thoughtful and then decided;

"I think I'll call her. If dad went to the bar, right now he's sleeping or enjoying his hangover. Yes... I'll call her."

At that moment the intercom rang.

Abner let his sister know, said goodbye and went to answer.

"You can let her in." He allowed the doorman and ran to the door, waiting apprehensively. When the elevator door opened, he expressed himself in amazement, with a smile.

"Mom! You here?"

"Hello son. I had to come." She hugged him for a while. Then, wrapping him around her waist and him with his arm around her shoulder, they get in.

The lady sat on the sofa, put the bag aside and asked;

"Are you ok? Did your father hurt you?"

Abner sat in an armchair that was almost next to the sofa. He seemed a bit confused. He did not expect that visit nor did he know what they would talk about.

"I'm ok, mom. It was nothing." He replied

"Your face is red, your lip is swollen."

She leaned and wanted to touch him. He generously took her hand, kissed it, and held it between his until her mother took it.

"I'm fine. Do not worry. It was nothing."

"I came here because I got tired of calling and... First, no one answered. I went to do my things, take care of your father... You know how he comes after drinking, right? I tried again and the line was just busy."

"I was talking to Simone. She called me as soon as I arrived. As I left, I took a walk to cool my head and turned off the phone. Sorry if I worried you."

91

"When I got the busy line again, I decided to come. I decided not to wait any longer." The young man took a deep breath, looked at her and asked politely;

"Mom, I need you to forgive me. I know what every parent expects from a child. They raise you as a man, they give you all the education based on the sex of the physical body, but... In my case, I'm not what you expected. I tried, I swear I tried, but... When I dated a girl, it was something very contrary to my nature... I can't explain it. I suffered a lot, it took me a long time to admit it... It was and is very difficult for me." Without any expression, the mother listened carefully. He continued; "I can imagine how difficult it has been for dad, for you... It has to be very sad, very embarrassing to face the neighbors, family and friends who find out and come up with offensive jokes or even outright offenses. That's why I left the house. I left out respect for you two, because it is not your fault what I am. If I could, I would go far, so that others would not know and make you suffer, be ashamed of me." Absolute silence reigned for long minutes. She was watching him closely and Abner didn't know what else to say. Still, he tried to explain. "It's not dad's or anyone's fault. This condition is not the consequence of any trauma. I already researched it. I spoke with qualified mental health professionals such as psychologists, psychiatrists... I looked for answers in religions…"

"Son." She interrupted. "Do you think God is evil?"

"No. Of course not."

"I'm pretty ignorant, Abner, but when I don't understand a situation, I let my heart explain it to me. I understand that when you are something, you live in a state... I mean…"

"You live in a condition." He helped her with words.

"That is. When you experience a condition, that condition is nobody's fault. If it is necessary to live like that, this state or condition happened with God's permission. Let the ignorant blame

God for anyone's conditions, because that is what prejudiced people do. When prejudiced people curse, offend, discriminate, mistreat someone because of their condition, they are offending and blaming God who allowed someone to be born that way. If they curse, offend or discriminate against someone because of color, sex, difference, special need, because they are fat or thin, tall or short, that prejudiced person will have to deal with God. So let others speak. Do not wish them evil with words. Don't offend them for being ignorant. But don't demean yourself either. Raise your head and go on with your life. I'm ignorant, son. I don't know how to speak properly, but... I don't hurt or offend people because of the way they live."

"How is that, mother?"

"The world is modern, but there is something that bothers a little, especially for someone my age or someone raised like me."

"What do you mean?"

"The other day I was at the mall and I saw a boy and a girl kissing. Son, that wasn't a kiss, it was... it was a sexual act!" She said in dismay. "Despite being a boy and a girl, the scene was too much. I was embarrassed. If it was one of my children, I would have noticed. Give each other a kiss, a peck. I've even done it in public. But the way I saw those two... It was too much. So if I see two boys or two girls kissing, I will be surprised. I think the vast majority of people are not ready for this. For that reason, I ask you: watch your behavior when you are in public. That is what gives reasons for others to offend people with their status as... homosexual."

"Today, a public place where heterosexuals can kiss is also valid for homosexuals. I will not say that it is common, but it is easy to see homosexuals dating or living together in marriage, walking side by side, holding hands, shopping in stores or supermarkets."

"I know. I have also seen many. And I confess that I saw many well educated and respectful people around you. They seemed to live the way they wanted and didn't bother anyone. What I tell you is what I already told your sisters. Look in the past, the woman was very repressed by her parents, and then by her husband. That was in my time. Later, when the woman began to feel freer, more comfortable, many felt too comfortable. Many women have become vulgar for walking with one man today, tomorrow with another... I know girls from good families who have prostituted themselves to pay for college. The moment she becomes a vulgar and easy woman, even when she dates a married man, does not pay attention to what she is doing. But then, over time, over the years, in her conscience, there will be regret, pain... She will want to go back to everything she did and won't be able to do so. This can cause nervous breakdown, depression, pain in the soul and that disorder that many live today and at such a young age. Normally, and I speak from life's experience, these couples who constantly cling, rub each other and give outrageous kisses in public... These couples don't last long. They do it by showing off, to assert themselves. Just as it is not pleasant to see a man and a woman rubbing and kissing, it is not pleasant to see two women or two men doing the same thing. At least that's what I think. The world still does not understand what homosexual is and it will be more difficult to understand if these people impose themselves disrespectfully."

"I understand what you mean. But I didn't need any guidance on this. I don't want to expose myself. Not in that way. I will not deny that I'm gay. I have suffered a lot for denying what I am. However, I do not want to impose my homosexuality on others."

"You know, son, sometimes when I see that in gay parade, a lot of guys show their bodies and expose themselves so much, I think it's no different from those women who expose themselves naked or semi-naked in the carnival parades. It surprises me a little, both situations. I can't tell if it's right or wrong. They don't need to do that. I think that's why some people rebel. I've seen a lot of guys with that girlish look, with those delicate lines, using paint, pulling out the eyebrows... This is more common, acceptable, since each one dresses and groom himself as he wants. But in those gay parades, with naked people or at the carnival with those naked girls... Ah...! I do not approve of that."

"I don't recall seeing naked people at a gay parade. At carnival, it is more common. Mom, I think the gay parade is a way to ask for rights and acceptance. With that, people realize that there is homosexuality, that these people are people and they have their rights like everyone else. There was a time when homosexuals were taken to the stake, to die in concentration camps, in the holocaust. Until the 1970s, psychiatrists considered homosexuality to be a mental illness. It wasn't until the early 1990s that the World Health Organization (WHO) removed homosexuality from the list of mental illnesses. It was a victory, but everything is very recent and there are a lot of misinformed people. They think that a homosexual needs treatment. Today it is known that it is not a mental illness, it is not a psychological disorder. Even by law, health professionals trying to cure someone of their homosexuality are prohibited. Homosexuality is a different way of being a man or a woman. There are cultures, like India, that believe in reincarnation, that also believe that homosexuality is a third sex. So much so that there are three elements in the forms of public government procedures for the person to specify the gender or sex to which they belong."

"How is that?"

"When we make a form in which we need to identify ourselves and put personal data on how to obtain a driver's license, for example, in some forms, in this country and many others, there are two elements so that we can indicate what gender we belong to: M for men and F for women. In India, there are three: M masculine, for men; F female, for women, and T for transgender." The mother didn't say anything and he continued; "Sometimes I think they are

95

more accurate. At least, more accurate than those religious fanatics who criticize and want so much to cure the homosexual, ignoring his true nature. In fact, religious practices, false promises to cure someone to make them heterosexual, should be prohibited. They should have more to do. Provide comfort to those in hospitals, to the elderly who are in nursing homes, joy to hospitalized boys, participate in organizations that collect food and provide education and culture to those who do not have it, to help social inclusion. There is too much to do. But no. They insist on spreading the cure for homosexuality. That is homophobia and homophobia is a crime."

"It is homo... what is it?"

"Homophobia is any type of prejudice against homosexuals. It is non-acceptance, contempt, aggression, physical or verbal offenses, moral or psychological restriction. There are numerous cases of homicides of homosexuals due to their sexual condition or orientation. Despite being a crime, the laws should be stricter."

"The laws on all kinds of prejudice should be stricter, son." Then, the silence was absolute for a while, until the lady justified; "Abner, I came here to see how you were. I was worried about the way you left the house and... And to tell you that I'm your mother, however you are. I only ask you one thing." Seeing him in silence, she continued. "Do not prostitute yourself. Do not corrupt yourself. Don't vulgarize yourself. Don't become anyone. Be a decent person. I think it is not correct for a person to be promiscuous. I don't know if you want to go to a gay parade or not, but... Think about it, son. Everyone can ask and protest for their rights. This parade should be a protest against such homophobia and tell the world that you have the right to be what you are, to love whoever you want, because God has given you free will. When it comes to sexually transmitted diseases, they exist for everyone. We have to be careful and that's it. It is also necessary to remember, son, that everyone can dress as they want, speak and gesture however they want, but it is good to remember that homosexuals are not animals, they are people and people should value themselves. I saw on television, at these parades, those who tear their clothes and have sex or imply that they are having sex on the street, like animals. That is not true. No one needs to expose themselves to such humiliation to claim their rights. Act like a civilized human being. One day, you might want to dress differently, but dress like a person."

"I know it mom." She smiled. "I'm not going to do that. I'm also not in favor of this kind of attitude, for anyone."

Mrs. Celeste opened her loving arms to him and called out to wrap him. Abner accepted and responded immediately, going to her. As they hugged, the mother was overcome. At that moment the bell rang. The son walked away and, somewhat embarrassed, commented.

"To come up here without being announced, it must be David."

Immediately, Mrs. Celeste understood who he was and asked;

"Come on, ask him to come in. After all, I only know him by phone."

"Perhaps I did not want this experience for my son, but what could I do but accept him with love. Fighting, yelling, offending, distancing would do nothing. It would only serve as an aggression that would cause him to suffer immense negativity that would stand in the way.

It is up to us, in all circumstances, to lean unconditional love through acceptance. They are people like everyone else, who seek to understand their doubts, fears and desires.

Who of us does not seek balance? Who among us does not seek to be understood?

We are not superior. It is not for us to judge. We must measure the part of responsibility that we have before those who come our way, be it an old man, a boy, a special person, a disabled person, a heterosexual person, a homosexual person or whoever.

It is not enough to be heterosexual to say that you have balance and calm, especially when it comes to sexuality."

When Abner opened the door, he didn't have time to say something, because David came in saying;

"When you called me, I was at the market with my mother. She was mad that you didn't come to our house. She sent you that chicken tart and…" He stopped when he saw the lady standing in the living room.

"This is my mother, Celeste." Said Abner, introducing them. "Mom, this is David."

"Hello Mrs. Celeste. How have you been?" He greeted normally, as he approached.

The woman opened her arms and, when he hugged her, she said;

"Then you are David! We just talked on the phone, right?" As she stepped back, she took his hands and continued; "You are very different from what I imagined, son." She smiled. "You are a very handsome young man."

"Thank you, Mrs. Celeste. You are very kind and friendly. You have a beautiful smile. In fact... smiles are my specialty."

"You are a dentist, right?"

"Yes, I am. When you need my services, just let me know." Whispering, he said cheerfully. "I won't charge you for anything. Just look for me. But don't tell anyone."

"If you offer it, I'm going, huh? I'm needing it."

"And to get there, take my card." He took the card out of his pocket and offered it to her. "And just call and make an appointment. I will be very happy to help you."

The lady looked at the card and put it in the bag. Abner was totally embarrassed. He had never imagined himself in that situation.

Soon the lady said;

"I'm leaving now. It's late."

"No, mom. Stay." Asked the son.

"My mom sent this cake to Abner." Going to the dining room table, David showed it and said; "It is still warm. Don't you want to eat a piece?"

"I won't be ashamed, boy. This cake is very fragrant. I want a piece and then I'll go."

Abner spread a tablecloth on the table, opened a soda, set plates, cutlery and served the cake. So, Mrs. Celeste decided.

"It's late. I really need to go."

"I'll take you home, mom."

"Let's go in my car." Said David. "It is parked on the street. It is closer."

On the way to Mrs. Celeste's house, Abner ask;

"Mom, how is my father?" He wanted to know.

"You know how he looks after drinking. Hangover, headache and liver pain... You can't take him. I said a few things to him before I left."

"I don't want you to fight because of me."

"You know me, son. I do not fight. I always leave your father talking to himself. However, when I want to, I know how and what to say."

* * *

At home, Simone was worried about her family's problems, despite having enough in her life.

That day, after returning from her parents' house, where she had gone with the intention of telling them about the condition of the baby she was waiting for, she did not find her husband.

After talking to her brother on the phone, she called the in-laws' house, but Samuel wasn't there. Concerned, she called her husband's cell phone and was surprised to hear the phone ring in the bedroom.

She went there, picked it up, smiled for a moment, and opened it. She discovered that there was another missed call besides the one she had just made.

Checking the list of missed calls, she noticed a name: Marrie.

It was strange to see an unusual name. Recalling the memory, she remembered Marrie, a professor who taught at the same university as her, the previous semester, the same university where her husband was director of the history course. She remembered that she was a not so beautiful woman, but she dressed well and knew how to behave. Even better. She and Marrie weren't friends and when she saw her talking to Samuel it kind of annoyed her.

It had been a few months since Marrie left the university. What could she want with Samuel? Why would she have his cell phone number? After all, if for some reason she went to work there again, she should call the university or go there. There was no point in calling Samuel's cell phone, especially since he was the principal of another course and not one that Marrie could teach.

Smart, Simone decided to check the box for messages sent and received from his cell phone. Weird. All messages were deleted. Her husband was not the type of man to worry about. His cell phone was always full of messages, and she was often the one that deletes them at his request.

Also, he had deleted the messages recently, because the day before, she sent him one. It bothered her a lot.

She took a shower, turned on the TV, and tried to distract herself with a movie when her husband arrived. Samuel, silent, passed the room and barely looked at her. Not even to go over and give her a quick kiss, like always.

"And well...?" She says, calling his attention. "Something happened?"

He returned, faced her and replied;

"I went out with friends. I was stressed out and needed to relax a bit."

"And my kiss?" She asked, smiling as if she wasn't hurt, resenting his cold attitude. The husband approached, kissed her as usual and Simone realized. "You have a sad face."

"I'm tired."

"Samuel." Seeing him facing her, she said. "Today I went to my parents' house, but... I couldn't tell them anything". The atmosphere was a bit tense and... It was not a good time. However, tomorrow we are going to your parents' house and then to my parents' house. They need to know about the baby.

"I don't want to tell them anything. Tell them yourself."

The woman got up, approached and said in a soft tone;

"What about our son? If you are suffering, so am I."

"We already know what is going to happen to him, right? Therefore, it is better to consider that we do not have a child. Pretend that he doesn't exist. That way we will suffer less. Imagine that you are sick and that in a few months... I don't know... You will have surgery and everything will be as it was before."

Simone couldn't stand at it and yelled.

"You are a monster! Realize what you just said! How can you be so cruel? So insensitive? So, what? How absurd, Samuel! What happened to you?

"I'm being realistic, Simone. Realistic! I know that if he is born, he will have little time to live. Weeks or months…"

"There are kids with this syndrome who are ten years old or older."

"And do you want that?! Are you sure you want a boy with serious mental and physical problems who will live for a few years? Do you really want a son with a horrible face that will last ten years? I do not want it!" He yelled.

The woman was shocked and speechless. She felt bad about her husband's insensitive and perverse reaction.

He turned over and went into the room, leaving her alone.

Confused and extremely sad, when she heard her husband turn on the shower, she could not bear it and called her friend Cláudio, who listened attentively and comforted her with generous words.

Simone and her husband no longer spoke. There was nothing to be said after the rude opinion he expressed. She felt hurt. She was incredulous, her husband was always a kind, loving and understanding creature. Now she didn't know what to say to him when she discovered the cruel heart her husband has.

6.– THE FAMILY'S ACCEPTANCE

ON WEDNESDAY, as agreed, Abner arrived at the sister's home early to go with her at the doctor's appointment.

As soon as he saw her get into the car, he noticed that she was very nervous. After exchanging greetings, he wanted to know;

"Are you alright?"

Simone took a deep breath and, with teary eyes, answered in a low voice.

"Nothing is okay. I can't deal with this anymore."

"Was it Samuel? Did he say or do something that hurt you?" The sister told him about her husband's opinion.

"He got another woman. I'm sure." She declared.

"That can't be…" He said, incredulously. "No. Samuel wouldn't do that."

"I'm sure, Abner. I got unanswered calls on my cell phone and yesterday I saw a message that he didn't delete. It is Marrie, she was a professor at the university. A very intellectual, slim and elegant woman. She is not pretty, but she has a strong presence. However…"

"What?" The brother asked about the pause.

"I can't judge her, but… Do you know that kind of woman who, just by looking, you know she's worth nothing?" Abner was silent, expressionless and she continued; "I never liked seeing her talk to Samuel. I felt like Marrie offered herself."

"What did the message you found on his cell phone say?"

"Give me a call. L.Y." I think that L.Y. means: love you. That is what was written. I'm devastated. My life is over. Besides saying what he said about our son, not respecting my feelings, my sensitivity, he got another woman. Earlier today, I reminded him that there was an appointment, but he didn't say anything. He got ready and went to work."

"Samuel really loves your son. He is upset with the baby's condition and cannot cope with the situation. He is not ready."

"Neither was I." Then she looked at her watch and said; "Let's go, we are late."

"Okay, let's go"

Abner accompanied her to the appointment, as planned, and did not leave her sister's side, supporting her all time. Especially when the doctor explained the difficult conditions and even the characteristics of the baby.

She cried a lot and her brother, seeing her in that condition, suggested to the doctor a medical leave for work, since, as she was emotionally touched, she could not teach. The doctor agreed and provided the consent, because, in addition to her very touched emotional state, there was a risk of miscarriage.

Then they went to Mrs. Celeste's house. Abner did not enter, he left her there and went to work.

Mrs. Celeste noticed that her daughter wasn't well and received her warmly.

"Come on, Simone. Sit here." Seeing her settled, she asked. "What happened to make you like this?"

Simone couldn't resist and told her all about the baby's condition. She talked about her research on the Internet, about the syndrome and even showed the documents she had printed. In the end, she cried a lot and Mrs. Celeste, hugging her, cried too.

Without being seen, Mr. Salvador heard all of it.

First, the man was stunned. After a while, he perked up and went into the living room. Sitting next to his daughter, he said;

"That's why I don't like those stupid tests. If it were in the past, in such a case, you would only suffer after seeing your child born and not before. Now look at you... You will torture yourself until you see the little boy. This is bad. These doctors don't know anything. Come here..." Pulling her to lean against his shoulder, the father caressed her affectionately. Seeing her more composed, he advised her. "Let's see if you don't stay like that. Stop crying. Your child does not deserve to suffer."

"But, dad, he..."

"He does. You have to take good care of him. I have seen many reports that each baby, even in the mother's womb, feels everything that happens with her and with the environment. For not understanding or knowing what it is, he feels fear, fear, rejection..."

"I didn't want everything to be like this..." She got tearful.

"Nobody wanted, daughter." Said the mother. "But if that is what God wants, we will do everything possible to respect his will and take care of this baby."

"Samuel is weird. He doesn't want to get attached to his son." Simone partially recounted her husband's opinion and the father said;

"So, Samuel, who is a learned man, is more ignorant than I am. I never thought that..." He did not finish and decided. "Then you will not return to your house. We take care of you here."

"I can't stay, father. I have my house."

"But didn't you say the doctor gave you a leave of absence? So…"

Said the man. Mrs. Celeste, more thoughtful, added;

"You don't have to leave your house completely. You can stay here with us during the day, and at night Samuel comes and takes you. Staying there all day looking at the walls and thinking nonsense will not be good. Actually, you were already going to stay here during the recovery, what will change is that you will come here earlier."

"I can't decide just like that. I need to speak to Samuel."

"But he doesn't even care about you, much less his son." His father murmured.

"You don't have to talk like that, Salvador." His wife scolded. "Samuel is confused. Just that. It will pass by." Despite the pain and sorrow she felt at the news and at her daughter's fragile state, Mrs. Celeste took a deep breath and tried to appear firm, proposing. "Simone, enough suffering. Your child is and will continue to be loved. This is all sad, but it doesn't change how we feel about him or you. Isn't that right, Salvador?"

"Yes, it is. Here you will have all our support."

"So, daughter, go inside, take a good shower… I'll borrow some of your sister's clothes for you. Then you will eat something and rest. Later, we will call Samuel saying you're here. Is that okay?

"I'll do it myself. I'm so tired…" So, it was done.

Much later, while Simone slept, her parents were sitting at the kitchen table in total silence until Mr. Salvador asked.

"Is the baby really like she said?"

"Neither she nor the doctor would play with such a thing. Today, Abner went with her and saw the ultrasound exam."

"I heard what you read from those documents and I saw those photos from a distance… But I don't even want to see them

106

again. I wonder... Why does God allow a baby to be born like that?" Not hearing an answer, he continued. "I already read in the Bible, when Jesus says that a man's blindness was not the fault of his father or mother. He was blind by himself. But if the man was born blind... Where did he go wrong or sin to be blamed for his blindness?"

The wife, extremely sad, did not listen to him and lamented.

"My little grandson..." She screamed. "My first grandson... I didn't expect this..."

"I just thought that these things happen in the neighbor's family." Getting up, Mr. Salvador stood behind his wife and said, caressing her back gently. "I didn't want this either, but if it has to be like this... We need to be together and give Simone strength."

✻ ✻ ✻

Later, after a restful sleep she hadn't had for a long time, Simone was lovingly awakened by her mother.

"Daughter, it's after four. I think that if you sleep more, you won't sleep well at night." She woke up, sat on the bed, and her mother suggested. "Come into the kitchen, I made you a cup of lemon balm."

"Mom..."

"What's the matter?"

"Sit here, mother." She asked, putting her hand on the bed. Mrs. Celeste obeyed and her daughter said. "I don't like the way Samuel is. He has got another woman."

After listening to the whole story told by her daughter, Mrs. Celeste said;

"Don't jump to conclusions. You haven't seen anything. He did not change you with another woman."

"I'm going to talk with him. What do you think?"

"Talk, but do it calmly. Don't blame your husband."

"What if it is true? What if he has another woman?"

"Have faith, daughter. You need to pray and ask God for strength to support you. Pray to Mary, Blessed Mother, to protect you and keep you with her veil." Seeing her daughter distressed, she asked her affectionately. "Do not cry. It will transmit bad emotions to the baby. This is not good. Come on, get up and let's go to the kitchen. Then we'll walk around the block and you'll see that bad feeling go away."

Right after dinner, Samuel arrived to pick up his wife. He was received by Mr. Salvador, he barely greeted him and sat on the sofa, waiting for his wife.

Sitting habitually in his chair, the father-in-law said;

"Simone told us about the baby." The son-in-law said nothing and continued watching television. "She also told us about your opinion, thinking that she is sick."

"Look, Mr. Salvador, this is a very particular problem that I don't want to share with anyone. My vision is realistic. I don't want Simone to suffer. We must face the facts and that is it."

"You're making Simone suffer more than the news of her son. You have to think about her feelings."

The son-in-law didn't say anything about it. He got up and asked;

'Where is she? I need to go soon."

"She is in her sister's room. They are all there."

Samuel, in silence, went to Rúbia's room and entered after calling at the door.

"Simone, ready?" When he saw them gathered together, he greeted them from a distance. "I have to get up early tomorrow."

The wife did not reply. She got up and went to get her bag. Meanwhile, Mrs. Celeste explained with apparent naturalness.

"The doctor gave Simone a leave of absence. She has no emotional conditions to work. Tomorrow she will take care of the documentation. So I told her to stay here at home. I think that, alone, in your house, it will be worse for her emotional state."

"Simone will not be alone. The maid is there."

"It is not the same thing. My daughter is suffering a lot and she will find comfort in the family. It will be better."

"I agree with my mother." Said Rúbia. "We have to take care of Simone's emotional state."

"As you wish. That's fine for me." He agreed, but took a deep breath showing dissatisfaction.

"It'll be like this: you bring her here in the morning and pick her up at night." Proposed Mrs. Celeste.

"It can be. If she can't drive, it can be."

"She can even drive, Samuel, but going home at night is difficult." Said Rúbia. "You never show up until eleven o'clock. It won't be great for her to leave early and be alone. However, if you leave from here after 10 or 10:30, it's too late. Is not safe."

At that moment, Simone arrived and said;

"Let's go."

He did not reply to his sister-in-law. He was annoyed. Seeing her ready to go, Mrs. Celeste remembered.

"Daughter, tomorrow, don't forget to bring some clothes to make you feel comfortable."

"Okay, mom. See you tomorrow. The blessing." She said; "Goodbye."

"God bless you."

109

Mrs. Celeste accompanied them to the door. Then she returned to Rúbia's room, saying;

"Jeez...! I can't believe what's happening. I've never seen this guy so cold."

"He is, mother. How strange is Samuel. He does not look like the same man."

"And you don't even know the worst thing."

"What?"

"Your sister suspects that he got another woman."

"Another woman?"

Mrs. Celeste told them everything and then got angry.

"She's a shameless scoundrel who wants to take advantage of the situation! That naughty woman who does not have the ability to find a free man and is destroying the home of others."

"Maybe she is his friend."

"Friend?! The married man has no female friends! The friendship of a woman should be with her partner, even so... This is the thing of a woman waiting for a destroyed home. She is a naughty vulture! I didn't say any of that to your sister so as not to hurt her more, but..."

Rúbia felt her heart sink. In a way, she thought, her situation with Jefferson was similar. He still lived with his wife and children, and she was just someone waiting for the destruction of a home.

She didn't know what to say.

Sad and bitter thoughts corroded her. She was not raised to destroy someone's home. Her family gave her basic moral principles. What happened in her life was contrary to her education and morals.

"Rúbia! I'm talking with you!" The mother said when she saw her daughter distant, without paying attention to what she said.

"Sorry... I was so far away."

Mrs. Celeste continued as if she had heard.

"Like I said, I want you to talk to your brother. If you can't, if you don't have the ability to understand Abner, just accept him."

"Are you in favor of what he is?"

"I'm neither for nor against. I just understand and accept it. He is my son. That is what God has entrusted to me."

"Only if God has entrusted this to you and not to me." Protested Mr. Salvador, who arrived unseen. "I'd rather have a boy in jail or dead than a fairy son, a pedophile."

"You don't know what you're talking about, Salvador!" His wife scolded him. "I love and accept our son exactly the way he is!"

"Only if he is your son, because mine died the day I knew about his evil! If he shows up here, I'll cut him in half! He died for me! It's no use coming here even when he's sick. Yes, because as he has become what he has become, he can only hope to catch these diseases that are out there!"

"Stop being ignorant. The diseases you are talking about exist for everyone, not just homosexuals."

"I do not care. If he appears here..."

"Stop, please!" Asked Rúbia. "You are going to start fighting over something..."

The phone rang and Mrs. Celeste answered, ignoring her husband, who continued.

"I support my children, but I will not admit a pedophile son and a lost daughter, a random woman dating a married man or dating one and then another man. Never!" He yelled and went out of the room.

Once again, Rúbia was invaded by thoughts that hurt her badly.

If her father suspected she was dating a married man, he would kill her. He would take her out of the house and he would no longer want to see her. He would do the same thing he did with her brother.

Her mother's comment and her father's harsh words about having an affair with a married man did not leave her alone. She felt bad and wanted to cry. She needed to decide what to do with her life. That wasn't what she wanted, but she thought she liked Jefferson very much.

Although recently, especially when she complained that he hadn't done anything about the divorce, Rúbia perceived him as very dissatisfied, apologetic, and even a bit distant.

Remembering Jefferson's behavior, she experienced a fear that she had never felt before. A bad feeling squeezed her chest and choked her. She couldn't bear the burning thoughts and decided to call Jefferson's cell phone, but it only went to voicemail.

So, she had to endure the painful anguish she felt.

✳ ✳ ✳

As the days passed, Simone began to sleep at her parents' house. Every day it was for a reason. Sometimes it was late and Samuel said he was too tired to go pick her up. Others, he needed to get up too early and if he left her there before going to work, he would have to wake up even earlier.

When Simone noticed a significant distance from her husband, she sought him out and was very direct when she asked him:

"Is there another, Samuel? Do you have another woman?" Very surprised by the question, he tried to hide it.

"What is that?! Where did you get that idea from?"

"From your strange and distant behavior. From the messages I found on your cell phone, the ones you received from a Marrie."

"Have you been searching my things...? Searching on my cell phone?"

"No. It was a coincidence. You weren't here, I called your cell phone and it rang in our room. I went to turn it off and removed the missed call so it didn't beep every five minutes. Suddenly, I saw a message and went to see what it was. I'm not the type that sniffs shirts or takes phone calls. Although I noticed that you deleted all existing messages and calls, something you generally don't do." The husband said nothing and she insisted. "So? Is there another woman, Samuel?"

Simone felt shaky inside, but she held her ground until he answered coldly, looking at her.

"I'm confused about our marriage. I think your pregnancy..." He stopped. Faced with the silence, even confused, she said;

"We planned everything in our lives! I didn't get pregnant due to carelessness."

"You are not understanding. We didn't plan a disabled and weakened son. I'm touched. I'm not ready."

"And do you think I am?" She asked firmly. "Do you think it's easier for me than for you?"

"I guess not. If you want, you can solve that problem. Abortion is allowed, in your case."

"I can't believe you just told me that." She said, hurt.

"That's what I think, Simone. I can't take it anymore."

"You can't stand it, why?" Without waiting, she said; "Why did you cry your bitterness with a scoundrel who consoled you and made you forget that you have as much responsibility as I do with this child?"

"Do you want to know?!" He spoke rudely and nervous. "Face it as you want. I never thought about the possibility of having a child with problems. It shook me and I couldn't talk about it with you. Plus, Marrie showed up at the university the week we found it out. I was depressed and we talked. I expressed it with her. She knew how to understand me and see the situation from my angle. As for you... Every time I see you, I feel a burden. And I can't stand it."

"A burden?! I've never complained to you about anything."

"No?! The hospital, doctors, laboratories, exams... I don't want to continue any of this!"

"If your son was perfect, would you accompany him?"

"Of course! That's the truth. And if you want to know more: I'm disappointed, ashamed of this situation. I don't know how to confront family and friends, especially when they ask me about your pregnancy, about the baby. They will feel sorry for us. They will see us as unfortunate people and many will only want to speculate. I hate speculation!"

Simone was shaking from head to toe. Slowly the wife sat down on the sofa. Incredulous and not knowing what to do.

The husband cared little about her feelings, her sensitivity in that delicate state. He went to the bedroom. Although confused, she picked up the phone and called her brother.

"Abner?"

"No. One moment." The voice of a man answered. When he returned, said; "Abner is in the bathroom. Would you like to leave a message, please?"

"Who's this?" She asked in a shaky voice.

"I'm David."

"Please, David... This is Simone, his sister."

"How are you, Simone?" He wanted to know politely.

"No... I'm not well and..." She fell silent.

Noticing her heavy breathing, as if she were crying, he wanted to know.

"Abner told me that you are pregnant. Do you need help...? Do you want me to go there?"

"Yes, I need you to help me. Ask my brother to come get me at my house as soon as possible."

"I'll tell him. Calm down." After a moment he asked. "How do you feel? Do you want me to call an ambulance? Maybe it will go faster. Or if not... if you want to talk to me..."

"No. Thanks, David. I need some clothes. I have to go. I'll wait for my brother here in front of my house."

"It's okay. As soon as he gets out of the shower, he'll go there."

"Thanks. Goodbye."

"Goodbye."

David warned Abner to hurry.

Meanwhile, Simone picked up two bags, put on some clothes, and went to wait for her brother on the sidewalk in front of their house, without saying anything to her husband.

Abner wasted no time in coming with David, who quickly got out of the car and went to meet her, taking her bags.

Wrapping her in a hug, the brother kissed her forehead and felt concerned. When he led her to the car, he asked her.

"What happened, Simone?"

115

"I will tell you later. Take me home." They did as she said.

Upon arrival, she had a strong crying attack for a long time. The brother made her some tea and chilled it. Serving it, he talked to her with an affable tone in his voice.

"Drink a little. It'll be good for you."

After she calmed down, she told him everything that happened and finished.

"I didn't expect that from my husband."

"As I understand it, you left the house and didn't warn him, did you?" David observed.

"It was just that. I had nothing else to say. What else can I say?"

"In that case, silence is the best choice." Abner mentioned.

"I told mom and dad about the baby."

"I've heard so. You did well."

"I never thought dad was going to act the way he did. He was so generous, understanding, loving... He surprised me. I have yet to tell my in-laws."

"Don't you think it is better to leave that responsibility to Samuel?" The brother proposed.

"Abner, I don't know what to do. I'm confused, stunned. Sometimes I don't know..."

"Sorry for intruding. I know you didn't ask for my opinion, but..."

"Please, David, you can give your opinions." She asked, looking at him.

"Simone, I think the moment is very delicate and that is why you must prioritize everything you are going to do. I believe that your priority now is your wellness and the wellness of your child. You

116

must pay attention, a lot of attention, to your physical and mental health. Arguing with your husband will not bring you peace. To the contrary. You noticed that he had a very harsh and wrong reaction. Perhaps he will not change his mind, because he was not prepared at all for this experience."

"I also don't think I should talk to Samuel so that he can accept our son's condition. It would just wear me out. But... what do I do?"

"You need comfort, support, protection. You have to strengthen yourself, mentally and psychologically, to know how to deal with your child's condition. It may be that he needs you a lot. So... Enjoy all the welcome offered by your family and get together. After everything has settled down, you and your husband can talk better." Said David.

"It is not fair that a scoundrel person destroys my family, my life. I want to look for her and..." She screamed.

"Will it work? Do you have all the energy and willingness to seek her out and fight, curse, exchange offenses? Yes, because that's what will happen if you find her, don't you think?" Said the cautious man. Simone fell silent and looked at him thoughtfully. And he added; "As I said, you have a good family and they are willing to receive you with all their love and affection. Seek, together with your parents and siblings, the strength for the most important step, which is to welcome your child. That first. Then look at your husband's position. He is likely to look for you and apologize. Samuel had no structure for what happened, and maybe he can see it for himself and regret everything."

"I can't stop thinking about him with that woman. How could he betray me in the midst of everything that is happening to us?"

"You will be thinking and talking about it until you have used all that energy of anger, of annoyance. That's normal.

However, as soon as you can, direct your approach, thoughts and attention to other things more peaceful and pleasant. Watch TV, a telenovela, pay attention to what you see. Go out, walk, preferably in a square. Look at the trees, birds, the blue sky. This will distract your mind from an obsessive subject that is bad for you." David advised.

Simone seems calmer, although nothing was solved in her life.

Looking at the young man for a long time, in total silence, she seemed to think hard about those important tips. Then she offered him a slight smile. Despite that, you could see sadness in the shadow of her eyes.

He smiled at her too, spread his hands and asked;

"Get up, take a deep breath, and wash your face. Abner said that today he will prepare a delicious natural sandwich for us."

"Did I say that?!"

"Yes! I heard you just said it." He laughed. Abner smiled and agreed.

"I really will. I bought ingredients for that. If it will work... That's another story."

"Abner." When the brother looked at her, she added. "Can I stay here today? I will sleep on the couch. Do not worry."

"You can. Of course, you can."

"Thanks. It's just that I don't want to go to mom's house. Samuel must go there and I don't want to see him. So, I will call her to let her know I'm here. If you want, you can tell her."

"Make yourself at home, Simone. My home, your home."

"I will not bother you?"

"Not at all. Keep calm." He replied, hugging her affectionately.

Later, Simone realized her request and thought it would embarrass her brother and David.

She thought that David would sleep in the apartment and she would take away their freedom. At the first opportunity to see Abner alone, she commented;

"I think it would be better to take me to mom's house today. David may not be comfortable. I didn't think of that before."

"We are not living together. If that's what you want to know."

"I thought so..."

"That's the idea. But not now."

"Sorry, Abner. The subject is... delicate."

"It's a new topic, so it's strange to have to comment on it for you and for me. In time we will get used to it."

"Thanks for your help and support."

"I say the same."

David came into the room.

"It's late enough. My mom is alone. I need to go."

"And your brother?" Abner asked.

"Cristiano has not arrived yet and she is worried. Today was not going very well. When he panics, he leaves. He always does that when he's not okay and that's what he did today, but he hasn't returned yet. My mother..." Mrs. Janaina. "She is distraught and has already called me three times since she was unable to speak to him. The cell phone only gives voice messages. I'll tie a whistle to Cris. He will see." He tried to joke in order to dispel the concern.

"What's wrong with your brother?" Simone was interested.

"My brother was in a very violent car accident. He, his girlfriend Vitória and her brother Vanilson. They were handing out the latest wedding invitations. The brother was driving, Vitória was

119

next to him, in the passenger seat, and my brother in the back seat. The car was quite old, but it was in good condition. Vanilson was speeding and another vehicle, driving through the red light, hit the side. The car rolled several times. Vitória was thrown away. She was without a seat belt and died on the way to the hospital. Her brother died at the time of the accident. Cris, who was wearing a belt, was the only one who survived. He fractured his skull and was in a coma for more than a month. When he woke up, he didn't even remember his name. Little by little he regained his memory, but he began to have strange dreams and horrible nightmares. He would wake me up screaming... I had to check on him. It was then that during the day he began to have strong crying spells. When he remembered everything, he was not satisfied with what happened, mainly because it was him who decided to go in the back seat, asking the girlfriend to sit in the front. My brother had surgery, he recovered from multiple fractures, including his skull. He did a lot of physical therapy, but he did not recover from his soul. He has not been able to go back to work. To this day he has not been able to return to work. The doctors say he suffers from post-traumatic stress disorder and panic syndrome. There are times when we see him pretty normal, but there are times when he panics, gets depressed and gets really bad. When he talks and talks a lot, he says he gets better. I make myself available to talk, but there are times when he doesn't want to. It is not easy to understand."

"Is he being treated by a psychiatrist, psychologist...?" She asked.

"Yes, he is. Psychotherapy once a week and takes black-label medications, recommended by a psychiatrist with whom he has appointments at least once a month. In addition, care is taken with alternative medicine, such as homeopathy, color therapy, and flowers. Everything we can try. He even spends time in the Spiritist house. He has been improving, but very slowly. Whoever saw him at the beginning thinks he looks great now."

"Which was his job?"

"He was also a dentist. But he still can't go back to work. I insisted that he can work with me." He smiled. "Even Abner proposed himself as a guinea pig, but... He panics and fails."

"But... What does the accident have to do with the panic he feels when he tries to return to work? Is there any explanation?"

"According to him and the psychologist who treats him, they have come to the conclusion that it is the fear of making mistakes, of making decisions. He believes that when he decided that his girlfriend would be sitting up front, he decided on her death."

"Does he know why they were speeding?"

"Cristiano says that his future brother-in-law started speeding up and he asked him to go slowly. After that, he can't tell what happened. Only the lightning of the moment when the other car struck and nothing else was glimpsed. Certainly, the impact was strong and there was a rollover due to the high speed. You know, we don't have a father, he died five years ago. It is my mother and I who take care of him. Is not easy. In recent times, after recovering from fractures with many physical therapies, Cris is having panic attacks. He says he gets better as soon as it goes away. Then he leaves the house, walks ten or fifteen kilometers, and then comes back. But that worries us. When it happens and I'm away, my mother is desperate thinking that something has happened. It gets worse when he forgets or doesn't answer his cell phone. It is not easy."

"You have to see him, Simone." Abner interrupted. "Speaking with Cristiano, no one says that he is experiencing such a serious, worrying disorder. But when he goes through a crisis, he is unrecognizable."

"He really liked Victoria. Even today he cries a lot for her."

"Now I need to go." Decided David.

It was then that Abner spoke;

"Your mother called me to go for lunch there tomorrow, but we better save it for another day. Can you tell her about it?"

"No. There is no way." The sister decided. "You can leave me at dad's house and then you go for lunch."

Turning to her, David added.

"I would very much like you to meet my mother. Do you want to go there tomorrow? It will be a massive pleasure for us."

"Well…" She hesitated.

"Let's go, Simone. You will like Mrs. Janaina." The brother insisted.

"But not for lunch. I'll just go to meet her."

Abner and David looked at each other and smiled. They knew it wouldn't be just a quick visit. And the brother agreed.

"Then it's okay. Just a short visit."

"See you tomorrow." David said goodbye, approaching Simone and kissing her on the cheek. Looking into her eyes, he caressed her face with affection. "Take care, huh? And take care of that big boy too."

Offering a simple and sad smile, she thanked him.

"Thanks for everything. You helped me a lot."

"Then, take care dear." He said.

After David left, silence reigned for a while until she observed.

"Are you sure you two are gay?" The brother laughed out loud.

"Why are you asking that?" He said.

"Because it doesn't seem like that. I could introduce you to a friend or have Rúbia go out with David."

"Homosexuals don't need to be mannered."

"You two are so beautiful." She said with a soft and gentle voice. Abner was amused and she commented. "You are like our father, but taller. Fair skin, honey eyes, light brown hair... Rúbia and I look like our mother. Our skin is darker…" When she saw him smiling without saying anything, she asked; "does his mother know about you?"

"That we are homosexuals? Yes. The mother, the brother and some relatives know about it. And that we are together too."

"Was there no discrimination or prejudice from his family when he assumed he was homosexual?"

"David says that at first it was very difficult. The father was alive and did not want to talk about it. Despite that, he respected him, treated him the same as his other son. But he didn't want to talk about it. When the matter arose, the father retired. Mrs. Janaina, I think that, like most mothers, in this case, she was more understanding. She never disrespected him. She is a very loving woman."

"And when you two... How can I say it... you started dating?"

"I went to the office he and his brother shared. We became colleagues. Then I did the architectural plans for the office renovation. I started going to his house... We became friends. Mrs. Janaina likes me very much. We never said anything about our relationship with his family. No one has witnessed any intimacy between us. We keep showing up, one in the company of the other. Those closest to us, who knew we were gay, assumed we were together, getting to know each other better, dating."

"I think it is more difficult when the person is homosexual and looks straight."

"I also think so. The longer it takes a person to discover or assume that he is homosexual, the greater the impact on him and

123

others. When you have a manner, you talk, you dress, you look different from childhood or adolescence, it seems that it becomes easier, no one is afraid when they see you with someone of the same sex."

"I confess that it is quite strange to hear that from you. Precisely due to the lack of aesthetics, something never introduced." There was a brief pause and she asked. "If his family knows, then... tell me, how did you introduce yourself to them? Was there prejudice?"

"It was like this: we met, we became colleagues, friends and shortly after the accident with Cristiano, we began to appear together more often and everyone noticed, especially his mother. No one has criticized us or made any comment, at least not in front of us, because we gave no reason to do so. Over time, they got used to us."

"Abner, I'm sorry for my curiosity, it's just that I want to know you better." The brother smiled and she asked; "Have you dated another man before?"

"Yes, I have." He simply answered.

"So, you are really sure about what you want... talking in terms of feelings…" She did not know how to express herself, but she organized the ideas quickly. "If there was a stable union between homosexuals, the so-called homosexual marriage, would you marry?"

"Yes, I would. There is a very strong feeling between the two of us. This leads us not to want to abandon each other, under any circumstances. I believe that it is important that homosexuals have duties and rights before them and society. Homosexuality has always existed since the world is a world. For centuries people have mistreated themselves, suffering, feeling guilty for being born with this sexual orientation, with this sexual condition. They hide in order not to be rejected, killed, ridiculed, humiliated. In recent

124

times, with many groups demanding freedom and rights, the time has come to set ourselves free and also demand our rights. It is necessary to end prejudice and discrimination against LGBT: lesbian, gay, bisexual and transgender. In the same way there are laws against racial prejudice or against people with disabilities. We're all human beings. Some are different from others, created by one God, the same Father. We must end intimidation or bullying at school, prejudice at work, discrimination on the street, whatever. No more suffering for everyone. Know that it is not a comfortable situation for homosexuals to see that we are rejected by people due to their ignorance, rejected by irrational religious dogmas and people who claim to be conservatives full of false moral conceptions. You know... I started to study the Spiritist doctrine a bit and if everyone tried to know a little about reincarnation, there would be no prejudice. Today we are born a man; tomorrow woman. In the past, one may have been homosexual and today heterosexual. One may have been black, today white or Indian. I don't know. Someone who was rich and abused what he owned, trampled, usurped, was fraudulent, stingy, greedy, today he was born poor and unable to improve his life, lives depending on donations from others and government grants as a gift and that, bag that and another."

"And someone who mutilated, mistreated, was an executioner or mistreated his own body with drugs and other abuses, can be born with a sick body, sequel... Like my son." She said, sadly.

Abner went to his sister and, sitting down beside her, spoke in a low voice;

"Don't try to find out now why this happened. That will only make you suffer. If it were for you to know, you would already know. If it is a rescue, I think that we are already rescuing. You know, Simone, I think I'm gay because I need to make amends for the past. Or I got to the point of understanding and feeling love for everyone, regardless of gender. I don't know. At first, I thought that I should abstain from sex, sublimate that energy. I thought about it a lot and concluded the following: I'm not a promiscuous homosexual, I never prostitute myself. When someone came, I thought: what now? We get along, we love each other. So, I decided to have good morals, to have integrity. I'm not going to hang out with one and the other. But I have the right to be happy with someone I love, who loves me. We respect each other. For some Law of God, which I don't know, if I'm going to abstain from sex, I'm sorry, today, in this life, I still cannot. However, I will have a clear conscience not to prostitute myself. I will not think about the past or the future. I will live the best for my conscience, now. Respecting myself, above all."

"The most important thing is to take care of you and leave everyone with their lives." Abner smiled and hugged her, kissing the top of her head.

7.– RÚBIA'S DISAPPOINTMENT

THE NEXT DAY, Abner and Simone arrived at David's home, where they were greeted with great affection.

Mrs. Janaina was a very nice woman, short in stature, a small woman, very thin, very agile and lively during her sixty-two years. Short and very gray hair, well cared for, because her white hair had a soft bluish color that gave her a classic, special tone. Her beautiful, cheerful face was marked by expression lines, signs of time and life experiences.

After the greetings, Abner asked;

"I was going to call yesterday to find out, but I was talking to my sister and when I looked at my watch, it was too late. And Cristiano arrived well?"

"He arrived safely. Now he is in the bathroom. Yesterday that boy disappeared and drove me crazy. I was so worried! He always tells me, but yesterday he didn't let me know and it took too long."

"When I got home, Cris arrived with me. I didn't even have to call the police or the army." David joked.

Changing the subject, Mrs. Janaina asked, speaking in a pleasant tone;

"What about you, daughter? Are you ok? Is the pregnancy going well?"

"I'm fine, thank God."

"Do you know what it is?"

"A boy…" As she answered, her eyes filled with tears and her voice cracked. She looked at his brother, asking for help.

"Did I say something wrong?" Said the lady when she saw her reaction.

"No. Not at all." Abner said. "It's just that she's a little sensitive and…"

"Is the baby okay?" David's mother was interested again.

Simone could not bear it and leaned her face on the shoulder of the brother who wrapped her around and explained:

"The baby has Patau syndrome. It is a genetic problem that has serious consequences for physical and mental health."

"I'm sorry." The woman lamented, approached her and stroked her arm.

"It has been very difficult for me. Not only my son's problem, but… my husband's non-acceptance. As my brother said, I'm very sensitive, worried and still do not have the support I expected from Samuel. Among other things. Worst of all, the kids with this syndrome who are born alive have a very short life expectancy. Patau syndrome is very sad for the baby and the parents."

"Good morning." Cristiano greeted, shyly and quietly, when he reached the room. He was the youngest son of Mrs. Janaina. He was a tall boy, six feet tall, with a well-built body, white skin, black straight stubborn flowing hair. Dark eyes, a very close beard that, when brushed, gave a bluish tint to his white face. He had been experiencing severe psychological disorders since the accident he suffered. For that reason, he introduced himself without smiling and somewhat embarrassed. After the greetings and introductions, the boy simply asked. "What child was born with Patau syndrome?"

"He is not yet born." Simone replied, looking at him sadly. "As you can see, I'm pregnant and my son has this syndrome, which is very rare. Do you know it or have you heard of it?"

"Yes, I know. As you said, it is a rare syndrome. I was a volunteer in an institution that cares for and helps kids with this and other disabilities. I was providing dental treatment there. It is really something that surprises those who are not prepared."

"He is my first child. It has not been easy for me."

Seeing Simone sad, Mrs. Janaina felt encouraged to change the subject.

"I'm making a special lasagna for our lunch. You are the first person in Abner's family to come and meet us, so we deserve a very special lunch."

"I don't want to bother or give work."

"It is not a hassle at all."

Despite being somewhat embarrassed, Simone liked everyone's reception and welcome. She feels good in the company of such a lovely lady.

After a pleasant lunch, the healthy conversation made her forget her difficulties. Much later, she sat on the recliner and fell asleep watching television."

She was startled when she felt a light blanket against her skin.

"Sorry. I didn't mean to scare you." Said Cristiano and covered her.

"No... I must not sleep. I have to go."

"Abner, my mother, and my brother are troubleshooting a plumbing problem in the barbecue sink. I think it will take time."

He smiled and joked. "All three are highly skilled technicians for the job. So, I didn't even go to help them."

She smiled and asked;

"You are a dentist and you have an office with your brother, is it right?"

"Yes, it is... but... I'm not working."

"Did you say you treated boys with Patau syndrome?"

"It was only for about three or four years. Then I had to stop."

"I really admire volunteer work. I have heard about this syndrome, but I didn't remember. Maybe I didn't pay any attention. I was terrified. I thought about the treatment, the cure, but I found that there is nothing that relieves it. It ended up with me, my husband and even…"

"Even…?" He wanted her to continue.

"It even ended my marriage. My husband did not accept all of this. He is upset and goes to seek comfort in the arms of another woman."

"Jeez...!" He exclaimed in a low voice. "I imagine how difficult it must be; however, we must accept and do our part when we have nothing else to do."

"Cristiano." She said; "My first college degree was in nursing, but I did not exercise the profession, I gave up. When I finished, I went to do economics. Something completely different. I totally disconnected from the health area. I have seen boys with special problems, but I have never seen, at least I do not remember seeing, specifically, a boy with Patau Syndrome, except on the Internet when I did search about it. I understand that you met a boy with this syndrome very closely and…" She was nervous. She wanted to ask but was afraid of the answer. "Can you tell me if it's too difficult or...? How is the life of such a boy and the life of his family?"

"I can't tell if the correct term is degree. However, to understand us, I would say that there are different degrees regarding this syndrome. Some are born with many disabilities that are quite compromising. So much so that they don't have much time to live. You already know that."

"Yes, I know."

"Others, with a lower degree, live longer. The vast majority have a cleft lip and palate, this causes serious problems in the dental arch, if any, when they reach a certain age."

"What do you mean by a certain age?"

"In those who reach the age for the first teething and, if any, a second early teething. The teeth are damaged, very weak and dental treatment is very difficult. The patient needs to be sedated."

"Answer me something, if you know. Are kids like vegetative? Or do they understand something?"

"I really think all of them understand and feel. In different degrees, of course. However, without doubt, all of them understand. I realized that despite the mental retardation they were aware of what was happening and could recognize us, feel us. In addition, they conveyed their feelings and wishes. They all had a will of their own."

"My husband doesn't think they feel anything. He says we shouldn't be together. He even commented that I was supposed to consider this pregnancy as a disease and that in a few months I would recover and..." Her voice broke and she held back the crying.

"It is a life. It is a being that grows and, when it is born, it will need care, food and, consequently, it will need love and attention. I still say that it is necessary to love him now."

"I'd like to get in touch with kids with that syndrome. Do you think it is advisable?"

"Why do you want that?" He was surprised.

"To find out now what I'm going to deal with. I want to have a more lively, practical and real notion of what it is to have such a small boy in my arms."

"I don't see anything wrong, if you are prepared. As I said, it is not easy, since it is not common to see it."

"But I'm going to have to see, face, and deal with my son, right?"

"Won't that make you suffer beforehand?"

"Can I suffer more?" Facing the silence, Simone asked. "Can you give me the address of this institution?"

"I can even go there with you, if you want."

"Yes, I want to. If someone is with me, I will feel more secure."

"Tomorrow I can call there and confirm the visiting hours. I haven't contacted them in a long time. Maybe, there was a change or something."

"Is it far?"

"No. It's in the neighboring neighborhood. Close to where we have the office. Can you leave your cell phone number? As soon as I have information, I will call to make an appointment." Cristiano took his cell phone, wrote Simone's phone number and saved it, promising; "You can let me call and I will schedule to go."

"It will help me a lot."

"Hope so. You are being very brave. There you will also find kids with other syndromes and disabilities. All the work done is very good. They have physical activities, for those who can. Games, physical therapy, psychomotor skills, occupational therapy and many other things. Most of those who accept the task are volunteers: doctors, dentists, pedagogues, teachers, psychologists, but that does not exclude valuable volunteer tasks that have no university education. They help with some care, games, reading... Most of the time, they are retired or they are people with some free time. Or people of good will who take the time to take a few hours of their time to help others."

"Are kids hospitalized there?"

"Yes, some of them. These are the ones that were unfortunately abandoned by the family. Others have families, but cannot offer them the necessary treatment and care. As transportation from home to institution is difficult and expensive, these boys only spend weekends and holidays with their family, since the parents work. Only a very small number arrive there in the morning and go home early at night, as they live closer."

"Are they all together?"

"No. They are separated by age and also by needs, as much as they depend on other people."

"Interesting. I've never known a job like this."

"It exists and it is a beautiful work."

"Why did you leave?" She simply asked.

"I had an accident. I'm still in psychological treatment. I couldn't fully get over the trauma. It is something involuntary, since I have always liked my job, but I cannot do it. When I tried, I panicked, got sick and couldn't do it."

"How many times have you tried to go back?"

"Two, three... When I insisted, I was so ill that I suffered a very intense panic attack. I almost fainted. Then I went into depression. It was psychosomatic symptoms that took months to alleviate, so I'm afraid to try again. I do not know what happened to me. I always liked what I did."

"Have you considered doing something else?"

"I'm thinking about that. I signed up for a landscaping and gardening course."

"¡Landscaping and gardening!" She admired and smiled. "How nice! What a different area. For those who did dentistry…"

"I have always liked it. I think I'll do it to occupy my time. I'm tired of medical, psychological and physical therapy treatments. Did you know that I have done more than two hundred physiotherapy sessions so far?"

"Are you kidding?!"

"It's not. I think I already did physio for the whole body."

"You look good."

"But I'm not one hundred percent. I still have limitations. I had four surgeries after the accident. It terrifies me to think of hospitals and doctors."

"I see... And your work is also in the health field."

"That's true."

The subject of both was interrupted by the conversation of those who approached.

"And? Did you fix everything?" He asked when he saw David.

"No way. The pipe is leaking into the wall. But this is simple." Abner replied.

"Simple for those who understand the subject, have the appropriate tools and materials." David said cheerfully.

"In the middle of the week, I'll bring one of the guys who works with hydraulics at the company and he'll do the job."

"Thank you, son." Said Mrs. Janaina. "It has been a problem for a long time. That is why the water tap on that side is closed all the time. And that leaves me without water at the other tap on the patio as well."

"Ah, mother, I already told you to call someone. I don't know how to change it, nor would I want to try. I can't hurt my hands. I really need them. The last time I started doing a job like this, I ended up with a huge cut and I was out of work for almost three weeks. Fortunately, at that point, Cristiano took care of my patients who couldn't wait." David said.

Abner looked at his sister and called her.

"Let's go?"

"Let's go."

"It's early. Stay a little longer. I'll make coffee and bring cake."

"No, Mrs. Janaina. No way. I ate a lot today. I can't hold it anymore." Simone said. Getting up, she approached the lady and thanked her. "Thank you so much for everything. I had a very good morning and afternoon. The best of recent months. I felt very good at your home and I loved you and your children. In fact, Cristiano will accompany me to the institution where she helped some kids and, if possible, the day we go there, I will stop by to see you."

"Are you going there?!" Said the admired and worried woman.

"Yes I'll go. I need to do it." She convinced herself.

Mrs. Janaina looked at Cristiano, who considered.

"She wants to know. Maybe, it will do her good." Seeing the same astonishment on her brother's face, Simone said;

"Do not worry about me. I want to prepare myself to receive my son. I don't want surprises. I need to live reality, in some way." No one said anything, and after a moment she decided. "Well... I have to go. Thank you all for giving me such a pleasant day."

"Come back whenever you want, daughter. We need to talk more. Ah! I have some instructions for woolen jackets and shoes that are beautiful. I'll do some for your baby."

Touched, Simone offered her a simple smile and hugged her again. Then they said goodbye and left.

When she was alone with David, the mother was surprised and commented.

"I don't think Cris will accompany Simone at the institution."

"Nor I. Every time I asked him to go back there, he was sick. One day we came to the door and he almost fainted. We had to go back. My intention was for Cris to be encouraged to provide help, which she liked so much. Volunteer work, in cases like hers, greatly helps the psychological state."

"I know about it. It was strange, right now when I looked at your brother, I was so sure. That's weird."

"Maybe, the time has come for him to react, and perhaps he does not need our support for that. He may even need to be in charge, control the situation. In this case, he is the one who, alone, will take Simone, who is fragile and sensitive. This will be great, because he is the one who will have to be strong to set an example, to control the situation."

"It is true. So, let's not say anything."

✳ ✳ ✳

On the way to her parents' house, Simone continued to praise Mrs. Janaina and her sons. Abner listened to her with satisfaction and added generous comments to that family.

When they arrived in front of her parents' house, she called.

"We are going in."

"There is no way."

"Abner, mom would like to see you."

"But not dad."

"Do you mean that you'll never visit your mother again?"

"I don't know. Never is something very definitive. Let's say, for now, it doesn't work." He kissed her face, smiled and got out of the car to pick up the bags with his sister's clothes. When he was in front of the door, he asked. "Do you want me to talk to Samuel?"

"No. Do not do that. Please."

"Maybe, who knows... A short talk can help."

"No, Abner. What I'm going to do is find my in-laws and tell them everything. I need to do that as soon as possible."

"One more thing... Are you sure you want to go to the institution with Cristiano?"

"I'm completely sure. Yes, I want to. If I don't want to see other kids with the syndrome, how am I going to look at my little boy? I'll go there with or without Cristiano. Tomorrow or later I will go home to look for my car, so as not to depend on anyone and take action on my reality. I don't know what happened to me today, I felt very strengthened after our conversations, after meeting Mrs. Janaina. They lamented the condition of my son, but did not see him as a poor thing. They didn't even treat me like a poor thing. I admired when Mrs. Janaina said she would make him a jacket and shoes... She treated him normally. She did not wonder if he would be born alive, how he would be born or how long he would live."

"This is called living in the moment. It is important not to regret the past that was not good or turn it into a chest of good memories that are gone and never return, constantly living it to escape reality. It is also important not to live anxious, worried about the future, with situations that have not yet happened and probably will not happen. The person is more balanced and happier when living in the present, one day at a time, trying to do well. Doing the best for yourself and others today, here and now. Do not accumulate tasks for tomorrow or live from the past."

"It is true. I understood it very well. Thanks Abner. Thank you for everything." She hugged him tightly and lovingly.

"When you need me... You know where and how to find me."

"Thanks."

✳ ✳ ✳

After entering her parents' house and telling them everything that happened between her and her husband, Simone decided to go to her sister's room.

Standing in the doorway, she saw Rubia sitting on her bed, her elbows on her knees. She held the cell phone in one hand, using the other to muffle his voice. Her hair was loose on the sides of her face and she spoke almost in a whisper.

"We need to talk! What is happening to you to act like this?" There was a brief pause in which she listened. "And your wife, isn't she? Is she the one bothering you?" There was another pause and she said; "You said you two lived in the same house, but were separated from bodies. It doesn't matter! You look different! Where is the divorce that was going to accelerate? We need to talk urgently! I need to talk with you. I'm serious!" Another silence. "Jefferson, pay attention: I won't be holding this situation alone! Where are your feelings for me? Where is your vow of love?" Silence. "I can do something crazy! I can tell your wife everything!"

Simone felt herself freeze when she figured out what her sister was talking about.

"Jefferson! Jefferson? Hello!"

"Who were you talking to? Who did you talk to like that?" Simone asked firmly, watching her with a repressive gaze as she approached and surrounded her.

The sister was clearly nervous and lost control.

"Don't stress me, Simone! What do you want?"

"I want to know who you were talking to. Why did you say you were going to tell his wife everything? Is that what I'm thinking?"

Rúbia found herself cornered. She didn't know what to say. There was no way to lie or hide and she began to despair.

Trembling, she went to the door, closed it, clearly shocked.

"I started dating a man. He is the director where I work. It was with him that Abner spoke to get an interview for me." A few seconds later she started wringing her hands anxiously. "I didn't know, I swear I didn't... Until a friend told me he was married. So... He doesn't live well with his wife and they are already separated. They just live in the same house."

"Separated living under the same roof?" She said, dissatisfied and upset.

"Yes, but..."

Simone didn't even let her finish and asked irritated;

"And you fell in love with him?! I can't believe it!" She walked a few negligent steps, running her hands over her head in a nonconformist way.

"It is not what you are thinking. His mother is ill and does not accept the separation. They just share the same house and..."

"I doubt it! I really doubt it! When love ends, I doubt that a man and a woman could live in the same house, especially with their financial situation. After all, he is a director of the company, earns really well. The wife must work and... Rúbia! Are you crazy?"

"You don't understand!"

"No, I don't! I don't understand how you, a clever and cunning girl, got into it! A man who is married and lives with his wife under one roof will never end the marriage because of you! If they were to separate or get divorced, he would have done it already!"

"It is not like that."

"It is not like that?! This man just wants to take you to bed, cheat on you, go out with you on display, use you. Only after using you as he pleases will he discard you and return to his wife. It is with her that he sleeps every night! You are just an object. You're just the other one, the frivolous one. You're just an ordinary person with whom he varies the menu. Therefore, this man will never want an official date with someone ordinary."

They were nervous, almost screaming. However, they tried to muffle their voices so as not to be heard.

"Do not say that! It is not true!"

"You are being vulgar! How can you lend yourself to such a low, poor, and disgusting role." She revealed. "My marriage is being destroyed by someone who is not different from you."

"You are offending me!"

"You are the one who does not value herself. You should have had the courage to say no, the moment you discovered all the mess you were in. We were raised with good morals, with principles." Discontent, she walked aimlessly around the room, but couldn't help herself and continued; "The guy is a scoundrel, a bastard... I guarantee you that he must live very well with his wife and even with his children." She thought for a few seconds. "Does he have children?"

"Two."

"Rúbia! What happened to you?"

"Don't talk to me like that. You don't know how it all happened. We love each other." With an ironic tone, Simone asked indignantly;

"Oh, really?! You love each other?! You say that you love each other to convince whom? To convince me or you?" There was no answer. "The way I saw you talking to him just now, how can you tell me that there is any feeling of respect between the two of you?" Without listening to her sister defend herself, after connecting the ideas, she asked; "Abner knows that, right? He knows and he came to reprimand you for it. Then you offended him and ended up letting dad know about him, right?" She was firm in saying it.

"He knew." Said Rúbia aggressively. "Who is he to tell me if I'm right or wrong?"

"He is someone who has morals. Our brother is not frivolous, scoundrel or cheeky like you and Jefferson."

"Is he not?!"

"No! With him there is no betrayed wife, cheated boys, destroyed home. If our brother got involved with someone, none of them are engaged, no one is being betrayed or hurt in that story. What about you? How can you go to bed knowing that you are using a man who belongs to someone else, and as soon as he leaves you, he will go back to sleep and relate with her?"

"Shut your mouth!"

"I will not shut up! How come you can't imagine the two of them together after he leaves you? I'm disgusted with you! Betrayal hurts and always makes someone feel like trash. While the two of you are laughing and having fun, having dinner and hanging out, his wife is there taking care of the house, taking care of the kids, managing the life of the whole family. Imagine yourself as a man's wife and all of a sudden… a tramp appears to take him out of home, destroy everything you have built, destroy dreams, plans... destroy

141

a home! Think and put yourself in the shoes of the other and you will know what it is to feel stupid, idiot! Although you are already being an imbecile and an idiot for wasting your time and your youth." After a brief pause she asked; "Do you know what the worst of all this is?" She did not hear an answer and continued. "The worst of all this is that if he does that to his wife, with whom he has a commitment before the law and before God, imagine what he will not do to you... you that just are a frivolous adventure. What he does to his wife will be much worse for you if he ever stays by your side."

"Get out of my room! Get out of here!"

"Of course I will, so that you are alone with your sad and unhappy conscience. I doubt that you feel good about what you have done and are doing."

Saying that, Simone turned and left, leaving her sister alone. Confused and disappointed with herself, Rúbia took the pillow, threw it, and threw herself face down on the bed.

✳ ✳ ✳

As the days passed, Rúbia was not satisfied with Jefferson's strange behavior and began to push him. She couldn't bear to be involved in such an unstable and unpleasant situation.

"You're cheating on me, you're using me, making me lose my youth. You're just wasting my time."

"Enough! I'm tired of your demands."

"Demands?! You said you were going to file for a divorce, but so far, nothing. You said you would tell your mother, but you didn't. You always make excuses. I already told you that I don't want to be the other one. This is really bothering me."

"You are not being sympathetic."

"It is not the same. Enough! We can't go on like this anymore!"

"If you say so…" Jefferson got up from his desk and left the room, leaving her alone.

Rúbia felt very bad. Her siblings were right. She was just a fling. Indignant, she returned to her section. The next morning, without waiting, she was called to the company's Human Resources department, where she found out that she had been fired."

Incredulous, she did everything she needed and went to her section to get her personal things.

"Fired? You?" Talita asked, alarmed.

"Do not tell me more. I do not want to cry."

"Raise your head and take a deep breath. It's an unpleasant surprise, but you will get over it."

"I hope so. I'm devastated, disoriented. I don't know what to do."

"You better go home and rest." Talita said.

"Tomorrow I have to do the medical tests... I'm leaving now."

"I don't know what to say, girl. But the best you can do is go home and rest." She said really anguished, because she liked her colleague.

"Will you call me at night? To talk for a while…"

"I will."

They said goodbye and Rúbia left.

Upon arriving home, it was not pleasant to face his parents and break the news of his dismissal, mainly because of the pertinent question.

"Why did you get fired?"

"Why, dad? They never tell you."

"You were doing everything right, weren't you?"

"I was. Now I need a shower. I'm lousy. I want to rest." However, the worst of all for her situation was yet to come.

Rúbia underwent the required medical tests at the time of firing and discovered that she was pregnant.

Looking for Jefferson, she felt very bad and humiliated when she heard;

"Get rid of this pregnancy as soon as possible, you understand? You are irresponsible! Or, a smart, opportunistic one!"

That blow was too hard. She didn't think she would bear it. Without saying anything, she left him alone in the restaurant and left.

Upon arriving at her house, Rúbia went to her room and did not leave that place. She didn't want to talk to anyone. She didn't even look for the company's documentation to find out what her situation would be like going forward.

"Daughter, for the love of God, why are you like this?"

"Nothing, mother. I want to be alone."

"You need to eat, get out of this room... Losing your job is not the end of the world." Said Mrs. Celeste, trying to comfort her. "Look, have this soup I made for you."

"I don't want it."

"Is something else happening besides the layoff?" The daughter began to cry. At that moment, Simone entered the room and sat on the bed next to her sister. Stroking her hair, she asked;

"What's going on? We can help, we are your family and we love you."

"No one can help me." She stuttered.

"Tell me what's wrong, daughter." Mrs. Celeste insisted.

She realized that she could not hide that fact from her family. Not for much longer. She sat on the bed, wiped her face with her hands and said in a whisper;

"I'm pregnant."

Mrs. Celeste looked for a place and, sitting up slowly, stammered.

"Pregnant? Daughter..."

"Are you sure?" Said Simone.

"Yes..."

"And your boyfriend, daughter? We don't even know this guy." Said Mrs. Celeste.

"He doesn't want his son. He told me to get rid of the pregnancy."

"My God! He has to assume what he did. This can't stay like this." The mom was worried.

Nervous, Rúbia confessed with tears running down her face.

"He's married... he's not going to assume anything."

"My God!" Said the mother, alarmed.

"Calm down, mom. It's not the end of the world." Said Simone. "It is a difficult situation, but it is not the end."

"And dad? How is it going to be when dad knows?" Rúbia cried and Simone replied;

"He will be nervous and angry, but he will have to accept it."

"Your father won't accept it. God of heaven!" The mother was nervous "Daughter! How did you let that happen? With a married man?! What did you have in mind?!"

"Stop mom. Stop it. Now I know. It's done and I can't change anything."

Stunned, Mrs. Celeste left the room, and as she passed the living room, the husband asked.

"And Rúbia, did she eat?"

"No." Mrs. Celeste watched him for a few moments and decided to tell him before she cowered or tortured herself any longer. "Rúbia is devastated. Not just because of the dismissal. She found out that she is pregnant."

"She is what?!"

"What you heard. Rúbia is pregnant!"

Mr. Salvador got up from the sofa, faced the woman and asked angrily.

"Where's the bastard boyfriend?!"

"He doesn't want to take care of his child. He's... he's married." She practically whispered.

"I will kill Rúbia!!!" He screamed. "Shameless!!! Scoundrel!!!" Furious, he cursed several flatties and headed for his daughter's room.

Simone, seeing him so angry when he entered, she stood in front of her father, otherwise he would attack her sister.

"I did not raise a daughter to be a cheeky, frivolous bitch!!! You are not worthy to live in this house!" After yelling and offending a lot, he screamed. "Get out of here!!! Get out!"

Simone and Mrs. Celeste tried to restrain him and drag him into other room from where he yelled;

"I'm leaving, but if I come back and this bitch is here, I'll kill her!!! I'll kill her!!!" Lying on her bed, Rúbia cried, crouched and terrified, listening to everything.

As he said, Mrs. Salvador turned his back on them and left.

Mrs. Celeste regretted having told him, but it was done. She knew her husband would react that way anyway.

Back in the room, when she saw Simone sitting on the bed next to her sister, patting her on the back, she thought she needed to calm them down and decided to go make some tea.

In the kitchen, while the water was boiling and she was washing some lemongrass sticks she picked from the garden, she was anxious to know what to do. She would have to be strong with her husband, she would not allow him to expel her daughter, especially in that state. It was enough for Abner not to visit her again. She missed her son, she felt bad about that situation.

At that moment, Simone reached the kitchen, pulled out a chair and sat down at the table. When drying her hands with a cloth, the lady approached and asked;

"Daughter, are you okay?"

"I'm nervous, mom…" She said, shaking.

"My God… You can't be nervous. The lemon balm tea is almost ready and…"

"I thought dad was going to hit Rúbia."

"He just didn't hit her because of us. I shouldn't have said anything."

"At any moment, you would have to tell him."

"How is she?"

"She was calm now. She didn't say anything else."

"How could your sister get involved with a married man?! She had a good education. She had principles, religion… Did she become disoriented because I did not pay the promise I made to get her a job?"

"Why, mother? How absurd! Our Lady would not be cruel to punish her just for not making her a promise. I only care about one thing."

"What?"

"What will happen when dad comes back?"

"God will have to give me strength to face your father. Since he will return even more drunk. He will not expel Rúbia from here. It is not the same." The lady got up, took the tea, which was getting cold, and sweetened it. She picked up the cups and served Simone, then she said; "I'm going to take this cup to your sister."

When she reached her daughter's room, to her surprise, she did not find her. She called her in the hall, looked for her in the bathroom and throughout the house. No sign of her.

"What happened mom?" Simone asked and went to meet her.

"Your sister has left."

8.– SPIRITUAL INVOLVEMENT

IN GETTING INVOLVED WITH A COMMITTED MAN like Jefferson, Rúbia couldn't imagine the bitterness and lower spiritual energies that drew her.

She did not recognize the spiritual signs that arose from the anguish, because of the discomfort in her conscience every time she remembered that Jefferson was married. Those feelings were an alert, signaling the unfortunate path taken.

Furthermore, she ignored the spiritual company that sustained her adventure in false pleasure and her escape from spiritual obligations to contribute high moral values to the ascension of the human spirit. They were spirits of low moral value, frivolous, desirous for energetic nourishment and for a greater number of incarnates to join them for the lowest demands.

By undergoing the influence of these spirits, she received their stimulus through the force centers, the chakras, where the sex and the stomach meet. When she made her choice and decided to be an adulteress, she unknowingly chose for companies she spiritually desired.

She thought that she could live a false happiness, because Jefferson deceived her and she was deluded, she was deceived.

No one cheats on us without our permission. This happened because she had no opinion of her own, because she did not renounce the inconsistent side, because she did not take a moral position.

One is not really happy when someone is betrayed, cheated, or harmed. One is not happy when one is irresponsible with the life and happiness of others. One day, certainly, the unconscious side of morality and responsibility will knock on your door and conscience will call you to harmonize what you have disharmonized.

Now, after so much disappointment, resolving to abandon her inappropriate behavior, Rúbia had new spiritual companies, different from the previous ones. They were vulgar personalities attached to the lowest energy resources, created by the inevitable vibration of their thoughts and the energy of everything that happened. The dark observers of the moment demanded a posture that even they could not practice, in earthly experience, for moral and spiritual elevation.

They were adulterous spirits who lived in the circle of afflictions. They considered themselves educators of those who strayed from the best way forward. However, they refused to make the adjustments they needed with their own conscience, believing that by punishing and making those who lost their way like them suffer, they would free themselves from the conscious terror of the demands they needed.

Finding herself defenseless, Rúbia walked aimlessly. She could not hear, but she felt in her soul everything that the lower spirits desired.

Her mind, then, insecure and fragile, impressed her with tremendous conflicts and morbid ideas due to spiritual suggestions.

"Scoundrel! Bitch! Come on idiot! Did you see what happened to date a married man?"

"Yes, bitch!" Said another, in addition to other offensive, deplorable and unpronounceable names. "Now you're carrying a bastard! Scoundrel! You should die!"

"That's it! Shameless since you have to die to find us here! Then you will learn! Bitch! Die, miserable!! Die!!

"Your father is going to kill you! You have no home, there is no home, no one else. That wretched traitor only knew how to suck you and kick you with his foot!"

"Die, you idiot!"

These and other inspirations were directed to Rúbia, who had more and more confused thoughts and conflicting ideas.

"Bastard! If she had been fooled by him... but she wasn't. She knew and was adulterous with him! She wanted to build happiness in the misfortune of others' homes!"

"Yes! He hadn't left the family for her to be with him! She was filthy! Worthless kind of woman! She has no morals!"

* * *

In her house, next to the small church she had and where she placed some images of Catholic saints, Mrs. Celeste lit a candle to the Blessed Mother and began to pray.

"My God, help my daughter. Bring that girl back. Our Lady, you are a mother and you know what I feel. You know what is good for our children. Light up my daughter's mind..."

Although her heart was tight, the woman continued in sincere prayer, asking for light and intercession for her daughter for a long time.

* * *

Rúbia didn't care where she was.

151

She had walked a lot during the night and a thin cold drizzle began to fall.

In the middle of confusing thoughts, unhappy ideas arose, inspired by the spiritual companions of the moment.

"It would be better for me to die. It would solve everything. It would end all this suffering. What am I going to do without work? Without family? Am I going to live on the streets? I better die." She thought.

She was walking on a bridge that overlapped a major avenue with very busy traffic, mainly trucks.

As she approached the wall, she rested her arms on it and stared.

"It would be better for me to jump in as soon as possible. If I don't die in the fall, a truck will solve everything... It has to be very fast... there is no problem. Only then will I give everyone peace, especially my father who, now, is so ashamed of me. He will die of remorse for what he told me... Jefferson, bastard... He cheated on me, he abandoned me... He ended my life... I want him to die of remorse for what he did to me." She thought, imagining these people's reaction.

The energies of Mrs. Celeste's heartfelt prayer served as a protective force manipulated by friendly entities to distance the commotion made by the lower spirits that vibrated in the same harmony as Rúbia and nurtured those desires.

Her mentor enveloped her, inhibiting the action of those evil personalities. However, the lower thoughts continued due to a lack of faith in God and hope in divine manifestations that changed a whole trajectory when we decided to stand up and act better.

Seeing her with a fixed idea of that unhappy purpose, to put an end to everything, Rúbia's mentor needed to act quickly. And it did it with the help of other spiritual friends. Taking advantage of a good pedestrian passing by, it turned into his spiritual protector, and they quickly engulfed the incarnate in an almost involuntary and unexpected action. As a result, the man was annoyed by Rúbia's posture in front of the wall and her gaze that was lost in the panorama of vehicles speeding by below.

Without thinking much about what he was doing, the stranger approached her and asked;

"Young lady... how are you?"

"She was startled. She looked at him in surprise, but said nothing."

"Are you alright?

"Yes." She murmured.

"Sorry for the inconvenience. It's just that you're pale, holding on there... I can ask for help, if you're not feeling well."

"I'm a little confused... I lost my job. I don't know what to do." She stopped.

"Do you want to come with me? I think we are going the same way. Not many come through here because of the cold and the drizzle. If you are not feeling well, you may fall and someone will need to help you. Come on." Proposed the man.

She did not reflect and followed him mechanically.

On the way to cover the rest of the bridge, the friendly spirits who enveloped her with beneficial energies, especially the energies gathered by her mother's vibrations during prayer, tried to protect her, but it was difficult to protect her from her own thoughts.

"I'm going to the church." He said, trying to talk with Rúbia. "Today is a novena day for Our Lady and I have much to be thankful for." After a moment, he said; "You know, I was unemployed and in a very difficult situation. I got sick and couldn't get a job. My wife took me to church and made a promise to Our Lady. That day, I felt that something had happened to me. I was

153

very touched. I regained my health and right after, I got a job. And, by the way, a very good job." He laughed. "Since I did well, I will rise to the occasion… I try to be the best employee. Since then, I have been a devotee of the Blessed Mother and all day of prayer in devotion to Saint Mary, I come to thank her in the church across the square. I feel very good!" After a brief pause, he continued talking. "My wife was supposed to be with me, but she is a nurse and was on call at the hospital today, so she couldn't come." Seeing her very quiet, he understood that she was suffering from something and tried to console her. "I know how you feel. I also thought about a lot of bad things when I lost my job, got sick and had to be supported by my wife for a long time. You know, girl, when there is something bad, but so bad that happens in life, we believe that it is the end, that we cannot take it anymore. We think a lot of trash. However, these bad things that happen to us are for our good in the future. What happens makes us stronger. There's always a way out."

"And when you don't have a job, or a family, or the support of those you believed in and still don't have anywhere to go and you're pregnant?"

The man, in all his noble simplicity, stopped, looked at her, and replied;

"We pray. Look for the house of God and go pray. Our Father does not abandon us." After a moment, he proposed; "I'm on my way to church now. Come with me and pray. You will get a solution or an idea. Have faith and believe."

Dazed, with tired and fragile thoughts, Rúbia followed him without saying anything.

Upon arriving at the church, several people were gathered before the prayer service for Our Lady began.

On the spiritual plane, without the incarnates being able to see, there was an immense beam of light, heavenly vibrations and healthy energy that bathed everyone as if it were the fine drizzle that fell outside.

The harmony of the people saturated the environment with sweet magnetism, although there were only a few dozen incarnates. Unlike the physical plane, there were hundreds of spirit companions full of help and love. Candidates for relief service, sublime participation, magnetic cleansing and all kinds of help and support worked for the incarnate brothers and sisters present to pray, ask or give thanks, that day scheduled in advance.

It didn't take long, and the service began with lovely, lively songs of devotion and thanksgiving. Immediately, each of the mentors reached out to their protégés and donated uplifting energies. This eased worrying thoughts and sustained them by increasing her faith in God and a better future.

When the prayers began, although not all those present were concentrated on the prayer, there was an intense luminosity from top to bottom and, upon reaching the center of the place, they were transformed into magnetic waves that lovingly enveloped each of those present, supplying them with innumerable resources of which they needed.

A higher entity was present and the most radiant fluids were soothing the place with generous force. It was an imposing and beautiful scene, yet serene and humble and majestic. Indescribable for the plane of the incarnate.

During the prayers, Rúbia's thoughts calmed down and were left without the impregnations of the old observers. His mind was weary, scorched by countless worries, but now attached to a thread of hope.

A delicate entity, like a form of light floating in space, approached Rúbia with tenderness and humility. Feeling the higher radiation, Francisca, her mentor, gave her space.

"Every prayer is heard and I'm here at the request of your mother." Said the great spirit. "The door of salvation is the narrow one, the painful one, the most difficult to pass. Most of the time, the being wants to overcome it instead of making a great effort to overcome the difficulties, it is necessary to resign and move on. To think of abandoning the challenge is to want to go through the wide door, the door of ruin, where the path leads to evil, to the ruin of the spirit. No more through the wide door, down the path of bad passions. Make a responsible commitment to harmonize with your own conscience."

Serenely, it placed its luminous hand on her and a beautiful burst of radiant light was made on Rúbia, who was moved and cried for a few minutes without knowing why.

With an angelic physiognomy, the noble spirit smiled at the mentor Francisca and happened to be close to another incarnate.

With her eyes fixed on the altar, Rúbia, totally exhausted from fighting a fervent battle with her own thoughts, concluded;

"I made a lot of mistakes, my God. I cannot blame others for my wrong decisions. I must assume that half the fault is mine. I made as many or more mistakes as Jefferson, because I knew it was wrong to be together. Wanting to die, disappear, kill my son as I thought, will be another big problem among the many that I already have. I shouldn't have let this happen, but now... Now, after everything that happened, I must be responsible and do my part. Give me strength, Father! Make me find a way out. Help me!"

As she looked down, she found a church liturgical pamphlet on the floor, where the gospel passage of Jesus and the adulterous woman was transcribed. She took it in her hands and when she read it, she felt moved, with the help of the Master Friend who defended the woman when everyone wanted to stone her. One sentence stood out 'Go, and never do wrong again.'

"If Jesus knew how to understand the error of the adulterous woman in those days ... Why would he abandon me now? I think it's like that man said: he meant who took her there. When you don't know what to do, you should... pray. Conscious of being worthy to receive the benefits of prayer and to do what Jesus ordered: go, and never do wrong again." After those thoughts, Rúbia began a prayer that was more of a conversation with God, asking for support and light because he knew what to do in that condition. She received help and with that she promised to correct her mistakes and continue with perseverance and faith, with high morals, doing her best.

Despite being mentally exhausted, in the end, mechanically, she got involved in the prayer that those present said and it was noticed much better, surrendering to the irresistible call of love.

Despite everything, she was still worried. What to do? Where to go? She was broken and with only the clothes she was wearing. She could ask her brother for help, but she thought she shouldn't. Now she felt ashamed because she didn't understand his situation when it was necessary. She couldn't go home due to her father. He was gone, he was probably drunk. If when he was sober, he did not accept it, under the influence of alcohol it would be worse. She thought of Simone, but her sister was having problems with her husband and was sleeping at her parents' house.

Time passed and she noticed the cell phone vibrating in her pants pocket. It was weird. She didn't even remember it there.

She picked up the device and looked at it. It was one of those text messages sent by the operator to thousands of customers.

By then, the service was over and some were still meeting.

Rúbia went where He was. She passed between the benches and went to the central hall, turned to look at the altar, bent her knees slightly, and made the sign of the cross, mentally thanking Him.

As she left the church with her cell phone in hand, she called Abner's cell phone, but the call went to voicemail. She tried calling her brother's apartment, but no one answered.

Again, that feeling of emptiness, of abandonment, of not knowing what to do.

She couldn't stay there, at the door of the church. She walked down the steps and onto the sidewalk when the same man who had led her there approached.

"Girl!" He tried to catch her attention. Seeing her standing up, he reached her out and asked. "Are you okay?"

"Yes, thanks. I'm better than when I arrived. Although I still don't know what to do."

"Sorry for not being able to help..."

"You helped a lot. You can't even imagine."

"Look, Father José must be in the rectory. If you have nowhere to go... We can talk to him. But I don't know if he can help you."

"Thanks, but... I don't know if I should. I want to try talking to my brother. I don't think he denies help, but he is not home now."

While they were standing there, the same cold thin drizzle fell as before. They remained a few minutes without knowing what to do. Long enough desired by spiritual friends, because, at the same moment, a car that passed slowly stopped, opened the window on the passenger side, and a voice was heard saying;

"Rúbia?!" He seemed surprised and saw Ricardo, her brother's friend and partner. Sitting in the driver's seat, he practically lay down on the passenger seat.

"What are you doing here in this drizzle at this time?" Without waiting for an answer, he wanted to know. "Do you want me to give you a ride?"

"He's a friend of my brother." She said to the man with more joy.

"Go see if he can help you! Come on! Go!" He enthusiastically encouraged her. As she approached, she leaned close to the vehicle.

"Can you take me to Abner's apartment? I'm without a car."

"Come in!" Ricardo agreed and opened the door for her to get in. Rúbia turned to the man who helped her and thanked him, holding out his hand.

"Thank you very much Sir. Thank you very much. I think it was Our Lady who put you in my way."

"What is that? I did not do anything…"

"What's your name?"

"Jorge."

"My name is Rúbia. Thank you very much Mr. Jorge. May God protect and bless you."

"Go with God. May Our Lady cover you with her mantle. After getting into the car, Ricardo greeted her and notice;

"You are all wet and only with this top! You're not cold, are you?"

"Just a little."

"And your friend? Where is he going? Don't you want me to give him a ride?"

"I don't know… I met him while he was coming to church. He is not my friend, even though he acted like one."

"What is his name?

"Jorge."

Ricardo drove the car slowly towards the man and called him:

"Jorge! When he saw the man looking at him, he asked; "Do you want me to give you a ride? Do you live nearby?"

"Yes, I do. And I would appreciate it if you do it." He said, going to the vehicle door. Upon entering, he commented. "The drizzle is getting thicker and today I didn't think it would be this way. I came without an umbrella."

"Where do you live?" Ricardo wanted to know.

"Take that avenue and get down on the second lighthouse."

"It is nearby. Let's go." Ricardo said.

During the short trip, Rúbia, embarrassed, thanked again.

"Thanks Jorge. I did not know the power of prayer. I was never religious... I was so distraught when you found me."

"Don't thank me. Reciprocate with another person in some way, sometime and when you can."

"I thought it was strange to see you there in church. Are you okay, Rúbia?" Ricardo asked.

"All good... it's nothing…"

When Jorge saw the car enter the street he wanted, he asked;

"You can stop right here."

"Is it ok here?" Asked the other.

"It's perfect. I live there." He pointed to the end street. "In the fifth house. Thank you very much. I would have gotten soaked if it weren't for the ride."

They said goodbye and after seeing him gone, Rúbia asked again;

"Ricardo, could you take me to my brother's apartment?"

"What happened? Everything is quite strange. Not that it's my business, but…"

"I feel terrible. A lot has happened... and it's even embarrassing to talk about it."

"Embarrassing, why?"

"I was fired."

"And is that really embarrassing? Why, Rúbia?" He smiled generously.

"What's behind this is embarrassing. Now, after all, I don't have a job, my dad kicked me out of the house, I just put on my clothes and..." She closed her eyes, leaned her head against the seat and murmured. "I'm pregnant."

"The situation may be difficult, but it is not embarrassing."

"The father is a married man." The friend took a deep breath, thought and said;

"The situation is still difficult, but not shameful. Shame is not in the mistake made, shame is insisting on the mistake. And is this the case?"

"How is that?"

"Are you still together with this man? Will you insist on staying with him?"

"No! Of course not!"

"Then don't be ashamed. Now... let's get out of here. I'll take you to your brother's house and we'll talk on the way."

During the trip, Rúbia told him exactly everything that happened to her, up until the moment she found herself there, in front of the church where he picked her up.

In front of the building where Abner lived, they said, at the entrance, that he was not there. They insisted on calling his cell phone, but there was no answer.

"Wait..." Asked Ricardo, pulling out his own cell phone. "I think I have the number of Mrs. Janaina, David's mother. Let me see... Yes, I have it!" He said, exhilarated. When calling, he was answered by the lady who treated him very well. Then, upon

161

request, she passed the phone to his son. After the greetings, Ricardo asked. "David, do you know about Abner? I'm trying to reach him, but he doesn't answer the phone."

"He went to a Congress of Civil Construction, Architecture and Urbanism in Joinville, Santa Catarina. He will be back next week. Did you forget it?"

"Jezz. It is true! Now I remember. He told me about it a week ago and I forgot."

"Something urgent?"

"No... I can talk to him later. Thanks David." Hr said goodbye and after hanging up, Ricardo turned to Rúbia.

He was very anxious and apprehensive.

"Abner is in Joinville, Santa Catarina. I had forgotten."

"Oh my God... What should I do?" She thought for a while and asked; "Can you give me David's phone number? I'll see if he has a key to my brother's apartment." Reflecting a bit, she asked; "If you talk to him for me, thank you. I wasn't very nice the last time we spoke."

Ricardo called him again and explained.

"Hello David. It's me, again. Look, here's the thing: Rúbia had a family problem. She doesn't want to go home and has nowhere to stay. Do you have the key to Abner's apartment? I don't think he cares if she spends the night here. We are in front of your building."

David thought for a moment. Worried, he decided.

"Ricardo, I'm going to ask you a favor: bring Rúbia over here. I have the key to Abner's apartment, yes. But I won't give it to her. Do not say anything to her. I insist that she stay here at my house. I don't know what happened, but we will help her."

"But... David…"

"Pay attention, don't say anything. I know you are by her side. I will not rest easy knowing that Rúbia is alone in that department. Think with me: if you had problems and cannot return to your parents' house, something very serious happened. And it must have been serious, because I know the last person in the world she would ask for help would be Abner, since they are arguing. So, it is not good that she stays alone, especially in his apartment. You never know what a nervous person is capable of and feels like a dead end. Bring her over here. I'm sure my mother won't mind. We will talk and give her all the support."

"You're right. I'm going over there." He hung up. Turning to her friend, he commented; "Let's go there."

Rúbia thought that they were going to David's house just to get the key, because Ricardo didn't say anything.

When they arrived at Mrs. Janaina's house, she received them with great satisfaction.

"So, you're Abner's little sister! Nice to meet you! I'm David's mother." They greeted each other and, as they settled into the room, the lady observed. "Girl, what happened? You are all wet. Don't you feel cold?"

"Just a little." She replied shyly.

David came to the living room, greeted them both, sat in an armchair and asked, directly and simply;

"Rúbia, I'm sorry but I must know. What happened to you that you need to stay in Abner's apartment?"

"Many things. Among them... My father kicked me out of the house. I lost my job and..." She stopped, looking down.

"For losing your job your father kicked you out of the house?" David was concerned. Looking into his eyes, she almost cried.

163

"I'm pregnant. When my father found out, he did not accept it. I left the house with the clothes I was wearing." David took a deep breath and looked thoughtfully.

"A pregnancy always changes everyone's plans, when it was not planned." After a reflective moment, he decided. "I see that you are nervous, confused and disoriented. I have the key to Abner's apartment, but I don't think it's a good option for you to be there alone and as you are. It is late and, with the worries you have, loneliness will not be good company for your thoughts. Today, you stay here. It will be very good for you and even better for us, won't it, mom?"

"Of course! She stays with us." Getting up, the woman reached her and said; "Your clothes are wet, you can catch a cold. Let's go in and you'll take a hot shower and we'll put on some clean clothes. Then we'll have a soup that I made that is delicious."

"But…" Rúbia tried to say something, but she didn't know what. She looked at Ricardo as if asking for help. And he replied;

"I also think you better stay here. You will have company and… From what you told me, you must not be alone now. I'm sure you will love Mrs. Janaina. Wait and see." He smiled.

"You too, young man." The lady said to Ricardo. "Stay for soup with us. No one has eaten yet. Cristiano hasn't come out of the bathroom yet."

At that moment, the youngest son entered the room and greeted them. When he shook the hand of Rúbia, who was introduced as Abner's sister, he noticed.

"Jeez! You look like your sister!"

"My sister…? Do you know my sister?"

"I know her/ Your brother brought her here and we had a nice afternoon together." Rúbia was surprised, but said nothing.

Nothing more was said and they tried to change the subject.

"Come on, come on!" Encouraged Mrs. Janaina. "Let's go up there. I'll find a sweater that fits you. You take a hot shower and then we'll have dinner."

Shrouded in a fog of shame and still dazed, Rúbia did not think clearly and, without alternative, followed her.

Ricardo, much calmer, decided.

"I don't miss that soup at all. It's unfortunate that your mother invited me." He said laughing and rubbing his hands.

✳ ✳ ✳

Rúbia ate little, despite Mrs. Janaina's insistence. They all spoke animatedly and, after dinner, Ricardo said;

"I'm going to act like a skinny dog. He finishes eating and leaves."

"What about your son, Ricardo? How is he doing?" Asked David.

"Renan is fine. He is going to a camp next vacation and is very anxious. He can't wait to go. It is the first time he travels alone."

"His mother is the one who should be worried. An only child...!" Commented the lady.

"She is. We talk about it a lot. Although very apprehensive, I also believe that it is time for Renan to be alone and away from home, from his father, stepfather with his mother, relatives and among friends and colleagues. This will be good for his independence."

"It will." Said David.

"Well guys... I really appreciate the welcome, the great soup... In fact, it was the best I've ever had! I appreciate everything. I would stay, but I have to go."

Getting up, Ricardo said goodbye.

The lady and David accompanied him to the door and, upon returning, the generous woman proposed.

"Let's go watch TV, daughter? It's good to get distracted a bit."

"What about the dishes? I will help you."

"No! Today is Cris and David's day to clean the kitchen." She laughed. "I don't miss that stewardship at all. Let's go. Then I will prepare a very warm bed for you to sleep in."

"That's right, Rúbia. Come on, keep calm." David encouraged as Cristiano remained silent.

The younger son did not know why the young woman was there. He did not understand or was interested in knowing. He would withdraw into his own thoughts and, for the most part, be silent.

Going to the living room, Rúbia asked;

"I would like to call my mother and let her know that I'm fine. She must be very worried about me."

"It is true. Yes, call her."

This was done. After telling her mother that she was fine and among friends, Rúbia accepted the lady's invitation to watch television, despite not being able to pay attention to anything she saw.

9.– CULTIVATE THE SPARK OF GOD IN YOU

THE NEXT MORNING, Cristiano was preparing a fruit smoothie in the blender, when Rúbia slowly made it to the kitchen.

"Good morning." She greeted shyly, not wanting to scare him, since he hadn't seen her.

"Good day. I hope I didn't wake you up with that noise."

"No way. In fact, I didn't even sleep well."

"Do you want some?" He offers the smoothie.

"No, thanks."

"It would be good if you take it, it'll be good for you. You will be more willing, take a little." He insisted, taking another glass.

When he was about to put the smoothie in a glass, she said;

"No, please. Thank you. I really don't want it."

"If that's so…"

After a few minutes, Rúbia asked;

"So, you know my sister, right?"

"Yes, I know her. A very kind person." He picked up a cup from the cupboard, offered it to her, and showed her where there was fresh coffee and hot milk.

"Thanks." She accepted it. "Simone is going through difficult times. But very different from me. She didn't seek difficulty, I did. I'm ashamed to be here. I never thought that someone like your brother, after everything I said to him, would still welcome me."

"Good morning." David greeted, reaching the kitchen. They both answered and he asked; "And mom?"

"She went to buy bread." Replied the brother. He let the coffee brew and left.

"I think you found someone to talk to."

Looking at David, with some embarrassment, Rúbia thanked him.

"Thank you. Thank you for all that you are doing for me. I never thought of going through such a situation and being so welcome, especially after that day we talked in my brother's apartment."

"Forget it and don't thank me. I just did what I would have wanted someone to do for me."

"You really don't want to give me the key to Abner's apartment? I'm sure he won't find it wrong."

"He won't find it bad, but I insist that you stay here. Like I said, it won't be good for you to be alone now."

"Did I take too long?" Mrs. Janaina asked, smiling when she arrived.

"I know what happened! You went to help bake the bread!" David teased, kissing her face.

"I ran into a friend and we were talking. We agreed to go to the center tonight. That will be a good talk."

"I just can't go. I have to see a patient."

"You haven't been to the center in a long time, huh, son."

"I know, mother, but at the moment I can't. It's not out of bad will. But I make sure that God lives in my actions."

"Today I will go with Simone to the institution." Said Cristiano. "I'm going to invite her to go to the center. Will she accept?"

Rúbia didn't understand what he was talking about. In quick words, Cristiano explained, then she said;

"She will accept it. Simone has already attended a Spiritist center. She even took courses. She left everything because of her husband. Samuel didn't like it at all, not a bit. In fact, he has no religion at all. I think that's why he acted that way when he heard about his son with a problem."

After a few moments, she commented; "I just don't understand why she wants to go to that institution. Isn't it enough to know what the baby has? Does one really need to see others in the same state?"

"Her will must be respected. She wants it. If she gets there and wants to give up, if in the middle of the visit she doesn't want to continue, that's fine. We will be back. She won't be forced to do anything." Said Cristiano simply.

"Will she come here?" Asked the other.

"I agreed to go find her. I'm taking a bus to her home, because I haven't been driving lately. Do you want to go?"

"No. I'm not ready."

"I don't think it's a good time for you either, daughter." Said Mrs. Janaina. "Pregnant women are very sensitive and should not force themselves in certain situations."

"Are you pregnant?" Asked Cristiano.

"Yes, I am."

"Sorry for inviting you to the institution. I did not know that."

"If you want, you can go to the center with me tonight. They said the conference will be great." Said the mother.

"Despite my sister's insistence, I never went to a Spiritist center. But I like to read Spiritist novels."

"In romances we don't always learn a lot. The best thing is to go to a Spiritist house. And there is always a first time. I don't know why, but I'm sure you will like it." Said David, smiling.

"What will the conference be about?" Rúbia asked.

"A speaker studies a topic from the Gospel of Jesus and talks about it." Said Mrs. Janaina.

For Rúbia to understand better, David exemplified:

"For example: in the Gospel of Jesus, according to Matthew, Chapter V, verses 44 to 48, there is the passage where the Master Jesus tells us about being perfect. Then Jesus says: *But I tell you, love your enemies and pray for those who persecute you, that you may be children of your Father in heaven. He causes his sun to rise on the evil and the good, and sends rain on the righteous and the unrighteous. If you love those who love you, what reward will you get? Aren't even the tax collectors doing that? And if you greet only your own people, what are you doing more than others? Do not even pagans do that? Be perfect, therefore, as your heavenly Father is perfect.*"

"You memorized it well, huh?" Cristiano joked.

"Yes, I did. I love that passage. So, this Gospel passage, in the lecture, will possibly explain it as follows: Jesus says strive to evolve. He teaches that it is useless for me to be alone with my class, only with my friends and not give the slightest importance to people who do not belong to the same social, religious and philosophical group as me. If we begin to do good to a stranger, to help without any interest, to help even if the other belongs to another social, religious, philosophical group, etc. we will get closer to God. We will be more connected to Him. When we do good to those who hate us, that is, when we love our enemies, we pray for those who slander us, we practice the greatest of all virtues: charity."

"It's hard to pray for someone who slanders us." Said Rúbia.

"It's only hard at first, but then it's so much easier." Said David. "We feel good. You don't get that heartbreak that comes with the feeling of hatred, anger. Praying for a person who speaks ill of us and wishes him the best, makes all the light, all the peace, all the blessings of the Father come to us, something beneficial that does not pay money. Prayer with love, it is not bought with money. When you practice the charity of loving prayer for an enemy, he is no longer your enemy, even if he is in his head. By doing so, you get up, because with this kind of charity, which is prayer, you get rid of two gigantic vices; selfishness and pride."

"Selfishness and pride? How is that?" The young woman was interested.

"Usually, we are selfish as we would not pray if it weren't for ourselves, asking for all the blessings in the world just for ourselves. And we only do it when we need it, otherwise we don't even remember God." He smiled. "We are proud to pray only for family members, close friends, believing, consciously or unconsciously, that the enemy does not deserve our praise, our love, our compassion. It is as if the stranger, the different, the one who does not share our opinion, does not deserve peace. We only begin to be perfect and to get up when we love our neighbor, even though he is a stranger, despite that annoying neighbor who turns on the radio at the highest volume, not respecting your need at that moment, be it a headache, studying for an important test or the simple need for silence to reflect. If this neighbor has no education, if he still lives in ignorance and stupidity, get up and pray with all your heart, so that he can have peace and know, as soon as possible, the love for his neighbor, showing respectfulness, through a low sound."

"You will agree with me that it is difficult to understand the neighbor who turns on the loud sound or makes noise that annoys

171

us. Not just the neighbor, but also that person on the street who turns on the car stereo at the highest volume, annoying everyone." Rúbia commented.

"Yes, it is difficult, but think: if he makes such a loud noise, the sound goes up to the highest volume, it is because he cannot stand on his own. He must be that kind of person who needs to make noise because he can't bear his own thoughts, because everyone who has good ideas, happy, good and healthy thoughts, they don't like noise, loud sound. These people enjoy having their own ideas, with their own thoughts. But those who do the opposite generally have problems, they are disturbed. So, we must pray that the person has peace with himself."

"What if the person doesn't have that kind of problem and decides to make noise, turn on the sound anyway?"

"If he does not have problems and does it until he irritates others, then it follows that he has not evolved, he is someone rude and he also needs compassion, prayer so that he enlightens his conscience and thinks about the right to peace of others." When he saw Rúbia thoughtful, he added; "You know, in our daily life, we have countless opportunities to practice charity on the way to perfection. When we cross a street and a driver almost runs us over, instead of calling him miserable, unhappy and wanting him to crash the car, you think he can have serious problems, because doing so, he has problems. Then ask, in your mind, that the light of Jesus illuminates your conscience, so that you can be a better and more educated person. When another car closes yours, out of ignorance of the unhappy and rushed driver, pray, in quick words; "God guide that person, give him peace". Just do that. In that way, you don't create negative, bad and heavy energies in yourself that will permeate your mind and consequently make your body sick. All illnesses and health problems that happen to us are due to our negative thoughts. And don't think that negative thoughts are just those ideas that something is not going to work. It's not just that, the negative thought is the one you swear to the guy on the subway that pushed or squeezed you. Or wish your neighbor would die because he dumped the trash in front of your house, making you mad about it. Wanting the other to crash the car because he was aggressive behind the wheel and somehow assaulted or scared you. Wishing the colleague at work would be fired, sent away just because of an unfortunate comment he made or some behavior that upset you. All of this and more is negative thinking, ideas contrary to the Divine essence that is within you. If God created us, we certainly have something of Him in us. We can call this something of the spark of God. That spark, that flame tends to grow, to spread as you practice good charity. And know that the best practice of good, the best practice of charity is in our vibrations of love, in our wishes for peace with our unknown brothers or with those who do not share our tastes."

"Our David…" Cristiano smiled after thinking. "What a lesson! Days ago, I was very angry with a guy who appeared on television because of a crime he committed and... I started to think differently now."

"Change any bad or unhappy thoughts you have about someone right away. Correct yourself when you want the other's harm. Think that person is sick. If that person is not sick in body or mind, he is sick in soul and is unhappy for having done what he did, even if he doesn't know it yet. So, pray fast, hoping that love is born in your heart. Just that. It's that easy. This way you are not permeated with the heavy energies of sad vibrations. If you wish evil, you will not correct a person or the world, but you will certainly be diminishing the flame of that spark of God in your heart, causing yourself suffering."

Rúbia took the opportunity and asked;

"And when do we know about a cruel murderer? If he used a lot of evil to kill someone, there was suffering, torture, can we not want him to suffer as the other did?"

"Justice belongs to God. If you want the other to suffer what made someone else suffer, how will this feeling of hatred, aversion help you or help the other?" She didn't answer. "What good is it to vibrate negatively towards someone? After all, if you believe in God, you know that He will provide justice at the right time for that individual's understanding. On the contrary, one should think; "God, enlighten the mind of that creature with peace and love. In that way, your heart learns to be tender and to love your neighbor. If you do exactly that, that good vibration, before addressing another person, will pass through you, as if it were an antenna that receives the Father's blessing to address the other who is so in need. The energy received is from God and, if God is with you, my friend, no one, incarnate or disembodied, may be against you. Only something according to the Father's will, something can happen to you. Now, if you want evil, revenge, you want the other to be condemned... I'm sure that God will not be with you. When you are someone who generates bitter, sad, anguished and suffering energies, when you wish evil, to any degree, it will not be God or your guardian angel who will be by your side, but unhappy and suffering spirits. They vibrate at the same frequency, permeating with lower energies that cause innumerable physical and emotional suffering."

"So, I shouldn't wish evil even for a murderer who has cruelly assaulted someone?" Rúbia insisted.

"Instead of focusing on the murderer, why not say a heartfelt prayer for the victim's relief? After all, that person is the one who most needs peace and relief. Also, I'm sorry to remind you that God doesn't make mistakes. If that victim is experiencing so much suffering, then, there are two ways: or it was an evolved spirit and, for some reason, accepted to go through what happened, or it was a spirit that needed to suffer what it suffered to harmonize what it did in the past. Nothing is by chance. I'll give you a classic example: Jesus suffered what He suffered for a cause. Jesus had a purpose when He allowed himself to be arrested and brought to trial. A high spirit like Him could only seek something very dramatic, at a time when the human creature was so rude, to draw attention to such a noble cause. Look, He was very knowledgeable and vibrating very high. Others who suffered on the cross, like him, ended up there only for crimes they committed, they went through what others went through. They were not innocent, but spirits who, incarnated, needed a sad and painful experience to learn not to do to others what they did. I cannot believe that an innocent person experiences painful or sad consequences, they will face very intense suffering, because I believe in a good and just God. Therefore, He would not let you or me suffer what we do not need."

"Very often we only learn from suffering." She reflexively concluded.

"That's right." At that moment, David saw his watch and said in surprise. "Wow, guys! I need to go. I'm late."

Getting up, he approached his mother and kissed her. Leaning towards Rúbia, he also kissed her cheek. Then he put his hand on his brother's back, saying goodbye and went to change to go to work.

David was absolutely right. Our negative thoughts are worse than all our enemies together trying to do something against us.

Rúbia was impressed by the clear explanation. Looking at it from that angle, life events began to make sense. Everything we experience has a reason for being. We need to evolve, but we only evolve when we practice the charity of the desire for good and harmonize the situations that we disharmonize.

175

* * *

That afternoon, as agreed, Simone and Cristiano went to the institution that cared for boys with special needs. She was apprehensive. However, she insisted on visiting the place. The receptionist gently and politely asked;

"Are you sure you want to see all of our wards? Sorry to ask, but it's not common for a pregnant woman to visit us. In fact, I don't think we ever had a visit from a pregnant woman. Not that I remember." He said with a smile, generously.

"My baby, who is going to be born... I hope, has Patau syndrome. I was desperate when I heard it. I was not aware of this syndrome. Now, after much crying and despair, I understood that I had to face reality. After all, I will see my son, take care of him, love him and do everything for him, as God wants. So, I decided that I wanted to meet other children with this and other syndromes. I want to know the reality, because, for me, this is the way to create an organization for life. A firm and real organization."

"If that's the case... let's go." He smiled, retaining his admiration for the firmness of that woman. "And you, Dr. Cristiano, haven't come to visit us in a long time, have you?"

"That's right. I had an accident and since then it has been a bit difficult to come here."

"I heard so."

They kept walking until they entered the rooms where the children were, beginning with the youngest.

At one point during the visit, Simone inadvertently grabbed Cristiano's arm and gripped it. When they passed the benches, she was impressed with what she saw.

The young man put his arm around her shoulder and, in a generous voice, asked politely, almost whispering;

"Do you want to go back? There is no problem. We can go back now, if you want. Bete will understand it." He referred to the employee who accompanied them.

"No. Let's continue." She decided.

During the visit, Simone asked a few questions about treatment, food, basic care for some needs and everything. She seemed a little more comfortable, more confident.

After a while, at the end of the visit and near the exit, she asked;

"You introduced me to those women volunteers. How do you offer to be here?"

"The person has to fill out a form with the home address. Of course, we cannot accept any volunteers. We need to take care of the safety and well-being of our children, so there is a rigorous evaluation. It is necessary to have good will, punctuality, good spirits and other qualities necessary to help others."

"I see."

"Most of the time, they are women who are willing to preserve the place, that is, cleanliness or the more specific care of local hygiene. Those who have worked as nurses, babysitters, teachers, mainly kindergarten teachers, school chefs who help with educational services and other tasks, especially with children, they can help with specific tasks such as food, food preparation, activities with games for those who have better conditions. There is always a ward that needs someone to help and there is always someone who needs to volunteer to take care of themselves."

"I saw Mrs. Matilde, Mrs. Josefa and others repairing donated clothing that can be used in the institution. I found the work so beautiful!"

"It was Mrs. Matilde who started this work here." He smiled while saying that. "She was depressed. The husband had passed away and her world was over. After a long time in a horrible state of depression, panic and many psychosomatic symptoms, she told us that her psychotherapist told her to do something, to do some work. Very dejected, she came to us. We couldn't put her, in the state she was in, with the boys. Then one of the cooks suggested that she could help in the kitchen. Mrs. Matilde started, but she turned out to be very sad, she had depressive attacks and was crying. One day, when she was walking through the reception to leave, she saw a woman who wanted to donate clothes of many boys, but said that they were dirty and that others needed repairs. The woman at the reception said that wash those clothes would not be a problem, but that we did not have a sewing service. So, Mrs. Matilde volunteered. She took the clothes home, washed them, and started mending them. She was distracted by the service and when two friends went to visit her... I don't know how to explain it... but the friends liked to sew the clothes, because many of the services were by hand. Then it all started. Mrs. Matilde's house had no space, so we fixed the room where they work today. Other volunteers arrived. Today, they repair all the clothes and still make embroidered kitchen towels, embroidered tablecloths, and bath towels to sell at our bazaar and raise funds for the institution."

"Jeez! I saw you so excited. What about her depression and panic syndrome?" Simone was interested.

"What depression! What panic, nothing!" He laughed heartily. "It's over. Now she is a cheerful, lively and productive person. Very productive. Full of ideas and good will."

"It's hard to believe. Depression is degenerative." Said Simone.

"And I know about that." Cristiano murmured. Then he admitted. "I'm the one who needs to overcome depression and panic to get back to normal."

"It will pass, doctor. It will pass." Bete tried to cheer him up.

"Yes... we will see. It is not easy." He sighed and forced a smile.

"Dr. Alcides has been asking for you these days."

Looking at Simone, he said;

"Alcides is the doctor who accompanies dental treatment, as some boys need to be sedated."

They talked a bit more, and then left. On the way, Cristiano asked;

"Do you want some juice? There is a big juice house there."

"I don't know... only if you want to."

"Let's go." He insisted. "It will be good if you distract yourself a little more before we return. Also, it has been a long time without you eating. You have to worry about the baby."

"Then, it's okay." She smiled, nodding.

When they got to the juice house, Cristiano ordered and waited, sitting at a table in front of the place.

Looking at the back of the establishment, she did not believe what she was seeing. She paled and did not pay attention to what the other said, until the young man realized.

"Simone? Are you okay?"

"There... in that table..." She looked and said, whispering, her voice trembling; "He is my husband. It is my husband who takes that woman's hand and kisses her... It is Samuel." She spoke as if she was in shock.

"My God..." The young man repented in a whisper, not knowing what to do. Lowering his head, he thought for a while and suggested. "Let's go."

"No. We are going to stay." She was determined but was pale and visibly shaky.

The waitress brought the juices. She barely touched the glass two or three times with her mouth, and Cristiano, worried, did not even touch the drink.

They said nothing. Simone couldn't help but look back and see her husband smiling, hugging, and sometimes kissing that woman's hand and lips.

"You don't seem well. Let's go." Said Cristiano.

"Won't you drink the juice?" She wanted to know, trying to impose a cold mode in her speech.

"No. I'm sorry I brought you here. We are leaving now."

"Don't you want the juice anymore?" She insisted in the same tone.

"No, why?" He was surprised.

"Then we can go, but first…" She got up and went to Samuel's table, who was surprised to see her standing there beside him. "Good afternoon!" She said in an energetic tone.

"What are you doing here?!" The husband asked, turning away from the other woman.

Looking at one, then the other, Simone noticed Cristiano at her side and introduced him.

"This is Cristiano, my brother's friend and now also my friend. He accompanied me to give me more information about how our son, who has Patau syndrome, can be born. Son that God entrusted to us both, Samuel. Not just to me!" After a moment, she asked; "And what about you? What are you doing here with kisses and caresses with this one?"

"Simone, don't you…"

"I'm leaving, Samuel. I feel sorry for you. I'm sorry I was wrong, thinking that I married a man, when, in fact, I married a coward, a poor man. I suffer, but at least I understand and accept my suffering. You don't even know what to expect." Addressing the woman accompanying him, she commented contemptuously; "As for you, Marrie... There's no point in saying anything. I see that you are so far from me, so low, so inferior that you will not understand anything I say to you." Turning to her friend, she added. "Let's go, Cristiano. Please."

They turned and the young man led her to the car. They both tried to hide their nervousness, but when she settled in the passenger seat, Simone couldn't bear it and had a crying fit. Cristiano was silent until he composed himself and only then he say;

"I'm so sorry, please. It was my fault because I brought you here."

"No, no it wasn't, Cristiano. I already knew... I just saw it with my eyes. Now... I want to go... Take me away, please."

The young man was startled. He hadn't driven since the accident, but he couldn't refuse. After all, the friend seemed in no condition to drive a car.

He closed his eyes for a moment, took a deep breath and, even with shaking hands, started the car and moved forward. When he found out, he had parked the vehicle in front of his house. He didn't even know how he got back. When Mrs. Janaina saw him, she exclaimed incredulously to Rúbia;

"Oh my God! It's Cris and... driving!"

"And my sister's car!"

Trying to stay calm, the lady opened the door of the house and went to greet them very naturally.

"I'm glad you came! I made a delicious yucca cake."

"Hello Mrs. Janaina. Is everything alright?" Simone greeted, still stunned.

"Yes, daughter. How are you?"

"I'm well."

181

The sisters hugged and greeted each other for a long time. Looking at the son who was walking by the vehicle, she asked enigmatically;

"How are you, Cris?"

Cristiano, seriously, did not respond. He kissed her as usual, but there was nervousness in his gestures. Perceiving the young man trembling and pale, the mother called him.

"Let's go inside. Rúbia and I were in the garden looking for mint. I made coffee now, but figured I shouldn't have it due to the caffeine. So, I came to get mint. I'll make a very tasty tea for us. Peppermint calms. I think we need it."

Then they entered the house and Cristiano followed his mother into the kitchen. They knew that the sisters wanted to be alone.

Sitting on the couch, they hugged until Simone asked;

"Are you alright?"

"Now I am. Mom and dad?"

"Mom was calmer when she heard you were here. I said I knew Mrs. Janaina and... I told them who they were. I was sure they were taking care of you. As for dad... You know how he is. He drank, talked a lot and resigned himself. But... it will pass."

"I don't know what to do with my life. I thought so much nonsense..." Rúbia confessed.

"For some things, only time brings the solution." There was a brief pause and she mentioned; "I just found Samuel laughing, joking, exchanging kisses and caresses with Marrie."

"Are you kidding?!"

"No. I wish I was. Cristiano was with me and saw everything."

"And you?! What did you do?!" The frightened sister asked. Simone explained what she had done and, when Rúbia was going to offend her brother-in-law, she remembered what David said to her that morning and considered. "Samuel hasn't woken up yet. He is out of touch with reality. Poor."

"Yes…" She sighed. "You're right. Thanks for looking at it that way and not getting mad. I wanted to face him, but no. I thought of my son. Somehow, the baby will feel and be damaged by my nervousness."

"What are you going to do now?"

"I will think of me, my son, and I will do the most unlikely for Samuel."

"What is that?" Said Rúbia.

"I'm going home. Hire a lawyer and file for divorce. Hopefully, I can get a divorce before the baby is born."

"Simone!"

"Yes." She gave her a bitter smile. "God help me and give me strength." Cristiano arrived and said;

"My mom is making coffee."

They got up and went to the kitchen, where everyone sat at the table.

"Today is a victory day for Cris." Mrs. Janaina was delighted.

"Oh, mother… please, enough." He said, unsatisfied and embarrassed.

"Why?" Simone was interested.

"Since the accident, Cris hasn't been to the institution and today he has. He hadn't driven since the accident, and he did today. I didn't see him interested in anything either and I'm seeing him interested today. We have a lot to thank God for."

Cristiano felt himself blush and Simone asked;

"As far as I knew, you weren't behind the wheel in that accident. Still, you didn't want to drive?"

"No. I didn't want to drive. Since the damn accident, I panic about all situations, or most of those in which I have to make decisions or be responsible. Driving is one of them."

"I didn't know... I'm so sorry." Simone muttered.

"But now you can, right, son?"

"Yes..." He agreed with uncertainty. "My concern is to go back to work as a dentist, since I need to have a lot of responsibility for the health and even the lives of the patients. I fear for an unexpected and risky situation."

"You couldn't go to the institution and you did. This shows that, little by little, you will overcome these fears that you have never had before."

"Why didn't you tell me?" Simone asked.

"Although I have dealt with those boys and girls countless times, without any feeling other than love and the willingness to help, when I thought of them, there was enormous sadness, inexplicable despair. So when you came here and I saw you with the courage to go there, in your state, with all the difficulties that you are experiencing... I said to myself: have courage! Ahead! Face the fear!" He smiled and revealed; "I won't tell you that I didn't wince when we got there. I was shaken up when I had to drive out of the juice house, but I kept going and saw that I could."

"I didn't mean to bother you. I'm sorry, Cristiano." Simone said in a simple voice.

"Why...? You did me a favor. You were an instrument in my life. I cannot live as I am. I need to seize opportunities and bring out the best in me."

"He's made great strides lately." Said the mother in a complimenting tone. The phone rang and the young man stood up.

"Let me answer. Excuse me."

When she saw him go to the living room, Mrs. Janaina commented;

"I have never seen Cris as good as in recent weeks. Especially after meeting you, Simone. Your willpower, your willingness to overcome difficulties, moved him. It seems that it gave my son courage. He didn't even smile like that months ago. He even reduced his outings and those walks alone, which worried me a lot."

"What do you mean?" Rúbia asked and Mrs. Janaina said;

"As soon as he recovered, he went out for a walk and said he was relieved. He says that he feels desperation, something unbearable and that when he walked, it relieved him a lot. But it has decreased a lot too."

"What he feels is a kind of tension. This tension is an energy and when he moves, he walks, he manages to expend that energy and feels less nervous, less tense." Simone explained.

"When Cris went out for a walk, he seemed immensely sad, upset. I was very scared. These outings had neither time nor day. I prayed a lot and my prayers were answered. In recent weeks, he has only been walking with his brother, who is a weekend athlete." She laughed.

Upon returning, Cristiano commented;

"It was a friend who wanted to know how I am. It was good to have called, it reminded me of today's lecture." Addressing Simone, he invited her; "Come to the Spiritist center with us. We know tonight's speaker is great."

"Today?"

"Yes."

"I'm going. I accept. I haven't been there in a long time."

"Awesome! I love having people here." Mrs. Janaina rejoiced. "I will prepare a very tasty dinner and after dinner, we will go."

"No, Mrs. Janaina, I can't bear to eat more!" Rúbia said. They laughed and continued the conversation.

10.– WHAT IS REALLY CHARITY?

THAT NIGHT was very beneficial for the spiritual participation of all who opened their minds to the very important topic: *Love your neighbor as yourself.* This fulfillment is the greatest charity. It is the most complete expression of charity, because we do to others what we want them to do to us, when we are in their place. This practice is the end of selfishness and pride. If we do not love others as ourselves, we cannot love God above all else. By loving our neighbor as ourselves, even though that neighbor still lives in the practice of disharmony with Nature and the Father, in many cases, we are exercising benevolence, brotherhood, understanding and elevation of spirit. Love is the divine essence that exists in us.

As we are taught in *The Gospel according to Spiritism: loving your enemies is absurd for non-believers. He for whom the present life is everything, only sees in the enemy a pernicious creature, disturbing his peace.* For those who believe in the teachings of Jesus, and those should be, mainly, spiritists, to love our neighbor is to understand that we need to atone for the past, to think that we don't know what we were in other lives. Perhaps even worse creatures than today's discontent. Also remember that there is a future and we never know what tomorrow holds. We don't know how much our enemy can help and love us today.

Therefore, we cannot complain about what we experience because of what others do to us. We should not complain about those who serve as instruments for us to develop patience, love, resignation, and the opportunity to pray. This way of acting and thinking leads us to forgiveness. We feel, then, more willing to be generous, prudent, consequently, we get up and stay away from the negative and inferior energies that could reach us.

Some say they can't do charity as they don't have much to share. The truth is that charity can be achieved in many ways: in actions, uplifting words and good thoughts or a prayer. And no one is so poor that he can't practice it through a thought, a prayer with a desire for good, for prosperity. This is impossible not to do, unless you don't want to. There, we show how selfish we are.

No matter who we are, what we are, how much we have or in what conditions we live. What matters is the love we have and the love we address on a daily basis to all the brothers along the way, especially the love that we naturally address with our thoughts. All the Doctrine of Jesus is summed up in love.

The lecture was magnificent. It made many people reflect on their feelings and actions.

Mrs. Janaina, seated between Cristiano and Rúbia, leaned over to her son´s side and asked Simone;

"Did you like today's lecture?" She whispered.

"I loved it." She whispered too. "This passage of the Gospel was very well explained."

Cristiano turned to Rúbia and commented;

"Now is the time to receive the passes. People who want to receive passes are in that line." He pointed out. "They will be taken to the pass chamber where there are other pass workers. The intention is for the pass-giver to apply, that is, to transmit the healthy energies that he receives from spiritual friends who work here in the name of Jesus. There will be no physical contact, only the laying on of hands. I like to remember that the pass-givers seek to do the same as Jesus when he extended his hands over the needy and alleviated their pain, especially those of the soul. Some came to heal themselves. This is the purpose of the pass applied here. Do you want to receive it?"

"Yes, I want to." She whispered with enthusiasm. "I loved everything I saw, heard and felt here. I haven't felt this good in a long time."

When they stood up and headed for the passing line, they were surprised by David's appearance, all in white, as he had come straight from the dental office.

"Son, you came." Said his mother.

"I arrived at the beginning of the lecture, but there was no place near you, so I stayed there." Then he greeted Rúbia and Simone and said; "One patient from the afternoon got lost and the other arrived earlier and... I didn't have class today... Anyway, I ended up having a little time and came straight here."

After the passes, Mrs. Janaina explained to the two sisters about the work in the house of the Spiritists and they listened attentively.

"So, they make basic baskets, baskets for needy pregnant women, teach fabric painting, embroidery, crochet and other things. Everyone who teaches here does it voluntarily. There are those who also help in the canteen or bring some sandwiches to sell. What is collected helps to pay some of the bills of the Spiritist house, such as water, electricity, telephone, cleaning material, toilet paper, material for workshops... We also have Spiritist studies courses. It is always important to know and understand Spiritist Codification better."

"I didn't think there was such a thing." Said Rúbia. "I had no idea."

Suddenly, Mrs. Janaina looked up and saw a friend, who was also a housekeeper and who was some distance away, walking towards them. At that moment, the lady turned to David and recommended;

"Son, here comes Mr. Raimundo. Let him say whatever he wants, ok?"

"Keep calm, mom. I know how to deal with him."

He was a big man, tall, almost serious. He always seemed unsatisfied when making his comments, especially when it came to criticism.

"Good evening." Said the gentleman as he approached. They all responded and Mrs. Janaina introduced the sisters.

"These are our friends, Rúbia and Simone. This is the first time they have come here. This is Mr. Raimundo, a colleague here at the center."

"Glad to meet you." Said the man as they shook hands. "Apparently you should introduce the house not just to them, because there are people who haven't been here in a long time. They might not remember anything else." He said wryly, looking at David.

"It's just that I have a lot of work, Mr. Raimundo." David responded politely.

"You know we shouldn't think about work, dear. We cannot depend only on money. This is greed and even selfishness, pride, arrogance in some way, because you think you have nothing to learn here.

"Don't judge me, Mr. Raimundo. I have a human commitment. I have taken an oath and I must attend to those who need my services. After all, my patients are taking care of their health through me. It would be a lack of charity, on my part, to say that I can't help them because I'm going to the Spiritist house. I go to graduate school three days a week, at night, so I only have two nights left to help those who only have this time available. One of those two days that I have left coincides with the day of the conference here at the center."

"Do the brother spirits, or rather, does God understand your supposed difficulty?"

"Oh... God does understand. And the spirits understand why, if they are spiritual harnesses, they are watching everything I do. And as for God, he understands because he is God." Looking at his mother and the others, David said; "Shall we go?"

There was no time for response, as the very critical man seemed very dissatisfied with David's response and decided to find a way to criticize, immediately broadening the topic.

"You can do a million things, dear, but you are indebted to your presence in the house of God. You must attend more often, participate more, do some homework, study, and give yourself here. Living the life you have... You will be a victim of yourself in a short time."

"Mr. Raymond, I'm trying to be nice so that you understand me. This moment in which I live is a phase. Now, studying and working, I cannot be present in the Spiritist house."

"Mainly being the provider at home. I'm not working." Cristiano remembered, interfering in favor of his brother.

"So, David, you can't say that you are a Spiritist and that you frequent a Spiritist house. You are far from the house of God."

David took a deep breath, looked down, then looked at the arrogant gentleman and said in a soft, polite tone.

"Mr. Raimundo, it is very common, in the middle of a Spiritist group, to hear the question; which Spiritist center do you attend? I always wanted to answer this question as I'm going to do for you now. Before asking, you need to ask some other questions such as; is it possible to limit the Divinity to a few square meters surrounded by cold masonry? Is it possible to reduce and compact the message of the reviving Gospel, to the point that a simple physical space can contain it? If the question is so restrictive, I think the answer will be simple: I don't go to any center. But if the interlocutor believes that the consoling message of the Gospel is something sublime, born from the heart of God and as immense as his love, I believe that the answer goes further. Kardec clearly states that the true Spiritist is recognized for his efforts to become a better person, but in no way does he confine the field of these efforts to the four walls of a Spiritist center."

"Our body." He continues with a calm tone. "A temporary residence of our spiritual individuality, must be consecrated to the intense and uninterrupted work of self-improvement, as a temple of praise and adoration to the only God. Therefore, each word, each gesture, each attitude towards life and towards the similar, must be a hymn of gratitude to the eternal God, who does not support us only in the Spiritist center or in churches, synagogues and other houses of prayer, but rather in every moment of our life; in the illusion of fleeting happiness or in the clutches of desperate sadness. God supports us all the time."

"It would be to despise the Divinity." He continued in the same tone, looking at the other with a generous eye. "Trying to impress our merely human imperfections, to try to reduce the Creator of the Universe to the mediocrity of anthropomorphism; to seek to dedicate (many times, to redeem ourselves) our conscience in just a few hours of our daily work, while he envelops us in His Infinite Love, from our first breath of life, the crumbs of time offered on a stone altar, never on the altar of our hearts."

"Yet, even though they know that God is important to be adored in spirit, many, like you, feel completely at ease with the Creator, for devoting the minimum of their time to religious service, whatever it may be. Poor human being who is grateful for the abundance with which God provides him crumbs. Poor servants, who think they are faithful, as they close their eyes to a prayer and think of the tasks that await them when they get home or what they must do the next day."

"Fragile religiosity, which the slightest breath of adversity throws away, exposing the truth under a subtle layer of piety... Don't you think so?" The man said nothing and David continued; "Look around you. Try to cover the greatness of the Divine creation with only one glance. Listen to the song of the birds, see the light of the dawn and the shine of the stars that illuminate the immensity of the heavenly dome. Think of the air that you breathe and that many insist on polluting. Billions of plant lives work incessantly to clean up what humans insist on irresponsibly polluting. And can we, little human beings, somehow give God even one atom of oxygen that our organism needs so much? Could we pay, if charged, for one drop of drinking water? And with what would we pay the Creator of the Universe? What coins would we use to trade with the One who, in the words of Moses, called himself I AM?" Total silence in the brief pause "Do you dare to haggle with the few minutes you have left with the One who is the Creator and the Maintainer of Life, the alpha and the omega, the beginning and the end of everything that exists, existed and will exist?"

"And it is this God, this Father who is sovereignly just and good, who offers you abundantly everything he needs. His love is not measured by restrictive human concepts. If you want, in some way, to thank the Creator for everything you receive, if you want to dedicate something to the One who gave you everything, don't spend minutes. Dedicate your life to the fullest. Establish your home, your work, the street where you walk, wherever you are, a temple where you can worship your Creator with the purest love of your soul, poured in the cup of your heart. Let every gesture, every word, every act of yours be made as if on your knees before Him who created you, no matter where you are or with whom."

"Follow the footsteps of Jesus, who was Christ in every moment of his life and was rarely in the temple. Can you think of a bigger example than yours? Can you conceive of Jesus restricted within the cold stone walls, no matter what religion he is?"

"So, Mr. Raimundo, do not try to reduce the sun's brightness to the miserable flickering of a candle. Seek God in daily tasks, in conversation with friends, in work that will allow you to maintain your life, because that is what I do every day, every minute, wherever I am. And when you understand, when you are sure that the universe is God's house and every creature in it is your brother, your whole life will be imbued with Christian precepts. Then you will be able to live in perfect harmony with yourself and in permanent communion with the Great Plan. From now on, your words will be prayers, your thoughts will be light, and you will worship the Lord your God with all your heart, with all your soul, with all your understanding, and you will love your neighbor as yourself, wherever you are and whoever your neighbor is and wherever you are."

"Yes, my brother..." He sighed at him and smiled softly. "Wherever you are. Men only created the temple because he forgot that God resides within him."

As he said all this, David, with a simple expression, looked into his eyes. He was blushing and didn't know what to say.

Mrs. Janaina touched her son's arm, but David still said;

"By the way, loving your neighbor as yourself was the topic of today's talk. If I were as wrong as you are, as arrogant, selfish, and proud, I would want to know from someone what I have just told you. I would stop, reflect and reform myself intimately. And, without a doubt, I would be grateful to the friend who loved me and was faithful to me, warning me of my failures. Remembering that criticism is a terrible addiction, Mr. Raimundo, it is the mother of discord, prejudice, hate and many other evils in the world."

"Son…" Murmured Doña Janaina, calling him.

"One minute, mom." Turning to the man again, he said; "I have not stopped being a spirit in my heart and in my practices. Nor am I far from the house of God, for I make my world the house of the Lord." Turning to his mother, he called. "Let's go. It is already late." Then he said goodbye. "It was a pleasure to talk to you. Until another day, Mr. Raimundo."

"See you…" He turned his head down, shaking his hand.

When they left the center corridor, Mrs. Janaina asked in order to scold him.

"David, what was that?"

The boy stopped, turned to his mother and explained with a soft smile and tenderness in his voice.

"I could have offended him, pointed out all his faults, talked about his destructive criticisms, but no. I spoke calmly, courteously, everything I needed to review. I didn't offend him at any time. Right?"

"Let's go." Said his lady, looking angry, dissatisfied with her son, but not making a fuss.

David exchanged glances with his brother and both smiled. When they were near the cars, Ricardo called them.

"Hello, people! I thought I wasn't going to catch up with you." He said breathlessly, greeting them.

"Where were you? We didn't see you." Mrs. Janaina asked.

"Selling snacks in the canteen. I couldn't get out of there and there was no way to call you."

"Are you a volunteer here?" Simone asked, smiling.

"I am. Not long ago I took up the task." He smiled and said; "Today, during the conference, I was in the background and I saw you, but you were far away." Turning to Rúbia, he asked interested; "And you, how are you?"

"Better than yesterday."

"Did you talk to your brother?"

"I was only able to call today at lunchtime. He also thought it was better for me not to be alone in the apartment. He asked me to wait for him at Mrs. Janaina's house."

"That's right. It will be good for you. Besides, there is no better place than the home of this lovely creature." He praised, putting one arm around the lady's shoulder and bringing her slightly closer to him. Laughing when he found himself without a theme, Ricardo decided. "We'd better go. It is already late." He said goodbye and promised; "On Saturday afternoon I have a walk around your house, Mrs. Janaina, that is, if you don't have any problems."

"No way. Go ahead and we'll be waiting for you."

"Agreed."

As soon as Ricardo left, the sisters said goodbye. After promising to return to the lady's house to take some clothes to Rúbia.

Simone decided to go home, as she was determined to resolve her situation with Samuel.

* * *

Upon arriving home, realizing that her husband had not arrived, Simone called her mother to let her know where he was and to tell her what happened that day.

After the conversation, she went to her room and took a shower. She took too long and Samuel arrived.

She was waiting for him, sitting on the living room couch, strangely quiet, sure of what to do.

On the contrary, the husband was very surprised to see her.

"Simone? Are you here?!"

"Of course. It's my house, isn't it?"

"Yes... It's just... About today..." Interrupting it, she clarified.

"I don't want any explanation of what I saw today. Nothing that you can tell me will change my mind. In fact... what you say can hurt me, hurt me even more. So, please, don't tell me anything."

"So...?"

"Then," She interrupted again. "I came here simply to take what is mine, by right, until a judge decides for us, who will keep what things."

"You mean that..."

"Divorce." A tear rolled down her face. She never thought of saying that word to her husband. Firm, looking austere and not showing emotion, she continued. "The best thing now is the divorce. I know that, if it is friendly, it will be quick and less painful."

Samuel walked around the room a few careless steps, thought a little and asked;

"Won't you fight for me?"

"Fight for you?!" She smiled with some irony. "Fight for a man who abandoned me at a time when I needed a friend, a shoulder, a partner the most? Only if I was unbalanced. That's absurd. When my world fell apart, you could still throw a bomb at me and stomp on me. You couldn't respect my feelings. You didn't even have a drop of consideration, of respect for me. This child is not just mine. God has entrusted him to both of us, as I said, but you have proved to be such a cruel, wicked creature that you have turned your back on both of us. Coward! Fearful of facing reality, even sad, you went to seek comfort, through your selfish heart, in the arms of a frivolous person. If you bastard had a shred of morality, of decency, you would have come back home to your family, which is your son and I, so that we can support each other, strengthen each other and move forward in doing God's will. But that's not what happened. I pity you, Samuel. Your college degrees did not alphabetize your morals or your spirit for the love of God. They did not open your eyes to the responsibilities of your existence. Materialistic and proud, you could only show off your son if he looked normal. That is not love."

"I won't let you say that!" He got angry. She didn't seem to hear him and continued.

"There is no good in a beautiful residence and two beautiful cars in the garage. Everything is very beautiful... However, it is useless to have planned everything in our life, if we didn't plan the most important thing. The main thing was to have each other, friendship, love, respect for difficult moments. I made it wrong, I made many mistakes. I saw in you a hard-working and studious man, who is very interested in updating himself to be always in line with the needs of the labor market... But unfortunately, I forgot to see if you had, within you, love and respect for God, see if you had a merciful heart, respect for others, love for others and so many other virtues that we miss so much in such an important moment."

"What do you want me to do? "

"Stay by my side, next to our son with love and faith, that's all!" A brief pause and, looking at him, she continued; "There's a moment in life when money is nothing. We need God in our hearts to support each other. We need to have someone by our side who loves us unconditionally and respects us. Money doesn't buy that."

Samuel lowered his head and the silence was absolute for a long time. Worried, he asked;

"What do we do now?"

"I will not give up what belongs to me. I fought hard, like you, to have what we have. I'm pregnant, so now, more than ever, I need the comfort and security of my home. Our child is going to be born and needs a home. And our home, our home is here. So, I'm not leaving here and you can stay as long as you want. Just in the other room. Tomorrow you're looking for a lawyer and we're getting a divorce."

"Like this? So cold?"

"Exactly. There is no other way."

"So, you came back here to keep the house?"

"I came back to give our son his due. It is not fair that I leave this place and stay in my mother's house, when everything I fought to achieve, to live better, is here. Everything here is mine and our son's and we will use it. Unless a judge says otherwise, I doubt it. I was not the one who strayed from the moral duties that bound us together."

"Are you sure you want a divorce?"

"Yes, without a doubt."

"Then I will provide and also demand what is mine. Half of everything here belongs to me." He replied, turning his back and going into the room.

While her husband was taking a shower, Simone made his bed, which was in another room. As soon as she finished, she showed up.

"You can stay here." She said, pointing to the bed in the room with the door open.

Samuel said nothing, even when he realized that all the clothing he was going to wear the next day was also there, ready for him to wear. Upon entering the room, he closed the door and left her alone.

When Simone found herself alone in the double suite, her heart felt tense and sad.

For a moment she wondered if she was doing the right thing for her and her son.

A deep bitterness invaded her as never before. She never imagined experiencing a situation like this. She needed to talk to someone. She thought about calling her mother, but she no longer wanted to worry her. She was already distressed about Abner, Rúbia and herself. The three siblings were going through difficult times. She didn't want to take on any more anxiety than she already had. She wanted to call Cristiano, but she was afraid, the friendship was recent and the boy already had his own challenges. She remembered Claudio, her colleague, a professor at the same university.

Her heart sank into despair and anguish overcame her. Without resisting, she picked up the phone and called.

"Cláudio? It is me…"

She cried. She could not bear the weight of all that had happened to her.

"Calm down, my dear." Asked the other with compassion. "Think about the baby. He needs to feel that you are calm. Relax, take a deep breath and think of something very good. When he heard her in silence and perceived her serene, he suggested in a tender voice. "Imagine a beautiful flower garden, a blue sky with fluffy white clouds, a soft breeze touching your face and relieving all tension. Now you are lighter. Your breath is calm, soft... Your body is relaxed…"

His story continued until Simone felt very calm and said;

"I'm better. Thank you. I'm sorry to call you at this hour. But I had to talk to someone."

"Don't apologize. Maybe someday I'll need you and I won't look at the clock." He laughed. "Come on, tell me what happened for you to be this way."

Simone told him about her day, from going to the institution to her asking for a divorce, and was moved when she reported her husband's coldness during the conversation.

"The best thing you did was go home. I don't know how many laws there are, but it's good to guarantee your rights and your child's rights."

"I said I want a divorce, Cláudio."

"Of course you do! That's what you felt when you saw the betrayal. Worse than knowing that you are betrayed, is catching your partner in the act, with the other, as you saw. After all, it would be very difficult for you to accept and be fine with your husband as if nothing had happened. What would your conscience be like when you sleep next to the man you know was with another? It would certainly be the saddest and most unfortunate thing to do."

"I can't stand to be with him anymore. I don't want him to touch me. Do you understand?"

"Absolutely. He must respect your will. I know how sensitive you are due to your condition. Even more emotional because of concerns about the baby. No matter what others say, the priority now is to respect yourself, to do what is best for you."

"Do you think I did it right?"

"If you do not want to sleep next to someone who doesn't respect you, doesn't love you, is not a friend, then you have done the safest thing in this world. Do not worry. Now all you have to do is pray. Pray with all the strength and love you have in your heart."

"I went to the Spiritist center today. I told you, didn't I? It felt so good. Too bad I stopped going to a spiritualist house because of him."

"It's always time to go back. If you feel good, enjoy it. Remember that moment of peace. You must have received a lot of strength, light and peace from God if you felt that good. This is what you will receive now with a beautiful prayer, with a very sincere conversation with God." There was a brief pause and he said; "I'm not a spiritist, I'm a sympathizer. I have been in a center over and over again and I like to read spiritist romances. So now I remember a story that came to my mind. It was told by a speaker. This story says that, once, in the spiritist center where Chico Xavier held the meetings, a woman arrived, among many others. She went to greet dear Chico and complained of having a severe headache. Chico, as always, very kind, asked the lady to sit there, next to the table. The speaker said the meeting went smoothly. After the first few minutes, the woman told one of her colleagues that her headache was going away and that she was very happy. Moments later, the pain was completely gone. In the end, much better, completely different from when she arrived, the woman was happy. She thanked him, said goodbye and left happily. Then Chico, humble, turned to the other companions and said that this lady, before arriving there, had had a very ugly fight with her husband. He offended her very much and wanted to hit her with a slap. He said the man hardly attacked her, but his will was so intense that the spiteful and hateful energy entered her ear and lodged in her head. Chico said that, even psychographically, the spirit Emmanuel, her protector, asked her to see the bad energy that the spirit Dr. Bezerra de Menezes extracted from the lady's ear because she was in true prayer, wishing good and vibrant love." After a moment Cláudio said. "I feel very impressed when I remember this story and I remember it every time I start feeling angry or hurt by someone. I think, certainly, that the person was also angry with me. Then I change my vibration. I go into prayer, at first for myself, so that my heart becomes softer and I can understand the other. Then I pray, with all my love, wishing peace and light on the other person's mind so that they can rise up and understand me."

"Do you think Samuel is angry with me?"

"I don't know if it's anger, but he's not satisfied. Think that your husband is not a creature sufficiently evolved to become strong, to assume the role of man of the house, of the patriarch, of the maintainer, to give you security and confidence. He may have several academic titles, but he is still poor in spirit. Let's remember, my friend, that you can't demand it from someone who doesn't have it, right? Both he and Marrie are not happy with you. So... pray, friend. Pray asking God to give you enough strength and love to love and wish good to those who don't understand, who will hurt you. Wish them well, that they have peace and light in their consciousness to follow the right path, without harming anyone. Doing this will not have the bad, stressful, sad and painful energies of any negative feelings that someone may wish for you. Remember the wife who got rid of the headache, generated by the hateful energy of her husband wishing her harm, because it vibrated with good, with love. She was in prayer, so the spirits helped her."

Simone took a deep breath and told her friend;

"It is not easy, Cláudio."

"But it is not impossible, my dear. Start praying. Your guardian angel will join you and everything will begin to flow naturally. Think or say the first words of desire for good and you will know what it is to love the enemy as Jesus taught. The important thing is to begin, the rest, the love you have in your heart, will manifest."

"Thank you, Cláudio. This conversation did me a lot of good."

"I'm the one who needs to thank you. Call whenever you want."

"Thank you."

Then they said goodbye and hung up.

Despite the challenges to be solved, Simone felt much better, more confident. While her friend guided her, she really prayed for him, her husband and Marrie. And it was in this way that she removed the painful energies that could be impregnated in her spiritual or physical body and even manifest in the form of disease.

11.– ENLIGHTENING CONVERSATION

UPON ARRIVING FROM HIS TRIP, Abner was surprised by the news about Rúbia. They were at Mrs. Janaina's house and he was talking to his sister alone in the room.

"That's what happened." She said after telling him everything. "I don't know what to do. I have no place to stay, I lost my job... Simone brought some of my clothes... I don't have anything else."

Rúbia was dejected. Her appearance showed great concern, however much she tried to disguise it. She did not seem as excited or ordered as she was. Her curly hair was tied back, like a tail, and untreated. The absence of makeup and the growing eyebrows gave her an almost sickly look on her dull face and without the smile she had before.

Observing her well, the brother responded;

"Of course, you can stay in my apartment. Without a doubt. As for work... You can't fire a pregnant woman, except for just cause. Which is not the case."

"But I don't want to go to work anymore! I don't know how to face it! What face will I show there? I'm going to quit." She said almost desperately.

"You can do that, but it's not right. Let's think about one thing at a time. First, let's go to my house. Mrs. Janaina and her children are wonderful creatures, but we should not bother others for too long with our problems. Secondly, I'm going to have a little chat with Jefferson."

"No! You will not do that!"

"Let's go home, Rúbia. Then we'll see what to do, shall we?"

"Only if you promise not to talk to him."

"This is not a good place to discuss. Let's go. Then we will solve this." So decided, Abner took her to his apartment, setting her up in the room where he had made an office. He provided a single bed and placed it there.

That night, when they sat down again to talk about it, Rúbia declared;

"I don't want to set foot in that company, I don't want to see Jefferson's face."

"Think about it. Working will entitle you to maternity leave, medical assistance, a health plan, and also, you will have money and so many other things that you will get only if you are employed. It wouldn't be good to be out of work now. What do you plan to do? After all, you have a child on the way and... To be honest, I can help you, but it will be very difficult for me to support you in everything, especially when it comes to spending on quality doctors and hospitals. It won't be pleasant for me or for you to depend on public services."

"I don't know what to do." She admitted disconsolately. "Dad doesn't want me home and you won't be able to support me all the time. After all, you have your life. You've achieved your independence. I have no right to ruin it."

Perhaps, Rúbia said this upon hearing from her brother that she would not be a problem and that he would help her in everything and for as long as she needed. However, Abner was honest in making her see reality and assume her responsibilities. In certain situations, too much help causes accommodation. Then the young man answered"

"You said it right. I can help you for a while, but I have my life. That's why I advise you not to quit your job."

"It's as if I don't have the strength. I feel a weakness when I think about showing up for work and... Jefferson doesn't want the pregnancy."

"You're not going to do what he wants again, are you?"

"No. In the moment of despair, when dad threw me out and I had nowhere to go, I thought about it. I wanted to die... But then... I can't let Jefferson determine what I should do to be free of charges. I would never forgive myself. I wouldn't have peace of mind for the rest of my life."

"See, I can imagine how difficult it would be to go back to work. However, it will be a boring or perhaps embarrassing situation just at the beginning. Then you get used to it and people lose interest and stop asking you questions."

"No one knows that Jefferson and I had an affair. People will want to know who the father of my child is."

"If you don't want them to know, be firm and don't say it. Before I ask something about someone's life, I ask myself: what am I going to do with that information? Why do I need to know that? If the information is not useful to me, then I'm being indiscreet and inconvenient. Then I don't ask anything. When someone asks you about your private life, ask yourself: what will that person do with that information? If it doesn't help you, then allow them the right not to reveal anything about your private life."

"And what do I say if someone asks who the father is?"

"You can answer: I know very well who the father is. You don't know. It's no use talking about it. In fact, it's not a good time for this conversation, don't you think?" He thought and added.

"When you answer an indiscreet question with another question, you disarm the person."

"It is not easy."

"Rúbia, think about it, do you want to give up the money you will receive for maternity leave, do you want to give up health insurance, hospital, doctors for you and your child and other rights for the sake of others? Now... Please...! Damn the others. You have to think of yourself."

"You don't want me to stay here, do you?"

"That's not what I said. Of course, you can stay here as long as you need to. But I don't think it's right to settle down and lock yourself in this apartment. I want you to organize yourself to be independent, and to do that, you have to move now. The most practical and quickest way to do this is to face the situation you caused. The truth, Rúbia, is that you looked for it. It wasn't for lack of warning that it went wrong. Now you must take responsibility for your actions and your choices."

The sister was embarrassed because she knew he was right. And she expressed;

"It has not been easy for me."

"I know. I guess it's not. But you have to be in control of the situation, of your life. Not going to work, leaving it's escaping responsibility, it's losing control of everything."

"What if Jefferson pushes me?"

"Try to avoid it, at first. If there is no way, be firm. Say you won't give up your employment rights and that you will take care of your child. And, for now, you have nothing to talk with him or anyone else about the issue."

"Abner... I'm so confused. I feel so weak."

"Pray. Ask for strength and inspiration to know how to do it well. Pray for clarity of thought."

"You said you were going to talk to him, I beg you, please don't go."

"As you ask, for now, I'm not going."

Silence reigned for a few minutes while she reflected. Soon Rubia said ashamed;

"I'm sorry for everything I said."

"About what?" We didn't understand.

"The last time we spoke, well... I offended you. However, now, you are the only person who can help me. If it weren't for you, I wouldn't have anyone. I wouldn't have anywhere to stay. I'm sorry for what I said." Seeing him with a low, silent look, she asked; "Of course I hurt you, didn't I? "

"I don't know if hurting is the right word. I was sad, of course. We've always been very connected and maybe I expected a different reaction from you. I thought you were more understanding."

"I'm sorry... forgive me." She asked, touching his hand. Looking up, Abner confessed.

"It is not easy to assume homosexuality on your own. It is not easy to assume for friends, family, or society. The dramas, the intimate conflicts are gigantic, painful, because they are different from the majority. At least, that's what happened in my case."

"Is the homosexual unhappy?"

"No. No way. I'm not sad about being gay. I'm sad about the prejudiced reactions, the non-acceptance of people. It's so good to live well, it's so good to be welcomed. Homosexuality is something natural, one is born that way, as I said. The problem is that many people think this is an aberration, the end of the world."

"When Jefferson started treating me differently and I found out I was pregnant, I thought about it a lot."

"How so?"

"I was so against your homosexuality. I didn't accept it. I thought it was absurd... However, I was frivolous, spineless, and immoral for agreeing to have an affair with a married man. I was aware it's not the same as yours. I could have avoided it. What I experienced was a false happiness. I knew that every night he went back home to his wife. I had to make do with the crumbs, the rest of him, the leftovers. I was proud. I didn't want to listen to your advice when you tried to warn me. Vain, selfish. I thought I was good enough to get him out of the house, out of his wife, out of his children. I didn't think that, if I had taken him out of the house to stay with me, he would have had regrets. Today, seeing with other eyes, I understand that no one can be happy when he destroys someone's happiness. No one is totally happy when they destroy a home, hurt, betray, cheat… No one is happy by being selfish. If he had left his family to be with me and our child, I could have been falsely happy right now, but in time, I would certainly take responsibility for the sadness I have caused for the wife and children he has with her."

"You would attract a series of painful consequences to your conscience." Said the brother.

"Today I understand that, and I can see it that way, but when I was with him…"

"The truth is that you have not made a mistake on your own. Be sure that he made a mistake too. But you can fix everything in time. I don't know if correction is the right word, but... I think you can harmonize what you have disharmonized. And you can do that now. Keep working. Have your child and take good care of him. Knowing what guy of man he is, unworthy of being called a father. If I were you, I would not ask him for anything. That is a good start."

"I'll confess one thing: I still don't think I'm pregnant. I don't see myself as a mother. I don't feel like a mother."

"It's just that other things are boiling in your head. Time will pass and you will think about your child differently."

"Why is it necessary to suffer in order to learn?"

"Suffering is part of our evolution, when we do not want to learn gently. The person who does not suffer, does not cry, is not sensitive, is far from evolution, far from understanding feelings, far from loving himself and others. Let us remember that even Jesus wept. The harsher, the more retarded the spirit is, the less sensitive he is and the sensitivity of others bothers you. Tolerance, patience shows the evolution of each one. All criticism is an absence of tolerance. When we criticize someone and it happens out of habit, we must immediately correct ourselves. Then think that, if that person does that, there is certainly some reason within his evolution. And we, who are criticizing, have the opportunity to elevate ourselves, first, by modifying our thinking, by correcting ourselves. Second, by wishing that person to be right in life, to correct himself, to rise up to stop doing what he is doing. Everything we do," He continued. "Has a purpose, a reason, because everything we do is in accordance with our moral and spiritual growth. Remember that we will always be called to account for our actions and thoughts."

Rúbia was thoughtful.

She was calmer and also more aware of her responsibilities. In spite of her wounded pride, her fear of the uncertain future, she would do her best, facing life head on, doing what the Father said, in the booklet she found in the church: go and make no more mistakes.

✳ ✳ ✳

At home, Mr. Salvador was not satisfied with his children's situation.

Simone, the daughter who was supposed to have a good life, had to be strong to face the problem with her son and that was unfair to her. He did not accept what Rúbia, her youngest daughter, had done. In addition to getting involved with a married man, she let herself get pregnant. This was unacceptable. That was not the education or the life example he gave her. As for Abner, he felt unhappy about him. His only son had taken on homosexuality and would never forgive him for it.

Especially when he drank, he had the spiritual companionship that made him even more enraged.

"Life is really ungrateful." He told his wife. "I have worked all these years. I fought like a convict to raise my three children... Now, all this happened"

"Problems and difficulties are not our children's privilege. Everyone faces this. If you loved your children, you wouldn't have done what you did to them."

"Simone has my full favor, I did nothing for her. As for loving, I do, but in my own way. I'm not forced to accept little, shame or mischief from anyone. This is not what I taught them. They stopped being my children when they started living with mistakes."

"Living with error or not, they are still my children. Despite all the good things I taught them, if they wanted to stray... They are still my children. I will not support what is wrong, but I will respect and guide as I can."

Mr. Salvador said nothing. He stood his ground.

✳ ✳ ✳

As the days passed, Rúbia returned to work.

Guided by her brother, she tried to avoid the subject of her pregnancy with her colleagues. She was embarrassed and realized that no one knew that the child she was expecting was from Jefferson. One day, calling her to talk, he demanded;

"You are irresponsible!" He exclaimed in a whisper so that others would not hear him. "You want to ruin my life! What do you have in mind? Get rid of that pregnancy. There is still time. If you want, I'll pay you the best service."

"I'm not going to do that. It's against my principles. I will not kill a child, especially not my son."

"I see!" He said ironically, irritated. "You want a pension and to be guaranteed for the rest of your life. You are very smart."

"And you are a scoundrel!" She attacked in the same tone. Approaching, without her expecting that, he took her by the arm and squeezed hard, saying between his clenched teeth;

"Get rid of that pregnancy, or…"

"Or what?" She reacted by pulling her arm in front of him.

"I'm going to lose my head with you, Rúbia. I don't know what I'm capable of." She felt herself shaking. A fear invaded her, giving her an unpleasant feeling. Trying to be firm, she looked at him with contempt, turned and left. When she reached the bathroom, she found Talita.

"Is everything okay?" Asked her friend, noticing that she was pale.

"I'm so…" She shut up. She opened a tap, washed her face and took a deep breath.

"Do you want to talk?"

Taking paper towels, the other one dried her face, faced her and breathed.

"I can't stand it. I should have quit. I can't bear to find Jefferson."

"Why?"

"He's the father of my child." She said, it was no surprise to Talita. She was already suspicious of both of them. Still, she marveled at the confirmation of the truth.

Approaching Rúbia, she caressed her friend, passing a hand over her arm. In a soft, touching voice, she asked;

"He doesn't want the baby, is that it?"

"That's right. Besides, I wanted to quit, but Abner kept reminding me about the needs I will have with doctors, hospitals, maternity leave... On the other hand, my brother made me realize that I can't be a burden to him."

"How so?! Are you in his apartment?" Rúbia told her everything and Talita said; "Wow! What a problem!" After some hesitation, she said; "You're not the first woman Jefferson has fooled with. Some time ago he did the same thing with another employee. I heard she got pregnant, but then she took the baby out and was fired. The guy is a coward."

"I'm afraid of him."

"If you felt threatened, I think you'd better file a complaint at the police station."

"Are you crazy?"

"No. I'm trying to open your eyes."

"He won't be crazy up to that point."

"Rúbia, you may not like to read newspapers, because your father already reads and looks at everyone for you, but it is impossible not to know the cases of great impact in the media. Women who died or disappeared because of their lovers, boyfriends, husbands... I think that they, like you, did not consider the risk they were taking. They endured a threat today, another tomorrow... I think it's good to be smart. Such a man is capable of terrible things, when contradicted. If I were you, I would go to the police station to file a complaint. If you are ashamed, go to the woman's police station."

"And then? Then he kills me."

"If you file charges and say you felt threatened, Jefferson will be called and questioned about it. He will not be able to deny what he told you or that he squeezed your arm. Look at the mark." She showed it to her friend who hadn't even seen it. "He may be angry, but he'll be smart. He'll know that if something happens to you, he'll be the first suspect."

"I don't have the courage to do that."

"You must have the courage to protect your life and your baby's. Talk to your brother. I think Abner will guide you better."

"The weather here at the company is bad. Everyone is asking, looking at me... I feel something when I walk around Jefferson... I can't even work properly."

"I can imagine. But I don't think you should worry about the bad things that he can do. Think about yourself, your labor rights."

"I can't concentrate on work."

"Try to do what you can. It will be good to make an effort, so that you are distracted and your mind is not full of useless things."

"Please, Talita, don't talk to anyone about Jefferson and me or about him being the father."

"Of course not. You are my friend."

✳ ✳ ✳

Embarrassed, Rúbia did not press charges for the threat and assault she suffered.

215

However, as the days went by, she was intimidated again. She was threatened. Her arm was squeezed again and she was slightly pushed.

When she arrived at the apartment, she told her brother that he convinced her to report it and accompanied her to the Women's Emergency Centers

Although she was embarrassed and even upset, she filed a complaint against Jefferson, who was furious when he knew that he had been called to provide clarification. However, this attitude of Rúbia's made him walk away from her.

✳ ✳ ✳

A few days passed and the sisters spoke quietly in Abner's apartment.
"So that was it. He was a beast, but he walked away from me."

"Are you going to find his wife to tell her everything?" Simone asked.

"I thought about that possibility. Then I considered that she had nothing to do with it. Why should I look for her?"

"What do you plan to do? Register the boy in his name? Does he require a pension...?"

"I didn't want anything at first. But I thought better and understood that I didn't make this baby alone. Jefferson also has his share of responsibility. In addition, I cannot deny my child his rights. I can't hide his background and last name either. I must do everything out in the open. However, there are times when I think about myself. Taking care of my life away from this boy and the more distant from him, the better. If I do everything the law allows me to do: register him in his name and apply for a pension, I will always be linked to Jefferson. I don't want that."

"This is a very serious decision." After thinking about it, she asked; "What about prenatal care? Are you doing it right?"

"I am." She smiled. "You still can't tell if it's a boy or a girl. Jeez! It's very exciting to hear the little heart and see it beating... I think that's when I realized I'm a mother." Then she asked; "What about your baby? How are you guys doing?"

"Well as possible. The doctor said we will only know when he is born."

"What about Samuel?"

"More and more distant, especially after he left the house. The last time I saw him was at the lawyer's office about twenty days ago. He doesn't even call and wants to know if I'm okay. It hurts a lot. After all these years together, I think I deserved more consideration. I'm very stressed out, Rúbia. My nights are unsafe, full of fear and a lot of loneliness. Every day seems worse... I still think a lot... I wonder if I will have the strength to endure everything alone until the end. It would be good to have Samuel by my side, helping, encouraging, giving strength... Certainly, everything would be lighter, less sad. I feel worse pain than if I had become a widow, because that would be by God's will. I understood that *losing* someone doesn't just happen with death. To lose someone is to have the other one distant and unprepared. Losing someone is when the other goes away and takes security, joy, support, happiness, faith in life, love, balance. To lose someone is to have a great emptiness that does not fill anything. And being afraid of tomorrow. That is horrible. Worse than death. When I remember that I saw him with another woman, thinking that he had the capacity to betray me, I feel like a piece of garbage, that I'm not. And Marrie, so short, so light, to be able to destroy a home, to make him leave me in this condition. And as for him... A creature so weak and poor... Today I understand that my marriage was already destroyed, although I didn't realize it. However, given the circumstances in which it all happened, I think that, because of my condition, the condition of our son, he might have had a little sense, consideration for me…"

Simone was sensitive and moved. She caressed her belly slightly as she unburdened herself with a lost look somewhere on the floor.

At that moment, Abner arrived in the company of David, Cristiano, Mrs. Janaina, Ricardo and his son Renán.

Surprised, they interrupted the subject and greeted everyone with expressive joy. Abner said;

"We are going to get pizza and come back to get you."

"I was already thinking about leaving…" Said Simone.

"What for? To be alone. No way. Come with us!" David encouraged himself, hugging her.

The night was lively and fun.

They talked a lot, which gave a break to the worries and sadness. Simone ended up sleeping at her brother's house, as they returned late.

The next day, it was agreed to have lunch at Mrs. Janaina's house. Rúbia and Simone prepared to arrive early to help the lady.

"You didn't have to be early. I will do something very simple. Nothing laborious."

"Even so, it would be impolite not to help you. Besides, it's very nice to be with you." Said Simone.

After lunch, Abner, David, Cristiano and Ricardo began to play dominoes at a table in the courtyard near the barbecue. It was a sunny and cool day, very nice to be at ease.

Gathered in the living room, which had the television on, Mrs. Janaina commented;

"I like to see my house so full of people. It brings a lot of joy."

"Christian looks much better, doesn't he?" Rúbia observed.

"Thank God. Much better." Said the lady. "He fell so down after the accident. My son was not like that."

"How old is a Christian?" Rúbia asked.

"He is twenty-nine years old and David is thirty-two."

"How curious!" Rúbia was funny. "I'm twenty-nine and Simone is thirty-two."

"It is true! What a coincidence." Agreed Simone.

"Cris is the youngest. I'm sure he will find the pleasure of living again. Sometimes, I think he was very attached to Vitória. They went out since high school. They went to college together. Once they separated for a year and a half. During that time, Cris went out with another girl, but it didn't work out. He returned to the date with Vitória. They got engaged. They established a house and decided to get married. Everything happened when they delivered the wedding invitations. My son was never a dependent. He made decisions alone. He was a completely different man. Shortly after the accident, he didn't even remember his name. I went crazy when he didn't recognize me. It was very difficult. I thought I would never recover. A little later after the hardest part of the treatment, surgery and physical therapy, he became very depressed. He didn't look like my son. For some time now, he has improved a lot. I thank God very much for that."

"Mrs. Janaina, as a spiritist, have you ever thought about the possibility that it was the spirit of the bride that bothered you or upset you?" Simone kindly guessed.

"I thought about it, daughter. Vitória was a spiritualized child, but I don't know... While they were talking, they couldn't see, but the spirit of Vitória was present."

219

When she became incarnate, she was a cheerful and witty child, interested in spiritist and spiritual matters. She was aware of the Spiritist doctrine. However, practice is often different from theory. When she suddenly disincarnated, the spirit Vitória was helped and taken to a station of spiritual help, where she woke up confused. She was extremely sad to realize that she was disincarnated. Not satisfied, she could not put into practice all that she had learned in Spiritism. Such was her misunderstanding that she was attracted to the incarnate, more specifically, to Cristiano.

The man, very surprised by what happened, sensitive by the trauma he suffered, let himself be wrapped by the sad and disoriented vibrations of Vitória's spirit. This caused the sad and confused fluids of that spirit to disorient him and drag him into a deep imbalance, making him fearful, unsure of making decisions, generating panic and a depressive state, so painful that it was difficult to let go.

Cristiano lost hope because of the sadness Vitória was going through, saying that nothing was worthwhile, that everything they had done was lost, worthless. When the man wanted to help Simone, because his situation moved him, he broke the dome of pitiful energies in which he let himself be placed. At that moment, he diverted his thoughts from psychic and emotional afflictions and focused on helping others.

For that, he had to overcome himself, overcome the opposition he had created for some situations. In other words, Cristiano faced fear, insecurity and acted, in spite of what he felt. It wasn't easy for him, but he insisted. He wanted to free himself from the bonds, from the mental prison that enslaved him in such despair and pain, that only he knew.

Even so, Vitória's spirit remained united to the plane of the incarnated, next to him.

"They're talking as if I'm not here. Everything they say about the spiritual plane is not true. Here you don't get rid of the pain, the anguish, the bitterness. The anguish is immense. It is a lot of pain. I have nowhere to go and no one to stay with. I wanted to be there with you."

Meanwhile, Mrs. Janaina said;

"I started to pray a lot for Victoria. She was always a good girl. But I don't know... I always prayed for her. I ask for light for her understanding and love for her heart."

"I have love. I love Cris." The spirit of Vitória answered as if she could be heard.

"If she is with my child, she needs to understand her new condition and agree to move forward. I even talked to her parents, but they think that Vitória and Vanilson, her brother who also died in the accident, are fine, in a high place."

"Are they spiritists?" Simone was interested.

"Yes, they are. As much as we try to get a sense of what it is like, we don't know the pain experienced when a child is lost. I understand that they wish and imagine, intensely, that their children are well. We learned from Allan Kardec, the codifier of the Spiritist doctrine, more specifically in *The Spirits Book,* that for the disenchanted God did not create predetermined places like heaven, hell or the purgatory. We know about the mental capacity that we all have, incarnated and disincarnated. For the disincarnated spirit, even more so, because it is free from heavy and complicated bodily matter. It is enough for him to think of moving in space or manipulating spiritual fluids with the use of will, of thought, to shape and form what he desires consciously or unconsciously. Then, regardless of the knowledge obtained when incarnating, a spirit, dissatisfied with its discarnation, or which is linked to some unresolved situation here, cannot go to higher levels. It does not evolve, does not learn or improve and suffers."

"I read in the book *Our Home*, psychographed by Chico Xavier, by the spirit André Luiz, that spirits can stay in Umbral or in colonies. The author of the book also talks about Relief Posts, about spirituality. Now you could tell me that the Spiritist doctrine explains that God did not create predetermined places like heaven, hell or purgatory. So, what the book *Our Home* says doesn't go against what the codifier showed us?" Simone was interested.

"The spirit André Luiz never said that the Umbral, the Spiritual Colonies or even the Relief Posts were structures created by God and that they are places destined for the feathers or rewards of a spirit. André Luiz described these places as groups of mental attunements. In other words, it is the union of minds, spirits or friendly personalities, with the same ideas and thoughts, with the same energy, with the same intentions. Soon the Umbral is still the meeting of minds that still suffer. They are creatures that have attached themselves to the physical body or the material plane, or are not even happy with what they should have left behind. These are intolerant, prejudiced, selfish, proud creatures without faith in a good and just God. Therefore, just like the more evolved colonies, like the colony Our Home, they are collectivities created by more enlightened, kind and loving spirits, interested in evolving and helping the needy, the disoriented, the lady wisely explained."

"But the spirit André Luiz informs us that the colony Our Home has protective walls, has buildings... He really describes a city with water and everything." Said Simone. "How is this possible? After all, the buildings we have here on Earth are made by man's hands and what is not made by man is provided by nature like water, for example. The human being just collects it and treats it, nothing else."

"If you are really interested..." Mrs. Janaina got up, went to the shelf, took The *Spirits Book* and came back. "I want to see... I was reading yesterday..." She read a little and said; "And here. Question 279 says: *Do all spirits have reciprocal access to each other?*

And the answer is: *The good ones go everywhere and it must be so that they can exercise their influence on the bad ones. But regions inhabited by the good are forbidden to the imperfect, so they do not lead to disturbances of bad passions.* See how interesting, here, in *The Spirits Book*, it states that there are regions, in plural. This means that there is not one place, but several places inhabited by good spirits, and these regions are forbidden to the imperfect spirits. This interdiction, this prohibition, must be done in some way, with walls, for example. There is nothing more natural than the existence of a barrier, like walls, to make us understand the limit, the prohibition against imperfect spirits yet."

"Excuse me, Mrs. Janaina, I know very little about Spiritism. If you can explain it to me... I understood that there can be walls or limits for unevolved spirits. However, how can these walls, water and other things be done in spirituality?" Insisted Simone, eager to learn. "Well, my dear, I think there is a Universal Fluid that we, as incarnates, cannot always see. This fluid is the fluid. Also, here in *The Spirits Book*, we are taught that this fluid exists in various modifications. Question 27-a, teaches us that electricity, for example, is a modification of the universal fluid and that it is a more perfect and more subtle matter. In another book of Spiritist Codification, *The Genesis...*" She stood up, took the copy and returned to the place she had been, continuing; "Here it is. In Chapter XIV, point 14, it says; *the spirits act on spiritual fluids, not by manipulating them as men manipulate gasses, but by using thought and will. For the spirits, thought and will are what the hand is for man. By thought, they print those fluids in any direction, agglomerate, combine or disperse, and organize with them sets that present certain appearance, form and color; they change their properties, as chemical changes that of gasses or other bodies, combining them according to certain laws. It is the great workshop or laboratory of spiritual life. Sometimes these transformations result from an intention; often they are the product of unconscious thought. It is enough for the Spirit to think something, for it* to take place, for it is enough to shape an aria, so that it reverberates in the atmosphere." She continued; "By analogous effect -that is, by similarity- the thought of the Spirit creates fluently the objects that he is accustomed to use. A miser will handle gold; a soldier will bring his weapons and uniform; a smoker, his pipe; a farmer, his plow and oxen; an old woman, her distaff. For the Spirit, which is also fluid, these fluid objects are as real, as they were, in the material state, for the living man. So, look, if a very imperfect spirit succeeds in creating mentally its gold, its jewels, weapons with which he killed, a wooden stick to wrap a thread, can you imagine a conscious, high and educated spirit? An entity of this level is capable of thinking of much more important and necessary things for the collective wellbeing, such as protective walls, electric shocks, water, houses, shelters..."

"Wow! What a lesson! That explains it all." Said Simone smiling. "I was always curious about all this, but I never found anyone who could explain or show me a perfect justification in the Spiritist Codification."

"It is good to remember that it is the spirits that are qualified for great collective works, in order to help others. In the case of the colony Our Home, walls were needed so that the lower, unclear spirits would not disturb those who were there to be helped, clarified or that were working for humanity. In the Spiritual Colonies, food and water are also needed. I believe that no one, psychologically speaking, is able to understand that he does not need water or food during the night, just because he died, he became disincarnated. Disembodied spirits also have needs for energy and liquids, just as the body of flesh needs protein and other nutrients. Therefore, I believe that the water in Our Home and other high colonies, created by very high spirits, should be pure, healthy, medicated, and wholesome. Only a pure and healthy mind is capable of such a creation."

"I see." She smiled with satisfaction. "It is just that I heard a fellow spiritist say that he disagreed with other fellow spiritists who believed in the creation of objects, water, clothing and other things, in spirituality, because the coder, Allan Kardec, didn't mention anything about it. He never saw a section of Kardec talking about buildings and food."

"That friend of yours is very ignorant. He needs to study the Doctrine better before saying things like that. This shows his ignorance." While turning the pages of a notebook that was among the books, Mrs. Janaina found what she was looking for and said;

"The study of the Spiritist doctrine cannot be limited to the five books of the Codification. I and other colleagues of the center have some important notes, especially for the cases of spiritist people who say that Kardec is not mentioned about the existence of everything that the spirit André Luiz reported in the book *Our Home*. Look... Here it is. Allan Kardec made a collection called Spiritist Magazine. Today we have all the Spiritist Magazines, by Kardec, published in books from 1858 to 1869. Each one corresponds to the year of his research, experiences, events... And in the Spiritist Magazine referring to the year 1859, September, there is the *Confession of Voltaire*, and a commentary of the famous English cardinal, Wolsey, from the time of Henry VIII, in which cardinal Wolsey informs; *It was thus, as I said, as a mocker and throwing a challenge, that I approached the spiritist world. In the beginning, I was expelled from the dwellings of the Spirits and covered an immense space. Then I was allowed to take a look at the wonderful buildings inhabited by the spirits and, in fact, they looked amazing. I was dragged here and there by an irresistible force. I was forced to watch and watch until my soul was dazzled by the splendors and crushed by the power that controlled such wonders.*" She read slowly to understand herself. She looked at her attentively, then continued; "As to the existence of food and flowers, in Kardec's works, it is in the *Spiritist Magazine* of 1861, March, about Henri Murger, in a Spiritist section, with colleagues of the Society. The report was; *the bigger the space of the heavens, the bigger the atmosphere, the more beautiful the flowers, the sweeter the fruits and the aspirations are satisfied even beyond the illusion.* We can find these reports in Kardec's publications, in the *Spiritist Magazine*, where we read about buildings, flowers, sweet fruits... Everything we find in the book *Our Home*, by André Luiz, psychographed by Francisco Cândido Xavier. Maybe your friend doesn't know much about Kardec's works, but it doesn't matter, he believes in evolution and he will get there." She smiled.

"Ah...! I'm delighted." Smiled Simone. "I'm not the type who has blind faith. I read the book *Our Home*, I read *The Spirits Book*, *The Gospel According to Spiritism* and I thought I knew enough. However, among the comments of some spiritists, I had doubts about this subject."

"Some people lack humility. That's why they argue. They may want to be on top, but unfortunately, they don't have enough knowledge. The most important thing is not what we have in the books, it's what we have in our hearts. That's why it's necessary, before we fight against something, to have a deep knowledge about it. In the case of the Spiritist doctrine, it is essential to remember that it is science and philosophy as Allan Kardec teaches us in the introduction of *The Spirits Book*. So, we should remember that the whole science starts small, because science is always born with a limited amount of knowledge at the moment it emerges. Only after much exploration does it grow, expand and develop. Take the case of medicine, for example, when some discoveries appeared, they were great for the time, but today we know that the knowledge was small and even defective. Over the years and centuries, after experiments and research, many things have changed in medicine. News has appeared and everything has improved and we know that there is still room for improvement. Spiritism is a science, therefore, it also tends to experiment with discoveries like the spirit that André Luiz and many others bring to us. What brought the codifier of the Spiritist doctrine, Allan Kardec, was the tip of the iceberg of everything that exists in the invisible world. The very spirits that collaborated with the codification works, in other words, told us that there were things that our capacity was far from understanding."

"It's interesting what you tell me. Now, thinking about it, I do not understand why some spiritists do not want the science of spiritualism to expand and develop with new discoveries on the spiritual plane."

"Some want material evidence about the subtle world of spirituality, even though here, on the physical plane, there are things we cannot study or understand."

"Things like what?"

"Electricity, for example. The other day, in the group of spiritualist studies in which I participate, we talked a lot about it. I understood that we could not isolate it in a test tube and simply save electricity for its study. However, it does exist. I mean, we see it and we feel it, but we cannot bottle this force, this fluid. Just as we cannot put it under a microscope to study what exists in the spirit world. You know, child, we shouldn't argue with people about this or that. Often, one wants to have more reason than the other. Let's take as an example our dear Chico Xavier, who never argued about anything or anyone. He has just fulfilled his mission. What counts is the confidence to do and feel right, to love God and our brothers."

"I understand that the spiritual plane is no different from here."

"No, Simone. There, the world is real. We can't be fake. We cannot hide who we really are or what we think or what we want in our hearts. We cannot be selfish or proud, we discover that we need each other even to evolve."

"We started this matter because of Vitória." Ssaid Rúbia, who had been listening carefully until then. "I also read the book *Our Home* and understood that some spirits that are not prepared for death, like André Luiz, go to the Umbral. Do you think that Vitória is in the Umbral?"

The woman sighed deeply, offered a soft smile, reflected and responded with the same serenity as always;

"The word Umbral means threshold, portal. This term was not used in the Spiritist Codification, but by the spirit André Luiz, from his first book, *Our Home*, so that we could understand what he was talking about. I understand, by Umbral, the limit between the two worlds: that of the living - of the incarnated - and that of the spirits - of the disincarnated. The Spiritist doctrine says that all, when we disincarnate, go through a state of disturbance; a kind of mental confusion. Some spirits are in this state for some minutes; others for hours, and others for years. I understand that being in the Umbral has a lot to do with this disturbing state that the codification tells us about. I believe that when it is disembodied, when the spirit is in that threshold, in that portal, and does not understand or accept its new condition, being in a state of disturbance, it is in a kind of portal or threshold, because it is very close to the earth's crust, but it is not incarnated. Then he remains between those two worlds. Because he is disturbed by his discarnation, lack of illumination, faith in God or belief in life after death, it suffers and sometimes suffers a lot. Some spirits, like the case of the spirit Andre Luiz, who sent countless rather enlightening reports, say that the consciousness of the creature itself generates too much suffering, demanding exactly all that he did or could not do. The laws of God are immutable for everyone. The Father does not protect one more than the other. Pride, selfishness, lack of charity and all our wrong actions will become pain in the soul and often in the spiritual body. These spirits gather for psychic attraction, in certain regions, and there they suffer, they are punished. These are extremely sad regions. Other spirits that did not do anything wrong, but did not spiritualize sufficiently, even though they had the opportunity or felt uncomfortable with their discarnation, may also remain trapped in the earthly crust, usually with their family. They experience great mental pain. They do not get up. They probably do not go to crowds or regions that are extremely sad and suffering, but are somehow disturbed on the Umbral, on the threshold between the two worlds, because they can no longer live incarnated, as they wish, and have no psychic conditions or elevation to move to a higher colony. What can happen, then, is that the spirit becomes very attached to the family or to an incarnate whom it likes very much. Therefore, it absorbs the fluid energies of the incarnate, generating regrettable fluids, that is, negative energies that the incarnate captures and understands as a vibration of pain, of misfortune. This gives rise to deeply sad thoughts. It causes, in a more intense way, despair, panic, anxiety, depression, neurosis and other things. If the incarnate one does not react, does not rise, does not change his thoughts, does not act, and gives in to lower ideas, this connection with the disincarnate one can cause illnesses in the physical body that will arise because of the spiritual fluids manipulated, unconsciously, by the disincarnate one, who regrets his fate and condition."

"That's why we shouldn't complain about life or illness." Said Simone.

"That's right, daughter. When we acquire the habit of complaining, we attract even disincarnated persons that we never knew and like to complain, they like sadness, pain, talking about sad things, tragedies, misfortunes and all that is bad. This is a mental attraction."

"So, you think that Victoria is in the Umbral?" Rúbia insisted.

"As I said, she was a great girl. She had spiritual knowledge, but not as much attention to spiritual life as she could. This is common because of her young age. She was a child who had dreams. She thought a lot about the future. She was committed to marriage and probably all that would keep her little heart away from God. I think she may have rebelled with her brother who, perhaps, was not wise. Although we cannot judge the boy, since we were not there to see. Who knows, maybe she wasn't content with having the idea of a future full of prosperity either, after all, she had a good profession, she was going to get married in less than a month? This could have left this girl very unhappy or even upset."

"Despite the knowledge she had?" Said Rúbia.

"If perhaps she believes she disincarnated too soon. It is likely that she is beside Cristiano and clings to him, who also, sad and upset by what happened, offered the perfect vibration for Vitória to continue in the state she is in."

"I don't know if I understand." Said Rúbia.

"Daughter, it is like this: if you are praying, asking God for much light and peace on your path, on the path of other people, spiritually speaking, who do you think is at your side in this moment of prayer?"

"Would it be too pretentious for me to think that it would be God or my guardian angel?"

"You are right. It's no pretense. Some emissary of God will be at your side, for sure. Now, if you are sad, crying, complaining, feeling angry, wanting revenge, wanting evil, do you think your guardian angel or some enlightened and inspiring spirit will be by your side?"

She smiled and responded;

"No. Of course not."

"Your mentor or guardian angel is probably at your side right now trying to protect you, as he respects your free will. Certainly, a high and friendly spirit inspires you with good thoughts, good vibrations, expecting you to react to bad tendencies, but it will not stay with you for long if it insists on inferior ideas and thoughts."

"In the last few days, I have learned a lot from you and your sons." Said Rúbia, with a slight smile. I was so disoriented when I met you. It was easy to hate, to scold, to think all wrong. However, I learned that I must love my neighbor, wish my enemies good and have good thoughts. She offered a wry smile and concluded; "Well... at least I learned, putting into practice is something else. But I will try."

"Good thoughts are very important, daughter. I believe that the main culprit is Cristiano being like this himself. Certainly, my son did not accept what happened. He was upset with himself for asking his girlfriend to use the front seat. He blamed his brother for speeding up. It all shows a lack of faith in God's purposes. I know this is hard to accept, but we must consider that the Father does not fail. Make no mistake. If it didn't happen that day, under those circumstances, it would be another time. It was supposed to happen. God doesn't sleep." The approach of Abner and the others interrupted the conversation. Ricardo, hugging his son, decided;

"We have to go."

"I'm going to make coffee."

"Not for me, Mrs. Janaina. Thank you. Renan and I are going to the mall. He wants a new shoe and maybe he can even get a movie."

"We also have to leave." Said Abner.

It is true. I have some things to pack. Tomorrow is Monday..." Simone agreed.

"Next week, I will visit the institution again." Commented Cristiano, looking at Simone.

"I really enjoyed the work done there. I'd even like to go back…" She said with a friendly smile, as if waiting for an invitation.

"If you want to join me…" He said.

"Did you call me the day before? If nothing is scheduled, I will. I'm waiting for the lawyer to call me to take care of some of the details of my divorce. I may have to go to his office."

"I see. I don't know what day I'm going to go. You can stop worrying."

Everyone decided it was time to leave. They said goodbye and left.

12.– THE UNION OF ABNER AND DAVID

AFTER EVERYONE LEFT, Cristiano sat down in an armchair in the living room and began to watch television with his mother.

The program featured spectacular feats, including vehicles and motorcycles climbing ramps and jumping on cars. Distance records were broken. At one point, a car made a miscalculated maneuver, came off the ramp and rolled over. Luckily for the pilot, nothing more serious happened than the scare.

At that moment, the Vitória spirit, together with Cristiano, remembered;

"It was something like this that happened to us. It broke us up. Our happiness ended and…" She shouted, holding on to him. "We were going to get married. We would have a lot to do together. So many plans…"

Cristiano immediately experienced an unpleasant sensation. He remembered the accident, the girlfriend, the surgeries, the pains of recovery, while a terrible fear invaded him.

Sitting quickly on the edge of the chair, he lowered his head, placed his elbows on his knees and clasped his hands in front of him. He thought he was going to faint. Despair took hold of him and he rubbed his face in an agonizing gesture.

"How are you, son?" The lady asked meekly.

"I haven't had that for a while…" He mumbled. "I think it was because of the accident I saw on TV."

"I don't understand that, but I don't think you can escape everything when you feel bad. In order to overcome the fear of flying, one must fly to lose that fear. If you are impressed by accident scenes, you should not avoid watching television and occasionally watching that scene."

"It just gives me so much despair. I'm sweating. I feel a terrible tremor. An uncontrollable fear."

He stood up. He was going to his room when his mother suggested;

"Shall we go for a walk, Christian? Don't go hiding in that room. You need to react and act when you get that thing. That way, your brain will understand that it should function normally when you see something that reminds you of the accident or makes you sad about the interrupted plans. Let's walk a bit." Insisted the mother.

"Yes, let's go. I'll go play tennis."

"Me too." Said his mom.

As they walked, Mrs. Janaina brought up one topic and another, occupying her son's attention with a common and healthy conversation.

"Son, when you started to react, and went to the institution, you came back to the spirit center and even drove!" She laughed as she emphasized. "You got better. Did you notice?"

"Yes, I noticed that." He smiled. "That day when I had to drive Simone's car…" He smiled. "I thought I was going to have a breakdown."

"But you didn't collapse at all. You faced your fear. When we face what scares us, we discover that we are stronger and more satisfied."

"I don't know why walking is good for me when I panic. Although I want to run to the room and be alone."

"I believe, son, that when you walk, you occupy your mind with the things you see and they distract you, they give ideas to you. Perhaps a spirit that is giving you sad thoughts cannot follow you."

"Do you think you can have this post-traumatic stress, this panic syndrome, due to an obsessor?"

"Not exactly. I think the accident terrified you. Then, extremely sad and unhappy about Vitória's death, about your interrupted plans... You had to undergo painful surgeries, facing the slow and also painful recovery. Somehow, I was disappointed with everything. I lost faith and I was upset with God's will. The truth is, I was confused, upset, and in conflict."

"Why do you say that I was in conflict?"

"Because you had to face the dilemma of not knowing what to do when you saw your plans fall down. Look, son, you always thought God was just and good. You always had a good life. Suddenly, you thought the Father had failed, seeing yourself as helpless. This is a conflict. They call what they feel like post-traumatic stress disorder, panic syndrome, they call it this or that disorder, but I think it disharmonizes your mind. You were confused, angry, upset. It was despair that made your mind sick. Just as our stomach can get sick from gastritis; lungs, sick from pneumonia, our mind gets sick from excessive feelings and bad thoughts like anger, hatred, annoyance, conflicts, despair. Think with me, when we eat what we should not and we make our stomach or intestine sick, we correct our food. We take care of what we eat, because only then will we recover. When we get sick of our lungs or compromise our airways, we take care of the cold, the polluted air, the fungi and mites that we can breathe in order to heal ourselves. Such care makes us heal. Now, if your mind is sick, what is the food, what care must you take to recover it?"

"Food for the mind is a good, peaceful and harmonious thought…"

"Besides, son, you have faith in God. Believing that everything that happened to you is for you to rise up, to grow morally and spiritually is important. It was not God who did this to you. You put yourself in that state."

"Why would I put myself in this state, mother?"

"To change how you act and think. To be sweet, calmer, more harmonious. I believe that when there is an unshakable faith, we do not have depression, panic syndrome, anxiety, neurosis and many other diseases of the soul."

Cristiano was reflecting for a long time while they walked in absolute silence. Later, he asked;

"Mom, you didn't answer. Do you think I'm having this panic over a dark observer?"

"The observer alone is not capable of doing all this harm to you or anyone else. The person is the one who lowers his own vibration. It is he who enters into despair, stops having faith and love in God and is equal to the same vibratory band as the observer or a disgusted and rebellious spirit, who does not have to be, exactly, an obsessive."

"I never thought to tell you this, but…" There was a brief pause. "Sometimes I come to think that Vitória did not accept very well everything that happened and induces me to have a thought that triggers these sensations, this despair, this panic and anxiety that I feel. I was never like that."

"If she doesn't accept it and she's desperate, sad, sure, you're up to it. Then, when you tune in, you are like that. When you disconnected, you reacted, you went to the institution, you helped

Simone, you drove, you faced life, despite what you felt, you lost the tune, the vibration and the bad thoughts. If this is caused by Vitória, it is also your fault, because you are at the same level."

Christian stopped, smiled broadly, and declared;

"No therapy session has done me as well or enlightened me as much as this conversation. Thank you, mom."

"I don't want to throw a bucket of cold water on your enthusiasm, but remember that you weren't so depressed, so terrified just by the accident. Sure, before the accident, you had many misconceptions about life. You thought that nothing bad would ever happen that would disturb your happiness. This is arrogance or lack of perspective on life. It will not be like this all of a sudden that you will come out of this state. You will have to change your way of thinking, acting and reacting. Remember that many people suffer serious accidents, and that does not mean anything. For those people, it will be another story to tell their friends. You need to change, son. Nothing changes if you don't do it yourself."

"I understand that. When there is a feeling of depression, panic, anxiety or the impression that something is going to happen, I should meditate, mentally, pray, have faith, try to do useful things."

"That's right, Cris. Also, pray a lot for Vitória."

"Do you think that...?"

"I don't think anything, Cristiano. But prayer is always a very good thing. It connects us with good humor. And it will never hurt anyone or anyone who receives it or who makes these good vibrations from a prayer."

He smiled and put his arm around his mother's shoulder, kissed her head quickly and continued walking.

* * *

Samuel had already left the house where he lived with his wife. So, not to be alone and seeing that her sister was not so comfortable in Abner's apartment, Simone decided to ask her to live in her house.

In a conversation, while indicating the room and where to place her things, she said;

"You can use that part of the closet. On this site here. She showed it. "There are still some things from Samuel."

Rúbia stopped, sat down on the single bed and spoke a little disconsolately.

"Once I was talking to Abner and, taking advantage of our father's criticism, I confronted women or couples who do not plan children and bring them into the world without first having a home, a good job...Now, look at my situation... Certainly, after I have the baby, I will be fired. I don't have a home and I don't know what to do next."

"There is no escape from what we need to experience. Look at my case: I planned it all. Today I'm not with my husband anymore, expecting a child with the uncertainty of being born or not, of having problems..." Her eyes filled with tears. Simone took a deep breath and snorted; "That was not under my control. I didn't plan it, I just understand that we must and need to plan our lives to have a more stable future, but there are situations that we must experience. We have to demonstrate this. This shows that we are not in control of everything. We need to have faith in God at times like this."

"You are living in a delicate moment. However, fortunately you planned your life as far as you could. Imagine if you didn't have education, didn't have a profession, a job, a house... It would be much more difficult and much more complicated. Today, I regret not having thought about all this, for not paying attention to the advice of our brother. What an idiot I was!"

Simone smiled and tried to joke.

"And I told Abner that if you didn't want to listen to my advice, don't ask for my help."

"You said that and asked me to come here?" She laughed.

"Did you see how the heart always speaks louder than reason? You are my sister. It doesn't matter what I say, but what I feel and do for you."

Simone approached and hugged her tenderly.

"Thank you, my sister. Thank you for everything."

"Why, Rúbia... Stop it. Now come on, we have a lot to do." They changed the subject and Rúbia commented;

"I'm enjoying the vision that I have of life through the spiritist perspective. The part about loving your neighbor was good for me."

"Jeez, I had so much hate in my heart and that feeling was getting so bad."

"It is very important to have a philosophy, a healthy way of thinking, like that of Mrs. Janaina and her children. With the way of thinking that she mainly has, we suffer less when we face difficulties."

"Mrs. Janaina said that Cristiano improved a lot after he started helping you."

"I'm discovering that helping others is the remedy for our ills. It's a shame I didn't discover this sooner."

Rúbia smiled and said;

"I believe that Cris has improved not only because of the help he gave to you. Don't you think he is too interested in helping you?"

"What are you implying?" She asked seriously.

"Ahhhh…" She made a sweet gesture. "I don't know. He looks at you differently…"

"Stop it, Rúbia. I'm married, or rather... I still have a husband. I'm pregnant and I have a child who needs me. Christian sees me as a friend."

"Yes, but... Besides being a friend, I think he sees you as a woman, right?"

"Enough." She was really angry. "Besides my son, I don't want another man in my life. Ever again!"

Remembering what she heard from her brother, she responded;

"Never is a long time."

"Please, Rúbia. Don't start." She said firmly. "It's not funny."

"All right. I'm sorry." A little later, she commented; "Now that he is alone, do you think Abner will take David to live with him?"

"I think so."

"This is still strange to me. I'm not used to their homosexualism."

"Let me tell you something; prefer to use the term homosexuality and not homosexualism." Said Simone."

"Why? Isn't it the same thing?" The other one was interested.

"Not exactly. Gay people prefer to use the term homosexuality for their condition. The term homosexualism was created by those who believed that homosexuals suffered from a pathology, an illness, and for that illness, the term homosexualism was created. The right thing to do is to avoid this negative concept of disease, disorder or something, because in the past people and even science did not know about aspects of sexuality. The term homosexuality is one of the possibilities of human sexuality."

"That's good to know. So... I still haven't gotten used to our brother's homosexuality." She corrected herself.

"When you accept that homosexuality is a condition, is a person's sexual orientation and not a choice, not a psychological disorder and much less an illness, you will begin to understand and accept it better."

"What if he is wrong about what he does?"

"It's none of your business. If Abner is wrong, it is God who he owes satisfaction, not you or me. Think about it: he's not hurting us at all, so let him live his own way."

"That's right. Let me take care of my life, because I don't even know about it." They laughed and went on to another topic.

✽ ✽ ✽

Time passed by.

After a few months, Abner called his mother to ask her to come to his apartment, agreeing to pick her up. For this, he prepared a good table with a good coffee and, after talking pleasantly about several topics, he decided to tell;

"Mother, I called you here because... Well, I want you to know that..." He embarrassed himself.

Smart, Mrs. Celeste deduced.

"Are you living with David, your friend?"

"No. Not yet. That's what I want to tell you. We simply decided that he will come and live here. It's very hard for me to tell you, but I don't want you to be surprised or scared when you come to visit us and we meet here. Do you understand?"

"Yes, son. I understand." Brief pause where they looked at each other firmly and she expressed;

"This is not what I imagined, what I dreamed for you when you were a boy. However, Abner, if this is your life, your condition in this life, if this is your way of being happy, then be happy, son. I will be by your side whenever you need me."

"Mom, when I understood my homosexual condition, when I saw that there was no way, I seriously thought about abstaining from any type of relationship. I even thought about becoming a priest, taking vows of celibacy." The lady smiled sweetly and he continued; "You must have realized that I spent many years without going out, without anyone... I told myself that I didn't need anyone. Time passed and... When David and I met, we became friends. I found out that he was also gay and that it was…" He stopped and looked down.

It was inevitable, wasn't it, son?

"That's right. You can't imagine how difficult it was for me. I thought a lot about you, my father, my sisters and even the rest of the family. What would it be like when you found out? What would it be like to face society... You know, it's not that easy for me... It's not because I want to."

"I understand. Yes, I understand." taking his hand on the table, she asked, smiling, so as not to see him so embarrassed: "When will David move in?"

"He will also talk to his mother and brother and... maybe in a fortnight."

"And what does his mother say about all this?"

"She is like you. She accepts. She loves her child."

"You're wrong about me, Abner. I'm not accepting just because of my love for you, no Sir." She smiled. "I don't know why, but somehow, I understand. I really understand."

"You are an evolved spirit. Undeveloped people are prejudiced, hard-hearted. Another, like you, may not understand very well, but respects it."

After a moment, he said;

"I also wanted to talk about something else…"

"What?"

"David and I bought that apartment together. We are both paying for everything and… this is because there is still no law that provides us with security in this regard. We have already seen cases where two gay men or two gay women live together, share everything, and in case of separation or death, one is harmed just because the property was in one's name. Since we are sharing everything, none of us will be lost."

"You're right, son. Do what you want. I'll respect it."

"Mother… What about Dad? Are you going to tell him?"

"In time, I will. Tell me something, Abner; can I meet David's family?"

"You can, of course. Mrs. Janaina will like it. She loves Simone and Rúbia. She will also like you." He said; "I will talk to her and one of these days we will make an appointment and you two will come here."

Abner was satisfied with his mother's understanding. He expected her to understand, but did not imagine that she would be interested in meeting David's family.

Mother and son continued to talk pleasantly for a while.

✱ ✱ ✱

Abner and David held a reception that marked the union of both.

243

On that occasion, Mrs. Janaina and Mrs. Celeste met and talked as if they had known each other for a long time. They talked respectfully about the subject which, for both of them, was delicate, but they never commented on their children. In fact, they did not even talk about the decision to live together, participating in the fraternization as if it was something very common for both of them.

That day, Mrs. Janaina invited and insisted that Mrs. Celeste visit her, and she promised to go.

✳ ✳ ✳

As the days passed, Mrs. Celeste called David's mother and they agreed to spend an afternoon together.

After showing her house, especially her garden and plants, Mrs. Janaina invited Abner's mother to sit in the living room. It was then, because they were alone, that the hostess commented;

"Well, Celeste, I don't think it's common for two mothers to meet in a case like ours. At least, I don't know of any similar situation yet."

The other one smiled when she agreed.

"It is true. It's nothing ordinary... But... We are here. I always imagined the most common thing, that is, meeting my daughter-in-law's mother, not my son-in-law's, in Abner's case." She laughed shyly.

Mrs. Janaina also had fun and remembered;

"They are our children. I believe that if he was born with this sexual condition it was because God allowed it to be so."

"You know, it wasn't a surprise to me when I heard that Abner was gay. You know, moms can feel some things. I knew he was different. When we talked about this, I asked my son that I wouldn't like to see any extravagant behavior. I'm still not well prepared for it. Perhaps because he had always behaved in the usual way for a man."

"Today I saw a very discreet and respectful behavior of both of them here at home. If I saw something compromising, in my home, I would reprimand it. I think we thought that way because since they were little, they didn't have any mannerisms. Cristiano, my other son, was going out and, one day, I saw him kissing Vitória, do you understand? I'm one of the old people. I didn't like it and I told him so. If I did it with Cris and his girlfriend, I would also do it with David. You know, Celeste, manners, the male or female form of some homosexuals are not an option either. The way they talk, walk and express themselves is not forced. It's normal for their psyche."

"Would it be, Janaina?"

"Of course. They don't do it for fun, for provocation."

"It's just that, before, it wasn't that common for people to assume they were gay. The prejudice was so immense that it was repressed. Today, although many people still do not accept homosexuality, society has become a little more flexible and homosexuals more courageous. You know, Celeste, I think we should respect what people are. In many cases, respect is synonymous with peace, love. We will respect our kids, we will respect people's differences. As long as they don't attack us, don't offend us, they have the right to be what they are."

"It is true. You are right."

"I had a very delicate situation here at home. Vitória, Cristiano's former fiancée, was against homosexuality. Whoever she was. When she found out that David was gay, she was shocked! You can't imagine. I was also shocked because she was young and young people are usually open-minded, more tolerant. But that wasn't her case. Vitória distanced herself, reduced her visits to this house and stopped talking to David. I didn't expect so much

245

intolerance, so much prejudice. We thought it was just at first, but no."

"Is it still far away?"

"She passed away."

"Oh…" She lamented. "Sorry. Now that I spoke, I remembered that my daughter, Simone, said that your son's fiancée had died and that he was still recovering from the trauma of the accident. I had forgotten."

"That's right. You have to know that, after Simone became our friend, Cristiano improved a lot. It was because of her that he resumed some activities. He is even rehearsing to go back to the office."

"And you also know that this friendship has gone very well for my two daughters. They tell me everything. Thanks to their conversations, Simone found the strength and structure to face the difficult situation with her husband and son. I have a lot to thank you for hosting Rúbia as well. Wow! I really have to thank you so much."

"I did what I wish someone had done for my children. When we help someone, we are actually helping ourselves. I knew that. And I was able to confirm when I saw Cris react, providing guidance and assistance to Simone. I really like your daughters."

While the two mothers were talking, the spirit Vitória, present without them knowing it, listened to what they were saying and lamented.

"All of this is wrong. Nothing was supposed to happen to me, and Cris wouldn't be like he is. The proof that the time was not right is that I'm here, trapped, close to the incarnate. I didn't see my disembodied relatives, not even my brother, who died with me in that damn accident. I don't like them talking as if I wasn't here."

Addressing Mrs. Janaina, as if the woman could hear her, she complained. "You keep saying I'm prejudiced, that's not all. I see that you are wrong. David is the way he is because of him, because of the family that has not corrected him since childhood. Gay is not natural. It's sinful. There shouldn't be people with such manias." At that moment, the guardian angel who had accompanied her since the beginning of her most recent incarnation lowered his luminescence and made himself known to her, who suddenly felt frightened by the call.

"Vitória?"

"Who are you?!" She asked apprehensively.

"You can call me Juan. I'm your mentor or guardian angel, whatever you want."

"Why did you take so long to come and get me?"

"It didn't take long. I was always by your side. But you couldn't see me because of your confused thoughts, stuck to appearances, to pride…"

"No! No way! If you are my mentor, you should let yourself be seen by me, that I don't have a body."

"Your thoughts are quite conflicting. Your vibrations are not high, so you could not see me."

"And why could I see you now?"

"In the last months, with the prayers of Mrs. Janaina and her children, you have received great energy. Together with them, who did not notice you, you improved your level, your anxious and excited reflexes became receptive to good vibrations. You calmed the heart. You left the discomfort a little bit and you improved your vibrations, your energies. Only because of it you are able to see me now."

"I have prayed and I'm stuck here in this house. Where are the aid Relief Posts? Where are the Spiritual Colonies? I learned this from Spiritism. But so far, I have not seen anything or anyone. Again and again, I think I see a figure or something. I have needs. I'm not well. Look how I look!"

"Due to so many prayers, supplications, gospel worship achievements, high thoughts, good cheer and much more, this home is a workshop for the spiritual work of goodness, in Jesus' name. You do not see it, as it is, because you are attached to the wailing. This place is protected by sublime energies and you are here, trapped, as you say, because you are being rescued. Know that your condition could be worse. Staying here is a relief."

"Sometimes I feel tormented, with a confused mind. I had a terrible dream. I seem to sleep for days. Then I wake up and everything goes on as usual. I must admit that the prayers of Mrs. Janaina and her children have helped me a lot. These are moments in which I feel a great relief."

"You let yourself be guided by the prayers made by them, because they are sincere prayers and desires for your evolution and understanding. You said you prayed, but your words, though beautiful, did not come from your heart, but from the rational side of your mind, trapped in the unnecessary beauty of materialism." He left her reflective for a minute. Then, politely, he asked; "Now, come with me." Vitória's spirit was carried away.

They went to a room in the house where, on the physical plane, there was no one. And he asked;

"Make yourself comfortable here. Feel that silence. Close your eyes and feel at peace. Empty your mind of worries and think of something beautiful. Try to remember a vision that reassures you."

"I always liked the sea…" She whispered, smiling.

"Then look at the calm sea. Soft waves. White beaches. Blue sky… Imagine listening to the murmur of the water gently hitting the rocks… Think of feeling the wind… It will make you relax."

Vitória followed the instructions and relaxed more. It was then that she allowed herself to be enveloped by the gentle and medicinal energies provided by her mentor. In a second, she seemed to be on a beach, her feet touching the water. She trusted the spirit that accompanied her and gave her security. She was silent. She didn't open her eyes. She did not let herself be influenced. Ando so, she entered a state similar to falling asleep.

13.– DO GOOD AND OVERCOME DIFFICULTIES

SOME DAYS HAD PASSED when the spirit of Vitória awoke.

She was lying on a bed and the generous light from the window touched her face, now serene. She felt warm. Very different from before. She moved, slowly uncovered herself and sat down. As she looked at herself, she recognized herself with a better, cleaner, more pleasant appearance.

Not long after, Juan's spirit entered the room with a slight smile on his serene face.

"How are you, Vitória? Are you feeling better?" He asked happily, seeing her well composed.

"Yes, I feel much better. As if I were different, lighter…" She smiled.

"Higher thinking, faith and true prayer always renew us."

"Where am I? In a Spiritual Colony?"

"No. We are still in the earth's crust, in the spiritual workshop that extends just above our sister Janaina's residence. This is one of the places of rest and restoration of some very select brothers."

"Why didn't I go directly to a colony? After all, I always believed and was aware of the spiritual plane."

"Ooooh... My dear, having knowledge and belief in spirituality is not enough. You should know that."

"I have always had a good life. I thought that when I died, I would be sent, rescued and cared for in a successful uplift colony."

"You are the one going somewhere. Lifeguards and spiritual mentors are only supportive. Vitória, my dear, you tried to live the right life, but your ideas, your opinions have always been too critical and your attitudes too harsh. You always acted as if you were only right, above all. Your mind, always agitated and anxious, disharmonized even the most perennial prayers."

"I always thought I was doing the right thing! I don't know where or when I made such a big mistake, as you say."

"There was no greater failure. There were many, small ones. You missed several opportunities where you could have practiced love through understanding and even silence."

"Can you tell me about some of these opportunities?" She was hesitant.

"Do you want examples?" He didn't think much of it and said; "Almost always you don't respect people's opinions. You could not understand the conditions of some and the limits of others."

"When was I so intolerant?" She asked with a faint, almost ironic smile. Such was her confidence that she had not failed.

"Some choices or decisions of Cristiano, in which he was always forced to give in so your will could prevail, for example."

"If you tell me that because I decided to choose the decoration in which we were going to live... I did it because he doesn't understand very well about the decoration of a house and... he didn't have such good taste."

"That's not exactly what I was talking about. However, it is good to remember that his opinion, in the decoration, was also important. After all, besides paying for it, he would live there with you. There is nothing fairer for him than having the opportunity to participate in it."

"Is that all?"

"Do you really think that's all it was?" Before she could answer, Juan remembered; "Your arrogance, your pride and vanity do not allow you to recognize your own faults. So much… that you cannot admit or remember what you did."

"I need to be stuck here because I can't remember or admit that I made a mistake?"

"Remembering and admitting that you were wrong is not enough. Because you didn't have humility, you stayed here. Didn't you ever hear about it when you studied the Spiritist doctrine?" Vitória said nothing and her mentor asked her; "Can you understand that, disembodied, your improvement was only possible by focusing on the prayers of Mrs. Janaina and her children?"

"I prayed, but…"

"Do you see your pride? You didn't exactly answer my question." She was silent. "It would be good to admit that your prayers were not from the heart. They were beautiful words, but weak, driven by despair and not by faith. You prayed without really believing in God, in the Father's help. You were trapped here by the silent accusations of your own conscience." Placing his hand in front of her forehead, without touching it, Juan's spirit concentrated and emanated healthy energies that clarified her thoughts and, consequently, brought back memories. Then he proposed; "Let's see some of your little defects with your intolerant behavior. Do you remember the last comments about your future mother-in-law? Were they fair?"

Vitória immediately remembered when, at the lady's house, with a cousin with whom she exchanged confidences, she complained.

"Mrs. Janaina is coming again. She can only cook, make delicious things to show her talents. I think she does it to show off or humiliate me, because she knows I'm not very good at cooking. If she is thinking that she will take food for her son after we get married, to intrigue us, she is very wrong. I will cut off her visits to my house very quickly." The cousin, besides agreeing, poisoned her with other unfair and unhappy opinions, and Vitória even said; "Mrs. Janaina spoils these boys a lot. That's why David became what he became. She supports her son's shamelessness. Cretin!"

In a calm tone, the spirit Juan asked;

"Do you know what Mrs. Janaina said about you?"

"No." She answered timidly.

"Look."

In that instant, Vitória could see, on her mental screen, as if it were a movie she was watching.

In conversation with her son Cristiano, the lady said;

"Vitória is a good girl. I liked her. She will feel overwhelmed by having to work in the office and take care of the house. Poor thing. Doing two shifts is terrible, I'm going to see if I can get a daily worker for her house. You can leave the key with me and I'll take a good look. Then, in the evening, you either have dinner here, then you can leave or come by and take some food to go, is that all right?"

"We don't want to bother you, mother." Said Cristiano.

"When we do something with pleasure, it is not work at all. I don't want her to get tired. I know what that is. I worked outside and took care of a house before you were born. I didn't have anyone to clean the house or do the washing and getting started was very difficult. Ah... As for your clothes, let me wash them. Most of them are all white. I'm used to it. Then Brígida, the woman who comes to iron clothes, can iron them along with mine. Vitória will arrive tired and still iron the clothes, it would be too much."

"Let's save that for later, mom."

In the eyes of Vitória 's spirit, there was a slight shadow of repentance when Juan said;

"Janaina loves you very much. She always loved you. She never disapproved of her son's marriage to you. She never spoke or thought badly of you. She tried to help in any way she could. Her proposals to make food or delicious things, as you said, were not to humiliate you, but to help you, to protect you from the exhaustion of a double shift working day."

"I misjudged her."

"The problem, Vitória, was that you not only misjudged Janaina, but also many people around you. Consider David's case, because he is a homosexual."

"That is wrong!" She pointed out.

"It is not." He answered firmly. "And if it is, what do you have to do with it? Why discriminate against him? Why prejudice? Why humiliate him? What did you gain from it? Didn't you have anything important to change in his own character?"

"It is wrong for a person to become a homosexual!"

"No one becomes a homosexual, my dear. The spirit is born in this condition. Sexual identity comes with the spirit and develops from an early age, in childhood, and usually settles or solidifies until about age twenty-five, and can go much further. Sexual identity belongs to the soul. Unhappily for those who do not understand this, and become intolerant and prejudiced. Poor this creature that certainly does not believe in past or future lives. He does not know what was in the past and ignores what will be in the future, perhaps even experiencing, firsthand, what he condemned. In this case, the person is generally dissatisfied with himself."

"Homosexuality is wrong. The person uses the body incorrectly. It is not right to decide to be homosexual."

"No one is born and becomes a genius, a super-intelligent creature. A person is born super-intelligent and can use his intelligence for good or evil, if he develops this intelligence. This is the tendency of the spirit. Then, the person is born homosexual, being able to use his homosexuality in such a discordant and shameful way as the one who is born heterosexual. We all have attributes and weaknesses, but we all have the strength to control our own will. It is not just because one is heterosexual that a child will not feel inclined to bad sexual tendencies, to compulsive, rebellious and promiscuous sex. It is not because he is homosexual that a person will be inclined to deregulate through vulgarity. Harmonious sexual life depends on the evolution of each creature."

"What about the intimate relationship between homosexuals?"

"The relationship between homosexuals does not necessarily indicate an attitude of imbalance. There are those who are homosexuals and, for personal reasons, do not have sexual relations with someone of the same or opposite sex. They refuse to have sex. It is a matter of opinion. What brings mental disharmony, what brings imbalance to the spirit, in relation to sex, is when one allows debauchery, depravity, multiple partners, addiction to abusive sex and becomes vulgarized, sexually speaking. It jeopardizes your chance of evolution in this field, whether it is heterosexual or homosexual. However, this is a problem for everyone. It does not concern us."

"In the case of promiscuity, that is prostitution." Said Vitória.

"Not necessarily. The usual sex trade is prostitution. The sex worker, the one who has the means to earn money or receive any other good or advantage due to the sexual practice, becomes a prostitute. This is prostitution, regardless of whether you are heterosexual or homosexual. There are those who, whether homosexual or heterosexual, practice sex without commitment, without respect for the relationship. Many, to assert themselves, by pure collection in terms of number of partners, they are the type of people who give themselves up sexually easily, those are the ones who practice vulgar sex. That will not be good for your consciousness, for your life experience, and you will certainly have to harmonize. However, remembering again, it is the creature's problem. What we can do, when we think something is wrong, is not to agree with that person. Nothing else."

"Yes... I discriminated against David." She admitted. "I was prejudiced, intolerant..."

"Did you know that David offered you prayers, vibrations of love and peace, sincerely and more often than some of your family members?" Since he did not hear an answer, he said; "This helped a lot in your separation from the physical body and even the fact of being stuck here, in this workshop that is extended in our sister Janaina's residence. Staying here means protection for you."

"I did not know. We went to the same spirit house, but he was absent. He would show up from time to time."

"A presence in a house of prayer is very important, but that alone is not enough. God must be present in our actions. Upon awakening, David's first thought is for God in gratitude for the day that is beginning, for the morning light, for the air he breathes... When he goes to bed, his last thought is also for the Father, thanking him for the challenges, thanking him for what he received well and asking for peace, support and good ideas, as well as a task for good during his physical rest. He always does this. What about you? How many times have you done the same?" Vitória was silent. She was embarrassed. "As for David's charitable practices... I won't even comment. Every word, every gesture is spilled out of love for his neighbor, wherever he may be. He treats others as he wants to be treated. Do you want a greater example of love for others? Without commenting on other tasks in which he spends his time, work and personal donation. What about you, Vitória? What did you do with your talents? You didn't even treat your nearest neighbor well. You had no patience with your grandparents, going to the extreme of yelling at them, leaving them talking to themselves, not paying attention."

"They were stubborn!" She defended herself. "Especially my grandmother."

"Psychological attacks are carried out through contempt, foul language, shouting, threats, impatience and many other forms. I can assure you that they carry the same weight as physical attacks. You were not like this just with your grandparents. You also did this to your brother when he was little, with your parents. You tortured friends at school with aggressive words, contempt, threats, bullying. You were proud and arrogant with the employees because they gave a service, were poor or had a different ethnicity. You were not educated that way. You didn't get this example from your parents."

"That was a childish thing."

"No. This is the attitude of a spirit that does not want to evolve. You want to justify yourself for what you did as a girl. What about your behavior after adolescence and adulthood? Was it right what you said and thought about homosexuals, for example?"

The memories of Vitória's spirit were very lively at that time. As her mentor spoke, scenes of events came to mind.

"Enough, please." She asked, agitated.

"It doesn't matter if we are straight, gay, white, Asian, black, Indian, handsome, ugly, short, tall... The important thing is *what* we do with our life, *what* we do with our home, our work, in the street, wherever we go, at the school where we study..." He stopped briefly. "The house of prayer is where we pray, reflect and learn God's laws. Apart from that, it is where we apply our learning, showing it in the way we treat our brothers, how much we worship God, with the purest love of our soul. As they say: we must give to life, more than what we receive. Many think that it is a matter of going to a house of prayer, praying, asking and, when they are disincarnated, they will receive help. No. To be helped, to help ourselves, we need God in our hearts and to have God in our hearts, it is necessary more than just going to a house of prayer."

"I regret it. I missed opportunities..." Her regret was not sincere and Juan's spirit was silent. She immediately asked; "When am I going to a spiritual colony? After all, I'm really disembodied, there is no way I can return to the physical body, not now. I need proper protection as soon as possible."

"Only a pure heart and a clean conscience lift the spirit out of this prison, which is floating on the earth's crust. When you are honest with yourself, when you really want to change, you can attract yourself to a better place."

"I read in books, spiritualist novels, that there are rescuers and mentors who help the spirits in the colonies."

"Yes, they do exist. However, they work with spirits whose consciousness has lamented the error of truth. No one is taken to a colony without being prepared. We must remember that the spirit is always attracted to the colony compatible with its moral level." In the silence, Juan recommended; "Take advantage of your recovery and try to follow the work of some spirits who serve, meet and compose themselves in the spiritual workshop of this home. You can learn a lot from them. But if you return to complain, are absent from prayer, or lose faith, you will return to the state of the days before."

"Just one question."

"Yes." He said carefully.

"The spirit André Luiz, in the book *Our Home*, was helped directly to the Colony Our Home, so... Why do I have to stay here?"

"The spirit André Luiz spent about eight years in Umbral and had no knowledge of what exists on the spiritual plane. Unlike you, who have a huge and considerable baggage in the afterlife. Let us remember that the spirit André Luiz, before being helped, reflected a lot on his earthly existence, on the existence of a just and good God. When he came to the conclusion that there was a God of love and goodness, he asked for help with the purest, deepest and truest feeling of his repentant and suffering heart." He waited for a moment. When he saw Vitória reflective he advised her; "You know, daughter, it is not enough to want or demand; it is necessary to do, to believe and to feel. You cannot deceive God."

Vitória's spirit had a lot on its mind. At that time, she found it very necessary to be humble, patient and honest with her feelings.

✳ ✳ ✳

As time went by, Mr. Salvador got used to the idea that Rúbia was a single mother, although he did not admit it. Especially after she moved in with her sister.

In the company of Mrs. Celeste, he began to visit Simone, who was almost in her eighth month of pregnancy. It was inevitable that he would not find the other daughter, Rúbia, who, in turn, spoke little, as she was ashamed of the belly that already seemed to be well.

One day, the worried mother commented;

259

"Simone, you should go home. It's close to the baby's birth. You shouldn't be here alone."

"I'm staying here, mom. And he won't be born yet. Don't worry. I'm taking all the precautions and, at night, Rúbia is here with me. I'm not alone."

"During the day, you are alone."

"No, I'm not. I don't stay at home." She laughed. "I go out a lot... I can still do that, because I feel really good. It's good to have something to do and feel useful."

"Do you still go to that institution?" The lady was interested.

"I go there at least once a week with Cristiano. He goes there, almost every day. You have to see what a beautiful job he did in the garden there. Impressive!"

"Has he returned to work as a dentist yet?"

"No."

"My tooth hurts." Mr. Salvador complained. "It's terrible trying to make an appointment. In fact, it's disrespectful what these doctors and dentists do to us. We call there and never find the time or day we want. We are forced to change our entire routine because of the time they have available. As if that wasn't enough, we arrive at the right time or even earlier and wait... wait... Sometimes two hours! This happened the last time I went to the dentist. So, I never went back."

"Do you see what he did? That's why your tooth hurts." Said Mrs. Celeste.

"It is disrespectful to leave the patient waiting so long." The husband protested again. "It is absurd. These doctors and dentists don't know what we do to be on time. What we had to deal with before we were there, we had to wait for hours, sometimes in a small room with that TV on a channel I don't like to watch. Plus, they put out old magazines and newspapers, horrible coffee, that is, when you have coffee!" He exalted himself. "Otherwise, there is hardly any freshwater. These professionals are insensitive. And when are those kids crying, or those annoying people who run and scream from side to side? And the mothers, without authority, careless, keep asking with that sweet voice: "So-and-so, stop! Come here!" He imitated. "Calling like that encourages the girl or boy to continue with what he is doing. They must be firm and educate their children better, but no!"

Then Mrs. Celeste suggested as if she had a brilliant idea.

"Maybe Cristiano would open his office just to see you, Salvador!" Suddenly, Simone was encouraged by the suggestion.

"Who knows?! I can talk to him! You would go, wouldn't you, dad?"

"Yes..." He said as if he accepted. Then he wanted to know. "Isn't he the son of that woman you went to visit, Celeste? Who is he?"

"He is the son of Janaina. He is that young man who had a car accident along with the girlfriend and her brother. The girl and her future brother-in-law died. He suffered a trauma and..." She said; "I already told you this story, but never pay attention to what I say." His wife murmured.

"Where do you know these people from?" He was interested. Mother and daughters looked at each other and Simone answered.

"They are our friends. Cristiano's brother, David, is also a dentist and Abner treats himself with him. Their mother, Mrs. Janaina, met Abner and made friends with him. When I was very sad to hear about my baby, I went to see Abner and told him everything. In the end, he was going to take me to your house, but first he stopped at this lady's house. I knew she could comfort me. And that's what happened. She is a kind and experienced woman.

While we were both talking, Cristiano showed up and found out that my baby had Patau Syndrome. Then he told me that, in his volunteer work, he had already taken care of boys in these conditions. I became interested and asked him to take me to the institution where he worked. This is how our friendship began. Then, after an invitation from them, I visited a spiritist house and it did me a lot of good. I returned to a spiritualist center and started to feel better, with healthier thoughts. I was excited to move forward, trusting God. In the midst of everything, I heard about what happened to Cris and I felt very sorry for him. I wanted to help, to encourage. That's why mom met Mrs. Janaina in Abner's apartment, when we met there. Mom knew what happened to Cristiano, she knew how much they helped me and... so... Our friendship was strengthened. Mom liked her, so they went to have a coffee... Anyway, we need good people as friends, which they are..." There was a brief pause and she got excited; "If I can get Cristiano to attend you, will you go?"

"I think I'm going."

"Your father is afraid of the dentist." Said his wife.

"No, I'm not." He defended himself.

"If you go to that appointment, which I will tell Cristiano is an emergency, you will be helping a good person a lot, I can guarantee it."

"Then I will do it!" Mr. Salvador agreed, encouraging himself.

"I will agree with David so that he says that he does not have time or that he must go to university. In any case, he will tell his brother that he cannot attend to you. Then he will leave it to Cristiano. He will have to force himself." She rejoiced.

"You can be sure that I will do it!" Said the man.

"I think David has a class tonight." Said Rúbia. "Why don't you call him now?"

"Yes! Let's do it!" Exclaimed Simone, satisfied. She picked up the phone and went to another room to be more comfortable.

Returning to Rúbia, Mrs. Celeste wanted to know.

"Why didn't you go to work today, daughter?"

"I went in the morning. I had a doctor's appointment after lunch and then I came straight here."

"Is everything okay with you and the baby?"

"Yes, it is. The doctor asked me to reduce or even eliminate the salt completely. My blood pressure is a little high."

"Daughter, be careful. Do what he says. High blood pressure can cause serious problems for you and your baby. It doesn't cost anything to take care of. Remember that it is a health problem. The biggest problem is not at home, it's when you eat things on the street, in a restaurant... Try to eat a good diet." Recommended Mrs. Celeste.

Father and daughter have not spoken since she left home. Unable to bear his curiosity, Mr. Salvador asked;

"Do you know what it is?"

"It's a boy." She responded shyly.

"A boy?!" The man smiled.

"Why are you so excited, Salvador?" Asked the suspicious woman. Because to make that expression, the husband would have something on his mind.

"If she is not married... The boy will only have her last name! Just so my father's name doesn't die. If I'm going to wait for Abner to give me a grandson so that my family's name continues... I'm lost." Addressing Rúbia, he wanted to know even more. "What name are you going to give the boy?"

"I've been thinking a lot about grandpa in the last few days. I even commented with Simone... I'm thinking of choosing this name: Bruno Dellago. I don't know if I can add Neto. We'll see."

Mr. Salvador's face was bright like never before. He couldn't help but smile until Mrs. Celeste asked.

"What if the boy's father wants to register in his name?"

"Rúbia has to decide! He has no right. They are not married!" He answered quickly, without anyone expecting it.

Despite this, Rúbia explained:

"I thought about it a lot. I see that the father of my child is not at all, not at all interested in this pregnancy. He wants to hide it from his family and... So, I thought I would do the following: I will register him only on my name. If Jefferson wants to give his name to the baby, he has that right and he can claim it even before the law and I won't be able to do anything against him, because the tests will prove that he is his son. But I doubt very much *that* will happen. I think about registering him in my name and when Bruno grows up and he can understand the situation, he will be able to decide whether he wants to claim his father's name or not."

"That damn... that Jefferson won't want to register my grandson on his name and it's good that he doesn't dare!" The man reacted. "And after knowing what that scoundrel did to his mother, Bruno won't want to have that bastard's name! You are not a fool, Rúbia. You don't want a pension. You don't want anything, since you won't need it."

"Things are not like that, Salvador." Said his wife. "Rúbia was very clear. There are laws that defend the right of the father if he wants to register the boy. Besides, later on, if Bruno wants to be recognized by his father, he has that right."

"But it's not going to happen. The boy will be called Bruno Dellago Neto or simply Bruno Dellago and that's it! It was a very wise decision."

Rúbia felt like laughing. She turned her face away, trying to hide her almost shaky mouth.

When Simone returned to the room, she communicated.

"There! Done. Soon David will go to the course. I agreed with him that I will call Cristiano to say that you are dying of a toothache and that you must be taken care of urgently." She laughed. "You will go, won't you, father?"

"I'll go. But let him be nice. I don't like to feel pain."

"He'll do it great, Dad. Don't worry! She was happy to get excited by saying what she didn't know.

"Simone..." Said her father, worried about the other matter. "Rúbia said that her son's name will be Bruno, the same name as her grandfather's. What name will you give your son?"

"I definitely didn't choose, Dad. I thought of some, but... I need Samuel's opinion, because..."

"Do you still think that sassy guy will have an opinion about anything? I think it's good for you to get used to thinking about you and your child. You should only claim what is rightfully yours and your child's."

"How funny! You told Rúbia that she didn't want a pension or anything from Jefferson, but for Simone, you want her to demand what belongs to her and her son! I don't understand Salvador." Said Mrs. Celeste.

"These are different situations. You can't see."

"No."

"Ahhh, woman! Stop."

"It's because of the baby's name, mother. Dad liked the idea of choosing grandfather's name." Said Rúbia, trying not to laugh.

"I know. I understood. I just want to hear it from him." Said the mother.

"It's a beautiful name! You can't deny it!" He said, emphasizing.

"Can I register him as Bruno Dellago Neto? After all, grandfather would be his great-grandfather and not his grandfather."

"Only Bruno Dellago is very cute, but if you want him to have Neto in his name, you can change to Salvador Dellago Neto."

"Ahhh, nooooo!" All three responded to a single chorus.

"Why not? Isn't it beautiful? - He insisted.

"Bruno is prettier, Salvador. In fact, it was the first choice, wasn't it?" Advised his wife.

"Does it matter?" He insisted.

"Yes, it matters. She must choose the name that she thought of, right?" Said Mrs. Celeste.

Mr. Salvador was happy. He was happy that his grandson was carrying his last name. That was enough for him.

They talked for a while until, at the appointed time, Simone called Cristiano to ask him to see his father because it was a dental emergency.

"Me?" He was surprised. "To attend to your father? In the office?"

"I can only count on you, Cristian. David already went to the course. I talked to the assistant and she said she can even help you. She will wait for my call to see if she should stay a little longer. It's just that, the dentist we know and trust, at the moment, is only you. Please…" Talked to a little voice. "He's in a lot of pain…"

Together with her son, Mrs. Janaina listened to the conversation. She heard about everything arranged by David and encouraged him.

"Oh, son... If there's a problem with a toothache, take care of the man, poor thing! The worst thing in the world is to have a toothache."

Cristian was concerned. He was nervous to ask;

"What if David sees you later, as soon as he gets back from college?"

"Your brother will be back very late. I talked to him." Said Simone. Then she pretended;

"Then don't worry... Poor dad... I'll see if I can call someone else... but right now... Without being a known patient, I doubt that anyone will answer..."

"Wait." He said, fearful. "Look... I can't guarantee... Let's go. I'll see what I can do..."

"Thank you, Cristiano! I knew I could count on you! So, I'm going to call David's assistant and ask him to wait for us, okay?"

"No. I mean..." The man, clearly nervous, explained; "It's like this: I can work alone. The fewer people around me today, the better."

"I understand that. I'll call the office and say you don't need any help."

"That's right. All good. I'm on my way."

Simone hung up and laughed like she hadn't done in a long time.

As agreed, she, her father and Cristiano arrived at the office at about the same time.

After introducing himself, the man reported.

"I prefer to attend to you in my brother's office, as the devices, equipment and instruments are sterile. The room that was mine has not been used for some time."

"What a beautiful office." Said Mr. Salvador. "This glass wall with a garden outside... It even has a fountain with lights and everything." He marveled.

"It was Abner who designed it." Said Cristiano. "It really looks good and functional. It's nice and calm. I'll plug in the font so you can see it."

This is how it was done. The man was distracted when he saw the waterfall, causing a soft murmur that harmonized well with the very calm ambient music.

Cris prepared himself. He went into the room and checked the equipment and all the instrumentation. It didn't take long and Mr. Salvador was taken care of.

It was difficult to treat Mr. Salvador because he wanted to talk a lot, which was not convenient during dental treatment. However, the conversation was interrupted, distracting Cristiano, who mastered the situation and ended up feeling completely calm, in control, as if he had never been afraid to treat anyone again.

When they returned to the waiting room, where Simone was waiting apprehensively, she asked;

"And there? All good?"

"Everything is fine." Responded Cristiano with a funny smile.

"Very good." Said Mr. Salvador. "It didn't hurt at all. I didn't feel anything. Look, I've never been to a dentist who paid so much attention and treated me so carefully. My mouth is numb, it's true, but I didn't even feel the anesthesia. You're really good, doctor!"

"Very good!" She said, patting him on the back.

"Thank you, Mr. Salvador. As I said, I need you to come back in a week, because…"

Mr. Salvador was so excited that he didn't let him talk.

"Of course, I will come back. I really enjoyed your service. Besides being on time, I didn't feel anything. You know, there are dentists and other health professionals who are not human. They treat us like animals. They don't respect our pain. They don't understand our feelings, our fears. They don't care about our emotional side. Also, I'm very surprised by the hygiene of the office. Wow! The hygiene here is impressive! Everything was plasticized, the parts of the orthopedic appliances were cleaned and changed in front of me... The last dentist I went to was holding the pen using a glove. He took notes, then put the same gloved hand over my mouth. Then his secretary borrowed the same pen and returned it. Then I understood that the microbes from the secretary's dirty hand were in my mouth, because the dentist, using a glove, took the same pen, which he put in the secretary's hand, and then put his hand in my mouth. The glove protection was only for him. So..."

"Dad." Simone interrupted. "It's not polite to badmouth another professional. This is not elegant."

"And I want to be elegant? It was true, doctor! It just happened. There are health professionals who do not have the slightest hygiene and this, today, is very important."

"Cristiano." Simone interrupted again. "When can we come back and what is the cost of treatment?"

The dentist sat down at the reception desk, turned on the computer, opened the calendar, checked it and asked;

"Can we make an appointment for next Friday? What is the best time for you?"

"Do I still have the right to choose the time? I don't think so!"

When she saw him smiling, she said;

"I prefer at ten o'clock in the morning."

"It is programmed. I will not anticipate service because I want to attend to you in my office. I need to prepare the cleaning, sterilization of instruments, material and an assistant."

"It looks great, doctor! It's perfect!"

"And how much is the treatment, Cristiano?" Simone asked.

"I didn't do the budget. I'm out of date. Let's talk about this another time, okay?"

"Good." She agreed and smiled. "Now let's go, right, dad?"

"Mr. Salvador, just one thing." When the man looked at him, he recommend; "As I told you inside, try not to talk too much. You are anesthetized and can bite your tongue without realizing it."

"It will be difficult for you to follow that recommendation, but... Thank you."

"She doesn't know what she's talking about. You can drop it, doctor. I will follow your instructions."

After waiting for the boy to close the clinic, they said goodbye and left. Simone was intimately satisfied. She knew that this opportunity helped her friend a lot.

14.– HOMOSEXUALITY IS GOD'S WORK

WHEN CRISTIANO ARRIVED HOME, he didn't take his smile off his face.

He walked in and kissed his mother as usual. She did not miss the opportunity and praised him.

"You look very well dressed, all in white, my son." Then she asked; "And there in the office, how was it?"

"Simone's father is quite a character. Relaxed. He is not afraid to give his opinion about anything. It was difficult to treat him. He talks a lot." He laughed. "I'm glad I took care of him. A little more and the tooth would be seriously compromised with severe inflammation. Still, he's going to need to have a canal done."

"I want to know about you, son." The lady insisted. Cristian threw himself on the sofa, dropped his body and, looking up at the ceiling, declared.

"I owe a lot to Simone. It was God who put her in my way through all that I went through." Then he calmed down better, looked at his mother and said; "I will not say that it was good. I was scared to death, at first. But when he sat down and I started to prepare him... I took the instruments... Mr. Salvador was talking, telling me what he felt and why he didn't like dentists and... My sense of panic was disappearing. Amazingly, it happened. I didn't even realize that, one day, I had such a horrible feeling. I started working normally. Everything flowed... When I realized, it was all over."

"Thank God, son!"

"Thank God, mom!" He agreed without managing to close his smile. "I even thought that I would never treat anyone again. Ah...! I already booked for him next Friday. I'll take care of activating my office. I don't know where the equipment is. I need an assistant…"

"You can't imagine what it's like for me to see you so excited, Cris." She interrupted, almost crying.

"Thank God and Simone, mom. If it weren't for her…"

"Do not despise yourself. She came at the right time when you were ready to return and gave that little indispensable push. We will always be grateful to her, yes, but don't forget to watch all your efforts to get back to assist your patients."

"Apparently, everything has its time. I just hope I'm excited like this next time."

"You will be, of course! Don't talk nonsense, boy. You need to think positive thoughts." Said the lady while getting up and approaching him. He thanked her.

"Thank you, mom. Thank you for believing in me, for the strength you gave me, for not giving up... I have a lot to thank you and David for being by my side." He said kissing and hugging her with strength and affection.

On the spiritual plane, Victoria observed them closely and commented to Juan;

"I went with Cris to the office. The gentleman he treated is a very critical man."

"But with a good heart. Cristiano, for him, was a stranger. He had no reason to help him. However, he agreed to become a patient, even though he knew the boy was going through a psychological disorder."

"Yes, but... They lied to Cristiano. They said that no one else would be able to assist Mr. Salvador. Many were involved in the lie and that was wrong."

"Victoria, do you really think that God is going to care about that insignificant lie, invented to force a Cristian to overcome panic? I'm sure that Simone, David and the others will still tell him the truth and everyone will laugh a lot about all this. You, my dear, need to be more attentive to what you do and what you think. We cannot judge without deep knowledge. Mr. Salvador is a critical man because he did not learn differently, but he is generous. He showed a great heart when the opportunity came to be useful."

"I love Cris. I didn't like to see him cheated."

"We must beware of love that stifles and destroys. Cristian was only able to surpass himself and perform all necessary procedures in his profession because you just stood by and did not repent, as he did. Your previous behavior helped your ex-boyfriend get trapped in a confused mind, while that critical man agreed to undergo treatment to help free the boy who, as he said, was a stranger. Think about that."

When she saw him take a stand, the spirit of Victoria called out to him.

"Juan." When she saw him turn, she said; "I'm in trouble. I have strong opinions, but I can't be different."

"You can have opinions, whatever they may be; however, you do not have the right to hinder another person's experience because of them. Having an opinion is one thing. Being dominant, wanting to subject the lives and opinions of others to your control, is quite different."

As she said this, Juan's spirit left, leaving her to reflect on the conversation.

Weeks passed.

The heat was excessive, especially for Simone, who had a huge belly. At home, sitting on the couch, she closed her eyes and stretched her swollen feet on the coffee table in the living room, trying to relax.

Not long after, Rúbia entered with a gift wrapped and said enthusiastically.

"I bought a perfume for Ricardo!"

"Perfume, why?"

"It's his birthday today. I forgot it. We were invited to go to the reception that will be in the ballroom of the building where he lives."

"Ah, you are right…"

"I can see that you are not excited at all."

"It is not the same. I'm so tired, Rúbia…"

"Ahhh... We're going, aren't we?"

Observing his sister's anxiety, she smiled and agreed not to disappoint her.

"Yes, we are. What time?"

"At seven o'clock. I asked Abner what cologne Ricardo used. He told me last night. I went to the mall today and bought it so the two of us could give it to him. Do you think it's bad?"

"No. We live together."

Rúbia rejoiced. She didn't want to make a mistake.

"Then I will take a shower. I still have this hair to fix." The sister laughed and said nothing. She continued resting.

✳ ✳ ✳

Much later, Ricardo was greeted for his birthday. Both sisters met some acquaintances and were introduced to other guests.

Mrs. Janaina and Cristiano were also there. And it was with them that Rúbia and Simone joined a table and began to speak animatedly.

The birthday boy, along with everyone else, noticed;

"Simone, you look huge! So pretty!"

"Thank you. But the heat is killing me." She laughed.

"I think a pregnant woman is beautiful." Said Ricardo. Rúbia closed her smile. After all, she was pregnant too, but the friend praised her.

Suddenly, two girls approached them and Ricardo stood up, kissing and introducing them.

"This is Eloah, my sister, and this is Suzana, her partner." Rúbia thought she didn't quite understand; however, she realized that Eloah was dressed in a masculine manner, had very short hair. She was a transsexual woman. Suzana, who was very feminine, was homosexual.

Smiling, they greeted everyone. Then they excused themselves and went to greet other people.

Ricardo also excused, since he had to receive other guests. Seeing them from a distance, Rúbia said, almost whispering;

"I didn't know his sister was a lesbian!"

"Don't use that term, Rúbia!" Immediately the sister scolded her, very angry. "What a horrible thing to say!"

"But isn't it?" She asked quietly, in a humble way.

"No. She is apparently a transsexual. Her partner is homosexual or you can call her gay, because the term is for either men or women. Don't call people with disapproving terms or

275

unpleasant meanings. Would you like someone to refer to you with a derogatory term?"

"Like what?"

"Do you really want me to say ii?" The sister was silent, lowered her head and Simone tried to correct herself. Touching her hand, she spoke generously in her voice. "I'm sorry. I didn't mean to offend you."

"You didn't offend me. You reminded me that I was the other one, the scoundrel who got pregnant by a married man... That someone could call me all this or worse."

Rúbia got up slowly, excused herself and walked away. Simone went after her, but Mrs. Janaina hugged her lightly and advised her.

"Don't try to say anything now. It can get worse. You will not be free to speak here."

"Me and my big mouth." Said Simone.

"Stay calm, sit here. Then you two will talk in a better place." Said Cristiano nicely.

"She's upset with me." She said, settling down and acknowledging the failure.

"Then let me go to talk to her." Mrs. Janaina decided, getting up and looking for Rúbia.

After a while, Simone asked;

"I haven't been to the institution in three weeks. Have you been there?

"Yes, I have. I began to see, with the pediatrician there, the possibility of my returning to work as a dentist."

"What good news. I'm happy."

"They asked for you. They said that you are missing."

"Imagine…" She hesitated and smiled. The times I went, I didn't do anything. I spent two hours sewing clothes, and when I didn't, I read them stories…"

"It's quite a job. Don't be modest. However, I see that it is not good for you to leave, now, in the final stages of pregnancy. Especially in this heat."

"Don't even talk to me about this heat! Today, I only came here because of my sister. She hasn't been out lately and was so excited today that I felt sorry for refusing to come." The approach of Abner and David ended the matter. Simone greeted them with hugs and kisses. Being very happy to see them, she asked them to sit with them.

"And Rúbia, where is she?" Asked the brother.

"She is there, talking to Mrs. Janaina." She pointed out.

"You seem dismayed, Simone. What happened?" David was interested.

"It is the heat. My feet are swollen... In fact, I'm swollen. Did you see that?"

"Still, you look pretty." He praised the other one.

"Thank you. I know you're just saying that to please me…" She laughed. "But thank you."

"Oh! Don't say that! I'm not a false person." He smiled, caressing her arm on the table.

"Tell us about it." Abner was interested. "Does my father continue the treatment with you, Cristiano?"

"Yes, he does, and he arrives on time!" He smiled in a funny way. Then he commented in a friendly way; "I owe a lot to him and Simone. If Mr. Salvador wouldn't agree to be my guinea pig, and Simone insisted that I treat him... Maybe I will still be like before." He laughed. "I'm already taking care of other patients too, you know?"

"David told me." Said Abner.

Simone looked at David in a mischievous way and they both began to laugh.

"What happened?" Cristiano was intrigued, suspicious.

"Should I tell him or not?" She asked.

"Tell him about it. I'm his brother. He will try to punch me."

"What happened?" Cristiano smiled curiously. In a cheerful and playful tone, Simone said;

"If I tell you, do you promise to remain my friend?"

"I promise. Just say it already. I don't like to be anxious." He asked with a laugh.

"Do you know all that drama I did for you to see my father?" Without waiting for an answer, she revealed. "It was the biggest trick."

"What?"

"Simone revealed the whole truth and, smiling, Cristiano joked;

"Bunch of traitors! I don't trust you anymore! Especially you, Simone! I never expected to see you lie to me!"

"Ahhh, Cris... Forgive me, will you?" She said in a kind way, caressing his arm on the table.

"No. No way." He continued to play. "Traitor!" He laughed and patted her on the shoulder. "I must admit that the plot helped your father a lot. His tooth was quite compromised."

"Ivan is over there. I'm going to say hello. Excuse me." Said Abner, standing up.

"I'm going with you." Decided David, walk with him. "Excuse me."

"Yes! Apparently, no one wants our company." Complained Cristiano jokingly. "Would you like another soda? A snack...?"

"No thanks. I have passed my soda amount today and I'm satisfied with my snack."

They talked some more. They spoke about the manner of Mr. Salvador, whom Cristiano found very amusing.

After a few moments, Rúbia and Mrs. Janaina returned, joining them. After a while, Simone kept silent and, much later, asked her sister;

"Shall we go?"

"But they didn't even sing happy birthday!"

"I'm so tired, Rubia." She said in a discouraged tone. Mrs. Janaina, very attentive, became interested and asked.

"Are you feeling well, Simone?"

"I'm worried about being here. I don't seem to have a position. It's tiring and I want to leave."

Solicitous, Cristiano proposed;

"Want a ride? Rúbia can stay. Abner can take her, when they are finished here, with my mother."

"No, I'll spoil your fun." She refused.

"I'm not very interested. For me it was enough. I'm also a little tired."

Simone hesitated and then decided.

"Well, let's go."

So, they did and Cristiano took her home.

Much later, Rúbia, excited, arrived telling Simone everything that happened after she left. Simone listened attentively. Then she apologized for being rude during the party, when she scolded her. Rúbia excused her and acknowledged that she was also wrong. They hugged each other as happily and friendly as ever.

* * *

That Sunday morning, Simone woke up scared.

The short sleep she had was a restless sleep. She got up and decided to take a shower. She was very sweaty and the heat was bothering her too much.

When she finished, she changed and realized that she really didn't feel well.

Going to the room where her sister was, she gently woke her up, calling in a soft voice;

"Rúbia…"

"What happened?" She asked in surprise.

"Everything is under control, but I don't feel very good. I think it's good to call my doctor and go to the hospital."

The other got up quickly and asked;

"Do you think it's better to call Samuel or Abner?"

"Honestly… I'm in doubt. I don't know whether to call Samuel or not."

"Is it your responsibility to call him, yes. Anyway, I think I should warn you: just don't expect too much of the guy."

"I also wanted to call Abner. Our brother has accompanied me in all the consultations and exams. He is very dedicated."

"So, let's go." She decided quickly.

They got ready, made the calls and went to the hospital where Simone was admitted. After examining her, the doctor decided on a cesarean section.

It was on that hot Sunday morning that her son was born.

She could barely see the baby after delivery, as the boy needed special care in the neonatal Intensive Care Unit.

Despite a quick glance, the mother could see that the boy had a cleft lip, an extra little finger in one hand and the other was clenching his fist, the hand was practically non-existent. He also had deformities in his ears and head that were displaced. She was told there was an infectious condition, jaundice, umbilical hernia, pneumonia and a kidney complication. It was later discovered that he had polycystic kidneys and heart problems. Everything indicated a marked mental retardation.

Even when hospitalized, it was with difficulty that Simone visited her son at I.C.U. because the cesarean section was still very painful and she could not stay there long.

Samuel went to visit her only once, but he did not want to see his son.

It was Mrs. Celeste the one who remained in the hospital as a companion every day her daughter was hospitalized.

Upon her discharge, Simone was very sad to leave her son still in the hospital. Despite her insistence, she did not want to go to her mother's house, but went directly to hers. The pain she felt was silent. She said little about herself and her son. She answered only what was asked.

Her in-laws, on one of the visits, knew in great detail how the separation between her and Samuel took place. They, believing the son's words, thought the marriage was over because she no longer wanted him, because she was disappointed in the baby's condition.

After the couple left, Simone was visited by Cristiano, who left the dental clinic and went straight home. She said to him;

"I don't think Samuel could have lied to his parents like that, so blatantly."

"Has he visited your child yet?"

"No. Nor was he registering him at a registry office. Next week, after removing the stitches, I will have to register him myself. Do you believe so? It's so hard, Cris... It's hard to be alone in this situation. Despite having my family and friends with me, I needed the father of my child to support me. There are moments when I think I won't be able to stand it. And a lot of tension, a lot to do…"

"You are not alone. You have family, friends... Everyone loves you, they will support you in everything." He was silent for a moment, observing the extreme sadness in her lost gaze and proposed; "Whenever you want, I can go with you to the registry office to register the baby. Have you already chosen the name?"

"Peter. I want to call him Peter. You don't have to worry. Abner or my dad can go with me to the registration office."

"Friends help each other, have you forgotten? I'll go with you. Look what you did to me. Do you remember how I was?"

"Opportunities have arisen and you have come up and reacted. No one had to carry you."

"But no one else had the idea to invent the biggest lie to see me work again. I won't forget it, Simone."

"What you will not forget? The lie?" She smiled jokingly.

"I will not forget either the lie or your initiative and concern to get me out of the situation I was in."

"That's enough."

"Then I go to the registration office with you and that's it. When are you going to get your stitches out?"

"Friday morning. I'll take the opportunity and visit Peter. Then I'll go to the registration office. I think that, due to the absence of the father, I have to take the marriage certificate, right?"

"I think so." After a moment he commented; I'm impressed with your husband's lack of preparation. I'm sorry to say it, but…"

"My ex-husband, you mean."

"He is someone who deserves pity from us, pity for being so immature, poor in spirit..."

"Irresponsible, cruel, ignorant, inhumane..." She said; "What surprises me the most is the fact that I didn't realize he was like that."

"It was a serious and important event for Samuel to reveal himself. I'm sorry to ask you, Simone, but... Do you like him like you used to?"

"No." She answered lightly. "My love for him went away like that beautiful glass vase that breaks, but you don't miss it. I think it was the contempt I received. I never expected this from Samuel and I was so disappointed, upset that I no longer feel anything for him."

At that time, Mr. Salvador arrived with his wife.

Mrs. Celeste had decided to stay with her daughter for a few days. However, that afternoon, she went home to take care of some things and her husband brought her back. The lady had entered from the back and went to collect clothes from the clothesline and took care of other tasks, so she did not even see her daughter with Cristiano.

Mr. Salvador went straight to the room and rejoiced;

"How are you, doctor? It's nice to meet you here!"

"You can call me Cristiano, while I'll call you Mr. Salvador. For your life experiences, I owe you respect and I have to call you sir."

"Look! This is an example of education since the cradle." Said the man who then greeted his daughter. Settling down on the couch, he continued; "Today it is difficult to see young people like you being so respectful. Parents have lost control over their children and the kids are out of control. They look down on us and

283

treat us badly because of our age and appearance. And look, I'm not even that old. They do this as if they'll never grow old. Maybe some of them aren't. Without the education of their parents and family, these young people drink, smoke, use drugs, and get into trouble because of bad company, and they end up dying early, getting sick early, or maiming themselves."

When education comes from parents with common sense, parents who control their children to guide them better, it rises to be better and more respectable adult humans.

"I agree with you. I had a controlled education, so to speak. When I was a teenager, my mother, who was very demanding, wanted to know where I was, who I was with and what I was doing. I thought it was bad. Over time, I saw how good it made me. I will be 30 next month and even today she knows where I'm and what I'm doing. It's a pleasure for me to have my mother as a friend who guides me, wants my well-being."

"My children are a little distant from me because of the truths I tell, but I raised them well. Everyone is respectful of me and others. It just didn't work out the way I wanted it to. Simone did everything right. She planned her life, but fate prepared her. Rúbia hit her head and now she needs to rebuild her life. Abner... When I think about my son, I want to disappear... I don't know where I went wrong."

Cristiano looked at him expressively and, although he knew what it was about, he asked;

"Why do you say that? I know your son, he is an excellent person, unbelievable!"

"As a person you can be amazing, but then you can just decide to go the wrong way. I'm very upset about that."

"Why don't you talk, dad? Tell me why you were disappointed in Abner."

"Why, Simone!" He almost got angry.

"My father began to think this way from the moment he heard about my brother's homosexuality."

"Simone!" He scolded her angrily.

"I understand, Mr. Salvador. Many conservative people do not accept, or feel uncomfortable when it comes to homosexuality."

"See? He understands me. I can't understand what happened to this son of mine." He said; "My only son, a man! I don't know where I went wrong!"

"You haven't lost anything. Homosexuality is a condition. It is not a choice or a bad form of education."

"Look, kid... don't you give me that story too. That's cheeky."

"I'm sorry, Mr. Salvador." He said calmly and respectfully. "I understand you and I won't say it's wrong to think that way."

"How so? You understand me, but..."

"But I don't agree. I understand your strong opinion because I know you learned that way. When that happens, it's hard to change your mind and convince yourself otherwise. However, if you can understand what happens in the face of facts and reflections, you can come to accept it."

"There is no one that can change my mind and accept such shamelessness!" He protested.

"I believe that shamelessness, as you say, exists in both the heterosexual and homosexual condition. The person does not respect himself, becomes vulgar, corrupts himself, becomes promiscuous or prostitutes himself, regardless of his sexual condition. The condition is how we come into the world as a result of God's permission. I firmly believe that the homosexual condition is a reason for prejudice due to lack of information, lack of understanding. After knowing the truth, it is a very logical reflection. I do not want to convince you of anything, but I would like to make you think. Homosexuality has existed since the world is a world. The lack of dissemination of information on serious and well directed scientific research on the subject complicates the situation. Lack of information is a major problem. In addition, many minds and hearts are strongly closed. Some people do not want to change their way of thinking, so they do not seek to discover everything that happened and is happening in the history of mankind, in nature and in the scientific world."

He looked at his daughter, then at the boy and asked;

"Cristiano, you said that homosexuality has existed since the world is a world... What do you know about the history of homosexuality? "

"I studied a lot about it to understand a very particular situation."

"Are you going to tell me you're gay?" Mr. Salvador was alarmed. The boy smiled and answered;

"No, I'm not. But because I have a homosexual case very close to me, I decided to immerse myself in knowledge to stop being prejudiced. I don't feel as comfortable commenting, but some time ago I didn't think like I do today. I was very similar to you. In my research, I learned that in ancient and well-civilized cultures dating back to the 5th century BC, mainly in classical Greece, there is evidence of the practice of homosexuality, although the terms homosexual and heterosexual are unknown in the Greek language of the time. For them, having a preference for boys or girls was normal, depending on age and circumstances. Innumerable images, sculptures, paintings, biographies, philosophical and ethnographic texts, speeches and many other documents prove the reality of these love relationships."

"No one was against it?" Asked the other.

"The Greeks did not judge homosexuality as long as the citizen had control over his passions. It was normal for a married man to have a wife at home, a concubine, and even to have relations with prostitutes and ephebes. The ephebe was a relationship between an older man and a much younger one. It was the male qualities of the younger man, usually an athlete with skills, strength, speed, stamina, that attracted the older man and the older man was respected for his wisdom, experience and mastery."

"What is ephebe?" Mr. Salvador asked.

"He is a boy in puberty, in his adolescence." Said Cristiano. "The youngest boy's family, called ephebe, gave him to the oldest, called tutor. To be accepted by a tutor was a matter of honor, of great pride. From then on, the tutor would make him a Greek citizen. This older man was supposed to protect him, educate him, and train him for later, he, ephebus, may also become a tutor. They should develop a mutual passion, but they should master that passion which was the basis of this ephebic system. Along with all of this, the two were sexually related. Greek society did not approve of homosexual relations between men of the same age. In that same civilization, women were considered inferior creatures to men. Lower in every way: emotionally, physically, and intellectually. The relationship between a man and a boy was not judged, but they could not have female features. This was not accepted by society. To guarantee the active role of the man and his masculinity, he must have a submissive woman, a slave and an undeveloped young man, ephebe, and have relations with prostitutes."

"In Greece, were there any homosexual women?" Mr. Salvador asked.

"As for female homosexuality, which has also existed since the world is one, there are records in the 7th century BC of a woman, a poet, named Sappho, who lived on the island of Lesbo, a Greek island in the northern Aegean Sea. Sappho's poems are addressed to women, something always highlighted in her works.

In reference to the island of Lesbo, the island where Sappho was born, homosexual women are called lesbians. She was the object of much criticism by the poets of the time, but was acclaimed for her works. The macho society inhibited the knowledge about the life of homosexual women, so there are not so many details about their lives. Sappho had, among so many women, one of her favorites, her greatest lover, named Attis. There is a lot of controversy about her real life. Some researchers say Sappho fell in love with a man named Faon, whom she pursued with furious love. Unrequited, they say Sappho committed suicide by throwing herself off a cliff into the sea. Others say that there are records of her coming of age. She was an acclaimed woman, glorified by her poetic talent and called the *Tenth Muse* by experts and *A Bela* by Socrates. Both in ancient Greece and in the Roman Empire, nothing was against homosexuality; nobody judged it. There was only a good definition between male and female roles."

"Do you know *when* they started complaining about homosexuality?" Simone's father asked.

"There was a radical change with the arrival of Christianity. In the Middle Ages, fierce opposition was raised against homosexuality, since Judaism, from which Christianity originated, always abhorred that condition and considered it a practice punishable by death, included in the category of incest, bestiality and adultery."

"What is bestiality?" Mr. Salvador asked without hesitation.

"Bestiality is the act of relating to an animal, sexual pleasure with an animal, called zoophilia. Continuing… Although Jesus Christ never mentioned anything about homosexuality, Christians, obviously Christianity, considered that sexual practice was attributed to men only for reproductive purposes. Therefore, they considered that any sexual practice that did not lead to procreation would be a mortal sin against God. At that time, the name used for homosexuality was sodomy. By the way, the term sodomy was also used for masturbation, oral sex, interfemoral intercourse (sex on the thighs) or any other sexual activity that did not lead to procreation. Around the year 540, it was believed that because of the practice of sodomy and, mainly, the homosexual practice of some, nature rebelled against all humanity and caused plagues, earthquakes, tidal waves, floods, collective hunger, wars, betrayals of kingdoms.... that is, all collective catastrophes meant God's revenge for the homosexual practice of men. That is why the Byzantine emperor Justinian decreed the death penalty for all homosexuals. In the Penitentiaries, the so-called guides for confessors, the Church condemned homosexuality in the most varied forms. Not only homosexuality, but also other sodomy practices, including sexual relations with one's spouse during Lent. In spite of so much opposition to some sexual habits, it is known that in the clergy there were sexual practices with women, men, masturbation, bestiality, and everything that the high standards of the Church could not inhibit. The Church preached and believed that there was a universal flood, and the five cities of Sodom and Gomorrah were burned by the heavenly fire and their inhabitants were alive until hell, because of the practice of sodomy, but they did not stop it within the Church itself. This was not only with the Catholic Church. In other religions, pastors, Muslims, popular preachers and theologians also believed and preached the same thing, but they could not prevent this practice among those who had the same faith."

Cristiano was excited, it seemed that he liked to express all the knowledge he had acquired. While Mr. Salvador listened attentively, without blinking, the boy continued;

"It was around 1120, when it was decreed that homosexual sodomites would be burned alive. In England, King Edward I and, in France, King Louis IX established the death penalty at the stake for homosexuals. In Castile, Alfonso X decreed punishments and tortures to homosexuals in front of all people for three days, in a public square, after they were castrated and hanged by the legs until death. From then on, the persecution was increasingly fierce. Homosexuals were accused of witchcraft. They had to be removed from society by prison or death. Sin had to be eliminated from society by fire, said the motto of the Franciscan St. Bernardine. In short, in the Middle Ages, there were the most terrible punishments for homosexuality."

"In 1869, the term homosexual was created. From that moment on, they came to believe that homosexuality was a mental illness and entered the field of medicine, still believing that it should and could be treated. Even so, homosexuals were considered a threat to society as if someone was infected by them. Since then, they began to investigate the causes of this alleged disease, such as childhood trauma, corruption, immaturity, etc. Many studies have been conducted, but still not enough to make it clear to those who are closed-minded and to bring them to understand that homosexuality is not a disease. In Germany, shortly after the first support for homosexuality, there arose National Socialism which repudiated homosexuality by not allowing procreation and therefore not continuing with the superior race, the Aryan race, so it was considered a serious violation of that firmly homophobic policy: Nazis. Homosexuality was considered harmful by the Third Reich and it is believed that more than fifty thousand homosexuals were condemned and approximately ten to fifteen thousand homosexuals were killed during the holocaust. Tortuous medical experiments were conducted to find any hereditary differences that might cause homosexuality and its possible cure. Many other men were castrated by order of the German courts. Even Ernst Rohm, a homosexual, was killed by Hitler, his best friend. Not only him, but also many other homosexuals belonging to the Nazi Party were killed and it was the Gestapo who took care of that. At the end of

World War II, homosexuals were not recognized as victims of the Holocaust. They did not receive social pensions like the other groups of prisoners, Jews, gypsies, Russians and others, since they were considered criminals. Recognition of them as victims occurred only from 2002 onwards for some countries. After the war, homosexual survivors did not have much freedom to report what happened during the Holocaust. The world was still very homophobic. It is known that from torture and investigation, nails were pulled out, they were examined with splintered wood that pierced their intestines, and other unspeakable abuses. German shepherd dogs were trained to bite them, often to death. Homosexuals received these and worse treatments in concentration camps in Germany and other places dominated by them. Not only homosexuals were treated in this way, but bisexuals, transvestites and transgender people in general."

"It is difficult for me to understand some things because of the terms. They created many names like sexual identity, transgender, sexual orientation, gender, sexual role... it's so confusing!" Revealed Mr. Salvador.

"You're right about that. For those who are not used to it, several names are a bit confusing. I think this is because sex was hardly ever spoken of in the past." Agreed Cristiano. Patiently, he continued explaining. "I know that sex is biological sex, it's what we have in our physical bodies when we are born. We have male sex organs or female sex organs. With the exception of hermaphrodites or intersexes, who are born with both genitals. Therefore, biological sex is the sex we have in our physical body and with which we are born. The sexual role is the behavior, the appearance, more feminine or more masculine, independently of the sex of the physical body. For example, a woman who works in civil construction plays a male role, and a woman truck driver has a male role. A male make-up artist, the hairdresser is in the female role. You see, the sexual role has no connection with sexual desire, with sexual attraction. Women in civil construction, women in trucks are not necessarily homosexual. Like the makeup artist, hairdressers are not necessarily homosexual. The sexual role is the reason for much discrimination, because it is how society sees us, how we are perceived, and it turns out that it is seen in a way that is not common to our sex or the physical body. In the face of this, ignorant people are scandalized. This is a lack of education, a lack of information."

"I understand that. So, a man can be a cook or a dressmaker, which is the role of a woman, and not be a homosexual. While a woman can be a tile worker, that's the role of a man, and she's not gay."

"Exactly. And many people without knowledge notice that, and criticize or even offend. This is prejudice." Explained Christian.

"I don't know much about hermaphrodite." Said the gentleman, hoping the other would explain.

"The name hermaphrodite comes from the name of the Greek god Hermaphrodite, son of Hermes and Aphrodite, who are the representatives of the male and female sexes, Hermes the man and Aphrodite the woman. Hermaphrodite is the name given to a person, animal or plant that has the sexual organs of both sexes: male and female. The term intersex is preferable to the term hermaphrodite, because hermaphrodite was used for people who had visible male and female genitalia and was a reason for much prejudice. Over time, they discovered that there are intersex people, or hermaphrodites, who only have, externally, the male organs and, internally, the internal female organs: the female reproductive system such as the ovaries, the uterus, but the external female organs do not appear. In general, it is believed that this is due to an embryonic malformation. As far as I know, there are three types of human hermaphroditism or human intersex: true hermaphroditism or true intersex; male pseudohermaphroditism or also called male pseudo-intersex and female pseudohermaphroditism also called female pseudo-intersex. In true intersexualism, the boy is born with internal and external sexual organs of both sexes, complete with vagina, uterus, ovary, penis and testicles. This person has both sexual organs completely formed."

"Today, we know that, until the seventh week, after being conceived, the boy does not have his reproductive organs formed, that is, all organs are identical. Information attributed to sex can be found inside the cells, along with genetic information, called chromosomes. Females have two X chromosomes and males have one X and one Y chromosome. In the case of intersexualism, most boys are genetically female, meaning their chromosomes are XX. The existence or formation of male sex organs is attributed to reasons still unknown. In the case of male pseudointersexualism, the boy is born genetically with XY chromosomes, although his external sex organs are not fully developed. In female pseudointersexualism, the boy is genetically born with XX chromosomes, although the clitoris is overdeveloped and acquires a penis-like formation. It is believed that, in this case, the cause is not genetic, but is due to the effects of the drugs used by the pregnant woman, who often does not know she is pregnant."

"It is the chromosomes that cause the formation of sex-determining hormones. As females are born with XX chromosomes, they trigger certain types of hormones and in males, who are born with XY chromosomes, they trigger other types of hormones. Sometimes certain people are born with extra chromosomes or their chromosomes trigger the formation of hormones that blur the lines between males and females. In this case, it can lead to the development of female reproductive organs in males and males in females. Intersex is a condition. The person is born this way. It is not a sexual orientation or a choice."

"Ohh... I see." Replied the gentleman, who seemed a little embarrassed, as he had never discussed sex with anyone, especially his daughter. But he wasn't inhibited and wanted to know more. "What's with that of "sexual orientation"? Is that the talk... when we guide our children about sex?"

"No. Not in language about sexuality. What is offered to boys and girls is sex education. Sexual orientation is the desire, the attraction that a person feels. Let me see..." He thought a bit and explained better. "Someone's sexual orientation means: who attracts that person to sexual practice. Do you want to have sex with the opposite sex, the same sex or whatever? Sexual orientation should be: heterosexual, homosexual or bisexual. Or the person likes someone of the opposite sex and is heterosexual or someone of the same sex and is homosexual, or whatever and is bisexual."

"Sexual orientation is who I want to relate to, man or woman, is that it?"

"Yes. Who you want to have sex with."

"I thought it was the way parents guided their children. I blamed myself a lot for being wrong in the way I raised my son and that's why Abner became what he became."

"No. Nothing like that. The idea of giving or determining a sex for the boy and that the male or female gender can be learned was the subject of catastrophic research and application. The word "gender" has numerous attributes, if we look it up in the dictionary." Cristiano continued. "However, in this case, the term gender is used to mark the differences between men and women, not only physical, biological, but also attributions in culture and society. In other words, socially and culturally, the person is either a man or a woman. As I said, biological sex is the one we are born with, or we are men or women."

"I get it!" He was excited. "But... tell me, what catastrophic event happened?"

"It was believed that when a boy was born with one sex, one could change the gender. This was the theory of many, mainly a psychologist, sexologist, researcher and writer named Dr. Juan Money, who conducted research on sexual identity and gender biology. For him, gender was something that could be learned. For example, a boy could be raised as a girl, learn to be a girl, and naturally live as a girl and become a woman as long as his parents persistently reinforced the female gender in him. Dr. John Money was highly regarded and worked at the famous John Hopkins Hospital, considered one of the largest hospitals in the world, in Baltimore, United States of America. It happened that identical twins were born into a family. The two boys, about eight months old, went to the circumcision, a surgery in which the foreskin - the skin that covers the glans of the penis - is cut. During this surgery, there was a very strong electrical discharge in the surgical instrument of cauterization. It was so strong that the entire penis of one of the twin babies was completely damaged instead of being circumcised."

"This case was brought to the attention of Dr. Juan Money, who believed he had the solution to the problem. Dr. Money established that this boy should be operated on and surgically transformed into a girl. He should be taught to live with the female gender. For this reason, another surgery was performed where the testicles were removed. Dr. John also recommended hormonal treatment. Then the boy would grow up believing and acting like a woman. Remembering that this boy had an identical twin. This was the perfect opportunity for science to prove the theory that a boy born with one gender can be taught to live with another gender. This was because they believed that the homosexual was homosexual because of the way he was raised, because of a trauma experienced, that is, the person was homosexual because of external factors in his life or the way he was raised and created. For many years, Dr. Juan Money published scientific articles about the success of his experiment and about successful change. It later became known that all of this psychologist's statements were false. The boy was never happy. He never identified with the female sex. He did not act or behave in a feminine manner as a child. Attempts to socialize him as a child had failed! Upon discovering the truth, this boy, named David Reimer, was disappointed by the lie and tried, by all means, to repair the pain, the emotional suffering due to all the deception. As a teenager, he wanted to become a man again. He took male hormones, tried reconstructive surgery to rebuild his penis, but was unsuccessful. His life became very problematic, confusing, and sad. He faced numerous difficulties. At the age of thirty-eight, David Reimer could not take it anymore and committed suicide. When the truth of this fact was revealed, Dr. Juan Money's theory collapsed along with his image. In the United States, about five surgeries are performed daily on intersex boys, boys who are born with genital formations that escape the socially determined standards for men or women in order to assign sex and normalize the genital organs."

"They are designed for parents to be emotionally reassured and for intersex children not to experience the emotional distress of growing up differently. The worst thing is to believe that the boy will adapt to the gender, male or female, given, if adequately reinforced. Many disagree totally with these surgeries, as they can cause terrible damage, considerably diminishing the sensitivity of the genitals, which is detrimental to a healthy sexual life, or worse, they can reconstruct the genitals with a gender contrary to what is believed."

"How so?" Asked the gentleman.

"If the baby is a pseudo-intersexual woman, genetically, that boy was born with XX chromosomes, although the clitoris develops excessively acquiring a formation similar to the penis, and doctors, judging by the appearance of the organ, believe he is a boy with a malformation of the penis and has undergone reconstructive surgery of the penis, closing the gap between the penis and the testicles, through which urine came out, and by opening or leaving a hole at the tip of the supposed penis, which is actually a well-developed clitoris, he surgically transformed a girl into a boy. Only when that boy grows up will they discover the deception. There have already been many such mistakes that lead to terrible emotional suffering, mental anguish, despair, depression and can even lead to suicide. Intersex people are also considered transgender. When in doubt, and mainly without the consent of the transgender or intersex individual, no surgery should be performed. The person needs to be mature enough to decide what is best for him or herself. Worldwide, it is believed that about one percent of the population is born intersex, but there are those who believe that number is much higher."

"What about these transgenders? What is that? For me this has something to do with soybeans." Cristiano smiled and explained patiently;

"For the Spanish language it is transgender. Transgender is a name used when the expression of gender does not correspond to the social role, the sexual appearance, assigned to the sexual gender of the boy at birth. Trans means beyond, and gender in this case refers to physical characteristics. When a person is called transgender, it means that he or she is beyond that physical characteristic. It is a new term for bringing together intersex, transsexual, and transvestite people. In intersex, the person is born with both sexual organs. Whereas, in the case of transsexuals, the person has a body with a biological sex that is inappropriate for their mind. The male body of a male transsexual is totally inappropriate, averse to his female mind. The male transsexual thinks he is a woman, he feels totally female. She is a female soul trapped in a male body. That's why she wants to change sex, because, as a rule, she doesn't accept her body at all. And there is also the opposite, that is, a male soul trapped in a female body.

Transgender transsexuals are against the physical body from an early age. In the case of male transsexuals, the sexual identity is not in accordance with their physical and biological sex, so their sexual identity is female, even though their body is male. This person certainly wants a change, a surgery on his sexual organs, changing them from male to female."

"We know the sister of a friend of ours who is a female transsexual. She was born with the female sex, that is, the sex of her biological body is female, but her mind, her psychology is totally male. She feels like a man, she dresses like a man, she thinks she's a man and she's contrary to her physical sex. Despite her female body, her sexual identity is male." Simone recalled to exemplify.

"Exactly. Eloah is like that. I heard she takes hormones. She's undergoing treatment to have a different body from the one she was born with. She wants a male body. I just don't know if she's going to have the surgery. Being a transsexual wasn't her choice. It wasn't an option. She's mentally like that. It's her condition." There was a brief pause and Cristiano continued; "The transvestite is quite different. In the case of a male transvestite, he knows he's a man, but he wants to dress like a woman because of the feminine side that exists in his being. Generally, he can have two sexual identities, that is, he likes men and women, or he can only like men or only women. The transvestite feels like a man and a woman. The two concepts are united within him, although he only has one sexual organ, male or female. There are moments when you feel like a man; in another, a woman. But he doesn't want to neutralize any gender in him or in his mind. He does not want to give another definition to his body by changing his sexual organ, making surgeries for sex change. He usually adapts his body with silicone implants, applications and other resources to make the most of the other parts he doesn't have physically. According to most transvestites, who are men, we see that they want to have breasts, hips, full lips, but still have masculine characteristics. This makes them feel complete. They are complete by being men and women. Bisexuals are very different from transvestites. Bisexuals are physically and emotionally attracted to people of both sexes, with levels of interest varying from person to person. The bisexual doesn't necessarily have a different social role, that is, a bisexual man doesn't necessarily have to dress or talk effeminately or deal with a female sexual role in society. This is also true for bisexual women."

"Is he the homosexual in this story?" Said the gentleman.

"A homosexual is someone who is attracted to someone of the same sex. He or she does not necessarily need to have feminine or masculine attitudes, or dress differently than his or her gender, or assume different sexual roles from his or her sex. Therefore, his or her sexual orientation is of the same sex, that is, the homosexual person is attracted to someone of the same sex."

"And what is sexual identity?"

"Sexual identity is how a person sees and perceives himself. Only they themselves know in what image, within this universe, they fit. In her mind, what is she, sexually speaking? What do you like? What do you prefer? A gay man can have a male sexual identity, as well as a heterosexual, because he doesn't want to be a woman. He doesn't want to be passive. He only likes men. There is also the gay man, who likes men and wants to be passive in a relationship with another man, but doesn't want to become, surgically, a woman. If a person knows what his sexual orientation is, that is, what his sexual preference is, he knows his sexual identity."

"The world has changed. I don't accept that."

"It is good to be careful with intolerance, Mr. Salvador. Intolerance and prejudice come from ignorance. The truth is that there is a wide degree of contrast between the male and female extremes. Gender variation among human beings is not aberrant, abnormal or unnatural. Gender variation is purely natural. It is part of nature. We are living among beings that go beyond, far beyond the traditional category of male and female. Did you know that there are hermaphroditic or intersex plants?" The man did not answer and Cristiano continued; "In addition to countless animals that exhibit homosexual behavior such as giraffes, penguins, whales, chimpanzees, dolphins and others. Thousands of beings around us are hermaphrodites, that is, they are intersexual, have male and female sexual organs. The marine crustaceans, called barnacles, that live trapped in the rocks and in the hulls of the ships, are animals in which more than 97% are intersexual. Large percentages of starfish are intersex. Snails and slugs are hermaphrodites or intersexed and need partners to reproduce. In the sea, approximately one third of fish are hermaphrodites. There is a great diversity of gender and sexuality in the world, much greater than we imagine. It is estimated that almost half of the living species on the planet go beyond the known male and female categories. If we study it and know it in depth, we will discover that the variation in gender that is often seen as abnormal and rare is completely natural and not so rare. Transgender, homosexual, bisexual people are no different from the rest of nature created by God. They are the works of God himself. Certainly, for many, it will not be easy to accept this new reality of sex and gender. However, this is not the first time that the human race has been confronted with erroneous beliefs rooted in the culture. Let us remember that the Italian Galileo Galilei, physicist, mathematician and astronomer, faced the Inquisition, the Court of the Holy Office, which condemned him for affirming that the Sun was the planetary center and not the Earth, which revolved around him along with all planets. This contradicted some notes in the Bible, according to the Church. Galileo had to deny his ideas and was sentenced to prison indefinitely, even though he was very sick. He died blind and far from family and social life. Almost 350 years later, the Catholic Church absolved him, but I think it was useless."

"It is true…" Said the thoughtful gentleman.

"In this way, many other things considered unique, real, have already been unmasked and others have not yet been. The same is true for our belief in sexuality and gender. The world is not only divided between men and women and this is a matter of knowledge."

Cristiano paused briefly and considered;

"We can compare intolerance with homosexuality, bisexuality and transgender people with the intolerance and prejudice they had against women, in the past and even today. In many parts of the world, women are still submissive. They are of lower value than animals, which are treated better than they are. There were many struggles by women to get some of the recognition they have today. In some societies, when a girl was born in times of difficulty and scarcity, she was killed by her father or someone who controlled the situation."

"What is that?!" The man was alarmed, upset.

"Some African tribes, Eskimo families had these practices and probably still have them today. More isolated cases also occurred in European and Eastern societies. Only at birth women were killed. Throughout human history, we see women subjected to an inhumane work system, without access to culture, beaten, mistreated, sexually abused and without the right to complain. The search for respect, social, personal and professional dignity for women is very long, since the world is huge. In very recent times, we have seen this. In England, for example, two centuries ago, women alone were a social problem. Single women and widows expressed concern about the economic power that even considered sending these women to the English colonies to fulfill their role as women and to procreate. Something very animalistic, in my

301

opinion. If that happened in the middle of the 19th century, in England, a first world country, can you imagine the rest of the planet? The major feminist movements had to emerge for women to begin to be accepted."

"I think feminists are very aggressive." Said Simone's father.

"Perhaps they really need to be firm in claiming women's rights, because silence and submission achieve nothing. Being firm, perhaps, is confused with aggressiveness. That's where the term sexual role comes in. For a woman to be assertive in what she wants, in what she says, may seem different from the society that sees her, wrongly, as masculinized or something like that. It took, and still does, a lot of attitude and action on her part to guarantee her rights and also to recognize her sense of ability without destroying her feminine gifts. I still think they have a lot of struggle ahead of them. They are still not valued as they should even in our country and even less so in other cultures where, to this day, they are burned, stoned to death, exposed to all kinds of cruelty, humiliation and must be kept quiet, in total silence. You see, all it takes is an accusation of treason, without proof, to throw acid in a woman's face and deform her, kill her and get away with it, as if nothing had been done to the man who beat her horribly. I'm terrified when I remember what is happening today, there, in another country, for lack of common sense, at least."

"There are cultures, even today, that do not allow menstruating women to pray to God, because they believe that, in this condition, they are unclean, dirty and cannot pray." Recalled Simone.

"It is true. They forget that God created women with the condition of menstruating and believe that she cannot receive a prayer from His creation. This is inconsistent. I see the same kind of discrimination and prejudice practiced with those who assume their homosexuality, their intersexuality, their transgendered form. I only hope that something as terrible as what happened to women in New York does not have to happen to begin to recognize their rights."

"Are you talking about International Women's Day?" Simone asked.

"Yes, that's right. The date of March 8 was chosen to represent International Women's Day to symbolize women's emancipation because on March 8, 1857, in New York, workers in a textile factory held a march and then occupied the place where they worked, going on a big strike. They wanted better working conditions, they reduced the workload to ten hours, as the factory required them to work sixteen hours a day. They demanded a salary equal to that of the men, who were paid three times more for doing exactly the same job. They also demanded decent treatment in the workplace, vacations, maternity leave and other rights, which we can call human rights. They gathered in approximately 130 weavers and did not want to leave the factory until the owners promised to meet the requirements. With the arrival of the New York police on the scene, the factory was closed and the employers set fire to the building with all these women inside. Everyone was burned to death and no one was punished as they should have been. This fact had great repercussions at the time through the press. However, it was not until 1910 that March 8 was recognized as International Women's Day in honor of the weavers who were burned to death in 1857 for claiming their just rights. But the sexist universe is so intolerant that, only in 1975, if I'm not mistaken, that date was made official by the UN, United Nations."

"Some people say that this is a women's day and the other 364 days of the year are men's days. I hate that joke." Complained Simone.

"This date was not created just to celebrate women's day. It is important to remember the struggles and rights of women. Many countries, on that day, hold debates, conferences with the objective of inspecting and discussing the role of today's women in society and guaranteeing their rights. The purpose is to reduce, even one day, the prejudices and devaluation of women. Despite the achievements and some recognition, they are still subject mainly to male violence, lower salaries than men, financial and professional disadvantages, in positions similar to those of men, excessive working hours, not counting the other hours of domestic, maternal, matrimonial work…"

"The situation of the woman was so terrible that, in remote times, many believed that she had no soul, that she had no intelligence and that she was a creature much inferior to man." Simone said. "In our country, Brazilian women have only been able to vote since 1932. And the Brazilian Constitution has only offered the same rights to men since 1988. Human beings must be conscious that we are all equal in rights and duties. Not only in companies, industries, in the Constitution, but also within the home. In my opinion, household tasks must also be divided with common sense. I believe that the husband of a woman who works outside the home has a duty to help her with domestic services, especially when they have children."

"I agree." Said Cristiano, while Salvador was only observing and listening. "It was with my father that I learned to help with the household chores. After his death, my brother and I continued to help our mother. We need to end the prejudice that domestic chores are only for women. You mean the man who works retires and the woman doesn't? Women don't have the right to retire from domestic services? What an abuse! That thinking is wrong. Not long ago, the National Congress, in Brasília, was composed mainly of men. When the first women appeared, there was even the so-called lipstick counter, which was the object of mockery and prejudice in this policy exclusive to men."

"That was in 1987 and 1988!" Interrupted Mr. Salvador. "I remember that they even had to fight for the right to have a women's bathroom inside the plenary and they had to make a reform for that."

"Yes, it was like that. The press, at that time, only knew how to pay attention to elegance, beauty, costumes, as if they could only offer and represent that. They only knew how to see who was the most beautiful, the best dressed, the presentation of hairstyles and things like that. Until they managed to impose respect for the various performances. Soon, women had a higher rate of presence in the debates, not only presence, but quality participation. That made the difference." Said the young man.

"Article 52 leaves no doubt that the Constitution has offered principles of equality between men and women since 1988, but this is often quite different in practice." Said Simone.

Appealing to his good memory, Cristiano spoke from memory;

"Article 5a of our Federal Constitution guarantees that men and women shall be equal in rights and obligations; no one shall be obliged to do or refrain from doing anything, except by virtue of the law; no one shall be subjected to torture or to inhuman or degrading treatment; expression of thought is free, anonymity is prohibited; the right of reply, proportional to the appeal, is guaranteed, in addition to compensation for material, moral or image damages. Among other things, the Constitution also guarantees that freedom of conscience is inviolable. Even so, as I told you, women still suffer as if they were different, abnormal, less capable, which, above all, they are not. This issue goes a long way. There is much to tell, in the history of humanity, up to this day, about the prejudice, the discrimination that women suffer, due to

305

the fact that ignorant people think they were another race, besides the human race. Just as I see what happens to homosexuals, transsexuals, transvestites and others, today they are rejected in the armed forces, in many companies, institutions, religions… They are discriminated against in many societies and there is even a death penalty for homosexuals in Muslim countries. In them, someone is killed officially just because they are homosexual, that is, they are killed as a result of the laws. Although, in our country and in other countries, murder and personal injury are crimes, there are extreme homophobic groups that seriously injure and kill homosexuals and transgender people because they have this condition. This is absurd! They are living and thinking like those ignorant groups of people who killed and abused women because they were women."

"Ignorance is not only that. It goes beyond that. Have you heard that some Brazilian indigenous tribes today kill boys with physical or mental problems because they are born in this condition?" Said Simone.

"Yes, they even bury them alive. And it's not just kids with problems. In the case of the twins, it's the same with one of the boys, even though she's totally healthy. The one who should be dead is chosen by the shaman. Pajé or shaman, is the name given to the man of the tribe, usually the eldest, who is a spiritual specialist, a kind of doctor, sorcerer, healer and priest. He is given the power to communicate with beings who have died, whether human or animal. These are archaic, barbaric and wrong customs of ignorant, inhuman and cruel people. The same is true for homosexuals and transgender people. They are discriminated against, ridiculed, mistreated and humiliated as a result of ignorance and prejudice of people who are unhappy with themselves."

"What do you mean?" He was interested.

"I have this intolerance for me. Prejudices are practices of people who are poorly resolved, unhappy with themselves. Keep in mind that people who are truly satisfied and happy with themselves are not intolerant or prejudiced. They live well and let others live."

After a little reflection, Mr. Salvador commented;

"I didn't know anything about what you told me about the charred women on March 8 and I didn't remember the discrimination, intolerance and prejudice against women. But I still can't agree with homosexuality. God created man and woman, but he did not create a homosexual."

"Homosexual is a condition equal to that of heterosexual. The child is born this way. Most homosexual people have their sexual identity firmly established. Many are unaware that one was already born homosexual, intersex or transgender, just as one was already born heterosexual. It is not a choice."

"I don't agree, Cristiano. This is pure choice." He insisted.

"It is not a choice. And the destiny of the creature that God created. Otherwise, God would not allow a physical and material difference to exist when the human body of that being is being formed."

"What? Are you going to tell me that the gay body is different from that of normal people?" Said Mr. Salvador.

"First, we are all normal, whether we are gay or straight. Second, today, science has already identified the first anatomical difference, that is, the first physical, material difference, in the brain of homosexuals. For prejudiced academics in the scientific world, this still generates controversy, polemics, and many say there are several questions to be answered. However, research and studies, quite significant, recently carried out in Sweden, show that homosexual men and heterosexual women have a greater activity in a region of the hypothalamus, a region associated with emotions and sexual impulses, when exposed to testosterone, derived from male sweat. In contrast, heterosexual men have the same reaction when exposed to estrogen, the female hormone. This test was made possible with the use of new brain mapping technologies. In addition to countless other research and studies such as similar genetic markers in families with a larger number of homosexual relatives, which have not yet been approved. The most relevant is the study of the function and development of the visual areas of the cerebral cortex where it was possible to discover the first anatomical difference, that is, the physical difference in the brain of homosexuals. In the scientific world, there is much talk about mapping or isolation, to find the gene for homosexuality in the coming years. While some consider that homosexuality is not genetic, DNA research of transgender men: intersex, transsexual and some homosexuals reveal that they have a gene associated with the hormone testosterone that is less efficient. The reduction of this hormone can interfere with the development of the fetus' gender, which is still forming in the uterus, leading to a less masculine brain. Given the material, physical and anatomical discoveries in this small part of the hypothalamus and the reduction of testosterone, we can already say that, in homosexuality, there is the will of God or the body would not have these differences for that soul, that spirit would experience such duality. So, that proves that everything on Earth is the work of nature. It is the work of God. Therefore, any condition of living in this world, sexually speaking, is not a choice, but a destiny. In that sense, I'm not talking about attitudes, human behavior."

"I've heard that homosexuals should sublimate, that is, not have sex, abstain from sex. What do you think?" Simone asked.

"It depends on each one. In my opinion, I understand that sexual relations are the process, the act that guarantees the reproduction of the species. When we talk about the human species, we must understand that the sexual act is the mechanism responsible for the genetic and continuous variability of the species and, consequently, for the survival of the human race. If sex were used only for reproductive purposes, as some say it is God's will in the biblical passage: *grow up and multiply,* so heterosexuals should also abstain from sex, not practice sex when it was not for the sole purpose of procreation."

"How so?" Mr. Salvador wanted to understand.

"In the opinion of some, sex can only be practiced between a man and a woman because between these two the purpose of the sexual act would be to multiply. With this mentality, the heterosexual couple, who did not want to have any more children, should no longer have sex, they should also sublimate. I think that abstaining from sex is not right. Sex has a physiological, biological and unconscious function that results in many benefits. Sexual energy is creative. The problem is how to practice sex. Homosexuals, transgenders, and heterosexuals can misuse this act when there is vulgarity, promiscuity, and light living. This behavior will surely disturb your conscience one day. Some sex addicts need as much psychological help as an addict to alcohol, drugs, gambling, etc. whether they are gay or straight."

"There are many unhappy homosexuals who use drugs and drink because they are homosexuals." Said Mr. Salvador.

"Drug addiction and alcoholism are not exclusive to homosexuals - explained the young man. - You are wrong, if you believe that. What, perhaps, you see, and may happen is that a homosexual has a strict, intolerant, ignorant family and when that person discovers his homosexuality, he faces a great emotional struggle, an excessive concern for his condition because of the family he has. After much conflict, he does not know what is happening to him. Confused and trying to relieve stress and conflict, he may interfere with alcohol or drugs. He may begin to live a promiscuous life, corrupting himself. However, Mr. Salvador, many heterosexuals, in conflict, also choose the path of drugs and alcoholism, for countless other reasons, including in the sexual area. Let us remember that many homosexuals do not deviate from these addictions at all. What mistreats the homosexual most is the ignorant and intolerant rigor of the family, acquaintances, society and their own ignorance. What mistreats him is that he does not understand his condition." For a moment, Cristiano observed the thoughtful man. He waited for a moment and clarified; "I'm a spiritualist. Although there are many spiritists who are ignorant and even intolerant of the subject of homosexuality, what makes them is not the spiritist philosophy, but their own opinions and ignorance of the subject. The Spiritist doctrine, its codification, has no prejudices and practically does not manifest itself in this respect. Remember that the Spirit does not have sex and that we can incarnate a man today and a woman tomorrow. The Spiritist doctrine defends the thesis that the higher is the evolution of a spirit, the more use it has on lived experiences. This indicates experiences as a man and a woman, suffering conflicts, harmonizing their practices in different lives, in innumerable trials, exercises, attempts, tests, and all that God leaves at our disposal. We must live, whatever it is, with morality and unconditional love for ourselves and for others."

"Why are you born homosexual or transgender? Why this suffering?"

"We are all in evolutionary transit, so, as I said, we were born with the need for countless experiences. Being born in the homosexual or any other condition does not mean suffering or atonement. One is only unhappy and suffers when one does not accept what happens to oneself, when one lives in ignorance. By understanding and accepting his condition, a person can become a provider of blessings, light and love. The most important thing is not how the spirit reincarnates, but how it uses its conditions, its attributes. We are all entitled to choices. This is called free will, but when we depreciate ourselves in multiple relationships and lose a sense of balance, of self-love, we devalue ourselves, we become demoralized. This leads us to suffer and, I would like to remind you, that this is true for extramarital relationships in heterosexual marriages."

"They say God is good, but where is his goodness in that?" Asked the gentleman in a snappy tone.

"The goodness of God is found in reincarnation. It is through him that the spirit learns to love, not to do evil, to live well in order to evolve towards better worlds, because Jesus said that there are many abodes in the Father's house and I believe in him. When we reincarnate, we are born with all the possibilities necessary to grow. Even when we experience difficulties and difficult trials, these situations are for our evolution, for our good." After he said that, silence reigned for a long time. Mr. Salvador was thoughtful and said nothing during all that time. He seemed to revise his misconceptions and beliefs. He discovered that there was more to learn about the world and nature than he could have imagined. Cristiano smiled and concluded. "You know, Mr. Savior, I don't like to have blind faith in any subject, so I appreciate Master Jesus' famous sentence: *you shall know the truth and the truth shall set you free*. Think about all that we talked about. Try to reflect and question whether you are right or wrong. If you are wrong, admit it and you will see that you will be happier. Set yourself free."

At that moment, Mrs. Celeste entered the room and greeted the young man.

The theme changed. But Mr. Salvador had much to analyze about the whole very instructive conversation.

Meanwhile, in spirituality, Vitória and Juan observed them.

Some time ago, she left the spiritual workshop, which was an extension of Mrs. Janaina's house, following a more enlightened spirit to learn. That day, her mentor Juan took her to accompany Cristiano. After listening to all that was said, Juan commented;

311

"Sometimes, someone's homosexual experience is more of a difficult experience for other people than for the homosexual himself, who understands and accepts himself. Many do not understand that God's law is summed up in love. "Love your neighbor as I loved you." Although everyone has a spiritual reason for incarnating homosexuals, heterosexuals, transgenders or bisexuals... Although the reasons are different, they all share a common theme: a story that invites us to open our minds, eyes and hearts to consider and learn about the different forms of sexuality and the different genders that exist and are not accepted, not recognized, not tolerated, for now. Reincarnation exists through divine mercy. We are all subject to it. Sexual differences, in sexual behavior and sexual relationships, must be understood and balanced. There is nothing to eliminate or punish. The behavior of all belongs to him."

Surprised, Vitória marveled;

"How Cris has changed! How he learned! I have never had a class like this in my life. I started to understand that the biggest problem is not homosexuality, being transgendered or bisexuality, but prejudice." She thought about it and wanted to know; "Do you think that prejudiced homophobes can be reincarnated as homosexuals?"

"This is determined by one's conscience. The laws of God are recorded in the consciousness of the creature. When a homosexual is reincarnated, for example, logically, it happens with the consent of that spirit. Every earthly experience is for spiritual evolution, it is for individual or collective progress. No one ever reincarnates to go backwards in his progress. Never."

"Can you tell me why Abner and David are gay?"

"They reincarnated homosexuals by decision, by evolution, by mission. It may not seem like much, but the harmonious way of living is a work done, a mission, as an example to others. Observe, by behavior, that they are advanced spirits. They want to know what it is like to live this experience and to help others in the fight against intransigence. The evolved spirits often come to help in the work that some are trying to do, which is to demystify, remove the veil of prejudice regarding sex, gender. The world needs a lot to get rid of intolerance."

The spirit of Juan responded perfectly well. As explained in *The Spirits Book*, question 132 says; *What is the purpose of the incarnation of the spirits? - God imposes incarnation on them to reach perfection. For some, it is atonement; for others, a mission. But to achieve this perfection, they have to suffer all difficulties of the bodily existence: this is what expiation is about. The incarnation has another objective, which is to put the Spirit in a position to support his part in the work of Creation. To achieve it, in every world, the Spirit takes an instrument, in harmony with the essential matter of that world, to fulfill God's orders from that point of view. This is how, competing for the general work, it advances itself.*

Remembering that, in the sequence, the question 133 is completed; *Do the spirits that, from the beginning, followed the path of good, need the incarnation? - All are created simple and ignorant and are instructed through the struggles and tribulations of bodily life. God, who is just, could not make some people happy, without pain and work, and therefore without merit.*

In spite of having knowledge of the Spiritist doctrine, Vitória was reluctant to accept. She was not flexible and kept on questioning:

"But... Could an evolved spirit want to step back, in such difficulty, to try to help others in such complicated situations?" Victoria asked.

"Jesus, an incredibly evolved spirit, reincarnated in such barbaric times, so barbaric that he was crucified for preaching love. He did a lot to help mankind, didn't he?" He smiled enigmatically.

"They could be homosexuals and abstain from sex, right?"

"And what example of good morals, good behavior, respect and fidelity would you give to others if you did?" There was silence. Then, Juan explained; "Many times, one cannot go against plans of reincarnation. Reincarnated, with the blessing of oblivion, Abner, upon understanding his condition, intended to sublimate his sex life, to abstain from sex. However, when he found a similar soul, he believed that, together, they could evolve together and harmoniously. Without scandals, without unbalanced behavior, without depravity, they serve as an example to all those who accompany them. The particular reason for this, only interests them. However, they help to break down prejudices. The life of others does not belong to us. The important thing is to take care of ourselves, to observe our speech, our thoughts and our actions." After a few moments of letting her reflect, he asked; "Can we go now?"

She agreed and they returned to the house that received them with generous blessings. There they would continue with further explanations.

This conversation gave Mr. Salvador a lot of information that he ignored. He would have much to think about.

15.– PEDRO ARRIVES HOME

IN THE COMPANY where she worked, Rúbia felt a little more at ease. The embarrassment of the beginning, due to the pregnancy, had diminished and the colleagues got used to it, without asking more questions. However, when she met Jefferson, she looked away. She inhibited herself and, if she could, she deviated from her way.

It was early in the evening when, together with Talita, they walked to the subway station, huddled under a single umbrella and Rúbia commented;

"My sister is very worried about Pedro. He is still in the hospital."

"Poor thing. No discharge forecast?"

"I don't know. It's been a month since he was born and he never went home. Poor thing. It's so sad to see him there in the hospital."

"Did your brother-in-law visit him?"

"Only once, can you believe it?"

"I admire your sister very much. She is very strong. Good thing, right?"

"You know, she was the one who had to go to the registry office to register Pedro. Samuel didn't even do that."

"Are you kidding?!"

"My idiot brother-in-law didn't even do that. After my sister left the hospital, he didn't visit or call. What he did was deposit the

315

alimony into her account as if only the money was going to be offered. There is night and dawn when I hear her walking around the house. Sometimes she stands at the window of her room looking out onto the empty street." After a moment, she commented; "We have been in the Spiritist center with the owner Janaina and Cristiano. I feel that it does us a lot of good."

"If that's good for you, then go ahead."

"Going there gives me peace. My situation is not easy either. I live in my sister's house, I will have a child and I know that I will not be able to count on the father's help, I will probably be fired after maternity leave. This means that I will not have money, doctors, security... I will be even more dependent. Besides, I'm afraid of what Jefferson might do."

"After he went to the police station, did he ever come back to you?"

"No. He never spoke to me again. Still, I'm very afraid. I'm very worried about the future and…"

"Are you going to register the baby in his name?"

"At first, I thought about doing that, but now I'm changing my mind. My case is different from many people. For me, it's like Jefferson represents danger and…"

They were on the sidewalk, near the subway steps, when they heard;

"Rúbia!!!"

In the distance, they looked and saw Ricardo's car stop and someone running down the rain to the stairs.

They approached and he, from inside the vehicle, leaning on the passenger seat, asked aloud;

"Are you going home? Do you want a ride?"

"I do! If it doesn't get in your way..." Accepted the friend. Saying goodbye to Talita, who continued on her way, she got into the car and greeted Ricardo.

"What about your colleague? Doesn't she want a ride?"

"Talita is going in the opposite direction." Rúbia got into the car seat and then asked. "I couldn't even say hello to your friend properly because of the rain. Does he work with you?"

Ricardo offered her a generous smile. It wasn't the first time he had had that experience. Politely, he replied;

"*He* was my sister. She stopped at the company and, due to the unexpected rain, asked for a ride here."

Rúbia was embarrassed as never before. She didn't know what to say to redeem herself. Legitimately ashamed, she seemed to be begging when said;

"Ricardo... For God's sake, I'm sorry. I didn't get a good look at her... I was under the umbrella and... It's just that she's very thin, with short hair and... I thought..."

"You don't have to be like that." He smiled sympathetically. With a soft and meticulous speech, he explained:

"My sister is a transsexual. Unlike Abner and David, who are gay. She expresses this in the way she dresses, talks and presents herself. All of her sketches are male. She considers herself and feels like a man. She simply did not have surgery. Lately, she is undergoing hormonal treatment to get more hair, a thicker voice, and muscles."

"I remember... I saw her on your birthday. Sorry for the mistake."

"I must take you to Simone's house, right?"

"Yes, please."

He continued to drive while commenting;

"I have two sisters, Eloah and Bia. The one you just saw is Eloah. Bia is in New York and she won't be back until next month."

"Are you the big brother?"

"Yes, I'm five years older than Eloah and seven years older than Bia." Rúbia was silent. She didn't know what to say after the farce. After a while, when the friend understood her shame, she commented;

"I really liked your mother. She is very friendly."

"Now she is like this; friendly, happy... But, not in the old days. My mother was very serious. She didn't make jokes. She didn't have fun. She was a workaholic and very competent."

"What did she do?"

"She still does. She is a lawyer. She is a partner in a renowned firm. She is a very dedicated but strict mother."

"What about your father?"

"My father lives in Argentina. They got divorced and he remarried. I have a brother who is eight years old." He laughed. "Can you believe it?"

"How interesting," She smiled. "Does your mother live alone?"

"Only when Bia travels. Eloah does not live with her, as she has a partner and her own apartment."

"I understand." A while later, she asked; "You said your mother was more serious. What made her change?"

Ricardo smiled in a funny way. He looked at her and said;

"Since we have a good traffic jam ahead of us... I'll have time to tell you, if you want to hear it."

"Of course, I want to. Tell me." She smiled happily.

"Since I can remember, when I was a child, my mother was... let's say... a normal person. A few years after Eloah's birth, she started acting differently. She was more serious, silent. I should have been about ten or twelve years old and I remember when my mother went to various doctors and psychologists because of Eloah."

"Why?"

"Eloah had firmly established her sexual identity since she was a child. Around the age of three, she only wanted toys for boys. Mine, of course." He laughed, looking to the side and observing her friend's reaction. "She didn't like girl's dresses or accessories or ornaments like hair ornaments, bracelets, necklaces, rings or shoes with colorful details, no way. She used to take them off. She used to cry. She didn't want to wear them at all. Realizing this, my mother was not satisfied. She sought out pediatricians, psychiatrists, psychologists and nothing. When my mother saw that it was irreversible, she began to be closed. Eloah, after the age of twelve or so, could no longer be controlled. Everything about her was male, from her manners to her clothes. Once she cut her hair on her own because my mother wanted her to lengthen it."

"What about your other sister?"

"Completely different. Bia seems to have been born inside the most refined shopping center and already in high heels." He laughed. "She is feminine from head to toe. Only... Well, let me tell you about Eloah and my mother, then I'll talk about Bia." There was a brief pause and he continued;

"Being older, curious and observant, I realized that Eloah was a friend to girls and that it wasn't just friendship. My mother was upset. They fought a lot. This sister of mine graduated in Civil Engineering. It's not a female profession, in my opinion. I tried to take her to work with me, because she was a great professional, but she didn't want to. She started working for a big construction company, where she is today and very well. Some time ago, she met Suzana. They went out and decided to be together. That was

319

the last straw for my mother, who did not accept it. She argued, offended and did not want to listen to us when we tried to alleviate the situation, making her understand." After a few seconds, he said; "Abner and I were friends for a long time and I expressed a lot with him about my sister. It was at this time that I learned of his homosexuality."

"I never realized that my brother was gay."

"Me neither. To tell you the truth, I was a little impressed. I didn't think he was gay, but I saw that it didn't interfere with our friendship. On the contrary, he could understand my sister very well and helped to enlighten me immensely. We are still more friends than ever. It was thanks to Abner that I stopped being ignorant, understood Eloah better, and we became more friends because, despite accepting her, I didn't understand her. At that moment, my mother became more serious and close-minded than ever and immersed herself in work. Then, to make my mother's situation worse, Bia, my younger sister, began to understand herself better and discovered that she was asexual."

Ricardo was quietly waiting for the same question he always had, when he talked to someone about this subject. It didn't take long and it arrived:

"Asexual? What is that?"

"Asexual is a person who is indifferent to sex, to sexual practice. You do not feel like getting involved with anyone. She has no sexual attraction to the same sex or the opposite sex."

"I've never heard of that."

"But it exists. The asexual person is not gay. You don't have hormonal or physical problems. You are not transgendered. You don't have a disorder and you haven't suffered trauma. That person just doesn't want to, doesn't like to, doesn't need to, has no interest in having sex with anyone. They deprive… abstain from sex and they fight for their rights and that's it. There are even those who want to fight for asexuality to be recognized as the fourth sexual orientation, since heterosexuals, homosexuals, transgender people and now asexuals already exist. Some groups have already begun to appear in homosexual marches around the world, but they are much smaller groups than homosexuals."

"I don't know if I understand, but... If these people are asexual, I mean, they don't like sex, I think it would be easier to just not have sex and that's it. Why do they need to stand up for rights, raise the flag on the issue? Isn't it just being quiet enough?"

"It's not that simple, Rúbia. Asexuals experience a lot of prejudice from having this behavior. They think that's enough. Friends mistake them for homosexuals just because they don't see them staying in, going out, kissing, dating. There is always pressure from society in relation to the intimate lives of others. In daily socializing, at work, at the gym, at the club, and other places, over time, others want to know who you stayed with, who you went out with, who you had sex with? And when the asexual person has nothing to tell, does not reveal their particular life, they think they are gay or transgender. Among the asexuals or asexuals, as far as I know, there are two groups: the romantic asexuals, who can go out, fall in love, get married without having sex with each other, and even have children by artificial insemination. Maybe a kiss, for some. The others are non-romantic asexuals. They do not accept affection, do not fall in love, do not have any intimate contact, do not kiss or caress each other. Like everything that exists, there are always people against it, there are those who do not believe in the existence of asexuality, but it exists and research with animals such as sheep, lambs, rats and others can confirm that, in nature, these people are not alone, because there are, in other species, creatures in the same asexual condition. Let us remember that in the past similar statements have been made about homosexuals and transgender people."

"You told me that your sister, Bia, is very feminine. I understood that she likes to dress up and everything... How can that be?"

"Being asexual does not mean that you are no longer a man or woman, much less caring for yourself. In fact, Bia is very feminine. She's also very beautiful. But that doesn't mean anything. You need to know her to know what I'm talking about. She's extremely happy without sex and doesn't understand why, in today's society, everything is sex and sexuality. Asexuals don't want to have sex and that's it. Some even tolerate sex, but it doesn't mean anything, others couldn't bear the experience." Rúbia didn't ask any more questions and Ricardo continued. "When Bia arrived with this news, which for my mother was another scare, the house fell down!" He laughed.

"I think Bia should have been quiet, don't you think?"

"Ahhh...! If I had been her, I would have done the same. Do you know why?" Without waiting for an answer, he said; "My mother used her as an example of femininity to try to change Eloah's condition, as if that were possible. She also accused Bia, asking her when she would get a boyfriend, get married, give her grandchildren…that kind of thing. Then Bianca couldn't take the pressure and stepped up. She said she went out, kissed, had unwanted sex, and it was a horror. She no longer wanted to know about the intimate contact. She said she suffered a lot at first, especially during the period when she didn't understand herself. She saw the other friends excited, interested in the boys, but she didn't feel anything. When she tried to understand her condition, she found herself asexual. After she began to understand herself better and know who she was, Bia said she began to be really happy. She doesn't like sex and that's it. She lives well with that. Incredibly, she has an American boyfriend, who is also asexual."

Rúbia smiled and asked curiously;

"How can that be? Is it hard to find a good guy to go out with and she, who doesn't like intimacy, has one with a condition as rare as hers? How do they go out?"

"In this world we find everything. I was also interested in knowing how they went out." They laughed together. "One day I couldn't stand it and asked. She told me that they are romantic asexuals. They walk hand in hand, exchanging affection. At most a kiss like a little kiss. Nothing else. And she said they are complete and happy like that."

"Are you kidding?!"

"No!" He laughed willingly.

"How did she meet him?"

"The company he works for sent him to New York. He works at headquarters. They met there and, when she returned to Brazil, they started talking on the Internet and became great friends. When one of them discovered that the other was an asexual romantic: they started dating. He has already come to Brazil. He even stayed at my mother's house, who didn't have to see the two of them." He laughed willingly.

"Ricardo!" She scolded him and laughed together.

"And isn't it true? We hardly see them exchanging affection; barely they are holding hands. And look... Clearly, we realize that they are in love. Don't ask me how, just by seeing." After a moment, he commented; "You hardly hear of asexuals here in Brazil; however, they do exist. And I say more: you do not need to have a sexual relationship to understand being asexual. It's a condition and that's it. I understand it and I accept it very well. Just as there are people who are sexually compulsive and need sex every day or several times a day, there are those who are happy with sex once, twice, or three times a week. There are those who are satisfied with having sex once a month or twice a month. In between, there are also those who are perfectly happy without having any sex at all. It is that simple."

"What about your mother?"

"Well, at first it was chaos. My mother did not accept and my father, always absent, did not give his opinion. My parents' marriage did not go well for a long time and in the height of that period it ended. Time passed and Eloah went to live her life and Bia needed to stay there in New York. During that time, my mother became very ill. She was having problems and a very serious bowel obstruction led to surgery. After the surgery, she had complications, infection, and had to stay in the I.C.U. When she came home, with a drain and everything, she was very weak. She suffered a lot. She needed help with everything, including bathing. I couldn't help her, but Eloah, besides working all day, was not very good. She is more masculine than I am, I must admit. It was then that Suzana, her partner, took care of my mother, who could not say anything. She had no other choice. Suzana lived there with her for over a month. She helped my mother in the bathroom, in the bathtub, with the drainage, and the dressings… It was a lot of work. Suzana was great."

"They became friends and started to get along very well. Eloah returned to my mother's house and she became much more understanding, flexible and, in time, understood and accepted her condition and union. After that, her life changed and my mother became a different person. Happier, happier, more understanding, kind… She even got younger! Not to mention that her health was excellent. Psychologically speaking, I think the bowel obstruction occurred because she got stuck, closed, and was bitter towards people and herself. Unfortunately, she had to suffer a lot because of it."

"I understand. Sometimes we need to suffer in order to learn. I know what that is."

"Stubbornness." He said, smiling. "When we are stubborn, we show our pride, our arrogance and how much we are inferior spirits. We must keep in mind that the most important thing is to take care of ourselves, to watch our actions, our thoughts, our words and let each one take care of his own life."

"You know how surprised I was when I heard about Abner's homosexuality. I couldn't accept it at all. However, I could not see that I was more frivolous, more reckless than he was."

"Don't say that about yourself." He said, politely. "You don't have to mistreat yourself. Sometimes we have to make mistakes in order to learn and evolve".

"It is not easy to admit what we are or what we were. I admit. I acted very badly. I knew Jefferson was married and I stayed with him. You can't imagine how I feel."

She was silent for a long time, then she confessed;

"I regretted so much that it took me a long time to see myself as a mother, to accept my son. It was complicated."

"That phase of non-acceptance of the baby has passed, hasn't it?

"Yes, it has. Now I can talk to him, feel him as my own." She said with a beautiful smile.

"What's his name?"

"Bruno."

"Nice name! I like it."

"Thank you."

"And... And Jefferson accompanies you or helps you with something?"

"He didn't care and I didn't want him to. I decided not to register my son with his last name."

"I think you should put his name on it. Well... I wish my son had my name, even if his mother and I weren't together."

"You think so, but it's not your case. Jefferson wanted me to take away that boy, he was mistreating me, threatening me."

"Yes, I know."

"I will not hide his origin from Bruno. I will let him decide whether or not he wants his father's name on his papers."

"It is very strange for me to see a man reject his son, like what is happening. I can't see myself far from Renan. You know, when I got divorced... Jeez! For me it was the end of the world. This happened more or less when my mother was having surgery. That was one of the reasons why I got a little far away from her. I looked terrible and I didn't want her to see me like that."

"That's when you started going to the house, right?"

"That's right. I had nowhere to go. I was very upset and Abner, as always, gave me the greatest strength."

"Why did you and your wife separate?"

"It was sudden. Something totally unexpected. For me, our marriage was perfect. One day, like this, Flora said she was unsatisfied and needed some time. I thought it was a joke, but it wasn't. It took me a week to believe it. That's because she started sleeping in Renan's room, after putting a mattress on the floor. I went crazy. I couldn't work or eat. She didn't pay attention to anything. My life has become meaningless. There was no explanation. We sat down, talked a lot several times, but... There was no way she wanted a divorce. I broke down. I rented an apartment and moved out. I signed the divorce and accepted everything she wanted. I went into a depression and sought the company of friends, because I didn't want to be alone. A terrible fear of loneliness hit me. I also decided not to get involved with anyone else. It was at that moment that Abner took me to the Spiritist center and introduced me to Mrs. Janaina and her children.

We became friends, I went to your house and talked a lot. It helped me immensely. I began to go to the Spiritist center and I began to compose myself. Sometime later, I was devastated again when I heard that Flora was getting married. In time, I got used to the idea. Today, thanks to Renán, we maintain bonds of friendship. What gave me a lot of strength was the fact that I had my son. I needed to be on my feet because of him. We are very connected. We talk every day on the phone, and we see each other several times a week. I'm with him in everything."

"It is very important to be friends with your child, especially in case of separation. Do you get along with her current husband?"

"We respect each other, we treat each other well. That's good enough for me. I don't need to make friends with him. However, if one day it is necessary... There will be no difficulty. I'm glad that he is a good friend of my son. Renan is the one who says that."

"I believe that if I wait for Jefferson to take action, my son will never meet him."

"You are in a position to be a great mother. Provide education, limit, teach respect, affection, attention. Give it all and that's what you'll get."

"My father, in all his ignorance, says that the boy whose parents demand respect and limit, becomes a more docile teenager and a happy, more aware adult. I believe in that."

"It is true. Excess freedom leaves the boy uncontrolled, uneducated and disrespectful to others, especially the elderly."

"You know... I'm very scared, Ricardo."

"Fear?"

"Yes, fear of the future, of not being able to cope, of failure. I will definitely be out of work after maternity leave. I'm living at my sister's house and, for now, I can help with the expenses, but I don't know how long."

"The father must pay a pension. Nothing could be fairer."

"Our conversation has not been at all friendly lately. Ah... There are days when my head boils. It is not easy."

"I can imagine." Silence reigned for a while until he said; "We are here!"

"Let's go in, Ricardo."

"No. Save it for another day."

"So... Thank you very much."

They said goodbye with a kiss on the cheek. She got out of the car and went inside.

At home, she realized that Simone was not there. She probably went to visit her son in the hospital.

Rúbia felt a tightness in her chest and a lump in her throat. She was distressed and unsure. Her soul ached and she cried in silence.

She loved the child she was expecting, but she knew she would experience many difficulties. Everything might have been different if she had listened to what her brother had told her when he found out about her relationship with Jefferson. She knew that an affair with a married man could only end in pain, discomfort, frustration and much bitterness on both sides.

She lacked prudence and control of emotions. She was very impulsive when she gave in to false and ephemeral happiness.

She knew she had to plan her life, her future and have goals, but how? Without job security, without a supportive partner to help her, and with a baby on the way, it would be very difficult.

Sometimes she believed that her father would call her to live with him and her mother. She didn't like it either. She didn't feel comfortable with this situation. She would be dependent in the same way.

Now she knew the price and the burden of responsibility. The house, the clothes, the food, the medicine and so many other needs would weigh on her shoulders.

Suddenly, a noise took her out of her reflections. The front door opened slowly and Simone entered very slowly, carrying her little boy on her lap, wrapped in a blanket.

Seeing her sister, Simone smiled and whispered with satisfaction:

"Welcome home, my son. This is our home." Then she turned to Rúbia and said; "He is asleep. He was discharged today."

Behind Simone, Cristiano entered with a bag and an envelope in which he would probably have documents and hospital examinations.

Rúbia hurried to her sister and carefully lowered the fold of the blanket to see Pedro. The boy was sleeping soundly.

Now, very close, the aunt could see him better and his smile was closing, without him noticing. She began to be impressed by the appearance of her nephew.

His face had slight deformities. The ears were displaced, very low, near the jaw. He had a cleft lip, a clenched fist in one hand and an extra little finger in the other.

Feeling an indescribable bitterness, Rúbia tried to hide her impression when she saw the simple smile on her sister's face. She embraced him with careful affection, then she bowed to the boy, kissed him on the top of her head and murmured;

"Welcome Pedro. God bless you."

"Thank you, auntie." Imitating a low, childlike voice, Simone responded to her son.

329

After greeting Cristiano, she turned to his sister and asked her;

"Why didn't you say he would be discharged today?"

"They called in the afternoon from the hospital, reporting the discharge. I was going to visit him by myself. Since I knew that our parents had already gone to the doctor, I didn't even say anything about the discharge to them so as not to disturb them. They waited almost two months for this visit. I called Abner, but he was inspecting a job, so I didn't warn him. Before I did, he told me he was excited and very busy with something. I decided not to get in the way. I thought about calling Cláudio, my friend, but he couldn't, he was teaching. Only Cristiano was able. So, I took his clothes, called a cab and, having patients, Cris could only pick us up right now, early in the night."

"It's good to have friends." Admitted Rúbia with a slight smile. "Thank you, Cristiano."

"Why... I didn't do anything." He was embarrassed. Addressing Simone, he suggested; "Better put him in the crib, don't you think?"

"Yes, it is true." She kindly agreed. Simone went to Pedro's room while Rúbia, motionless in the room, did not leave.

Cristiano accompanied his friend. When he returned, he found the other one in the room, in the same position.

"What is it, Rúbia?"

She put her hands on her face, covering her mouth and partially covering her nose. She stood up slowly and cried in silence. She didn't want her sister to hear her.

The boy came over, sat down next to her and hugged her. Putting her face on his shoulder, he asked;

"Why are you like this, huh?"

"It is very sad. I'm impressed."

"Calm down. Don't be like this. You're sensitive because of the pregnancy and…"

"Simone can't see me like this." She said, wiping her face. Moving away from the embrace, she sighed deeply and confessed; "It is so difficult now… Before, in the hospital, with the glass and the distance, I couldn't see him very well."

"Try to be strong. It will be good for you and your sister. There is no way to correct Pedro's condition. There is nothing to comfort you now. That is why it is necessary to believe that God, in allowing this situation, has a purpose, and that purpose is the evolution, not only of Pedro, but also of all those who are close to him. We must remember that nothing is eternal. No suffering, no condition is eternal. God does not condemn us to endless suffering. In what we live are experiences of reparation. Sometimes these experiences are suffered, but never forever. This moment of Peter and all those involved with him, directly or indirectly in his life, will pass."

"Am I wrong to be impressed?"

"Why wrong?" Without waiting for an answer, Cristiano explained; "There is no mistake. It would be a mistake to shout, to exclaim "Jeez! How different he is! Look at his mouth as it is!" These and other observations are inconvenient, incorrect. We should not point out the differences of others. Being impressed is part of the surprise, whether it is good or not. You were surprised by your sensitivity."

"I was a little afraid?" She muttered.

"Of what?"

"That my baby was born that way. I told my doctor everything that was going on and he calmed me down. He explained it very well, but… In my head, sometimes I think I might have the same problem as Pedro."

"We always want our children and relatives to be born perfect and in good health, because we want their good. However, if this does not happen, we must respect God's will."

Standing up, Cristiano offered her a friendly smile, extended his hand and shouted;

"Come on, let's change our minds. Let's see if Simone needs help."

"It is true. Come on." She smiled and accepted the offered hand. When they entered the room in silence, they found a beautiful scene. The mother, lying on her side, caressed sweetly and lovingly the son who, by her side, was sleeping deeply.

16.– LOVE IS NEEDED
TO BE HAPPY

IN THESE LAST MONTHS, the spirit Vitória accompanied, as far as possible, some of the incarnates along with Juan or other spirits of the same elevation as his mentor.

When she went to her parents' residence, she did not feel well. They idolized her. They believed that she had evolved a lot and had countless spiritual missions as a spirit of considerable prestige. As a result, little prayers and good thoughts were directed to her. On the contrary, they made requests of her.

"They are wrong!" Vitória groaned in the shadow of great bitterness. "Juan, my parents believe that I'm fit to be a minister in some colony or, at least, a rescuer in spirituality. They think I live on very high planes, when, in fact, I'm still in the earth's crust."

"They were wrong. Because they are spiritists, they think that you…" She interrupted and joked;

"They think that I arrived with devastating spirituality, when, in fact, I arrived devastated! What a rage! They think I have a high moral quality. They think I qualify as a superior spirit, prudent or wise. Some people in the house of the spiritists continue to fill me with petitions, pleading as if I were a saint. I feel bad about that. Very bad. Even my parents and relatives beg me and my brother to intercede."

"That was a big mistake they made. However, don't blame them. The desperation of separating from a child is immense and makes parents lose control. In your case, they lost two, which is much worse. So, the best thing for you was to be in the spiritual post that exists in Janaina's house. The vibrations directed to you through David, Janaina and Cristiano, strengthened and protected you."

"And my brother? Where is Vanilson? How is he?"

"Better than you."

"And you tell me that... just like this!"

"What did you want me to answer, Vitória? Your brother is fine. He went to a colony. He was helped. In the next few weeks, he should move in with your grandparents."

"Wait, how so?! Vanilson was... he was... Diabolic! He killed us!" She protested.

"Are you sure?"

Her mentor's question sounded so serious that Vitória was silent for a moment.

The penetrating gaze of the mentor, fixed on her for a long time, shook her. Until she wanted to know;

"How so? Vanilson killed us. He was the one who was driving."

"Do you vividly remember the exact moment of the accident?" The silence was total. Juan's spirit continued to narrate, provoking mental scenes in Vitória, making her remember; "Everyone got into the car after Cristiano decided to sit in the back seat. Vanilson was driving and you were next to him. As always, demanding, nervous, dissatisfied and that was enough to connect with mocking brothers. You got into the mood and then decided to laugh, joke and play stupidly. Everything for you has always been extreme: either you laugh too much or you get too angry."

"Wait a minute, my brother was driving and he started running. I agree that I encouraged him, I said: Come on! Go! Cris is scared! At that moment, Cris asked Vanilson to slow down, but he continued. Cris asked again..."

"But not you." He said thoughtfully and seriously, calling her to account. "When you saw your frightened boyfriend, you began to scream, cheerfully and exaggeratedly to make your brother go faster. After all, like all controlling people, you wanted to terrorize Cristiano. This continued for some time. You laughed, screamed almost wildly. Cristiano even pulled your arm to call you to reality. But you didn't want to know. Believing that the speed was not enough, you loosened your seat belt and put your leg on the driver's side, stepping on your brother's foot on the gas pedal. The car wasn't modern or new, and it allowed you to do that. Then the accident happened..."

"No... it wasn't me..." She whispered disappointed, feeling very bad.

"It was you, Vitória." He confirmed, although he knew that the truth would provoke incredibly sad feelings.

The memories came alive and a deep pain sank into her chest. Unable to bear it, she began to cry and babble;

"I didn't want to... I didn't know that..."

"Anyway, the accident would happen. However, it was anticipated because of your attitude."

The spirit of Vitória said nothing more. Sad with herself, she decided to retire.

✳ ✳ ✳

As the days passed, again with the intention that his student would learn, the spirit Juan asked her to accompany the incarnate Janaina and Cristiano, who went to visit Simone and Pedro.

When they were there, Vitória's spirit was moved by little Pedro's condition.

335

"His condition is very sad." She said, without resisting her curiosity, she asked; "Juan, why did Pedro need to reincarnate like this?"

"Because his conscience asked for that kind of opportunity to have peace."

"Can you tell what he did in the past to wish for this difficult condition?

"There can be several reasons for a spirit to reincarnate in this condition. In Pedro's case, he was conspiring and also helped in tortures that disfigured his neighbor, compromised his organs, physical and mental health. Because spiritual evolution is one of the laws of God, when he came to understand how wrong he was, he began to feel the pain of others. He did not fit the capacity he had. When he saw himself, as a spirit, who had in the spiritual body the marks of all that he caused, in despair, he sought God and found him in the friends who picked him up. Very disturbed, he was attended and cared for by a dear sister who promised to help him out of pure love. Seeing his despair, this sister decided that, when he became incarnate, she would receive him as a son to help him relieve the pain, to help him recover from the consciousness that was punishing him so much. This sister, who is now Simone, his mother, received him as she promised, with much love and affection. Pedro is very relieved because reincarnation brings the blessing of forgetting the past."

"She prays for her son and also with him, as if the baby understands her words."

"You may not understand, but you feel the beneficial vibration that expands and envelops everyone during prayer. Prayer pours out a shower of sublime and blessed energies that soothe the mind and soul. How important this is. You are an example of this."

"Am I? "

"If it weren't for the prayers and the vibrations you received, I don't think you would be here." Having said that, they returned to the subject of little Pedro, which Vitória wanted to know.

"He's not going to stay here in the flesh for long, is he?"

"The less rebellious the spirit, the less its ordeal will be. There are those who are vigorous and stay longer. But this is not common."

Vitória was silent for a long time and just watched. Then she concluded;

"Cristiano and Simone get along very well. I have noticed this for some time. Did my discarnation occur so that they could be together?"

"You disembodied because it was necessary, whether they were together or not. After all..." He smiled. "They are not together. There is no romance between them."

"There is a very strong feeling. An energy of harmony, friendship, understanding... This is more than a romance. Something I didn't feel when we were together." After a brief pause, she asked; "Why did I disembody?"

"Why don't you and your brother talk about it?"

"How?"

"I heard that he would come to visit you today."

Vitória's spirit was overwhelmed by immense joy. She opened her big smile and asked with enthusiasm;

"When? Now? Will he come here?"

"Soon, at Janaina's house."

"Oh! I can't believe it!"

"Then don't believe it." Joked Juan happily with his joy.

337

∗ ∗ ∗

Much later, when she returned euphoric to the residence that served as a refuge, the spirit of Vitória was waiting for her brother.

"Vanilson!" She screamed when she saw him. Running into his arms, she wrapped her arms around him and burst into tears.

They hugged, kissed and, moving away from the hug, he asked, while holding her from her shoulders for a closer look;

"Are you okay, Vitória?"

"Now I am. What about you? Where were you? Why did we split up? Why didn't I go with you?"

"Calm down, let's talk about everything.' He asked cheerfully, with a beautiful smile on his face. They settled down and, less euphorically, she wanted to know;

"What about grandpa and grandma? I heard you're with them."

"I am. I don't know how or why, but I ended up in a colony." He laughed. "It was very funny. I woke up and thought I was in a hospital. First, I thought I was having a horrible dream. I vaguely remembered the accident, my body covered in blood, broken... almost unrecognizable. Then everything turned white. I heard an incredibly soft and beautiful song and I felt like I slept. When I woke up and looked at myself, I saw that I was complete. No plaster and everything in its place. It was strange, because I was sure that everything should be broken. Then... a kitten appeared." He said on purpose, and then corrected himself; "Oops! I mean…"

"Don't play!"

"I'm not playing. She was beautiful, really beautiful."

"Stop!"

"So... That angel appeared in my room, asking if I was okay. She gave me water... I wasn't even thirsty, but I drank." Vanilson said in a playful and witty way, without mischief. "I was just happy, happy."

And the sister got angry again;

"How could a mocker like you go to a spiritual colony and I don't? You are a scoundrel!" She spoke in a mocking way, with no intention of offending him.

"I'm a scoundrel with a good heart and good deeds, little sister." He laughed and hugged her warmly. "Now, I'm serious. I discovered that this beautiful and luminous creature was my mentor. Her name is Grace. Except that she was cruel, because then, after asking if I was okay, she smiled and announced: Welcome to the spiritual plane!" He laughed. "I almost died of fright, didn't I? Then she explained how it was and where I was. I stayed in that hospital for a while."

"When I had a kind of discharge and I thought that Grace would take me to her house... Nothing like that. I was thrown from there directly into an Education Center. I think they thought I was rude." He smiled.

"You have no way, Vanilson. You don't take anything seriously."

"I will. I like to play with good things. Play, joy and happiness, as long as it is healthy, is not something of an inferior spirit, unless there is evil, malice."

"And then? Tell me!" She asked excitedly.

"I spent a lot of time in school. I worked hard, see? I had to study and work hard, and I loved it! I asked about you, but they told me I didn't want to go there and I decided to tour here." He laughed. The sister grimaced at the joke and he finished; "Not long ago, I went to live with grandma."

"Unlike you, I got stuck in the earth's crust. I spent a lot of time mourning our death. The worst part was that I was tormenting Cristiano, crying on his shoulder."

"I heard…" He said this time very seriously. "I heard everything. I prayed a lot for you, Vitória. I vibrated to find peace of mind and to ascend to better places."

"It was very difficult. I was in a lot of pain, I felt the bruises… I was hungry, cold… I prayed, but…"

"You prayed out loud, didn't you?" Seeing her sad, he said. "I'm sorry."

"It was true. After a long time, I followed the prayers of Mrs. Janaina and her children. They intensified their prayers because they suspected that Cris was not well, emotionally, because of my presence. From then on, I felt more and more relieved, serene, and I even slept better. Sleep was refreshing and calm as before. I managed to get a better vibe and was able to see Juan, my mentor. I saw the spiritual aid station that exists in this house. I started to learn, to accompany some mentors, when they allowed me to." She smiled when she said; "I met new incarnated, or rather, new friends of Mrs. Janaina, who continues to make friends."

"Have you been visiting our parents?"

"Every time I went there, I didn't like what I was feeling."

"I heard what they do." Said Vanilson. "It doesn't bother me, it's good for them. At least they are not depressed because of us."

"It doesn't bother you because you're on a higher level."

"What you can also do."

"I was very saddened to learn that I was the one who caused the accident."

"Can I be honest?"

"Of course!"

340

"You were sad because you can no longer blame someone else for what happened."

"You too, Vanilson?"

"Me too, what? Telling the truth? Here one is neither happy nor uplifted when one lives in illusion. We need to know ourselves, assume who we are and recognize that we made a mistake, that something went wrong because of us. Do you understand? You know, seeing your condition and that of many others who said they were religious when they became incarnate, I understood that passage in the Gospel where it says: *Not all who say to me, Lord, Lord, shall enter the Kingdom of Heaven, but only those who do my will.* Father in heaven. The Gospel according to Spiritism teaches us that it is not enough to say "I'm a Christian" to follow Christ. The true Christian is recognized by his works. *A good tree cannot bear bad fruit.* Many want to shape the teachings of Jesus according to their ideas and convenience."

"What do you mean by that?"

"You always wanted everyone to fulfill your will. That accident was going to happen, but not that day. I was wrong when I played a bad game. I saw that the avenue was new and barely marked. I knew the traffic light was too far away and I started running. As soon as I decided to stop, I felt your foot on mine. The accident happened because of me, but you reinforced my mistake by wanting to see your will prevail." There was a brief pause and amused when he revealed; "The worst thing was that everyone thought I did that and that I still didn't have a seat belt. You let go of your belt to step on the gas pedal, and when you approached my seat, you accidentally pressed the button and let go of my belt."

"Wow! I did that too."

"I was reckless, but not as reckless as you think. Although it won't make a difference now."

341

"I think I understand it better. Everything had to be according to my will. I was always kind, polite, cool, but intolerant. I always did what I could to get people to give in to my wishes. I thought I was right and that my ideas were always the best." After a few moments, she acknowledged; "You, on the other hand, have always been the joker. The one who didn't get his head around it. You lived and let live. You were more respectful, considerate, even when you couldn't help. I remember I had no patience with grandma and grandpa. In my opinion, they talked a lot about unimportant things. On the contrary, you paid attention, you talked, you played with them…" She smiled. "You always brought the sweets that grandma liked… I remember you bought those word search magazines, crossword puzzles for them and the magazine about soap operas and artists that grandma always liked… and I said it was a gossip magazine, something useless. You were very useful to occupy their minds… On weekends, you used to go for a walk with them, without bothering with the slow walk. Even after grandpa had to stay in the wheelchair, you would carry him, regardless of the difficulties and obstacles. When our mother scolded you, I never saw you answer."

"Not when I was nervous, of course. Then I would look for her to talk and explain what had happened to me for doing something she thought was bad. Often, she was right, sometimes…"

"It's not just that, Vanilson. In countless situations, many details, you were better, much better than me. This shows your elevation and the merit of going directly to a good spiritual colony."

"It is not about the position, sister. It's not about being worthy of going to a colony. It's about the attraction. If you think like that, you won't go to a colony because you don't deserve it, not because you didn't do everything you should have done. If you did, no one would go to a good spiritual colony. Remember our great reference, the Andre Luiz spirit. He did not do everything right or

342

almost nothing right when he incarnated. He was very confused and disturbed. But he prayed sincerely and felt attracted to a good place, in spirituality."

"He may not have done everything very well when he became incarnate, but then... He transmitted so many lessons, so much knowledge."

"Then learn from your lesson."

"You know what's worse, Vanilson?"

"No."

"I don't even think I missed that much."

"You don't believe it, but your conscience or your unconscious does."

"Do you think I unconsciously feel guilty?"

"I think so. The laws of God live in you, in your mind, in your heart."

"I need to improve. I need to work on God's laws for me to think differently." After a moment, she asked; "What is God's main law?"

"I believe that God created one law. It is the law of love. If you think and expand your understanding, your comprehension, your reflection on love, you will find in this noble feeling, the basis, the foundation of harmony, peace, happiness, benevolence, bliss and, above all, tolerance."

"Why do you emphasize tolerance?"

"Because, as in your case, when we believe that we are full of reason and we believe that the other is wrong, the law of love is applied through our tolerance. We cannot always change the other, just as we cannot change the world. However, we can live in harmony, peace and happiness if we are tolerant and silence our strong, severe and aggressive opinions. Think about that."

After a few moments, the spirit of Vitória commented;

"If I had been more tolerant…"

"Don't regret what you couldn't do. Start taking action now or you will have more than you can regret."

"Vanilson?"

"Tell me." He smiled, as if he knew what she wanted.

"Can you tell me why I disincarnated so young and with so much to do?"

"Are you sure you want to know?"

"Does it have anything to do with Simone and Cristiano?"

"In the past, you did everything you could to separate them and you did. Leaving Simone in great difficulty with her little boy."

"So, Cris was also wrong to leave her. It was not only my fault."

"Simone was your sister and had been promised to Cristiano. They loved each other very much. They were going to get married and move in, but you didn't settle for that. A little later, with the death of your parents due to the flu that affected Europe, she came to visit you and spent a few days with you. Then, with the help of two other people who received considerable value in jewelry, Simone disappeared pregnant. She was placed in the hold of an English ship and taken from Europe far away to the new world that had just been discovered: the United States. With the help of these same people, you placed a tombstone in the city cemetery with inscriptions of your sister's name. Because of his wife's delay, Cristiano went to look for her and learned from you that she had contracted the flu and had died. He was dismayed for a long time. However, over the years, you achieved what you wanted: to marry him. You did not have a life full of happiness, because it takes the love of both parties for a couple to be happy."

"What happened to my sister?"

"She died in childbirth."

"And the child? Did he die too?"

"No." He simply answered.

"What happened to the baby?"

"He was a child and was adopted by a family that gave him shelter, food and turned him into an employee, practically a slave." He smiled. "He resigned himself to the difficulties and learned to take advantage of them, evolving and doing good as much as he could."

"What about me?"

"You couldn't be happy. You never forgot your sister and suffered greatly from succeeding in controlling your destiny. No one is truly happy when they cause situations that make others suffer."

"She would not be with him. She would have died in childbirth anyway, don't you think?"

"No. Simone died in childbirth due to the difficulties she went through, due to sadness, because she had nothing to do in such a distant and lonely place."

"So, did I die in the accident to taste the bitter taste of seeing my wedding plans sabotaged and seeing them together?"

"They are not together, as far as I know."

"We can see that there is a great feeling among them. They just don't realize it because of the needs of Pedro, Simone's son, who was born recently." Vitória was thoughtful for a moment, then asked. "What about you?"

"What about me?"

"Who were you? One of the two people who helped me put my sister in the hold of a ship in England and send her to the United States?"

"No."

"Who were these people, then? Did you know them in that last incarnation?"

"You knew them well. The two people who helped you at that time were our parents."

"Mom and dad?"

"That's right." He said softly.

"Were they with us at that time?"

"More or less." He smiled a little shyly.

"How so? Who were you?"

"Cristiano and Simone's son, who was born in the United States." He revealed, looking at her tenderly, waiting for her reaction.

"Oh! My God! No way, Vanilson. You've always been a great brother. You never fought with me and... You should hate me!"

"I don't hate you, there is no way. I love you and I can understand your evolution. Vitória, you have developed the intellect that along with your pride and selfishness forms an incredible obstacle to your own evolution. That is why you want to control situations and people. Instead, you must pay attention to moral development that includes feelings and emotions, which culminates in tolerance and the desire for good."

"I can't believe you don't hate me."

"When you learn to love, you will believe me"

"Don't say that." She said, almost in tears.

"Come here. Give me a big hug." He asked with a wide smile. Approaching and pulling her towards him, he wrapped her with affection, making her lean against his chest.

"Why are you so nice to me?"

"I already said. Because I love you unconditionally. And because I love you, I will not let you do anything wrong."

"How so?" She asked, turning away and trying to look him in the eye.

"I will become your obsessor!" He laughed willingly.

"What are you talking about?"

"Before you start crying again with Cris, disturbing him and making him unhappy, I will chase you to leave him alone. Only then will he have a chance with Simone." He smiled.

"Don't joke."

"I'm not playing. I'm waiting for this opportunity." Closing his smile, he spoke more seriously. "I wish that you would resign yourself and not repent again by his side."

"I'm not going to do that." When she saw him laugh, she asked. "Are you reading my thoughts?"

"I feel your vibrations, your energy. That tells me everything. The truth is that you want to control Cris. You don't want to see him next to Simone. You think that she doesn't look good because she's divorced, has a special child and... And a series of other notes that, in fact, are excuses to control the lives of others. Your time in the flesh is over. He who is incarnate, let him take care of himself. The time is now yours. Take care of yourself. If God wanted you there, with him, it would not matter his plan of reincarnation to die on the eve of the wedding, you would be there."

"Do you believe that?"

"Totally. There are countless cases of people, whose planning of reincarnation would be to disincarnate in a certain situation and age or with a certain health problem; however, because of what they realized nobly, earthly life was extended."

"I don't remember any such case."

347

"Sister Dulce is a great example. The famous earthly missionary who lived in Bahia and was so respected by everyone, without exception. According to the doctors, anyone who had that health condition, eating like her, would have died or stayed in bed a long time ago. But she did not. So, don't cry about your death, but your life. Look at the way she lived and change from now on."

With eyes clouded with tears of regret, Vitória asked;

"Will you help me?"

And Vanilson, with a wide smile on his calm face said;

"That's why I came here."

Holding her warmly, he slowly rocked her from side to side with tenderness and understanding.

17.– CRISTIANO CANNOT DENY HIS LOVE

AS THE DAYS PASSED, the abyss between Simone and Samuel seemed greater and the difficulties with little Pedro increased.

The baby needed doctors and medication constantly. He was hospitalized several times and needed a lot of attention.

Simone had turned to her ex-husband to help her help her son, but he refused, saying he was busy or wouldn't even take her calls. For this reason, she tried not to overwhelm anyone, trying as hard as she could to do it alone. But there were times when she couldn't do it, so sometimes she would call one, sometimes she would call another to accompany her to the doctor or the hospital. She couldn't always afford to take a cab, as Pedro's expenses were high and her budget was compromised.

Early that Saturday, she asked Cristiano to take her and Pedro to the hospital. The boy was burning with fever.

"I didn't even warn Rúbia. She is sleeping." She said, getting into the car with her friend's help.

"You did well to call me." Said Cristiano, who, after placing her in the back seat with the baby, closed the door and got into the vehicle through the driver's door. Then he asked; "What about your father? Has he improved?"

"Last night he had to go to the emergency room again. The doctor said he has pneumonia. That's why I didn't call my mother.

Abner took me to the doctor twice this week. David one. I don't think any of you can stand me anymore." She smiled. Then she said awkwardly; "Please, I'm sorry, Cristiano. I didn't want to bother you, but... Actually, I can't have a maid. If I had, I would ask her to come with me. Alone, I can't drive and leave my baby in the back seat."

"Stop. Don't even think about such a thing. Come on!" He almost got angry. As he was driving, he said; "My mother wanted to come, but I didn't let her."

"You did well. Every time we go to the hospital, it takes too long. It would be exhausting for her."

Pedro was seen and needed to be hospitalized. Apprehensive and fearful, Simone suffered in silence. She resigned. She didn't know what to say and just prayed.

Her heart was broken for leaving her son in the hospital again. She thought about how painful the needle sticks should be for the tests, to get serum and medication. Everything was very painful for that helpless boy who did not understand the reason for everything.

Upon leaving the hospital, the friend helped her into the car and got into the driver's seat. He seemed used to Simone's silence when she was worried and apprehensive.

Respectful of his friend's feelings, he said nothing, just drove. After a while, she asked;

"Can you take me to my mother's house, please?"

"Of course. It will be fine. There I can visit Mr. Salvador. I like to talk with him."

"Really?" She smiled when she asked.

"Yes. I do like it."

"How strange. Nobody likes talking to my dad. In spite of…"

"Of what?"

"I feel that you have some moral authority over my father. When you talk, he listens. He pays attention! He hardly ever interrupts you. In the end, he ends up agreeing with what you say or becomes reflective." The young man smiled and said nothing. Then Simone said;

"After that conversation we had at home, my mother said that my father started helping her with the household chores. Now he does the dishes, helps pick up the clothes. He even washed the yard and watered the plants without her asking. He was always very critical; he overestimated himself for what he did in life. Retired, he thought he didn't need to do anything else."

"You know... I think your dad is so critical because you just want to teach him critically. He hasn't learned what's right. When you give your opinion, you and your siblings don't want to listen to him and criticize him for talking that way. When I talk to Mr. Salvador, I listen and then calmly explain to him what I think is right. Then he pays attention and thinks. Sometimes he even changes his mind after he understands."

"I think you are right. I never tried to calmly explain anything." After a while, she commented; "I wonder how he will react when he knows that you are David's brother, Abner's partner."

"Let's live in the moment. When necessary, he will know. Don't suffer in advance." As soon as they arrived at Simone's parents' house, Mrs. Celeste received them with satisfaction. After hearing about the hospitalized grandson, they went inside and the woman scolded her daughter.

"You should have called me. When Rúbia called me and told me that you had left a note saying that you had gone to the hospital, I was worried. I called you, but... nothing."

"Pedro was being cared for, Mother. I couldn't leave my cell phone on."

"And only now have you been able to return, daughter? Jeez! How long it took!"

"It is always like that. I'm exhausted." She muttered, sitting on the couch. Leaning back, she closed her eyes.

"Sit down, Cristiano. You must also be tired. Just a little longer and I'll serve you dinner, son. It's almost ready."

"Don't worry about me, Mrs. Celeste. We had coffee in the hospital cafeteria."

"Haven't you had lunch?!"

"No. But that's not a problem. I'm worried about Simone. She is very pale. From what she told me, she hasn't been sleeping or eating properly in the last few days."

"Daughter... Take a shower while I finish preparing dinner."

"No, mom, thank you. I just stopped by here because it's on the way. I wanted to see dad. When Cristiano leaves, I will go with dad to enjoy a walk."

"Imagine! You leave the boy without lunch, just a cup of coffee and you send him away without dinner? You won't do that, right, daughter?"

"What about dad?"

At that moment, Mr. Salvador appeared in the room to greet them.

"Ooooh...! How nice...! How are you Christian?" He said really happy to see them.

"Good. How about you? Are you getting better?"

"I'm much better. This flu is terrible. It didn't help to get the vaccine. The flu hit me the same way."

"It's because the flu virus is mutant. The vaccine developed is for the type of virus that attacks most at that time. If you take it, you will be protected against that type of flu, but if the virus mutates before reaching you, you can get it. However, the vaccine is always welcome, since it will immunize you against the most aggressive disease. Can you imagine getting the flu twice?"

"Don't even joke about it." Addressing Simone, the father asked; "And Pedrito, daughter?"

"He was hospitalized again."

"You look pale. You need to rest."

"In what way?" Her voice broke, and she again closed her eyes and fell on the couch.

The father had a coughing fit and his wife complained.

"If he didn't smoke, it wouldn't be so bad. He's still going to die from that damn cigarette." She said, going into the kitchen.

"Are you smoking even with the flu and the onset of pneumonia?"

"I only smoked a little earlier today. He hadn't put a cigarette in my mouth since Monday."

"Why don't you take the opportunity to quit your cigarette forever?"

"It's hard, boy. You can't imagine how."

"When I go to do something that is very difficult, I reflect on the example of those who were victorious before me. If someone has already done it, I can do it too."

"I'm taking a lot of medicine."

"Cigarettes have a lot of chemistry, many drugs that intoxicate the body, leaving the person physically and psychologically dependent. The person who smokes dies little by little."

353

"We all die little by little. You have to admit that." He laughed, believing himself to be victorious in the teaching.

"Except that whoever smokes dies faster. However, the worst thing is not to die. The worst thing is to degenerate the perfect body that God has given you."

"You said you were a spiritist. Do you really believe in that reincarnation thing?"

"I think I do. How do you explain so many physical, social and emotional differences? Why are we so different? Why is one physically perfect and the other one can't see or walk or is missing an arm?"

"We are different because it is God's will."

"If it's only God's will that God is very cruel, don't you think?" Without waiting for an answer, he commented; "Yes, because my neighbor did nothing wrong, had an accident and was paralyzed. I had an accident, I was a little upset, but I'm getting better. I had no physical sequelae. If you believe that it is simply the will of God, then He is sadistic and likes to see his children suffer for nothing."

"Sometimes I think about it and don't have an answer."

Simone, without considering the matter, got up, excused herself and went to the kitchen. The two followed her with a look and Cristiano asked;

"How do you explain the condition of Pedro who was born with so many problems? Does God love me and you more than he does? Because he made us be born perfect, didn't he?"

The man breathed and breathed;

"I've thought about it a lot, but I don't have an answer."

"The only explanation is reincarnation. I believe in Jesus and he has always told us about a just, good, and merciful Father. Where is God's goodness, justice, and mercy if he does not let us correct, repair the mistakes made in life? If we were ignorant and made mistakes, would it be right to suffer eternally in hell, as some religions preach? If we only ask forgiveness for our mistakes, do we go to heaven and those whom we have harmed and made to suffer to maintain the harm? Is that right?"

It would not be fair. I agree with that.

"That is why I believe that God created us simple and ignorant. Through reincarnations, we learn to do to others what we want them to do to us. We learn to love and respect others and ourselves; to respect our body borrowed for this incarnation so that we can learn from the experiences of this life."

"And if I smoke, what can happen to me?"

"If you know that smoking is bad and you continue to compromise your health with chemicals that are so harmful and that you have in cigarettes, you will kill yourself more quickly, and worse, painfully, because smoking will cause you serious illness. Very painful, physically speaking."

"Many people have already died of cancer and did not smoke."

"Perhaps by harming one's own body or the body of another person in another incarnation or even in this life. The person who experiences cancer without having done anything in this life to cause this disease certainly did in another life and asked to live something strong to value the perfect body that God gave him. There are other reasons as well, but they all come down to loving yourself and others. Everything we do is recorded in our consciousness and, because we want to evolve and improve, we want to harmonize and to get rid of the burden of remorse."

Mr. Salvador was pensive. He had another coughing fit and as soon as he recovered, he asked in a deep, hoarse voice;

"Do you think my grandson did something wrong in the afterlife to be born this way?"

355

"We all did something wrong in another life. Some of us more than others. There are those who wish to evolve so much that they ask to reincarnate, harmonizing everything they did wrong. Then they are born facing immense challenges. Others prefer something softer, but the challenges span several incarnations. I cannot say what Pedro's purpose is. I just think he is a very brave spirit to decide to learn and harmonize consciousness all at once, facing so many challenges together. Besides, he is a very blessed child to have such a loving and dedicated mother, such attentive and helpful grandparents, a family that loves him and welcomes him with so much affection. It must have been very important for you, in another existence, to be so loved. You didn't know him in this life. He was born that way. He is different from someone who first enlisted the friendship of his loved ones and then had an accident." When he saw him pensive, he waited for a while and then said; "The good thing about this, according to the teachings of the Spiritist doctrine, is that Pedro's life does not end here. Like ours, it does not end now, in this life. Pedro is not like that, as we see it. He is like that, in these conditions. Certainly, in the spiritual plane, Pedro will be different, much better and even better in the next incarnation."

"In the next life, he will not remember us."

"I don't remember the last incarnation. I do not remember it. However, I'm sure that we met and somehow you were an important and very dear person to me, because I have very significant attention and affection, especially for you and, without modesty, I know that you feel the same way about me." Mr. Salvador laughed and he continued; "We do not need to remember, we need to feel." After a moment, he said; "Think about quitting the cigarette. I wouldn't like to see you challenged to learn not to abuse your own body."

Mrs. Celeste came to the room and called them.

"Dinner is on the table. Shall we go?"

"Thank you, Mrs. Celeste. Yes, I will accept." Said the young man standing up. Then he asked. "Where can I wash my hands?"

"There's a bathroom there, son." She said; "You can go there."

Soon everyone was at the kitchen table and the lady was serving them when Mr. Salvador wanted to know;

"And Rúbia?"

"She stayed at my house, dad. I just called her."

"And is she there alone?" Said the man.

"She said that Abner stopped by in the afternoon, had a cup of coffee and talked a little."

"She should not be alone."

"If you asked your daughter to come here, she would be with us now." Said the wife.

The husband lowered his head and said nothing.

"She really shouldn't be alone." Said Simone. "She's already on maternity leave and the baby can anticipate the birth. You never know."

"Do you want me to go get her? It's not far. I'll be right back." Offered Cristiano.

"No!" Simone answered immediately. "You have done a lot for today. You missed your Saturday."

"I had nothing to do. At least I was helpful." He said with a smile.

"Tomorrow you can come here for lunch. Come. Cristiano and Rúbia, we invite you."

"I appreciate it immensely, but I already have something to do tomorrow. It will be the next time."

Simone became restless. She didn't know what commitment her friend might have, but she said nothing.

After a while, noticing her daughter's behavior, Mrs. Celeste caught her attention;

"If you don't eat and get weak, who will take care of your child like you, Simone?"

"I'm not hungry, mom."

"You need to feed yourself. You lost a lot of weight. You don't sleep well…" Mrs. Celeste.

"Wouldn't it be a case of looking for someone to help you? A nurse, maybe?" Cristiano suggested.

"Yes…" She just answered. "It doesn't mean that the financial costs are going to be too high, aren't they?"

"You need to share tasks with someone. This will end up hurting you. So, as your mother reminded you, who will take care of Pedro like you?" The young man reasserted.

She did not respond and continued to stir the food with the tip of her fork.

At that moment the phone rang and Simone offered to answer to escape from the table;

"Leave it, I'll answer it."

Seeing her leave, the mother said;

"I'm worried about her."

"We are. And we don't know what else to do to help." Cristiano looked at her from a distance and said nothing.

"As soon as I get better, I'll stay at her house longer to see if I can help more." The father decided.

"Simone needs, in addition to material support, help with Pedro and emotional support. Mainly, emotional support." Commented Cristiano. "This experience is not easy for her. The presence of relatives, friends is immensely important. The ideal now is not to bring her insignificant problems or worries, things that we can solve ourselves."

"I understand what you mean. My daughter's burden is heavy enough. The worry and work with the boy, the divorce... It would be good, at this time, for her to see the family in harmony. It was good for Salvador to invite Rúbia to lunch here tomorrow. Ideally, Abner should be invited as well. That way, Simone would be happier."

"Don't start..." Grunted her husband with his mouth full.

"It would be good to have the family together." Said Mrs. Celeste. Simone's approach made them stop talking, and she said;

"It was Rúbia. I think my cell phone rang in the bag and I didn't hear it. She is alone and complains about it."

"I finished with the dinner. If you want to leave..." Offered the friend.

"Not without first experiencing some of the cake I made."

"Not for me, Mrs. Celeste. I'm satisfied. Thank you very much." Before she insisted, Simone asked;

"Mom, save it for another day. Cristiano, like me, is exhausted. The day was intense."

"Then he will take a little for him and Janaina."

"If so, I accept." He replied cheerfully with a mischievous smile on his face. "I love cake, but I ate too much." He said as a boy, rubbing his hands together.

Without delay, the lady arranged what the boy would take. They said goodbye and left.

When he was leaving Simone at home, her friend came in for a few moments. They stopped in the area and before she opened the door to the room, he invited her.

"Tomorrow there will be a party at the institution. A group of magicians and jugglers will give a one-hour presentation. Another group of women made cake, sweets and other things. Do you want to go with me?"

"I'm going to the hospital."

"At what time?"

"In the morning"

"I can go with you and then we'll go to the institution and..."

"What happens if Pedro is discharged?"

"I bring you both. I leave you here and go alone, because I promised I would. Would it be okay?"

"I don't know..." She answered in a discouraged voice, looking down.

"Simone, are you okay?"

"I'm very tired."

"I know. Since Pedro was born you have not stopped."

"It's not just physically. I'm worried and alert. Pedro requires a lot of care. You saw how difficult and sad it is to feed him. He never seems to sleep. I have to be on the lookout for medicines and countless precautions, because his immunity is always low. He has colds, respiratory and lung complications, his kidneys are never good, there is always a new infection…" Tears rolled down her pale face and she breathed. "I know I'm wrong, very wrong to say this, but... It is only then, when he is at the hospital, that I have a little rest... I can sleep a little... but my thoughts do not stop. I keep punishing myself, torturing myself because I feel some relief that I don't have as many worries that night as I will have the next day... He will be three months old next week and…" She cried. "I want to do my best for him, but I can't."

"Calm down. Come here." He asked, welcoming her with a hug. "I'm sure you're doing your best and that's all you can do. It's logical that you're wearing yourself out. You have nowhere to get your strength back. Everything has a limit, Simone, and you have reached yours."

Holding him tightly, she muffled the voice in his chest and cried; "The last time Pedro was hospitalized, I came home, took a shower and went to bed. I woke up sixteen hours later. I didn't know where I was or what day it was. I lost track of time. I was confused. I didn't remember leaving him at the hospital. I ran to the other room looking for him. I went to the living room and fell into despair. Only then I remember everything."

"This is physical and mental fatigue. You are overwhelmed. You can't blame yourself for that. It's a lot of work and a lot of worry."

"I'm afraid to go in, shower, sleep and forget about him tomorrow, where I left him."

"It won't happen, and if it does, I'll remind you. Is that okay?" He asked with a slight smile on his white face, which seemed bluish from his clean-shaven beard. Leaning slightly, he tried to look her in the eye.

Simone stepped away from the embrace. But Cristiano held her face softly and caressed it with tenderness and a penetrating look.

A strong emotion overcame them, making their hearts race.

Closing his eyes, he kissed her forehead for a long time, and pressed it against his chest again, feeling his breath altered.

While he was slowly moving away, Cristiano took her face again, caressed it lightly, bent down and looked for her lips, kissing them with tenderness.

Simone embraced him gently, responding with all emotion. In the next minute, she put her hand on his chest and distanced herself when she mumbled;

"Cris... no…"

"Why?" He asked in the same tone.

"I shouldn't… I…" She said softly, looking away.

"We are quite big. We know what we are doing and we can no longer deny how we feel about each other, Simone."

"My divorce…"

"So what?" He mumbled emphatically.

"I don't know. I have a son and…"

"I adore you. I love your child. I want to take care of both of you. I cannot and will not deny what I feel. Unless you don't love me and say you don't feel anything for me."

"I'm confused. I don't know what to say. What will my parents think? And your mother?"

"Do not create obstacles or impediments that do not exist. I doubt that anyone would suspect a stronger feeling among us, an interest beyond friendship. It will not be a surprise to anyone. Besides, we don't owe anything to others."

"I live in a delicate, worrying and very laborious moment."

"And I want to be a part of that more than I already am. I want to be by your side, next to Pedro. I want you to share everything with me."

Bringing her closer, he caressed her soft hair and looked at her for a moment. He bent down, kissed her tenderly and she answered.

At that moment, quickly and unexpectedly, the door to the room opened and Rúbia could not stop seeing them, even though her sister was moving away a little.

"Sorry, I…" Said Rúbia, ashamed and not knowing what to do. Then she greeted him as if she had seen nothing. "Hello, Cris, how are you?"

"Everything is good. And you?" He asked, breathing heavily, trying to hide his surprise.

"I'm more relaxed now. I don't like to be alone." That said, she invited; "Come on in."

"No. Thank you. I was just leaving."

"I just made an apple cinnamon tea. I learned to drink this tea when I lived in your house and I know you like it. Do you want some?" She smiled

"Alright, I accept. It just has to be quick. My mom is alone." Putting his hand gently on Simone's back, who looked down, led her to walk in front of him.

While drinking tea, Rúbia commented;

"Was Pedro hospitalized again?"

"He had another urinary tract infection." Said her sister. "I'm worried... unsure."

"The important thing is to know that you are doing everything with a lot of attention, love and care." Said Cristiano.

"I agree with you." Said Rúbia. "I see Simone day and night unfolding to take care of Pedro. The best doctors and hospitals within her reach are being consulted and..."

"Guys, excuse me..." Asked Simone, getting up and leaving them confused.

"What happened to her?!" The sister asked.

"Fatigue. She is tired, with many worries and... The truth is that Simone is dedicating a lot to something that she knows cannot have a prosperous, better and positive future. Today the doctor who attended Pedro said to her; *Mother, in spite of all your dedication and commitment, your little one has a very delicate and irreversible image. We will continue to do everything for him, but you must be prepared.*" It is not easy for a helpful mother to hear that."

"It is an immense struggle in which we know there will be no victory."

"Apparently, but no. Every struggle, every effort for good, for love, is a victorious struggle, even if it is lost. It is a fact that Pedro does not... He will not stay with us for long or for many years. I know this syndrome well. I believe that the attention, love and affection he received from us... Ah...! That will never be destroyed. That love will never go away. Both, he and we, will be better and stronger spirits than ever, as we have learned the importance of giving and receiving. We cannot limit our life to this experience alone. Today he needs us and so, we help him. Tomorrow, in another life, we may need him and he will be by our side."

"Thinking this way is the only thing that consoles me."

Cristiano's cell phone rang. He answered and immediately hung up. Standing up, he said;

"It was my mother. She was worried. Well... I'm going to see Simone and then I'll leave."

"Yes, of course. Your company is doing very well for her." The young man smiled, bowed and kissed her on the forehead, then left.

18.– BEYOND DEATH

ON SUNDAY MORNING, Simone, in the company of Cristiano, spoke with the pediatrician who took care of Pedro and visited the children's I.C.U.

"He is reacting well to the medication and if he continues to do so, our hero," Referring to the child; "Will be discharged tomorrow."

"I thought I'd take him with me today."

"I see in both of you very dedicated parents." Very seriously, Simone exchanged glances with Cristiano, but neither of them could correct the doctor who continued; "All the love, care and attention are important to him and to you. However, here at the hospital, we will resort to any emergency. Go home, rest, sleep, be distracted and go out with a smile. Why not? Here, Little Pedro will be well cared for, and tomorrow you will return, alright? "

"Okay, doctor. Thank you. We'll be back tomorrow." Cristiano extended his hand to the doctor and when he was given the chance, he thanked him.

"Thank you for everything, doctor."

"See you tomorrow."

As they walked slowly down the I.C.U. corridor in the hospital, the young man risked putting his arm on the shoulders of Simone, who did not care.

When they left the building for the parking lot, she hugged him and leaned against him. In the car, Cristiano proposed;

"Would you agree to take a walk around the mall? I need to buy something. Then, if you wish, we can have lunch together and go to the institution for your party. What do you think?"

Apathetic, without showing courage, she responded;

"That will be great. I need to be distracted." Looking into his eyes, she said with a slight smile of gratitude. "I want to thank you for all you have done for me and Pedro. Your help is great. Your support, your dedication, your presence by our side has a value that no one can imagine."

"Why... Stop." He asked uncomfortably.

"I will be very sincere: I expected this support, this dedication from Samuel. I never imagined that another person, outside of our family ties, outside of blood ties, could help and support us as you are doing."

Staring at her, he argued.

"In addition to family and blood ties, there are spiritual ties. These are much stronger and indestructible. They go beyond life and beyond death. I have no memory or knowledge of past lives, of what we lived together, but what I feel is much stronger than reason. And it is backed by this intense feeling and so, I find the strength and the will to be by his side."

"About yesterday, I…"

Cristiano saw her embarrassed, so he interrupted her.

"Let's worry about today. Caring for the here and now. Yesterday has passed and tomorrow... Well, tomorrow depends on today. We will not suffer or anticipate. I don't want to and I won't pressure you. I just need you to let me stay with you and Pedro."

Simone approached and hugged him tightly, hiding her face in his chest. He caressed her lovingly and kissed her head several times.

Then, moving away from the hug, Cristiano proposed with enthusiasm, wanting to see her more joyfully.

"Well... Shall we go to the mall?"

"Yes, come on." She agreed with a generous smile that had hardly been seen lately.

Her concerns about little Pedro made her forget about her commitment to lunch at her father's house with her sister. The boy had also forgotten, so they went to the mall, relaxed.

✳ ✳ ✳

Meanwhile, at Simone's house, Rúbia was worried. She knew that her father had invited her to lunch there that day and she didn't want to arrive at the last minute. She had plans to talk a little more, and get closer to her father. However, the sister did not arrive or answer the cell phone.

"Did little Pedro get worse?" She spoke to herself, walking from side to side. "Or did she forget?"

She never liked being alone. However, lately, she hated solitude. She simply did not accompany her sister to the hospital because Cristiano reminded her that it was not a healthy place for her condition. Otherwise, she would have left.

Restless, she called her mother who tried to calm her down.

"Calm down, daughter. It's not even eleven o'clock. She will soon be there."

"I should have gone."

"It is not a good place to go in your condition. I was the one who should have gone. I think we are abusing Cristiano's friendship too much. This boy lives helping your sister with little Pedro..."

"Maybe he likes it, mom. Or does he have any interest...?" She stopped in her tracks.

367

"He is dedicated like this because Simone helped a lot when he needed it. That must be that."

"Mother, have you ever wondered if it's not just that?" She laughed funny. "What if Cris is interested in her?"

"I already suspected that. If it is the destiny and the will of God... I pray that they will be happy. He's a good guy. If I knew how to support them in such a situation... Nothing more will be a problem for both of them."

"Apparently, everything will be fine. We just have to assume that they like each other." After a brief moment of silence, she said; "Mother, I'm going to hang up. Simone may call."

"It's okay, daughter. I'm waiting for you. Call as soon as she arrives."

"Kisses, bye."

Some anguish pressed on Rúbia's heart. She felt alone and did not like it. She wanted to love and be loved. She wanted someone by her side. Someone who would not use her. She regretted getting involved with Jefferson, being cheated. She thought her life would never be the same. She would have a child and many obligations on her behalf.

How could she find a man who would look at her and be interested, knowing that she had a child with another? Single, free and unhindered, she found it difficult to find someone interesting, available and interested in her.

What Rúbia did not know was that, by recognizing the mistakes she had made, correcting herself and trying not to make any more mistakes, her life changed. Attending the Spiritist center, learning prayer with attention and from the heart, the passes, were gradually imbuing her with the bad and regrettable energies she had acquired when she became involved with Jefferson. Spiritual companies, spirits of low moral value and frivolity, who were holding on to the energetic vibrations of that adventure in false pleasure, lost interest in being close to her and found incompatibility in her now healthy and changed vibrations. She was aware of following good principles, conscious of the responsibilities she had acquired, from which she did not want to escape. She had matured spiritually and this imbued her with wisdom, high thoughts and new beneficial fluids, which would make her attract good company to herself and consequently a better loving partner on her moral and spiritual level.

We attract energies and companies compatible with our thoughts and practices.

However, she still had some things to work out and leave the past behind her. Her thoughts were far away and she barely heard her cell phone ring. When she picked it up, she felt like she was freezing when she saw Jefferson's name on the screen.

What could he want? She didn't know if she would answer.

"Hello."

"We have to talk." Said a woman's voice, without even greeting her.

"Who is speaking?"

"My name is Cícera. I'm Jefferson's wife."

"Sorry. I don't know you and…" She didn't know what to say, as so much was the surprise.

"I know everything, Rúbia. We just need to talk. Can we meet today?"

"Meet…? Today…?"

"Yes, it can be in the food court of a shopping mall or in a cafeteria. In a public place, perhaps, you will feel better. Wherever you want."

"Look… To be honest, you took me by surprise and I'm not sure what to decide. Can you give me some time to think? I'll call back later."

"You can call Jefferson's cell phone, but please don't take too much."

"Okay. Talk to you later."

"Bye."

When she hung up, Rúbia was confused. She was disoriented. She didn't know what to do. She immediately called Simone, but her sister didn't answer.

She thought about talking to her mother, but thought she shouldn't. She called Abner's cell phone.

"I'm at the beach, Rúbia. Don't you remember? Yesterday I told you that I would come here."

"I forgot."

"Did something happen? Are you okay?"

"I'm fine. It is nothing. I just wanted to talk. I don't like being alone. So... Then we'll talk. Have a nice walk."

"Is everything okay?"

"Yes, stay calm." She didn't want to worry her brother, so she didn't say anything. "Simone is in the hospital and she should be here soon. Whatever, I'll call you later."

"You better!"

"Take care! Say hi to David."

"Alright. Take care! Bye."

Again, she felt alone and disoriented. What should she do? What could Cícera want with her?

She was afraid. Something strange began to occur, she thought that Jefferson's wife might mistreat her, subjugate her in some way. It would be easy to dispense with the conversation, but she would be worried and think too much about what the other would want. She needed someone's opinion or even the company if she decided to meet Cícera.

Her cell phone rang again and she became more fearful, thinking it was the same person. When she picked up the device, she smiled without realizing it and responded.

"Ricardo?"

"Hi, Rúbia. How are you?"

"Good. And you?"

"All good. Look, I'm sorry to call, but... Is Cristiano there?"

"No. He went to the hospital with my sister. They went very early to talk to the doctor who was going to visit Pedro and, so far, they have not returned. I called them, but it went to voice mails."

"It is because David is in Mongaguá and a colleague of ours, from the center, has a dental emergency, a painful tooth. He wanted to see if Cris would take care of it for him. However, it's fine. I will try later." Then he said; "I heard that you already went on maternity leave."

"It is true. The baby is about to arrive." Not bearing the pressure she felt, she decided to ask: "Ricardo, do you have a minute to listen to me?"

"Of course. What happened?"

She told her friend everything and he said;

"No way! You can't go to that meeting alone."

"I'm interested in knowing what she wants."

"Relax, Rúbia. What if the woman is crazy? She may react and... In my opinion, you shouldn't go."

"I don't know what to do. I need to call back."

"The truth is that you don't have to give anything back. You don't have to give in to what she wants. In any case... If you want to kill curiosity... I can go with you."

"Would you do that for me?" Gleefully.

"I would, yes. Book with her at that bar near the engineering and architecture firm. I'll go directly from here and meet you there."

"Then I will call her. I'll take a cab and meet you there."

"Why a cab?"

"I can't drive. I'm huge. The belly hits the steering wheel. If I put the seat back to give distance, my feet can't reach the pedals properly."

Ricardo couldn't stand it and started laughing. Rúbia got angry, but said nothing and decided;

"Call her and stay there, I'll pick you up, okay?"

"You don't have to do that. I'll take a cab."

"Ahhh...! Are you going to say you were angry with me just because I laughed? Stop being silly! I only laughed because I was imagining the scene."

"It's okay... I'll wait for you."

"I'm leaving now. Bye."

"Bye."

She returned the call to Jefferson's wife and quickly prepared. It didn't take long and Ricardo arrived.

When she got into the car, she kissed his face and thanked him;

"Thanks for coming. I'm very nervous."

"Let's go there. Let's get this over with." Turning to her with a mischievous smile, he asked jokingly; "Can you put your belt on or will you need a stretcher?"

"Ricarrrrrdo!" She expressed herself by emphasizing the letter "r" to playfully emphasize her anger. Then she spoke with a laugh. "If I didn't need you now…!"

"I'm just kidding. You're cute!" And then he praised again; "What a nice perfume. I love it."

"Thank you." She smiled with satisfaction. "And it is such a soft cologne, I don't know how you noticed."

"In terms of perfume, less is always more." He smiled and they continued talking.

Upon arriving at the bar where they agreed, Rúbia warned;

"I don't know her. She said she would come with a red blouse."

"Huuuuhm...!" he mumbled.

"Why?"

"Red... Color of war. She did not come in peace." He smiled as he looked at her.

"Don't joke. I'm nervous."

They entered and the friend led her with his hand on her back.

The receptionist went to meet them. At the same time, looking at a table, the only one occupied at the time, Ricardo told the girl;

"There is a person waiting for us. Thank you"

They went to the table where the woman in the red blouse was looking at them.

"Excuse me, are you Cícera?" Rúbia asked, holding her huge belly. The woman examined her closely without missing any detail. Then she answered;

"Yes, it's me."

"I'm Ricardo. Nice to meet you." He said, holding out his hand. The woman responded and he asked; "Can we sit down?"

"Yes, of course. Please." Then she said; "I was waiting for you alone. You are her brother?"

"We are great friends." He replied.

Cícera was clearly embarrassed by Ricardo's presence. She didn't seem to like it. Rúbia, visibly nervous, squirmed her wet hands under the table, when she asked in a trembling voice.

"Well... I'm here. You wanted to talk to me. You can talk."

"I hope you are great friends." Said Cícera in an almost offensive tone. "What I have to say is very personal."

"If you try to offend her, we'll go. I'm warning you." Said Ricardo, who didn't like her tone.

The waiter arrived and they asked for some beverages. When he left, in front of Rúbia, the woman attacked.

"I received an anonymous call and was told that you were my husband's lover."

"Wait a minute. I…"

"Let me finish, please." Rúbia sighed deeply and fell silent. Cícera continued;

"I didn't care, because I thought it was just one more."

"One more?!" She spoke in an angry tone.

"Jefferson can have as many lovers as he wants, because he always comes home and sleeps with me. It's best for you to know that."

When Ricardo realized that his friend had filled her lungs as if she was going to fight back, he took her arm slightly, pointing out that she would not say anything and remained silent.

"My husband had several women, but none were stupid enough to get pregnant. You should know that we have a financially reasonable life, and you certainly want to live on your child's support. However, I want you to know this: Jefferson and I are married with separate assets. All of our assets, that is, our house, which can be said to be a mansion, our beach house in a luxury condominium, our house in Campos do Jordão, our place in Ibitinga and other things that I don't even remember… Everything about us is under my name. What remains for you, or rather for your child, is nothing more than a very small alimony, as we have many expenses with our seven-year-old son, who is exceptional." Rúbia didn't know about Jefferson's third child, but she didn't say anything. And Cícera continued; "Our two eldest are fine, but the little one needs special care. He doesn't walk, he doesn't talk, he needs physical therapy, doctors, medication, a nurse for 24 hours… The list of expenses is enormous. For that reason, I doubt that any judge will take from that boy what he needs to keep yours alive while you are a healthy mother capable of working."

The soft drinks were on the table, but they didn't even touch them.

With her hands under the table and hidden by the towel, Rúbia was shaking. She didn't know what to say or how to act.

Looking at her, Ricardo saw that she was turning pale and decided to react.

"Mrs… Why is this aggression for? What is the cause of this gratuitous attack?"

"Gratuitous? Do you think that someone who sees her assets as a target of a… a… social climber, a scammer, to say the least, should remain silent? It's not the same! Before you go to the trouble of demanding the rights of the waiting boy, I warn you."

"Nobody asked for rights or a fat pension for their son." He defended her.

"Not so far!" She became aggressive.

"Wait a moment." Asked Rúbia in a hesitant voice. "Cícera, I don't know what you think of me and I don't care to know. I don't even understand what you want or know what I'm doing here. However, since we met, how about knowing the story with my version? Then draw your conclusions." Without waiting, she continued; "I went to work at that company where I met Jefferson. He wasn't wearing a wedding ring and didn't look married, because from the way he talked to me and other women, he didn't look like someone who owed his wife at home. We began to take an interest in each other. It was only after a long time that I learned that he was married. That's when Jefferson came up with that famous lie that he was breaking up, that he was getting a divorce… He wanted to break up, but he asked for a break. He said he loved me, that he was in love and I believed him. Idiot, I believed. I pressured him and threatened to end the affair. When I decided to do that, I was fired and found out. I was pregnant. I only stayed with that company to guarantee a good health plan, maternity leave, and other rights that I acquired. I didn't stay there because of your husband. He threatened me, demanding me to have an abortion, perhaps something he demanded of others, but I did not agree to kill my child. He threatened me again and I filed a complaint against him with the police. I don't know if you know this. Now, I want you to know." She said firmly, looking at her. "I don't want Jefferson or anything that comes from him. Make good use of your assets, your wealth, your fortune. Take care of your children and don't use what's special as a weapon to arrest your husband or sensitize others. I really admire a beautiful woman like you who seems respectable and intelligent, who submits to a husband who sleeps with someone and then comes home and uses her in the same way. The classification you give her lovers, as social climber, scammer and worse, also applies to you. Have a little more pride, self-respect and don't submit to this disgust. I really regretted getting involved with him. You can't imagine. Know that my son won't have any of his names. I would rather have him registered as the son of a single mother than have a scoundrel as a father. Forget you ever met me. I want to distance myself from you, because I feel contempt for a woman who lends herself to such devaluation in the face of a man who shamelessly betrays her. To have doubts, to give your husband a chance is one thing, to accept being betrayed constantly and to sleep with this man who is dating is to be insignificant. I was wrong. Yes, I did, but I didn't continue to do as you did. I'm qualified and I don't lend myself to that low role. Even with all the difficulties, I will not prostitute myself like you are doing. You are nothing, nothing different from those who sell, because you submit to this because you want to continue with your state, with your assets, and that is also prostitution." Rising abruptly, she said goodbye. "Excuse me. See you never again."

Perplexed by the scene, Ricardo stood up, sped up his steps behind his friend and didn't even have time to say goodbye.

When he reached her, outside the bar, he took her by the arm and turned her over, asking her;

"Calm down. Go slowly."

"Oh, Ricardo…" She muttered, rubbing her face with her hands in an agonizing gesture. "Take me away… I'm so nervous!" She said in a fragile way, very different from the previous minutes.

"Let's go. Let's go." He agreed, taking her to the car. Seeing her settled, he turned and sat down at the wheel.

"Who was that woman, huh? What did she want anyway?"

"I didn't understand it either."

For a moment she was silent. She took a deep breath, rested her head on the seat and closed her eyes while he looked at her silently. A few minutes later, she called out to him in a low voice.

"Ricardo… I think I'm not well."

"What are you feeling?" He said, worried.

"I think my blood pressure has dropped…"

As he touched her face, he could feel her cold and asked her;

"Do you have your health insurance card and documents in your bag?"

377

"Yes, I do."

"I'm going to take you to the hospital."

"There is a hospital that is in my health plan nearby." In a few minutes the friend took her there.

While she was being treated at the emergency room, he checked in at the counter. When he finished, he didn't know what to do or where to look for her. Asking for information from an attendant, she said with a smile.

"Mrs. Rúbia gave birth to a beautiful baby boy."

"What do you mean?! Gave birth?!"

"He was born beautiful and strong. They are fine, but it will take a few minutes to see them. You can wait here for the doctor to call you."

Ricardo began to laugh not knowing what to do. He even looked like his father. He walked from side to side and didn't take the smile off his face.

He stopped for a moment, organized his ideas and decided to call Rúbia's family. He soon realized that he didn't have Mrs. Celeste's phone number in his address book. He called Cristiano because he knew his friend was with Simone, but he didn't answer. He called Abner at the beach and told him what had happened. The friend gave him his mother's phone number and said he would be right back.

Calling Mrs. Celeste, he gave her the news. Then he was called to see Rúbia.

The friend was lying down, sleepy and connected to serum. Next to her, an empty crib.

"Hello…" He mumbled. "Are you okay?"

"I'm here. Everything went very fast. I was so afraid…" He kissed her on the forehead and took her hand, then asked her;

"What about the baby?"

"The doctors said they will bring him soon. They're just providing first aid." She slowly closed her eyes. She wanted to sleep.

"Rúbia... It was so fast!" He seemed admired, whispering. "As soon as I finished making your admission form and when I went to look for you, the baby was already born." He smiled. "A little more, he would have been born in my car."

She opened her eyes and smiled back.

The arrival of the nurse who was carrying Bruno on her lap woke her up.

"Look at mommy! Say hello to her again."

The drowsiness passed immediately. Rúbia straightened up, stretched out her arms and wrapped little Bruno with affection.

"Oh, my God..." The tears trembled in her eyes when a strong emotion overwhelmed her and she murmured. "Thank you, my God." She kissed him on the head and said; "It's beautiful! If..."

Ricardo touched him and caressed his face, removing his hair and putting it back with affection.

"Congratulations, mom. He's really handsome." Said the nurse with a generous smile. Turning to the young man, she asked; "Are you the daddy?"

"Unfortunately, not. I'm her friend." Ricardo only realized the answer when the nurse smiled broadly, so he tried to figure it out. "In a way, I'm an uncle, right?"

"Congratulations, uncle." She said; "If you need anything, just call us."

Rúbia didn't seem to have heard that conversation, she was totally focused on her son. Although her face was flushed, he came closer, caressed her arm and looked at Bruno, who was sleeping peacefully.

379

A little later, a few knocks on the door announced the arrival of Mrs. Celeste, who entered smiling and whispering;

"Hello daughter!"

"Mommy…" Rúbia was emotional.

The woman approached and, with her eyes clouded, kissed her and embraced her tenderly.

"I will not catch or kiss my grandson because of your father. He has the flu and I don't want anything to happen to my little angel." Then she greeted Ricardo and asked; "Guys, how did all this happen? Bruno wasn't going to arrive for another two weeks?"

Rúbia smiled and decided to tell what happened. They were happy and talking for a long time.

19.– BEYOND REASON

THAT SAME AFTERNOON, after the party at the institution, Simone returned home in the company of Cristiano.

They entered and she soon sought out her sister.

"How strange. She didn't say she was leaving." At that moment, she was alarmed. "I forgot! How could I?"

"What? What happened?"

"We were going to have lunch at my parents' house. I completely forgot. How could I do that?"

Cristiano was embarrassed. He felt guilty.

"I was tired, so worried... I should have remembered that too. I'm sorry for distracting you and asking you out. I wanted you to be with me so badly that I completely forgot."

"It was not your fault."

"Well... if she's not here, she must have gone to our parents' house. But the car is in the garage..."

"She hasn't been driving for the last few days. The distance between her belly and the steering wheel does not work. If she adjusts the seat, her feet can't reach the pedals." She laughed. When she saw the smile on Cristiano's face, she still joked; "Don't say anything near her, it's the model of the seat, the steering wheel." She laughed again.

"She must have taken a cab."

"Probably. I forgot my cell phone again." She said, checking the phone. "My God... Where am I with my head? I'll call my mom…"

As she approached, with a slight smile, Cristiano patted her arm, then her face, caressing her hair, asked her;

"Call soon."

Simone embraced him tenderly, leaning against his chest.

He kissed her head, her cheek and held her face gently. With a crystalline and firm glance, he invaded her soul for some seconds and murmured;

"I like you very much. I want you to stay with me."

"Me too…" She responded in the same tone.

Looking for her lips, he kissed her tenderly, embracing her with all his love. Inexplicably, surrounded by a very strong attraction, they could not control themselves. It was beyond reason.

They were two like-minded souls that had not known each other for a long time and had the most beautiful and sincere feelings.

The great cloud of worry dissipated in that magical moment and Simone allowed herself to be happy in Cristiano's arms.

Hours passed without them noticing. The rest of the world did not seem to exist. Lying down between the soft pillows, Cristiano caressed Simone's back, who was sleeping face down beside him.

Gently touching her shoulder with his lips, he felt the light and pleasant aroma exuding from her soft and delicate skin.

Moving her long, dense, slightly wavy hair away with his hands, he could look at her face with her eyes closed, and her lips which outlined a tender smile.

"I thought you were sleeping." He muttered in a deep, docile voice.

"And I am. I'm sleeping and having a beautiful dream."

He went over, hugged her and kissed her back and face. When he reached for her lips, she stopped him and asked him;

"Did you hear?"

"What?"

"It might be my sister."

"Did she arrive? I didn't hear anything."

"I did. I'm sure I heard someone coming in." She got up and looked for a robe that she put on quickly.

While Cris was looking for her clothes, Simone decided to go into the living room to see who was there. She did not have to go to the other room, because in the corridor, almost at the door to her room, she met her brother.

"Abner?! You scared me!"

"Hi, Simone. Sorry I scared you. Is everything okay?"

"Yes, but... what are you doing here? I..." As she was about to say something else, she saw David approaching the two of them. It was then when, clearly nervous and confused, she asked uncomfortably; "Let's go to the living room and..."

"Hi, Simone. Are you alright?"

"Yes, I'm, David." She replied, greeting him with a kiss. At that moment, the brother noticed her very embarrassed and worried.

He looked at her clothes and understood that she should be accompanied.

Without her seeing him, giving a sign to David, who followed Abner as he returned to the room.

On the sofa, the brother saw a man's shirt thrown away and apologized.

"Forgive me for coming suddenly." Without being able to take his eyes off the shirt and without resisting his curiosity, Abner asked; "Is Samuel there?"

"No." She answered, feeling her face blush.

At that moment, unexpectedly, the strong voice of Cristiano responded when he arrived at the room.

"I'm the one who is here, Abner." Without delay he greeted everybody. "So, everything's fine?" He looked at him a little uncomfortably, but firmly when he shook his hand.

"Cris?!" Her brother was surprised.

"What's up, David."

After greeting him, Cristiano went to his shirt, picked it up and put it on.

Simone was completely embarrassed and to change the subject so as not to see her embarrassed any more, her brother explained;

"I came to get Rúbia's clothes. She had the baby and…"

"Today!?" She was surprised.

"Just before lunch. We were in Mongaguá and Ricardo called me from the hospital asking for our mother's phone, because your cell phone was turned off."

"I went to the hospital to see Pedro and…"

"I imagine." He interrupted her. "Don't worry. Everything went well. Mom is with her now. But Rúbia needs clothes for her and the baby."

"The bags have been packed for a month." She laughed. "There were still two… almost three weeks to go. Is she okay? And the baby?"

"They are great. I've come from the hospital now. You don't even know what happened. She was nervous because Jefferson's wife called and…" He explained everything. "I'm glad Ricardo was there. Can you imagine what could have happened if she had been alone?"

"I don't even want to think about it." Said Simone. "Rúbia also… She shouldn't have gone." Then she asked; "Come here. Let's get the bags and…" She said as she walked. And Abner followed her.

Alone, with his brother, David couldn't stand it, he threw himself on the couch and laughed.

"If you make any comments, I swear I will explode you here and now." Threatened Cristiano, who also couldn't keep a smile off his face.

"I don't need to say anything. My silence and my laughter express more than a thousand words."

"You could have called, you know?"

"We called your cell phone, but no one answered. We didn't think you were here."

Cristiano looked for his wallet and car keys and found them on the dining room table.

In front of a sideboard mirror, he combed his black, stubborn hair with his fingers.

Simone and Abner returned to the room with the bags in their hands, he said naturally;

"Later, go to the hospital. She is in a private room and can be visited at any time. I will stay with her now while David goes to take our mother home so she can prepare everything for dad and then go back to the hospital."

"Is mom going to stay with her?"

"Yes, she is."

"I can't be with her, because…"

"We know, Simone. Don't worry." He said, interrupting her and stroking her arm.

"So... I'll be there in a while." She decided.

Still embarrassed and stunned, Simone didn't realize she hadn't asked what hospital it was, but David remembered.

"I left the address of the hospital with the room number."

"Ah! That's right. Here it is." Said Abner, handing her a note paper. Then they both said goodbye and left.

Cristiano approached Simone and wrapped her with affection as she hugged him by the waist, resting her face on his chest and confessing:

"I have never felt so ashamed…"

Not seeing her smile for remembering the shame, he responded;

"Neither do I. On the other hand, think of it... we are bigger and we don't have obstacles, right?"

"Also…"

Cristiano cradled her in his arms with extreme affection and kissed her. Then he traced her face with the tip of his fingers. With a strong and firm voice, he spoke in a low voice.

"You are not an adventure for me. We have nothing to hide and... I will always be by your side."

"I discovered that I have a very strong and special feeling for you. But I can't deny that I'm afraid."

"Afraid?!" He was surprised.

"There is a lot going on. I have to take care of my son, you know. All the responsibility for him is on me."

"I know about that, and I want to help you with whatever it takes."

"Look... You are single, free and unhindered. You have a great profession. Maybe, you should look for someone with the same conditions." Moving away from the hug, she walked a few negligent steps, sighed deeply and continued. "We will not be able to hang out with Pedro. I have no one to take care of him. You can't get attached because of me. You can go out, have fun without worrying... If you stay, you will be in prison with me... I'm divorced, with a child who needs me very much.

"I'm getting involved with the person I like, the one I like and the one I want to be with. I don't mind if I don't go out or have fun. That is not what I want. You are a person who is aware of her duties and I don't want you to change. I don't appreciate women who stay comfortable, need protection, and are totally dependent."

"David saw us today. He's open-minded, but what won't he tell your mother? Will she accept me? Divorced, with a son in Pedro's condition... And on top of that I'm older than you"

"Why, Simone! For God's sake! If you don't love me, if you made a mistake, just say so! Don't look for excuses with what my mom can or can't say! Have mercy!" He was angry. A moment of silence and he continued; "Both, your family and my family have nothing to do with us. Our happiness depends on both of us. Your father did not approve of Abner's condition or the fact that he had a partner. So what? He assumed his own life and is happy in his own way."

"And when my father finds out that David is your brother?"

"What about it?"

She settled down on the couch and he sat down next to her.

He caressed her back, made her look into his eyes and, in an almost sad tone, asked her with concern;

"Be honest. Do you like me?"

Hugging him, she kissed his lips. Then she looked into his eyes and whispered in a sweet, sweet voice.

"I can't see myself without you. I think this is my fear. After all…" She stopped and looked away.

"Are you afraid that I will change you for another? Are you afraid to try again what you have experienced with Samuel? Is that it?"

"In the end it is. I'm very afraid. I'm not sure, you're young, handsome... Like I said: single, unattached, with a good profession and…"

"Simone, don't compare me to him. Your life with Samuel was quiet and peaceful until the great difficulty with the baby appeared at the beginning of the pregnancy. It was different for us. We met when everything was very complicated in our lives. We have supported each other until now. I think the worst is over. If, in the midst of the challenges, we stay together... What else can separate us but God's will?"

"Is God on our side?"

"I firmly believe so. He made our paths cross, didn't He?" Simone hugged him tightly and he responded. They kissed and she decided;

"I'm going to take a bath. I want to visit Rúbia today."

"Go. I'll wait for you. I'm going with you to the hospital."

Allowing the warm water from the shower to spill over her head and back, she leaned against the wall and tried to relax, but could not. She felt her thoughts simmering.

How could someone live a romance fully if so many obligations and commitments called to responsibility? What would her father say? What would he think when he found out that Cristiano was David's brother? And what about Samuel? He might

388

even accuse her of an affair while they were married. At the same time, she remembered that she had the right to love, be loved and be happy. She had a lot to think about and decide. After all, would an affair be pleasant or would it be just another problem in her life?

She felt attracted to Cristiano for some time. She wanted him by her side. She always wanted him with her. She was grateful for his opinion and advice. She needed his help. She felt practically dependent and, why not say it, he was the one who was her friend at first and ended up becoming her lover. Why not admit that she loved him and wanted him by her side?

She looked like a teenager half her age, but with the responsibility imposed by the weight of twice the years she was living.

She didn't want to deprive herself of happiness, but she was afraid. A wave of doubts invaded her soul.

What if Cristiano had only attached himself to her because of her help, her encouragement of him? After all, she appeared in the young man's life when he was experiencing great loss and immense disorder.

"My God!" She murmured with the water hitting her mouth. "Guide me, Father, please."

After the bath, she went out to the suite and got ready. She dried her hair lightly with a hair dryer and entered the living room with the humidity still in her hair. When she saw Cristiano, with his eyes closed, lying on the sofa, she smiled with love.

As she approached, she cried out softly and tenderly;

"Cris…" He was asleep. "Wake up, honey."

"Hello…" He muttered in surprise, forgetting where he was. He smiled when he saw her and took her hand. Kissing her, he straightened up and stood up.

Holding her delicate face with both hands, smiling, he said;

"I want you to know that I adore you."

"I also adore you."

"I know you still have doubts about us, but that will pass. There's a lot going on right now. I just ask you not to rush into it."

"Ruch into…?"

"Wanting to be apart, wanting time to think or anything that keeps us apart. I don't want to and won't be away from you for anything in the world."

"I'm in conflict with many things, but I'm sure of one."

"What?"

"I want you by my side." She said sweetly and lightly with a beautiful smile. He kissed her and hugged her. Then he decided;

"Shall we go?"

"Yes, let's go."

✳ ✳ ✳

When they arrived at the hospital room, they found Abner, David and Ricardo.

Simone and Cristiano greeted them and then went directly to Rúbia, hugging and kissing her affectionately.

The sisters were emotional and hugged for a while, looking at little Bruno, who was sleeping in the crib next to his mother's bed.

"He's so cute! God bless you!" Said Simone. "Everything went very fast, Rúbia."

"Thank God, it was. I was so scared, remember? I felt bad. When I got to the hospital, I started to feel these strong pains. When the doctor examined me, he said the baby was already being born. I couldn't believe it. From the time I was admitted to the hospital until he was born, I think it took less than twenty minutes." There was a brief pause and she said excitedly; "Ah! I already fed him. Can you believe it?"

"Yes, I do." She said in a tender voice, looking bright and sweet.

Cristiano approached and, while looking at little Bruno, he put his arm around Simone's shoulders.

Seeing the scene, Rúbia smiled happily at her sister. She understood that they had assumed the romance.

A little uncomfortable, Simone asked what she already knew;

"Is mom staying here with you?"

"Yes, she is. She went home to get everything ready for dad. He needs to take her medicine on time and... You know. Dad's worried about this. David went there to drive her and he came back."

"When we get out of here, we can stop by and see him. What do you think?" Proposed Cristiano, looking at Simone.

"That's fine by me. If you don't mind…"

"Of course not."

Mrs. Celeste arrived and everyone enjoyed the reactions of the grandmother, who seemed very excited.

David and Abner decided to leave.

So, Simone decided to leave too.

On the way to her father's house, she was completely silent.

As he drove, Cristiano looked at her again and again. Annoyed by her quietness, he asked;

"Is everything okay?"

In front of him, she tried to smile, a smile that soon faded. Looking down, she responded weakly.

"All good."

"Why are you so quiet?"

"I know that nothing is by chance. Everything has a reason to be the way it is. Everything has a reason to exist. Only that…"

"What?" He insisted on the long silence.

"When I looked at Bruno sleeping... He is so beautiful! I thought…" Her voice trembled and she couldn't go on.

"Did you think about Pedro? Was that what you were going to say?" He asked in a warm voice.

"Yes…" She whispered. "I don't know if it's wrong, but... My son could be like his little cousin. I was imagining the two of them growing up together, playing, running, being friends... But it can't be like that... Is it wrong to want that?"

"It's not bad to want, to wish for something. It is wrong to rebel for what you do not have or to desire the evil of others."

"It's just that my son's situation worries me... It's not easy for me to look at him. You can't be happy with what I see. I'm being real. I sing, I play, I pray with him, but... I don't know how long it can last. How do you think I feel knowing it won't last long? Breathing problems, flu, infections... Everything indicates that Pedro is not going…" She cried. "I love my son. I wanted him to be healthy. The other day, when I was playing, I saw him laughing…" A sob drowned out her voice. "It took my son three months to smile. Do you know what that means to a mother? Sometimes when I sleep a little, I wake up and think it was just a nightmare. I ran to see Pedro and I saw that it wasn't a dream. He has problems and needs. Everything is very difficult. I can't entrust the care of my son to anyone. I couldn't even breastfeed him." She cried. "He can't suck and feed him like that is…"

Cristiano stopped the car in front of Mr. Salvador's house, turned to it and said in a low voice;

"God saw the right mother in you. The most perfect mother for him. You do not face difficulties, challenges as punishment."

"Isn't it a punishment, Cris? I did everything wrong and now I need to correct it?"

"What is the use of being worried and wanting to know the past? Nothing will help you. We can't change the past, but we can make the present better and the future better. If you were not a helpful, loving and caring mother with so many other attributes and Pedro did not deserve all your dedication and care, you both would not be together. Think of yourself as a special person to whom God has entrusted a special little creature. You have given your son the love he needs to receive."

She took a deep breath and tried to regain her composure. Then she said;"

"You give me so much strength…"

Taking her hand and kissing her, he responded;

"I will always be by your side." Holding her face firmly with both hands, he kissed her forehead for a long time and then said; "Let's see how your father is doing."

Mr. Salvador was happy to receive them. He liked Cristiano, who paid him a lot of attention.

As he looked at his daughter, he saw her bitter and immersed in her thoughts, perhaps sad. She had a blank stare and signs of discouragement.

"What is it, Simone? Why are you like this, daughter?"

"Nothing, father. I'm just worried."

"Were you visiting little Pedro today?"

"I went. I thought he was discharged, but no. It is likely that tomorrow…"

"You are very down."

"I think so too." The young man agreed.

"Mom will stay at the hospital with Rúbia. Do you want to go home?"

"No way. I can take care of myself. I'm not a boy. Your mother left everything in order here for me. Even the food is ready for tomorrow." A few moments later, not supporting his curiosity, he asked. "Have you seen Rúbia's son?"

"We did. He's cute. You have to see him, father. He's pink! He has blond hair..." She smiled with grace and sweetness. "He looks nothing like her."

"Your grandfather was blond, Polish. Bruno came out like him."

"Certainly." She agreed with a slight smile, not daring to bother him. She knew how proud the father was now and how difficult it was to accept that grandson.

"I think it's better for your sister to spend her recovery here at home, don't you think?"

"It's okay if she stays with me."

"She'd better be here." She said as if he hadn't heard.

"I see that you are much better, Mr. Salvador." Said Cristiano.

"I am. I stopped the cigarette and took the medicine correctly, but there are times when I want to..." He laughed. "I feel almost crazy. Then Celeste said I was supposed to be sucking candy or chewing gum. This is a little annoying."

"That's great! You can't imagine how happy I am to know that. I love to see determined people with strong opinions like you." He said with satisfaction to encourage him.

"I'm determined. You will see. I can do it." He replied proudly.

"To get rid of any addiction you need discipline and strength. The desire to have one more cigarette will be great, but if you resist once more, the desire will diminish until it is over. Then, in time, you will even be repulsed by the cigarette." Looking around, he suggested; "Why don't you disappear these ashtrays and throw away the pack of cigarettes, if you still have it?"

Standing up immediately, in a good mood, Mr. Salvador enthusiastically decided;

"I'll do it right now!"

Cristiano accompanied and helped him to throw everything away. Upon returning to the room, Simone decided.

"Dad, I'm leaving now."

"It's early. Order a pizza!"

"No, dad. I'm very tired. I need to be at the hospital early tomorrow and Cris has to go to work."

"Daughter..." He came closer, seeming to guess her thoughts, he commented. "You saw your sister's son today and... I saw how happy you were to talk about him. I know you are comparing Bruno with Pedro, but don't be sad. Accept your son as God has given him to you."

"Yes, dad. Why are you telling me this?"

"You are sad."

"In spite of the work, the fatigue, the despair that takes hold of me when I get sick, I accept the son that God has entrusted to me and that is why I would like you to also accept Abner, the son that God has entrusted to you, just as he is. After all, condition by condition. My child has one and yours has another. When the condition is imposed from birth, it indicates that God has allowed it." Cristiano immediately took her by the arm trying to stop her, but there was no time. Believing she said something unnecessary, she tried to redeem herself. "Excuse me, dad. I didn't have to say that. I'm exhausted and I don't even know what I'm talking about."

Mr. Salvador, who reacted, fell silent. He lowered his head and said nothing.

"We better go, right?" Cristiano asked.

"Oh, dad... I'm sorry." She said, with clear regret. Approaching him, she hugged him.

Caressing her on the back, the man said;

"Don't worry, Simone. I understand you."

When he saw them separated from the embrace, Cristiano insisted.

"Shall we go?"

They said goodbye and left.

✳ ✳ ✳

When they arrived at Simone's house, they entered and she thanked him.

"Thank you for everything."

"Don't thank me. Count on me. And... By the way, who's going to the hospital with you tomorrow? You won't be able to drive and return with Pedro if he's discharged."

"I will take a cab. Don't worry."

"Do you have money?" When he saw her eyes widened with the surprise of the question, he said in time; "I'm sorry if I want to know, but... a teacher must not earn well and... I see that the expenses are many."

Smiling shyly and finding grace in her own way, she responded;

"Don't worry. I have money. With the help that you and others have given me, I made a reservation for these emergencies. I simply cannot abuse or afford to take a cab every day."

As he approached her, he hugged her and she did the same.

As he had his face over her hair, he felt the tufts tangle in his beard and once again experienced that pleasant aroma she emitted.

"Do you want me to stay here with you?" He asked lovingly.

"I want to, I want to, but we shouldn't. Your mother is alone and..."

"I don't want to leave."

"I don't want you to leave."

Pressing her against him, he searched for her lips and kissed her with all love and tenderness. Then, they said goodbye.

Alone, Simone again gave in to doubt and insecurity. She felt beyond her limits and needed to be stronger than ever.

20.– RESPECT BETWEEN SIBLINGS

THROUGH THE SLOTS in the window, the rays of faint light came in, indicating a cloudy day, without the radiant glow of the sun.

It was autumn. A wind that came into the room all night made Simone feel cold all morning. She didn't have the heart to get up and wrap herself in another cover. This made her feel uncomfortable and her sleep was light and broken.

She didn't want to get up. She was curled up under the sheet and a very thin blanket. Extending her hand on the pillow beside her, she caressed it as he remembered Cristiano. No one had slept there with her except her ex-husband.

That time with Samuel seemed very distant, while the memory of Cristiano was vivid.

There was a force, a very strong feeling that attracted them in a way they could not explain.

How to live that love and be happy in the face of such serious difficulties and problems?

She could not neglect her son and she did not consider it fair that Cristiano should limit himself to getting involved in a situation that was not his job. He was young and unhindered, but they loved each other and wanted to be together.

She took a deep breath and felt exhausted. She didn't want to, but she needed to get up. She looked at her watch, sat up on the bed and felt a strange chill.

Forcing herself to get up, she decided to take a shower to cheer herself up, since she needed to go to the hospital and also see her situation at the university. She still didn't know what to do, since her leave of absence was ending.

* * *

Cristiano, lying in his bed, remembered the day before. He had slept little. However, awake, he dreamed a lot.

He couldn't undo the smile on his face. He was delighted. His eyes were fixed on the ceiling as he remembered every detail about Simone: her soft scent, her soft skin, her silky hair that she caressed with all tenderness.

A lot of time had passed, he wanted to hold her in his arms, caress her with affection and have her for himself.

It would not be the difficulties with little Pedro that would deter or discourage him. He liked the boy very much and clung to him without understanding why. He felt sad about his condition, but believed in future lives and that love, affection and attention would help him feel better and recover. He wanted to help him and give him all the attention he needed.

With a wide smile, which he had not expressed for some time, he jumped out of bed without worrying about the cold and got into the shower.

Shortly after, already in the kitchen, Mrs. Janaina was impressed by his disposition, which she had not seen in a long time.

"Good day mother!" He exclaimed, smiling, bowing and kissing her cheek as he always did.

"Good morning, son."

Sitting at the table, he filled a glass of juice while saying;

"Rúbia's baby was born yesterday."

"Yesterday! And you didn't even tell me? Why?"

"The day was busy. When I arrived, you were already sleeping."

"Why didn't you call me?"

"In the morning I went with Simone to the hospital."

"And little Pedro?"

"He is still in the hospital. After lunch, we went to the institution where we stayed for a while and..." He remembered and smiled, but said nothing. "As soon as I left her at home, Abner and David arrived there to tell them the news. So, we went to the hospital to see Rúbia and the baby. Wow! He's cute! You have to see him. Then we went to see Mr. Salvador. I took Simone home, and when I got here, you were already asleep."

"Did Celeste stay in the hospital with Rúbia?"

"Yes, she did. It was a normal delivery and so, tomorrow, I think she'll be discharged. Mr. Salvador wants Rúbia to spend her recovery at home." He laughed.

"How nice. I'm happy when the resentments and wounds are over. Tell me something; and Simone, how is she?"

"She's all right." He replied, not understanding his mother's intention.

"I know she is confident, lucid, understanding, but... As soon as she saw her sister's baby... Wasn't she upset?"

"I wasn't even going to tell you... in the hospital, she was fine. She acted normal. However, when she saw how Mrs. Celeste was with her grandson in her lap, happy and satisfied... I don't know if that was the case, because later, when we were alone,

Simone cried a little. Not out of jealousy or envy. She also wanted Pedro to be like Bruno."

"Every mother wants the best for her child. In her case, we don't even know what to say to encourage her." There was a brief pause. Then she thought and wanted her son's opinion. "Cris, what do you think of little Pedro? What are his chances?"

The boy closed his smile, sighed deeply and commented;

"Kids with Patau syndrome are known to have a very unstable and complicated health condition. As I understand it, that is, the doctor was not entirely clear, but he let it slip that naturally he has a low immunity. That's why he's so prone to infection and... We can't say that to Simone; however, I believe he won't be one year old. I don't know if I'm being too cold or realistic. I see her so committed, so concerned, doing everything she can to take care of her child and that gives me... I don't know... something. She is not wrong. In a way, I fear for her suffering when Pedro leaves."

"Last week, when I went there, I found Simone very depressed. Jeez! How she lost weight!"

"She hardly sleeps and has no time to eat properly. You heard that she fired the maid, right? She said the woman wasn't doing things right, but I don't think that was it. I think Simone is having financial difficulties."

"I thought so too."

"I don't know how to help, mom. I'm ashamed to offer anything and she is offended."

"Why do you feel compelled to offer something? Do you think you are not helping enough?"

Seriously, Cristiano looked up slowly and directly to his mother. He couldn't understand if she was upset because he was always with Simone and felt a romance between the two of them, or if she just wanted to try him.

"I can't say why I want to help more. I like Simone and Pedro. I don't want them to be in trouble. If I can... Why not?" Staring at her, he asked to test her. "Do you have something against our friendship or against what I do?"

"No, son. Somehow… I even think about going there and finding out exactly what's going on. After all, I consider her a lot. But she has her parents, her brother and sister. Abner is fine and…"

"What if he doesn't know? If he doesn't know, he won't help her."

"Well... you are always with her and you must know more than your brother. If there is anything we can do to help…"

Cristiano was suspicious. For a moment he thought his mother was not approving of his relationship with Simone. Perhaps she suspected something and didn't seem to agree. He decided not to say any more.

Actually, he finished his breakfast in silence and went to get ready for work.

✳ ✳ ✳

In the office, in the interval between one patient and another, David noticed that one of his patients had been absent and went to look for his brother. Seeing him alone, David asked him if he also had an absent patient.

"No, he called and said he was going to be late. He's on his way."

"My patient didn't even warn me."

"David, I need to talk to you." He went straight ahead, his voice thickening with tension.

"You're serious. What happened? Isn't everything okay with you and Simone?"

"It is a delicate moment for her. I will not pressure her in any way. Especially because, unfortunately, I know this will happen and I want to be with her when it does."

"I didn't understand. How so?"

"I'm talking about Simone's difficulties with her son, the divorce, the exchange of property and employment. I know that all of this will happen. When I say, unfortunately, I mean Pedro's condition. You know."

"Yes, I know." He agreed with sadness, looking down. "She is very close to her son. She will suffer so much."

"I'm very fond of him, David. I have been attracted to Simone for some time. I just didn't go near her before so as not to scare her."

"I understand." The brother smiled and confessed. "A long time ago, I saw that a romance was going on. I just didn't say anything because you never talked to me about your private and intimate life."

"Neither you with me." He said, staring at him.

"It's different with me, Cris."

"Today I understand that, in terms of love, affection and desire, there is no difference. When these feelings are true, they are strong and exist so that we cannot contain or explain them."

"We never talk about our feelings, our intimacy. I don't know what you think of me today. After all, I'm a homosexual."

"I understand and respect you. I respect you very much." David was moved. He looked away. He took a deep breath and fiddled with some things to hide it. Cristiano came closer, touched his shoulder, waited for him to look at him again and continued; "If I never talked about myself, about my intimate life, it was to avoid you to think that I wanted to tell you how it should be."

"Really?!

"Today I understand your condition. It wasn't always like this, I confess. I looked for a lot of information about it. I needed a lot of instruction. Mainly because…"

"Why?" Insisted David, wanting him to continue.

"Because Vitória was completely against your condition. I didn't accept it. I thought it was because she wanted to. Jeez! She saturated me a lot because of that. We fought a lot so I looked for information."

"When you didn't understand me, you didn't approve of me, you never said anything."

"You know me. I'm not the kind of person who criticizes, harasses anyone. After I stopped being ignorant, I saw it with different eyes. I know it took me a long time to understand and think differently. The accident helped me a lot, you know? I literally had to break my head to let something in. He smiled. I just didn't want you to think I was showing off, talking about women or wanting to teach you how to act, I don't know…"

"I wouldn't think that of you, Cris. You never talked about it."

"And why should I open up, huh? Why didn't you come to me?" David smiled generously and responded;

"I also don't know. It's a shame, maybe. How could I come here and tell you that I was attracted to boys and not girls? How could I say that Abner and I liked each other beyond friendship?" When he saw the other smile for understanding him, he proposed. "Let's stop what happened in the past."

The brother smiled in agreement and continued:

"Do you know what it is? I'm really enjoying Simone. I can't hide it from anyone anymore. Earlier today, I was happy that we both understood each other yesterday, since she also admitted that she liked me. I was going to tell mom that we get along, but... mom was a little strange. She arrived with a question like: Why did I feel obliged to help Simone? I didn't understand what she meant. It seemed that she was suspicious and didn't approve of the idea of seeing us together. I don't know if it's because Simone is divorced, has a child..."

"I wouldn't even tell you, but... Some time ago, mom came to me with some questions about you and Simone."

"What did she want to know?"

"If I thought you were doing too much or if your behavior was normal. What I thought of Simone. How was the connection between her and her ex-husband? She even wanted to better understand little Pedro's condition, whether it could happen in a future pregnancy or not."

"She even asked that?!" He was surprised.

"In short, she was interested in the possibility of a romance between you both."

"And what did you say?"

"That everything was possible. That you were a beautiful couple and mother laughed and agreed. You know, Cris, I don't think she's against it, she's just worried. You were always her favorite."

"There you go again."

"It is true!" He laughed. "Don't try to deny it. It doesn't bother me because you're a great brother. Being the favorite, you are full of care. She wants to protect you, to know if you won't be in trouble."

"How could I get in trouble?"

"As modern as she may be, she may find that divorce is stigmatizing, that it marks someone's life. For some people, divorce is simple. Separated, finished and ready to go. For others, it extends long ties to someone from the past."

"I know about that."

"Ricardo is divorced. He has a son with Flora and, whether they like it or not, that son will be a link between the two. Flora's current husband has to put up with her visiting Renan when he is sick and staying there. He has to see her pick up the boy and drive him back when he has to leave... among other situations when Ricardo and Flora need to be in contact for their son. In her case, the divorce is not so simple. Her current husband needs to understand, be patient, tolerant, because in his marriage, Ricardo's presence will exist. This may not be easy for some. There are people who do not tolerate it and then the fights begin."

"Simone's case is different."

"Her husband is far away for now." David recalled.

"Ex-husband." Corrected Cristiano, unsatisfied.

"Whatever. It's distant, but who guarantees it will always be so?" The brother said nothing and continued. "I know you're thinking the same thing I am. It's hard to admit, but the truth is that the connection, the bond between them, little Pedro, maybe, won't last long and Samuel won't need to have any more contact. However, the question of the house remains, as it seems that the judge let Simone stay with it while she was there with her son. In addition, the ex-husband may have a crisis of regret, wanting her to return to him, whatever... You have to think about everything. I think mom worries about that."

"I will not leave Simone, unless she wants to."

"So as not to have a strange atmosphere between you and mom, talk to her. Tell her how you feel and what you plan to do. This will reassure you."

At that moment, the assistant's weak voice caught their attention.

"Dr. Cristiano, the patient has just arrived."

"I'm going." Turning to her brother, he smiled and thanked him. "Thank you, David. Thank you. You helped me so much."

"Don't say that. You can always count on me." He patted his back and Cristiano left.

✳ ✳ ✳

When she was discharged with her son, Rúbia did not want to go to her parents' house. She decided to stay with her sister.

That day, Mrs. Celeste had come home to pack some things for her husband, who, because of his determination, was not to visit his daughter or grandson to avoid contaminating them with the flu, even though her husband was well recovered.

Simone's house, again, was the target of many visitors for the arrival of another baby.

Mrs. Janaina visited little Bruno and, in the room, together with the young mother, she admired the boy breastfeeding, while listening to the anguished cry of Pedro from another room.

"I'll see if I can help Simone." Said the pious lady. When she went to look for her, she found her in the living room, cradling her son with love, trying to make him stop crying.

"Do you want help, daughter?"

"I don't know what I'm doing anymore. Now it is always like that: he wakes up and cries. He doesn't stop." There was a short pause in which she caressed him generously and breathed. "I have a lot to do. There are dishes in the sink, clothes to wash and iron. I'm not even thinking about cleaning the house and, before, it was me who always liked everything clean and in its place."

"Let me take him for a moment." Asked the lady tenderly and held him very carefully. Looking closely at the boy, she saw his appearance and felt his sharp, impatient cry.

"Isn't he hungry?"

"I fed him just now." Exhausted, Simone sat down on the couch and watched the lady carefully cradle Peter. Then she asked; "Would it be a great abuse on my part if you stayed with him for a little while so I could cook and make soup for my sister?"

"Not at all, daughter. I'm staying with him." Pedro kept crying and his mother warned him;

"I know it's hard, but don't be upset, please. He just cries like that."

"Isn't he in pain?"

"Not even the doctor can tell. I've given him all the medicine for today. The first few times he did that I got desperate, but I found out that there is no way. I'm only sorry that it's an inconvenience to my sister."

"Come on, Simone. Do what you have to do. I'll take care of him."

Taking advantage of the help, she ran to the kitchen.

Finishing the work there, she hurried to wash some of her son and nephew's clothes and spread them out in the laundry.

When she finished, her mother arrived.

"Daughter, why didn't you leave me this?"

"I'm done, mom. Mrs. Janaina helped me with Pedro."

"How is he?" The lady was interested.

"He just cries. He calmed down a while ago, but it didn't last long."

Both went to the room and saw Mrs. Janaina caressing little Pedro, who slept for a few moments.

"He is silent." Whispered the woman. "When she got up to put him in the crib, the boy grunted, woke up and started crying again."

Patiently, Simone approached, took him in her arms and tried to calm him down.

"What is it, my love?" She spoke with a soft voice and a generous tone. "You are angry today. You didn't let mommy do anything and you just stayed quiet in your aunt's lap, didn't you?"

"Grandmother." Corrected Mrs. Janaina, smiling. "I'm past the age of being an aunt. You can call me grandma."

After greeting her friend, Mrs. Celeste tried to play with her grandson, but to no avail. The baby just cried.

"I'm going to take a look at Rúbia and Bruno. Are they in the room?"

"Yes, they are. Go, mom." Responded Simone, forcing a smile that faded as soon as her mother left the room. She had noticed that after Bruno's birth, Mrs. Celeste did not dedicate much to Pedro. In fact, it was not easy to contemplate. Without a doubt, it was much better to contemplate Bruno: healthy, perfect and beautiful.

Simone sighed deeply and had tearful eyes when she decided, amidst the weeping of her son.

"Come on, my love. Let's change this diaper. Maybe you're demanding that, right?"

"Do you want help, Simone?" Offered Mrs. Janaina

"If you can bring me some warm water, I'd appreciate it. The one in the thermos near the changing table must be cold."

"Of course, I'll get it"

Even after changing his diaper, little Pedro would not stop crying. He even seemed to scream more. It was a burning cry, like a high-pitched scream that started to bother her a lot. It was clear that there was something wrong with him, but she couldn't figure out what it was.

409

"It is worse than on other days. I don't know what else to do." Said Simone, almost desperately. "I think I'll take you to the doctor."

Mrs. Celeste and Rúbia went to the living room while Bruno was sleeping after his grandmother's bath.

"In fact, he's crying a lot, Simone. I've never seen him like this. Let me, please. Who knows, maybe in grandma's lap…" Taking him in her arms, she spoke sweetly; "Come to grandma, my love."

At that moment, they heard the sound of a horn in front of the house and Simone deduced.

"It must be Abner. He said he'd be here today. I'll have to go and open it, because the electronic door broke."

She went out and found out that it was Cristiano. Meanwhile, the other three looked through the curtain of the large window in the room.

When she opened the door, she received him with a smile. The boy was quick, kissed her on the lips and Simone responded.

At that moment, in the living room, Mrs. Celeste, very surprised, turned to Mrs. Janaina and asked her;

"Did you see that?!"

"I saw."

"Did you know?"

"No."

Rúbia said nothing and walked away, holding back her laughter. Simone, remembering that the others could see, spoke to him and seemed to whisper;

"Don't do it. Your mother and my mother are inside."

"It's time for them to know, don't you think?" Looking at her, he asked; "What's going on? Is everything alright?" Before she answered, he noticed. "You seem distressed."

When they came in, she said;

"Pedro has not stopped crying since yesterday. I didn't sleep a wink last night. And I'm also helping Rúbia with Bruno."

Upon entering the room, the young man greeted everyone with kisses and said;

"Let me go and wash my hands to catch this crying boy." He joked, looking at little Pedro in his grandmother's lap.

After a few minutes, he returned to the living room, taking the boy in his arms. In a generous way, he filled him with affection, but it didn't work.

"Why are you so angry today? Tell your uncle here." He spoke in a deep voice. He caressed his cheek, touching the side under his ear. Peter cried out painfully. Christian immediately asked. "Simone, give me a cloth diaper or some other clothes, heated with a hot iron, please."

"I'll be back just now!" It didn't take long and she came back delivering it. "Here. Check if it's not too hot."

With the boy in his lap, Cristiano sat down and placed the warm diaper over Peter's ear, which gradually diminished the crying and began to complain.

"His ear hurts." Said Cristiano, who, extremely generous and even paternal, took care of the boy with tenderness.

"My God!" He was silent and Simone was surprised. "How could I not have imagined this before?"

"Fatigue, stress and excessive involvement in a problem do not allow us to see alternatives. Besides…" He joked. "It was all solved with a man-to-man conversation. Aren't you a big boy?"

"What are you going to do now?" Mrs. Celeste asked.

411

"Ear pain cannot be cured with just a warm cloth. It must be inflamed and he must be medicated." Explained the young man.

Simone became discouraged, in her heart, when she thought about going to the hospital again. But, resigned, she said nothing.

"That's true, daughter." Agreed her mother. "It will be better to take him to the doctor now or he will have more problems at dawn."

"I'm going to change my clothes."

"I'll give you a ride." Decided Cristiano.

Mrs. Janaina didn't say a thing. She just looked at her son cradling the boy in his lap and smiled admiring the scene. She just wanted it to be different. Sitting next to him, she stroked Pedro's head with tender affection.

Soon Simone returned, lifting a bag with her son's things on her shoulder and asked;

"Are you sure you go with me, Cris? Won't it stop you from doing your duties?"

"No way. Come on." He said, giving her the little boy.

✳ ✳ ✳

It was late enough when Cristiano arrived home and thought his mother was already asleep.

He entered quietly, trying not to wake her up. But he was surprised by the light that came on.

"Hi mom! What a scare!"

"Jeez, son! How long it took! I was worried."

"After returning from the hospital, I stayed at Simone's house for a while."

Directly, Mrs. Janaina said;

412

"I saw you greeting Simone when you arrived at her house."

"Did you see?" He asked with a smile.

"Are you dating her?" In front of her, he said;

"We're dating, mother. Do you have anything against it?"

"Not against Simone. No way, I like her."

"So why do you look worried?"

"Because she is still working out situations with her husband. For having a child... Really, I don't even know why I'm worried. I think it's for you. I wish it were different."

"Since I met Simone, my life has changed. I saw someone with so much strength, so much determination and it was this, mainly, that helped me get out of the bottom of the well. You remember what I was like, don't you?"

"Of course. I'm very grateful for everything she did."

"Mother, if you managed to understand and accept David's condition, something very difficult for many parents... If you agree with his union with Abner... Why are you now, let's say... reluctant to accept my relationship with Simone?"

"I have nothing against your romance. It's her husband who I can't get out of my head, son. This man's attitude was very strange, don't you think? What if he suddenly decides he wants his wife back?"

"Ex-wife!" He corrected her. The mother said nothing and he said; "They are separated long enough. For her, I'm sure there's no turning back."

"It is the ex-husband who worries me about this situation. It's nothing against you. To be honest, at first, I was worried about little Pedro's condition. I was afraid that it was hereditary and that his next children might have the same problem."

"No, mom. This has nothing to do with it."

"I know. It is not hereditary. But you know how mothers are... They always want the best for their children. Your brother explained very well what this syndrome is. I'm sorry for thinking about things…"

Cristiano approached her, hugged her tenderly and caressed her short hair as she rested her face on his chest. He kissed her on the head and said;

"Stay calm, mother. I know what I'm doing."

21.– DAVID'S MEETING WITH MR. SALVADOR

IT WAS A SATURDAY AFTERNOON. The day was overcast when Cristiano parked his car in front of Simone's garage.

He got out of the car, walked around it and smiled as he looked at the door and saw Mr. Salvador standing there against a short wall.

On seeing him, Mr. Salvador opened the door and seemed satisfied, greeting him.

"I'm glad you came. I really needed some company."

"Is everything okay with you?"

"Almost everything."

"Why? Aren't you better?"

"Are you talking about the flu? Ah yes. I'm completely cured. However, just now, I got worse than when I was sick."

"What happened?" He just wanted to know, after he went in.

"When you enter, you will see. I just didn't leave because... I don't even know why. I'm outraged, to tell you the truth."

"What happened?" He became curiously interested.

"Neither Celeste nor the girls told me." He told his wife and daughters. "I know that Abner is living... You know. With a boy. I'm very embarrassed to tell you this, but... The truth is this. When

415

I got here, I found my son and a boy. That's when I realized he was his partner! That's absurd! I'm almost bored. I feel sick until now!"

"Did you see anything, any romantic relationship between them?" He asked with some care in his tone.

"No. It was just missing that! I was outraged."

The man was panting, blushing and visibly irritated.

"Are you sure he is his partner?"

"He can only be that. I heard a conversation about the trip to the beach that was interrupted because of Rúbia, who went to the hospital. This is a bit embarrassing!"

Cristiano said nothing and looked down.

This was the moment of truth. Either he would say that David was his brother or he would discover from others when they came back.

"Mr. Salvador." He said quietly and patiently. "We have already spoken about the condition of people like your son and David."

"David? So, you know him?"

"I know that very well. And sometimes you almost meet him, too, because the other room in the dental office is his."

"Wait a minute! You told me your brother was there!"

"Exactly." He confirmed with seriousness and calm.

"No! I can't believe it!"

"Well, you can believe it. David is my brother. Didn't you notice the similarity? We are very similar. If you look closely, I'm a little taller than he is."

"Now you're telling me…" He looked at him for long seconds. "Why didn't you tell me? Why? You're ashamed of him too, aren't you?"

"No, of course no. Somehow, it's about time. I was ashamed of my brother being gay. I stopped being ignorant a long time ago and got a lot of understanding about it. I love my brother. We get along very well. I respect him, I accept him, and I understand him. To be honest, I won't admit that someone mistreated or ignored him because of his condition. And this desire and defense, on my part, also extends to Abner."

"How can you accept that? They…"

"They have the right to do what they want in their lives. I'm not God to judge you or them. Understand that." The man fell silent… thinking. Cristiano suggested smiling, without giving him much time to reflect. "Let's go inside. You came here to see your daughter and grandson. So, get on with it. Do what you came here to do."

"I can't look at them."

"If that's the problem… Don't look. Let's go inside. You can't stay here all the time. Take advantage of the fact that I'm here and let's go have a coffee, let's talk." Putting his arm around the gentleman's shoulders, he guided him into the house.

Unexpectedly, the man stopped, opened his eyes wide and, looking at him, asked on impulse;

"You're not like him, are you?"

Cristiano smiled and held back his laughter to respond.

"No. Definitely not." He wanted to laugh. He thought he could tell him that he was dating his daughter. He would like to see the man's face. But he didn't say anything.

They entered and the man went directly to a corner of the sofa, standing next to the place where Pedro was quiet.

Through the presence of Simone's father, Cristiano kissed her face as he always did and he understood. The young man thought that the surprises of that day would be too much for Mr. Salvador.

Everyone was playing and talking animatedly when another visitor arrived. It was Cláudio, Simone's friend.

He was a gay man, medium height, thin, handsome, kind and very expressive. Very friendly and smiling, he greeted everyone, including Mr. Salvador, who was well hidden in the corner of the room, and went straight to play with little Pedro.

"Hello, friend." He addressed Simone with a gesture. "Can I hold him? It has been a while. Look at my little one!"

"Of course. Take him."

The mother took the boy out of the car and gave him to Cláudio, who was very good with the babies.

"Where is uncle's baby? Cutie! Uncle was dying, missing this beautiful boy! Where is the baby?"

Despite the deformity of the lips, little Pedro's smile was very clear.

"He smiled!" Shouted Simone. "He laughed with Cláudio!" She felt satisfied, truly happy.

Cristiano, who seemed jealous, got serious and came over to confirm.

Looking over Simone's shoulder, he gently complained.

"He never laughed with me."

"But he doesn't cry when he's in your lap." She said to comfort him.

"Oh, my friends! That smile was a blessing!" Exclaimed Claudio excitedly, continuing to play with the little one to see him laugh more.

Mr. Salvador sneaked away and, without Cláudio seeing or hearing him, he passed by Cristiano and murmured;

"That was all I needed to see." He referred to the young man, full of sadness.

Mrs. Celeste called her husband in the kitchen and offered him coffee. She wanted to get him away from the others, because she was afraid he would displease the visitor. As he was drinking his coffee, he asked;

"And Rúbia?"

"She is in the bathroom. Bruno should wake up in a while to eat."

"I want to leave. I can't take this anymore."

Cristiano went into the kitchen looking for something.

"What do you need, son?" Mrs. Celeste wanted to help.

"A glass, please. I'm dying of thirst."

"Here it is." She gave him the glass.

When he saw the young man, next to the filter, filling the glass with water, he asked;

"Did you see that?"

Cristiano drank the water and then answered;

"You know, Mr. Salvador, I think that's the way to go. Just as you and I, naturally, have our way of being and expressing ourselves. I believe that Cláudio is not forcing himself to do anything."

"Do you think that?"

"Yes, I think so. Even if you force yourself to have those manners, what do I have with that? It doesn't offend or attack me. So why do I care? Don't you think it's better to think that way?"

"And why should I think that way?"

Cristiano smiled and responded;

"To live more and better. There is no reason to be bothered by those who are not doing anything to you. Besides, why would you bother?" When he didn't hear an answer, he added; "Remember what I told you? People who are well resolved with themselves, people who are happy with themselves, have no reason to worry about anything."

"I think I'll be going."

"Don't do that. Stay and keep me company." Said the boy, running his hand behind his back.

He was happy and stayed. Still, he did not look at his son. He avoided him as he did with Cláudio and David.

It wasn't long before Rúbia got out of the bathroom, nursed Bruno and went into the living room.

It was then that the grandfather was satisfied to take his grandson Bruno on his lap and more at ease with David, who decided to take pictures to record that moment.

"Look how well you did on that!" David said, showing him the image in the digital camera.

Proudly, the man agreed and even told him;

"Bruno is my father's name, you know?"

"Rúbia told me. In fact, she had good taste. It's a very nice name."

"I like it too." Then, without realizing it, he brought up the subject. "Your brother told me that you are also a dentist and that you attend the other room there in his office."

"It is true."

"Why have I never seen you there? I'm his patient."

"I believe that the days when Cristiano attended you were the same days that I was taking a course."

"Ahhh…"

Everyone was talking a lot, laughing, joking and not paying attention to the conversation that started between the two.

"Apparently, Bruno likes his grandfather's lap. He has already slept." David noticed and smiled.

"It is true." After a minute, watching at the others, he asked; "Apparently, you have known each other for a long time."

"More or less. It was the last year that I met Rúbia and Simone."

"Has Abner known you for a long time?" The gentleman asked seriously.

David looked at him, also serious, and, gently, he said calmly;

"I have known your son for a long time." With his vibrant, almost greenish, honey-colored eyes, he invaded the old man's soul and fell silent. The man was surprised and looked away, rocking his grandson again.

After a while, so that the matter between them would not die, Mr. Salvador commented;

"My wife speaks so good of your mother."

"They are two angels! Your wife and my mother."

"You know, the other day, your brother gave me a very important lesson about women. I started looking and realized that I had retired, but my wife had not. It seems that she will never be able to retire from household chores. So, I started to help and... You know, in a house you have a lot of work."

"I know. It is important to help with domestic chores to give value to women and mothers. The man who is not very advanced, morally speaking, is the one who dominates the woman, and uses force, physical or psychological, to exercise his rights. In general, women are only physically more fragile because, for them, nature has determined some functions. God gave man strength to protect her and not to enslave her[1]."

"Your brother told me he was a spiritist. Are you one too?"

"I am."

"Don't you believe that Spiritism leaves its followers... I don't know if the name is followers or believers."

"Adepts, would be better."

"Doesn't Spiritism make its adepts very tolerant?"

"I believe that the adepts of the spiritist philosophy have more knowledge and that is why they begin to understand things, people and life better."

"I don't want to be rude, but... How does Spiritism explain *that*?" He pointed to Cláudio, who, on the other side of the room, laughed and amused the others by saying something.

David looked, took a deep breath, and straightened his stubborn hair. He thought, turned to him and responded calmly.

"Do you believe in reincarnation?"

"I don't know. I have no opinion."

"The Spiritist doctrine is a reincarnationist philosophy, that is, its followers believe in a just and good God and that He, the Father, does not destroy us after this life. Neither does it limit us to hell if we do a lot of foolish things. Neither does he send us to heaven if we ask for forgiveness of sins before we die."

"And the person who did everything right, doesn't go to heaven?"

---

[1] N.A.E -. In *The Book of the Spirits, in* Chapter IX - questions 817 to 882 - talk about the equal rights of men and women, under the vision of the Spiritist doctrine.

"And who, in this world, did everything right?" He asked, looking at him with a soft smile.

"I believe that the one who stepped on the earth and did everything right was only Jesus. And I remembered what he said very well: *throw the first stone to those who never sinned*. No one dared to shoot."

"But what does that have to do with the question I asked you?"

"Since I believe in a just and good God, I believe in reincarnation. Therefore, I believe that a reincarnated soul, often as a woman or a soul that, depending on what it has done in the past, can come as a female soul in a male body with different degrees of affectation to evolve, harmonize what it disharmonized or simply learn. It is probable that here, incarnated, we will never know the reason for this, since everyone has a different reason for entering into a certain condition. The important thing is to respect the will of God and to love your neighbor as yourself."

Rúbia's approach interrupted them.

"Did he fall asleep, dad?"

"Yes, he did."

"Let me take him and put it in the crib. I don't want this rascal to be crafty and just want to be held." She joked, kissing the little one on the forehead.

Carefully, she took him into the room. At that moment, Simone offered;

"How about a soda or coffee?"

"I'll take a soda, thank you." Answered David, standing up and saying; "Excuse me, Mr. Salvador."

The young man wisely decided to end the matter politely. He thought the man would drag it out and, apparently, was willing to be invasive, intolerant and might even want to enter into his private life with Abner.

Ricardo arrived with a gift for Bruno and flowers for Rúbia. To everyone's surprise, he was accompanied by his sister Eloah and his partner Suzana.

In the kitchen, preparing some sandwiches and cakes to put on the dining table, Simone turned to Cristiano and said;

"I've never had so many lively people in my house!" He laughed and commented.

"It will be an examination session for your father."

"It is." She agreed, smiling. "I hope he is not ashamed of me."

He came over, stole a kiss and whispered;

"Keep calm."

The movement in Simone's house was excellent. Suzana, delighted with the newborn, confessed;

"My biggest dream is to have a child. In fact, it's our biggest dream." She said, looking at Eloah.

"Do you intend to adopt or have artificial insemination?" Cláudio was interested.

"Here, in Brazil, today adoption is quite complicated for homosexuals. This is unfortunate, given the large number of homeless children growing up in orphanages." Responded Suzana.

"Ah, my love, there are many gay people who have already succeeded." Said Cláudio.

"I know, but it all depends a lot on who judges the right adoption. There is a lot of prejudice despite the National Civil Code Law of 2002, as well as the Statute of Children and Adolescents, which in no way inhibits adoption by homosexuals or single persons, as long as the adoptee is sixteen or older than the adopted child. Only discrimination and prejudice are great, depending on the state. In Brazil, the more conservative the state, the more difficult it becomes. They deny adoption to confine the young boy to the orphanage or institution with terrible treatments and then leave him to grow up without a home, without a family, without an education, without social and economic opportunities."

"When you leave there and then are free in the world, it is certain that most of them go to the world of crime and, later, to the penal institutions." Said Cláudio.

"That's the fault of religious dogmas and false moralists. As people with common sense realize and understand our condition, I believe our situation and our rights will improve." Said Eloah. "We will both try adoption first. If we don't succeed, we will go for artificial insemination."

"I think that discrimination against others is not worth it. The one who lives in peace is always happier." Said Cláudio.

The conversation continued and Ricardo realized that Rúbia had gone to the room and did not return.

Without being noticed, he went to look for her.

He knocked the bedroom door, gently, so as not to frighten his friend;

"Rúbia?"

"Hello Ricardo. Come in."

"Is he sleeping?"

"He woke up and babbled a little."

After looking at her for a few minutes, the young man asked;

"Sorry for my curiosity, but... Did you tell the father that he was born?"

"What father?" She asked with a slight disdain in her tone. "I don't even want to see Jefferson. As soon as my maternity leave ends, if I don't get fired, which seems right, I'll quit and forget I ever met him."

"It is difficult to forget something like this. I'm letting you know. Only in time will everything be fixed."

"What about Renán? Didn't he stay with you this weekend?"

"He traveled to Rio with his mother and stepfather. I'm worried. Flora's husband, Wilson, is about to accept the invitation to go to work in the United States. If this happens..."

"No chance of Renán staying with you? After all, the boy is used to being here. He studied..."

"I doubt that Flora will let him live with me. She doesn't abandon her child. I'm very nervous. I can't see myself without Renán."

"Don't be anxious. Maybe, Wilson doesn't accept the invitation, he changes his mind... Don't suffer in advance."

"It is difficult."

"Excuse me." Interrupted Eloah, turning to her brother and saying. "Let's go, Ricardo. It's getting late and they need to rest. They had many visitors today."

"You are right."

"No. It is still early." Said Rúbia.

"It is not too early. You and your sister must be tired. And this little boy is going to give some work at night." Said the other. "Goodbye, Rúbia. Congratulations, your son is beautiful." Said Eloah, kissing her and leaving.

"I'm leaving too." Decided Ricardo. "Goodbye. See you soon."

They said goodbye and Rúbia stayed in the room with her son.

It wasn't long before Abner and David left too.

Then Mrs. Celeste and Mr. Salvador went to the room where Rúbia was and convinced her to take her son, some clothes and things and go home with them. It would be easier to help their daughter, and Simone would not be too overwhelmed to take care of Pedro and have to help her sister.

Simone did not like the idea. She had already gotten used to Rúbia's presence. She didn't want to be alone.

Even so, it was done as proposed. Rúbia thought her sister was overcharged and decided to accept her parents' invitation, which made her very happy. After they left the house, it seemed empty.

In the living room, Simone began to clean the table and Cláudio helped her, while Cristiano put Pedro to sleep.

"Girl! How many dishes!"

"I'm fast at washing dishes. Leave it to me."

"Okay, let's wash and dry." The friend decided, taking a dishcloth. While washing, Simone commented;

"I thought my mother was going to stay. She usually has a lot of strength." She laughed.

"You're tired, aren't you, my friend?"

"Oh... And a lot, Cláudio. I mean it! I don't know what a full night's sleep is anymore. Not even the last time little Pedro was in the hospital did I rest. I had a terrible dream, I was very sad and I cried."

"Why didn't you call me? You know you can count on me."

"Calling you at three in the morning would be the icing on the cake!" She laughed willingly.

"If you need it, you know you can call me."

"The next morning, it passed. It always does. I found that everything passes." She smiled. Changing the subject, the friend asked;

"Does your father already know about Cristiano and you?"

"No. Jeez! Today I was worried. I thought my dad was going to embarrass me…"

"Girl…!" He laughed willingly. "Today your house looked like a congress of gays, lesbians and sympathizers!" He laughed and she did too. "What was that? There was the greatest biodiversity here! Did you do that on purpose?"

"No…" She laughed about her friend's funny way. "Oh, Cláudio… Only you being yourself makes me laugh like this."

After a moment, he commented;

"I saw your father talking to David… Does he know that David is Abner's partner?"

"I don't know. I was so nervous! My father was in a strange way. With a face… I think he was suspicious."

"He did not suspect. He knew." Said Cristiano when he arrived in the kitchen.

"How do you know?" She was interested.

"When I arrived, he came to talk to me and…" Cristiano told them everything and she was amazed.

"So, he knows that you are David's brother?"

"I told him."

"And then?!" She was curious.

"Your father had nothing to say, after that conversation we had the other day, when I gave him a lot of guidance. I was only worried when I saw him talking to my brother. But David is smart."

"Guys, it is very, very difficult for a parent to accept and understand their child's homosexuality. That hasn't happened to me until today. Since I was a child, I always knew that I was not masculine enough. I was different from my brothers."

"How did you notice that?" Cristiano asked.

"I did not like the same things as my brothers. It bothered me for a long time. I blamed myself and how I blamed myself! Sometimes, some mannerisms escaped and my father, always distant, used to come closer, but just to hit me. He would hit me on the head and say; *act like a man!*"

"And what happened then?" Asked the other.

"It was terrible. I suffered a lot because my brothers criticized me. No one accepted me and they fought with me a lot. I cried in hiding. I could not be what my parents wanted. I always had friends. The girls like me. But there was never any interest other than friendship. I felt identified with them. I was beaten up by school boys who didn't accept me." Cláudio stopped. He looked sad when he remembered and said; "I was cursed, ridiculed, humiliated... How I was humiliated..." His eyes were clouded.

They finished washing the dishes and Simone invited them to sit at the kitchen table and went to prepare the tea. Cláudio continued;

"I didn't know what to feel or how to act. My heart was aching. It was so sad that when I was a teenager, I wanted to die."

"Why?" Cristiano asked.

"I wanted to die so that my parents, my brothers, and my schoolmates would regret everything they had done to me. It wasn't my fault for being what I was, what I am. The others thought I was an aberration, that it was an aberration that I felt attracted to boys and I expressed myself with shadows without realizing it. I never attacked a man because of that, but the others didn't accept me because they thought I could do that, or else, that I could infect them. My grandmother, God rest her soul, didn't understand me, but she didn't criticize me. She was the only person in my family who accepted me as I was. I cried on her lap many times."

"Have you talked to your parents about it?" Simone asked, pouring steaming tea for the two of them.

"Who said they were talking to me? When my father talked to me, which was strange, he offended me and attacked me with words. My mother was silent. That's why I was depressed. I thought about suicide a lot, not because of my condition. I wasn't unhappy because I was gay, I was unhappy because of the way I was treated. In fact, any boy or teenager, gay or straight, who is treated rudely and critically by his parents, is unhappy and thinks about dying. So, not to be mistaken, I went to live with my grandmother, who was already very old. I decided to study to be financially independent. I began to look for an explanation of what I was, of my condition. I discovered that I was a homosexual and not a transsexual. I never wanted to become a woman. I don't want to have a woman's body as a transsexual. I want to be the way I am. It is that simple."

"What did you graduate from?" Cristiano got interested.

"First, I went to college in economics, then in architecture and then in the arts. In addition, I took two graduate courses and a master's degree. Today I teach several subjects at two universities."

"You never wanted to work in one of those areas?" Asked the other.

"No. It may seem absurd, but I like to teach." He laughed. "I complain, but I love it. Then he said; "For all that I have lived through, I can guarantee that it is very difficult for family, for friends, to assume homosexuality. I suffered a lot because of prejudice and discrimination. Psychological torture is worse than physical torture. I was fortunate to be independent and strong, emotionally, to face the prejudices. Not all doors open when you assume you are what you are, so I think there are a lot of people in the closet. For fear of the pain of rejection. I saw a lot of gay people thrown out of the house as teenagers. They had no support. They couldn't study or have a decent job. They ended up with a sad life, in prostitution, in crime, in drugs... They don't do it because they are bad people, they do it to survive."

"That is unfortunate." Said Cristiano.

"Abner did well to assume his condition just after he left home. That's my opinion." Said Cláudio.

"Much depends on the family. This was not the case with my brother."

"That is why it is important to teach the child to say no to prejudice, to say no to bullying, no to offensive nicknames. That will make her and others better adults." Simone said.

"It is true. There are people who want their child to be the best, but they don't correct him when he fights at school, bites his classmate and has no boundaries at all. This boy will grow up to be aggressive and consequently hated. The same happens with those who want a better world, a clean planet, but still throw candy paper on the street, a can of drink out of the car window… You can't get the maximum if you don't start with the minimum." Said Cristiano.

Pedro's crying interrupted them and Simone said smiling;

"My champion woke up. Let me run because he is very demanding." After she left, Cláudio commented.

"I'm sorry for her. Poor friend of mine. If I could help her more…"

"Being a friend as you are, you are already helping a lot. Shall we go and take a look?"

"No, Cris. I'm going to say goodbye. It's very late." He said goodbye to his friend and left.

Then, together with Simone, Cristiano asked;

431

"What's wrong with him?"

"I think nothing. This little wail is normal."

"Isn't it time to breastfeed?"

He looked at his watch and answered:

"Almost... I'm going to make the milk there."

"I'll take care of him." She said, lying on the bed next to the boy, caressing him.

Although extremely tired, Simone did not stop. She did not neglect her son and her duties to him.

He returned, and she fed little Pedro and placed him on the double bed next to Cristiano. He caressed the boy again, playing with him. She smiled at the scene and went to bed too, leaving her son between them.

"You're tired, aren't you?" Asked Cristiano, caressing her face lovingly.

"You can't imagine…"

The silence was absolute. Only the baby babbled sometimes.

Cristiano continued with his arm extended, caressing her hair and face and, without resisting, Simone fell asleep.

Carefully, he stood up and covered her with a blanket. He took little Pedro, turned off the light and left the room, closing the door.

He went to the boy's room and stayed there watching over him` all night.

22.– THE FIGHT BETWEEN SAMUEL AND CRISTIANO

ON SUNDAY, very early in the morning, Cristiano finished feeding little Pedro and huddled him up trying to put him to sleep.

"You barely slept last night, didn't you? I just want to know. You are so naughty." He spoke in a sweet, yet serious voice.

The boy looked at his watch and was glad that Simone was still asleep. After all, he knew she needed him.

As soon as the boy fell asleep, he carefully placed him in the crib. Suddenly, he heard a noise in the side hallway of the house.

Concerned, Cristiano went to the kitchen and opened the door to a backyard, where he could see the little house.

He was surprised by the profile of a man who opened the door of the room in the little house at the back of the courtyard.

"Hey, what do you want there?" Shouted Cristiano. The other one turned around almost as scared as he was.

"I'm the owner of this house. I'm the one who asks: what are you doing here?" The man spoke in a rude tone, very unsatisfied.

The young man stood at the kitchen door and Samuel went to meet him, asking him hard;

"Who are you?!"

"I'm Cristiano. Don't you remember me?" Without waiting for an answer, he said; "Simone is sleeping, exhausted from taking care of Pedro for days and nights. I would like you to come back another time."

"I'm going to go in and talk to her!"

Cristiano stood in front of the door, raising his shoulders, as if his chest were swollen, higher and higher than his six feet, and looked at him with a firm and deep voice;

"No! You're not getting in here! Simone needs a break!"

"Who do you think you are?" Shouted Samuel "Her couple?! Even with a sick son, she has no respect for herself and has already put a man in the house! Get out of my way!!"

When Samuel approached the other, Cristiano put his hands over his chest and pushed him hard. Samuel staggered and headed in his direction again, ready to fight. At that moment, Simone's voice sounded firm;

"Stop that! What's going on here?!"

"You are so easy! I left this house with everything because I was sorry for you and the boy! Now I see that it didn't take long to put a bastard in your bed! You ordinary woman! You scoundrel!"

"Look at the way you talk to her!" Shouted Cristiano. They tilted at each other. Simone grabbed Cristiano by the shirt, inhibited him and shouted.

"Shut up, Cristiano! And shut up, Samuel! You don't know what you're talking about! In fact, you are the ordinary coward who should be helping me take care of Pedro, because this child is not just mine! I haven't known what it's like to get a night's sleep for over three months! Tonight, was the first night I was able to sleep well and you came here to bother me. You don't know what it's like to take care of your child, take him to doctors, hospitals, take care of fever, infections, give him medicine, feed him! You don't know anything about that! You never fed him or saw what he looked like! It's desperate just to see! You don't know and you've never seen

434

your child's diaper changed! You left me pregnant, in the first few months of pregnancy, because you couldn't take the pressure! You ran into the arms of a homeless woman and as ordinary as you are, you just wanted something easy. Yesterday, I was exhausted like never before! I didn't say anything to anyone, but I felt very tired. Cristiano fed your son, changed his diapers and put him to sleep. I fell asleep. I don't even know how it was last night! If you knew your son well... he didn't let Cristiano sleep! It was the first night of sleep and peace I had and it wasn't thanks to you, Pedro's father! However, according to your ignorance, your demands... Who are you to demand something of me? Who do you think you are to demand something of the man who took care of your son? Who took your son to the doctor and to the hospitals several times? Where were you when we needed you? Now what do you want to demand? Why do you want to come into this house? Do you need to be more wicked and ruthless than before?" The silence was absolute. Still outraged, she cried out; "Come on! Come in! Let him in! Come in and see your son! Help me change the diaper and feed him." When she saw him standing still, she shouted. "Come in!"

Another silence until Samuel, awkwardly, said;

"I came here to take those books of mine that you said you put here in the little house. I don't want to bother you."

"You don't bother me. You disgust me." She said, turning around. As she entered the house, he called; "Come, Cristiano."

Closing the door so as not to see movement in the courtyard, he sat down at the kitchen table where he supported his elbows and covered his face with his hands.

Cristiano was going to stroke his back when Pedro started crying. Simone got up, went to the room, picked up her son and took him to the courtyard.

When she found her husband, who was leaving the house with a box in his hands, she went over and said;

"Look, son, this is your father. This is the only way he can meet you in person. When he saw you, he was behind glass in the hospital."

Samuel looked at the boy for a few seconds and turned his face slowly.

"I need to leave."

And he left without looking back.

Dissatisfied with what was happening, Cristiano went to her and asked;

"Give him to me. It's cold here for Pedro."

The son was delivered into the young man's arms. Sitting at the table again, Simone bent her head and fell, regretting having taken her son to Samuel to see him.

Very exhausted, she murmured;

"Contempt, emotional abuse is worse than any physical pain."

"It's hard to believe that there are people as selfish and insensitive as that. But... I shouldn't have taken him for him to see." He didn't say anything. Cristiano, leaning his face against the boy, sniffed at him and complained, playing with a funny voice. "Eeeeh...! Pedro took a dump! Now you need a bath! A very pleasing bath!"

Everything was enough to embitter Simone, who silently prepared the bath for her son, overcoming the difficulties of sad thoughts.

Often, she was distressed, weak and helpless, but she kept pushing herself and doing everything she could to offer her child the best.

✳ ✳ ✳

On that opaque and cold afternoon, Mr. Salvador dried the dishes that Mrs. Celeste had washed after lunch. Rúbia was surprised by her father's attitude, but said nothing, she just smiled.

It didn't take long and he wanted to know;

"You knew that Cristiano was David's brother, didn't you?"

"Yes, we knew, Salvador." Replied the wife.

"And why didn't you tell me?"

"I didn't see any need and I don't think that would change your opinion about Cristiano or about the condition of David and your son." Said the woman, who then commented; "I hope you were polite when you spoke to David yesterday. He's a good guy."

"To tell you the truth, I thought about telling him a lot of things. I just didn't do it for Cristiano."

"What were you going to tell him?" Mrs. Celeste asked, but she didn't let him answer and asked; "Were you going to say that he is very polite, kind, intelligent, hardworking, respectful? We can't complain about this kid's behavior, much less about our son. Their lives do not belong to us. In fact, we have nothing to do with anyone's life."

He was pensive and soon after he asked;

"What about Simone and Cristiano? Are these two having an affair? They haven't been separated lately and I saw them both together yesterday in the kitchen."

"Our daughter has the right to be happy. She doesn't have to suffer for everything Samuel did. If she and Cristiano get along, God bless them."

"I like him a lot. In a complicated situation like hers, he is always there for her, providing support, helping without any obligation. While Samuel..."

"I feel sorry for Samuel." Said Rúbia, rocking her son.

"Why? I don't understand." Asked the father.

"He avoids responsibilities with his child, he doesn't help Simone or visit Pedro. He can and is doing that now, but he forgets or ignores that life may call you to face a situation like his son's for a reason… and that you cannot avoid."

"What do you mean, daughter?" The lady asked.

"I began to learn that what we have to experience, no one experiences for us. We can escape from a responsibility, a situation, for a short time, only the day will come when we will no longer escape."

"I was very wrong about Samuel."

"We were all wrong, Salvador. Everyone. I'm surprised his parents don't give him any guidance, don't tell him to take on what he needs to do."

"He may not want anything else with Simone, but he must respect her and help her in whatever is necessary at least because of all the time they lived together, because of all they built. Money is not everything, especially because what he is giving does not help her and Pedro's expenses." Said Rúbia.

"Is Simone in trouble?" The father asked.

"I would not say *any* difficulty." Said the daughter. "It's just that the costs are so high. Expensive medicines, hospitalizations... There are tests and other procedures that the health plan does not cover and she had to pay for them herself. She takes care of little Pedro herself, since she has procedures such as injections, catheters... that, if she didn't know about breastfeeding, she should pay someone to do it. She is strong, I wouldn't have the courage to do what she does."

"How fate is…" Recalled her mother. "Simone went to nursing school and didn't like it. She didn't want to be a nurse at all. Then she went on to study Economics, working in that

438

company. She did a master's degree and went to teach. One day, she said that breastfeeding was a waste of time. Now, she had no use for it."

"It is true. I remember." Said the father. Then he observed; "I want to say something to you both. You may say that I'm rude and ignorant, but I make no difference between my two grandchildren."

"What do you mean, man? That I'm pleasing one more than the other?"

"Yes, you do. You arrive at Simone's house, take a look at little Pedro and then run to find Bruno. I have seen that several times. And I'm not even talking about the fact that Simone sees that and gets angry. I'm speaking for the boys. They both need our attention and affection."

"But I..."

"You have to stop with that, Celeste. I began to understand that Pedro and Bruno are the grandchildren God gave us to love in the same way. Without distinction. Without prejudice."

The daughter's eyes opened and she accepted;

"Dad is right, mother. Just yesterday, when you asked me to come here, you didn't even ask Simone if she wanted to come too or if she needed help. She is tired of working so hard. I haven't had little Pedro on my lap since Bruno was born."

"Did you see how right I am? Yesterday, who stayed there to help her? We left and left that mess there. I've never seen so many people in that house." Said the gentleman.

"It is true. Now I'm realizing it. There were so many dirty dishes..." The lady admitted.

"You just helped Rúbia pick up a few things. She took Bruno in her lap and left. Our daughter, on top of all that dirt and mess, had to take care of little Pedro. This is wrong. She doesn't even have a maid anymore."

"I will call her, then I will go there." Mrs. Celeste decided. When the lady called, Simone answered, and the lady found out that her friend Cláudio and Cristiano had helped her with everything, including taking care of her son. Simone decided not to tell her that Cristiano had slept there. Nor did she say that he and Samuel had a fight and she had to interfere. She said it was okay.

At the end of the conversation with her daughter, Mrs. Celeste returned and said;

"Cláudio and Cristiano helped Simone yesterday."

Mr. Salvador didn't say anything. He realized that of all those who were there, including him, left and that it was Claudio, that cheerful boy with an attitude he did not approve of, who stayed and helped his daughter.

Without saying anything, he went into the living room. Seeing themselves alone, mother and daughter commented;

"Dad is very changed, very different. What happened to him, mom?"

"I think it was some conversations with Cristiano. It's interesting how this boy influences your father. Salvador is much better, more tolerant."

"How nice! He complains less, understands and accepts situations better. He even asked me to come home." She laughed.

Mrs. Celeste was amused and commented.

"Yes... They say you can't teach an old dog new tricks... This is not the case with Salvador. Cristiano is the angel of goodness I asked for to guide Salvador. I have a lot to thank God for and ask Him to bless this boy."

They smiled contentedly and continued talking.

* * *

Leaning over the railing on the balcony of the apartment, David lost his sight in the distance and had distant thoughts when Abner approached, stood by his side for a while and only then asked;

"Isn't it cold out here?"

"I was about to go in when you arrived. I was thinking about your sister."

"What?"

David smiled when he said;

"Actually, I thought of both. Didn't you find Ricardo a little interested in Rúbia?"

The other one laughed when he agreed:

"Yes, I did." He said briefly, and then added. "As soon as he got divorced, Ricardo told me he didn't want more women in his life. But I don't think he will keep his promise." He said. "Did you know that his ex-wife and her husband are thinking about moving to the United States because of his job?"

"And Renán?"

"He will have to go with his mother."

"If that happens, Ricardo would die. He is very attached to his son."

"It would be good if he gets along with Rúbia. Also, because they make a beautiful couple." He wanted to know. "What about Simone? What were you thinking about her?"

"I wasn't really thinking. You know I notice a lot of things and…"

"What about her and your brother?

441

"Cris believes that Simone is in financial trouble. He wants to help, but doesn't want to offend her."

"Isn't that bastard Samuel helping?" Abner rebelled, outraged.

"Helping…yes, he is, but not enough. I began to suspect this when she fired the maid and started asking me to take her and the baby to the doctor, to the hospital…"

"How could I not have seen this before? If you ask someone to drive you, it's because you don't have money to pay for the cab."

"It would be good if you, as someone who doesn't want anything, take a poll to see how things are going. Did you know that she is selling the car?"

"No. I will talk to her and help her in any way I can."

"Do that. Simone deserves it." It wasn't long before David proposed. "Let's go in. It is very cold."

"Yes, let's go. How about we make some popcorn and watch a movie? I rented one. I think you'll like it."

"Great. I'll make hot chocolate. This cold will be fine." He smiled. Abner agreed. He put his arm around his partner's shoulder and they went inside.

✳ ✳ ✳

As the weeks went by, Simone was discouraged and more despondent every day. Her heart was punished by the wave of worries and difficulties with her son.

She felt that, inevitably, little Pedro's life was coming to an end.

In the last few weeks, she spent more time in the hospital than at home. She didn't know what else to do.

Even with the sale of the car, she did not have much money left, which was spent on Pedro's hospitalization and hospital procedures.

As if that wasn't enough, her ex-mother-in-law warned her that Samuel was trying to see the possibility of reversing the fact that she would take the house. She claimed that she was entitled to half of that property and that Simone had placed another man inside the residence. Samuel, knowing that his son was not well at all, was preparing for her to file a new application with the judge as soon as the boy died.

What to do now? She did not know if it would be possible for her ex-husband to get the judge's permission to sell the house to share the money. After all, that property was acquired by both of them and, in Pedro's absence, it would be the right thing to do. However, it was unfair. She cared for her son alone. He never helped at all. He only paid a miserable pension that was barely enough for diapers.

Sitting on the sofa, Simone dropped her body and closed her eyes.

She could not see; but in spirituality, Vanilson, Vitória, as well as other spiritual friends, were present. Vanilson's spirit bowed and kissed Simone's face for a long time, giving her a loving embrace.

"Did you know that she didn't have to go through all this with Pedro?" Vitória asked.

"I know. The situations that a person does not need to face, but, for love, for the greatness of his evolved soul, he faces, adds merits for his evolution and a better life. The whole morality of Jesus is summarized in love, humility and charity. In all his teachings, the Master has pointed out these three virtues as those that lead someone to happiness. He preached happiness to the merciful, asked to love others as oneself, and fought against pride and selfishness."

"I did everything wrong. Both in the past and in the recent incarnation. Now I recognize it. Even with all the knowledge I acquired in Spiritism about loving others, I did not admit that not respecting the feelings and opinions of others is a lack of love, charity and humility." Kneeling down in front of Simone, she put her hands on hers and asked her forgiveness. "I'm sorry for everything. If you were unhappy in the past, it was my fault. Don't be sad for your little boy. He is very well for having you as a mother, even in the present conditions. Be strong, for all this will pass."

At that moment, Simone took a deep breath, opened her eyes and murmured.

"God... give me strength…"

Spiritual friends put their hands on her and began to give her invigorating and strengthening energies through the spiritual passage.

The minutes passed and the phone rang, but before Simone answered, Vanilson and Vitória said goodbye to her.

When answering, Simone hesitated;

"Going to the center today? I don't know…" At Mrs. Janaina's insistence, she accepted. "Okay. I'll go. Will you come and pick me up?" Mrs. Janaina said yes. "Great!"

She got excited, went to take a shower and got ready.

✳ ✳ ✳

As soon as they returned to Mrs. Janaina's house, a place that served as a shelter, the spirit Vanilson turned to Vitória and asked her;

"Are you okay?"

444

"It saddens me that I was anything but flexible. Nothing humble. It is difficult to discover this."

"The evil of humanity is pride, selfishness, vanity, and these evils exist only when there is no humility. Vitória, it's good to know that we have a just, good, and merciful God, who gives us as many opportunities as necessary to evolve and be truly happy." After a moment, he revealed; "Today I have to leave. I must reincarnate soon to continue in my evolutionary journey. I need to continue where I left off."

"Reincarnation? Is that what I'm thinking? Will you be Simone and Cristiano's son?"

"We must continue where we left off." He smiled with satisfaction.

"Are you going to leave me here?" She asked sadly. He smiled broadly and invited:

"If you want to come with me... I think you're ready."

"Can I?! Can I go to a colony?"

"This must be your next step, daughter." Said the spirit Juan, approaching. "When the creature recognizes its defects, its errors, and wishes to change and improve with all its heart, the conditions for renewal appear. It is time for you to grow." He smiled, extended his arms and invited her to a fraternal embrace.

Vitória wrapped him up with strength and great affection.

It didn't take long and they went to a spiritual colony.

✳ ✳ ✳

As soon as they got Simone to go to the Spiritist center, Cristiano and Mrs. Janaina were excited to reveal something.

"We have a surprise!" The young man announced.

"I hope it's something good, please." She asked, smiling.

"Cristiano asked your father to go to the Spiritist center and he accepted." Said the lady.

"My father?! In a Spiritist center?" She was amazed. "I don't think so. My father doesn't even go to the Catholic Church when my mother invites him. And she insists!" She laughed.

"Well, believe me. We're going to get him." Said the young man. And then he said; "Mr. Salvador showed up at the clinic today, as if he didn't want anything. I told him I couldn't talk unless he waited because I had to see a patient. He waited and then we talked. Not much."

"What did he want?"

"The truth is that Pedro's condition still affects him. He wants to know why someone is born like him and another is born perfect. We have already discussed this, but I think it was not enough. He has doubts and ideas like many people. We talked about the evolution of spirits and the need for one to be born one way and another to be born in another way. And to talk about that, one has to talk about the Spiritist doctrine and reincarnation."

"Jeez...! Even without doing anything, Pedro does a lot." Said Simone, but she did not continue because her voice broke.

"Look, daughter, we all have an important task in this life. We do not exist by chance. You came to our house to get acquainted and to distract yourself, at the beginning of your pregnancy, because you were impressed, sad with the condition of your child. You soon met us because of him." She smiled. "When you talked about the syndrome he had, Cris said he knew about it and was interested in learning more. That is why Cris went to the institution with you. He overcame the difficulties, drove because of you, and saw patients again."

"If it weren't for Pedro's condition, I wouldn't know my ex-husband either."

"You weren't going to get along with me, were you?" Said the boy with a generous smile.

"Yes…" She smiled shyly.

"Did you see how important he was in many people's lives? Even in your father's life!" Said the lady smiling. "Speaking of him, how is he?"

"I went to see him earlier today. It's the same thing; with medications and serum."

A pain squeezed her heart and Simone fell silent.

No one else said anything until they arrived in front of the residence of Mr. Salvador, who was already waiting for them at the door.

The man was excited. His eyes were shining and he seemed anxious to know the doctrine that made him feel curious.

After greeting everyone, he was introduced to Mrs. Janaina and was amazed;

"You were on time, Cristiano! I like people like that."

"It's good to be on time. It shows our discipline. This is not always possible and we must be tolerant and understanding when it does not happen."

Addressing his daughter, he asked her about his grandson. After Simone's explanations, he asked;

"And back in college, daughter? What's your situation like?"

"Complicated. I can't go back to teaching with Pedro like this. The maternity leave is over. However, I have the right to leave to assist my son, as he is disabled, for a period of six months, extendable up to four years."

447

"If there was a way with your mother's help or I could look after Pedro until you are back."

"I know you can't, dad. There is no way."

The man looked at her with pity and patted her on the shoulder. It was difficult to see her in that situation and not be able to help her.

When they arrived at the Spiritist house, they cheered up a little more, greeted their acquaintances and presented Mr. Salvador.

The conference was excellent and the theme could not have been better: *Blessed are the gentle and the peaceful; love your neighbor as yourself.*

The speaker was very well involved in the spiritual realm. The topic included current problems such as bullying, racial prejudice, sexual orientation prejudice, offensive nicknames, bad jokes, cruel jokes that cause feelings of immense moral pain and extremely sad losses. The speaker spoke about the importance of teaching boys, from an early age, to respect others, whoever they are, and to say no to any prejudicial feeling, because the lack of guidance from parents in the education of their children makes rebellious and aggressive teenagers unhappy and cruel adults. Whoever is satisfied and happy is tolerant and knows how to respect others. He reminded that whoever acts with good, receives good and whoever acts with evil, receives evil. Therefore, one can say that happiness is not a matter of destiny, it is a matter of choice.

In the end, Mr. Salvador was very attentive.

When he saw himself far away from the others, he asked Mrs. Janaina;

"How did you forgive your son?"

"I did not have to forgive David. I love my son." She spoke simply and tenderly with her sweet, quiet voice.

Taking advantage of the distance between them, and Simone and Cristiano, he said;

"It's just hard for me to accept. I can't understand and this feeling is bad for me. I have pain in my heart for being rebellious. It is an anguish that I cannot explain. I want to understand and get it out of me."

"Mr. Salvador, I believe that all this anguish, all this pain is not because you do not forgive your son. It is because you hit him and no longer talk to him. It doesn't matter what he is or what condition he lives in. Love your son and show it to him. Find Abner and talk to him. You don't need to apologize. Forget the past and live as if nothing happened. He will understand and your heart will be lighter."

"I don't think I can ever do that."

"You will. You have a good heart, full of love. Since you have so much love, you feel this anguish of not talking to him anymore. You may not understand, you may not agree, but you can accept the condition of your children and respect them."

"How can I do that?"

"Don't criticize, don't fight and walk away. There is no need to accept and raise a flag of support, claiming that they are right and that the world should be like that. There is a need to treat them normally without reproach, without offense. This will be a big step. Living together ends prejudices, relieves the heart and makes everyone happier. Think about one thing: these are the children God has entrusted to us. It is up to us not to disappoint the Creator or our conscience or we will have to harmonize with all the pain and intolerance we cause."

The matter ended when Simone and Cristiano approached. The parents noticed that the man had his arm around Simone's shoulders, but said nothing.

"Did you enjoy the conference, father?"

"I liked it. I want to come here again. Can I?"

"Of course! How nice. I'm glad you liked it." Cristiano rejoiced.

"So, let's go. We have to get up early tomorrow." Said Simone, pleased with her father.

Everyone agreed and left.

23.– GOODBYE TO PEDRO

RÚBIA DECIDED TO STAY a few days at her parents' house with little Bruno. She would give less worry to her sister. Besides, she thought about the expenses Simone had.

She knew, quite well, that Abner was helping her financially and that made her feel more at ease.

As the days passed, at her mother's house, Rúbia received a visit from Talita, her friend, and was very happy to see her.

"Oh, how nice of you to come. I thought you'd forgotten me."

"Oh... don't complain. I called you. I just thought I shouldn't come in the first few days. I don't know... There are always a lot of people visiting and the house is full. This is exhausting for the mother, the baby and the helpers..." After a moment, she asked; "So... how are you?"

"Great. Despite not knowing what a full night of sleep is." She smiled. "It's rewarding to take that beautiful little thing and know that I did it." She laughed politely.

"Will he be sleeping for too long? I'm looking forward to carrying him."

"Bruno will wake up soon to breastfeed. He's a clock! He's very smart. You have to see him."

"And what about you? Have you decided whether you will go back to work when your maternity leave ends?"

"I think I'll be fired. Even if they don't fire me, I don't have the courage to go back. I'm hot-headed. I need to get another job. Now I have Bruno."

"What are you going to do? Get a daycare?"

"It would be ideal if I had a job which could allow me to afford it. What I get disappears into diapers, clothes, products for him... I didn't have the luxury of buying not even one face cream for me."

"Children are like that."

"And I was always complaining about people not planning to have a child. Oh, Talita, I paid for my tongue." She laughed funny.

"Nothing is by chance. Everything has a path. I'm glad you have a supportive family. Changing the subject, she asked; "What about Jefferson? Did you warn him?"

"No. Surely, he must know that Bruno was born, because of the date."

"I wasn't going to tell you anything, but... There's an intern there and he was having an affair with her, but…"

"As long as he has a woman who likes to fool herself, Jefferson will have a chance to get along. I want distance from him." She said, interrupting her.

"Wouldn't it be the case that you demand a pension? Teach the man a lesson."

"I thought about it like I told you. But I don't want my son to be exposed to that man. And if he wants to have the right to visit him, to walk with him... No! I wouldn't admit that. There are many parents who throw their children out of the window, stick them with needles, and mistreat them a lot. I see that he isn't a reliable person. Neither he nor his woman."

"Looking at it that way, you are right."

"I know the situation will be very difficult, but I must take responsibility. I will not try to share the task of raising a child with someone I do not trust, who has no character or good character. God knows what that man would be capable of doing.

"Like I was telling you... Jefferson was beating up the new intern and the case didn't go forward. He's not in good health."

"What's wrong with him?"

"He discovered a prostate tumor. He will have to have chemotherapy before he gets operated. He is far away. Since I heard that, it seems he has aged thirty years in one month."

"Oh, boy...!" She was astonished without being emotional. Then she confessed; "Do you want to know the truth? I don't feel anything. Neither pity nor happiness that it is so. I don't even know what to think."

"He used the sexual energy wrongly. He got involved with many women. He has worn out spiritually, unbalanced and energetically damaged the spiritual area around the sexual organs. It could only happen because of that, in this or the next incarnation."

"Thank God I didn't have any viruses or diseases. Although my tests were not ready, at the beginning of my pregnancy, I was not at peace."

"On second thought, I think it's better that you definitely forget about this man."

"I already forgot."

"So, let's talk about good things!" Talita was encouraged. At that moment, Bruno grunted, showing himself awake. Rúbia got up, picked him up and introduced him to her friend, who soon wanted to grab him too.

Talita's visit was peaceful and moved her friend.

* * *

Weeks passed.

Immersed in stormy thoughts, Simone sat waiting in an armchair in the cold hospital waiting room.

With her gaze lost on the ground, she felt powerless because of so much work and the restlessness that dominated her.

It was cold and her body was cold. She had spent the night there.

It was almost seven in the morning when Cristiano arrived, looking around for her.

As soon as he found her, he quickly approached her. When she saw him, she stood in front of him. Caressing her arm, he felt her skin freeze. When he took off his jacket and put it on her, he commented;

"I came as soon as possible. Why didn't you call me last night?"

"I feel bad for bothering you and others so much." In his sweet countenance there was a scowl. In her tired expression, her concern was clear. Leaning against Cristiano's chest, she wrapped her around his waist, squeezing him.

He embraced her tenderly, kissed the top of her head and stroked her back. He did not delay and asked;

"What the doctor said?"

With a sad and apprehensive expression, Simone looked at him and muttered.

"That he is not going well. I couldn't stand it."

Her face contorted and she cried. She cried a dull and painful cry.

Cristiano wrapped her in his chest, caressing her hair and said nothing. There was nothing to say. He tried to be strong to reassure her, but he couldn't. And without her seeing him, they cried together.

A few minutes passed and Simone wiped her face with her hands, sighed deeply and asked;

"Do you want coffee or water? I'll get some."

"Not for me. Thank you."

At that moment, Simone looked to the side and saw, walking slowly toward her, Dr. Nathanael, a doctor who was caring for his son.

A chill ran through her soul.

Standing up, she waited for the doctor's approach. Her eyes were drawn in surprisingly sad ways.

She knew it. Her heart warned. There was no need to say anything. Still, the doctor spoke quietly, in a serious and solemn tone:

"I'm very sorry."

Seeking help from Cristiano, she hugged him, hiding her face.

He wrapped her up tenderly, letting her cry as much as she wanted. Wrapping her in his chest, he cried in silence so that he would not see her.

As soon as he could, Cristiano informed Pedro's grandparents and uncles. He asked Rúbia to inform Samuel and his paternal grandparents. He also remembered her friends and told them, and they attended the funeral and burial with all their strength to show solidarity with their friend and not to leave her alone.

When she woke up, Simone was quiet, sitting on a chair. In total silence.

455

There she received the repentance and solidarity of all. There were many people, many university colleagues, friends of the institution and companions in the Spiritist Center who made a Reading of the Gospel of Jesus, followed by a brief explanation and the prayer that Jesus taught: Our Father Prayer.

Samuel attended; however, he kept his distance. Just before the funeral, he approached Simone, but said nothing. They just exchanged glances.

During the funeral, tears rolled down Simone's pale, swollen face. She rested her face against the chest of Cristiano, who held her cry and embraced her.

In the end, they walked slowly and hugged the car.

Simone decided to go home. She did not accept the invitation of her parents, nor of Abner or Mrs. Janaina to be with them. She politely said that she would like to be alone.

Only Cláudio, her faithful friend and Cristiano, accompanied her, at her request.

At home, she went to her son's room. She looked around, noting every detail, every ornament, everything she had prepared for him. After that, she closed the door and went into the living room. She sat down on the couch and closed her eyes.

Cláudio knelt beside her and was taking off his shoes, when she asked in a weak voice;

"What are you doing?"

"Anything to make you feel better." He took off his shoes, put on his slippers and asked;

"Don't you think it's better to take a bath? It would be good to get rid of this tiredness, this impregnation of the hospital and the cemetery, don't you think so, honey?" The friend did not answer and proposed. "Come on, I'll help you go to your room. Take a shower. I separated a very warm and comfortable outfit for you. It's up there on your bed. Cris is making tea and I think a soup too. Then you can eat some and go to bed.

She agreed. She decided to let herself be taken care of.

With the help of her friend, she got up and went to take a shower.

A little later, arriving at Simone's room and carrying a tray, Cristiano saw Cláudio kneeling on the bed, holding a hair dryer and finishing drying his friend's hair.

"It's cold and can hurt if you lie down with wet hair." He said when he saw Cristiano.

"It's true." Agreed the other. Then, when he saw him turn off the device, he offered him;

"I brought you tea. I'm making soup, but it's not ready yet." Simone was reluctant, but ended up accepting. After drinking the tea, she thanked them both and she huddled together with Cláudio.

Cláudio covered her with a blanket, hugged her over the blankets and kissed her on the cheek.

Cristiano found her friend's affection and dedication interesting. Perhaps the family members would not do the same. When he saw the other one walking away, the boyfriend approached her, kissed and asked her before leaving the door ajar.

"If you need anything, call me."

Simone did not respond and he went to another room.

✳ ✳ ✳

When he arrived in the living room, he saw Cláudio sitting on the couch and asked him;

"Do you want more tea"

"No, Cris. Thank you."

"Wait a moment. I'll put out the fire."

457

Cristiano went to the kitchen and then returned. Pouring himself a cup of tea, he took an armchair, almost in front of his friend, and commented;

"I thought Simone's parents would come here."

"Don't think badly of them. I saw Simone say that she wanted to be alone and then I heard Mrs. Celeste say that Bruno had a fever. She and Mr. Salvador were going to take the boy to the doctor with her daughter."

"Ooooh... That's why Rúbia went and then got back home soon. I didn't even have time to talk to her."

"Have you seen? Samuel was there and had the courage to be there with that other woman."

"I saw it. I'm glad he didn't dare open his mouth. I'm drowning with that man."

"I knew him, or rather, I thought I knew Samuel. Many years have passed. I didn't think he would do such a thing. He rejected the boy since the pregnancy! How absurd! It is good that God has put you in their lives to support them and be with them in the role of father and partner. Your presence was very important to her and Pedro. You replaced his father."

"That was not the intention. What I did was from the heart." After a moment, he asked; "You and Simone are very close. Have you known each other for a long time?"

"From the university. First, she took nursing and didn't like it. I guess she didn't know she was going to attend this university just to take care of the boy, or else the poor boy, perhaps, could only stay in the cold environment of a hospital, without love and affection. After finishing nursing, she started the year doing Economics. That's when we met. But we were not friends. She must have thought I was too picky." He laughed.

"When we finished the course, we went straight to a master's degree. We finished and were invited to teach. We accepted and... Only after a while did the friendship arise. However, it seems that we have known each other for years."

"She always talked about you."

"And about you too." Cristiano was attentive and Cláudio continued; "Look, Cris, I know you very little, but enough to see that you are a good guy. I hope you two get along very well. Always be honest and truthful. Follow your feelings..." After a brief pause, he continued; "It may seem a little curious, but... it doesn't matter what others think or say."

"How so?"

"Mmm... You can say things like this: she's older, she's divorced, she had a child... I don't know what else. Remember that the important thing is from now on. You two love and respect each other and that's enough. Don't listen to anyone's opinion. Be honest with each other." He laughed in a funny way and even said; "And count on me!"

"Thank you, Cláudio. What you told me was important. You know, it crossed my mind at first, as soon as I started feeling attracted to her, the fact that I'm single, without any obstacles... I have a profession. I like what I do and today I don't have any problems. However, I got involved with a divorced woman. I was helping to take care of her child instead of going out, having fun, enjoying life... Even the fact that Samuel confronted me and bothered me... I came to think that I didn't need this. But I couldn't get away from her or Pedro and, consequently, from the situation that involved them. I could look for another one without compromise and..."

"Go out after being engaged, at your age and with your financial situation, with a guaranteed future... Darling! You would only find selfish women. Ready to strike to stabilize themselves. A mature woman, with head held high, who has an amazing profession."

"I think those thoughts came to my mind because of obsessive and spiritual factors, because those ideas happened when we were together." Then he said; "I thought we were going to find problems with our family, but so far... Only my mother warned me about some things, but she did not continue."

"Family is fire!"

"Don't you have contact with your family?"

"No. Nobody wants to see me, not even in paintings! They'll only be interested in me if I win a jackpot in the lottery." He laughed.

"Are you alone? Is there no one?"

"Not living with me. Actually, I don't even have a boyfriend. After my granny died, I moved out of her house and found a place just for me. Thank God, I don't lack friends. That's why I don't feel lonely."

Cristiano looked out the window and looked at his watch.

"I made soup, I just need to take a shower."

"Make yourself at home. If she wakes up..."

"No. I'm not taking a bath. I don't have any clean clothes here. I need to go home. Could you stay here? I promise I'll be right back."

"Take it easy. I'll take care of Simone."

It was done that way. Cristiano left.

When he returned, Simone was already up.

Cláudio set the table for dinner and she, at the cost of much insistence, ate a little.

After dinner, the friend said goodbye and left. Abner called to see how his sister was doing

Much later, Mrs. Celeste did the same to find out about her daughter and they talked for a while. Cristiano decided to stay there. He couldn't leave her alone.

✳ ✳ ✳

The next day, when Cristiano had to go to the clinic and Simone found herself alone, it was the worst time.

She did not have a child to care for and did not need to go to the hospital.

A void filled her being and sadness silenced her soul.

She knew her son had serious health problems. She was aware of his difficulties, but she held on to him. She dedicated herself as much as she could and was the best mother while he was alive.

Now she felt alone, savoring pain, inexplicable fear and so many other feelings derived from sadness.

She was able to understand that her son only needed a short earthly stay and he complied.

What about her now? How to live with such absence? What to do? She went to her son's room and took another look.

Without delay, she went to the small house in her backyard, found some boxes and brought them to the house.

In Pedro's room, under the painful tears that ran down her pale face, she took all the things, all the clothes and the toys that she had bought with so much love and that she gave her so to play and have fun. And she boxed them up one by one.

In the end, the room was clean. Just unadorned furniture, no clothes, no grace, no life.

Simone put everything in the corner, closed the window and the door and left.

* * *

Cristiano visited her every day and decided to stay with her some nights. Her friend Cláudio also kept her company.

She even received visits from several supportive friends.

Samuel just didn't give her any news, but that didn't interest her.

Time was passing by.

Her boyfriend could understand her sadness over the death of her son, but he thought she was too attached.

She didn't want to go out. She only spoke a little. She hardly played. It was her friend Cláudio who made her laugh.

One day, Simone and Cristiano were watching TV on a Saturday afternoon when the phone rang.

He answered and handed it over, saying;

"They said it's from a hospital. They want to talk to you."

"With me?" She was surprised. She answered saying; "Who is speaking?" After the person identified himself and said what it was about, Simone stood up, took notes and answered.

"I'm going there as soon as possible."

"What happened?" He got worried.

"Cláudio is in the hospital. They can't say why. He was beaten and is seriously injured. He doesn't have his phone or any other address ID, he just remembered my phone number because it was easy."

"Let's go there. I'm going with you."

When they arrived at the hospital, they hardly recognized their friend, who was seriously injured, with a very swollen face.

Cláudio was brutally beaten by some boys. The aggression was without reason, without a reason to be.

Some bones in his face had been broken, where he had several stitch cuts. His arm, foot and two ribs were also broken. He could barely speak.

"Why did they do that? Did you fight or offend someone?" Simone asked, surprised to see him.

"I'm just one of hundreds of homophobic victims, my dear." He mumbled, trying to make fun.

"But why?!" She insisted indignantly.

"Just because he is homosexual." Answered the patient's doctor. "Homophobes are people with terrible emotional disorders. Deep psychological disorders and, above all, cowards. They are nothing but criminals. Criminals who will continue to act until we have more severe and harsher laws, with no protectionism for the wealthy. These homophobic groups that attack homosexuals are generally unemployed young people, without a family base and who need to revise their moral, social, spiritual and mental concepts. Simple things that balanced parents would give them. But nowadays, parents are often silent and misinformed.

"It's true." Agreed Cristiano. "When parents are irresponsible about their children's education, when they do not teach them limits and respect for others, their actions become aggressive and barbaric. It is time for the laws, the State, the penal institutions to fulfill the duty of parents. Then they cry and cry as if they were victims, when, in fact, they are to blame for their children being what they are and doing what they do."

"You're right." Said the doctor. "Parents are responsible for the frustration and insecurity of their children who, without structure, commit these crimes. Only someone who is frustrated and insecure can attack someone because of their condition. For no reason. It's absurd to attack someone for being a beggar, to set fire to someone else for being an Indian, to kill for being disabled. How far will we tolerate so much abuse? So much lawlessness?"

"I think it's a lack of religion." Said Simone.

"I don't think so. There are many who claim to be religious but are intolerant of homosexuals. They offend, assault and kill even in the name of God."

"It hurts so much." Cláudio complained.

"I'm going to ask to prepare some medicine for you. I will then prescribe pain medication and you will be discharged. I advise you to file a complaint at a police station. Make a police report."

Everything was done correctly and Simone took Cláudio home. She couldn't leave him alone in his apartment. Someone needed to help him.

Mr. Salvador was not satisfied when he found out.

When he visited his daughter, he was surprised and complained without the other one hearing him.

"You can't be here with him."

"And where am I going to send him? Besides dad, Cláudio is my friend. After my son's funeral, he and Cris stayed with me and took care of me. I will not abandon him now. There is no way."

"And what about Cristiano? What does he say about you taking care of a man in your house?" Simone smiled and asked.

"A man, dad? Please. Cláudio is my friend. Cris understands that." And so, the days passed.

✳ ✳ ✳

Simone lost her job at the university, where she taught, under the influence of Samuel. However, the friend, who was recovering at home, contacted another university to get her a new job.

The time she spent caring for Cláudio made Simone more active, without the depressed state she was in before. She seemed more excited.

Meanwhile, Rúbia had stayed at her parents' house. She was very worried about her own situation and talked about it.

"I need to get out and find a job. I'm sorry for abusing you, mom... I need you to look after Bruno for me. As soon as I start working, I'll put him in a daycare center and everything will be easier."

"And, daughter, we need to go to church to pay for the promise I made to get you a job."

"I'd like to go to the spirit center, mother. I'm learning a lot about this doctrine. Do I really need to go and pay for the promise you made?"

The woman looked at her seriously and remembered wisely;

"In my opinion, daughter, the Blessed Mother has no religion. Our Lady is neither Catholic nor spiritist, nor anything else. I know I made the promise and I would love you to understand my faith and come with me. This will be proof of tolerance on your part."

The daughter smiled and agreed.

"It's true, mother. It won't hurt."

"And your father, huh? Who would have thought? He did very well in the center. I never thought..."

"Why don't you go more often too? Keep him company."

"When my heart asks, I will. You know. I like to go to church. I respect and love knowing that your father found God in another way. It doesn't matter what it is. The important thing is to find the Father and have him in our hearts through our practices.

I'm very happy with Salvador. He has changed a lot and he has changed for the better."

"It is true. It doesn't matter about our religion. If we have God in our hearts, we are better off with our fellow man, with our family, with our community, in our work and before the world."

"Our daughter! You spoke well."

At that moment the bell rang. Mrs. Celeste stayed with her grandson and Rúbia went to answer it. However, Mr. Salvador had already received Ricardo and Eloah, who wanted to talk to Rúbia.

"Came in. Feel at home." Very excited, the gentleman invited.

"We don't want to bother you. We will be brief." Said Eloah firmly and quietly. "We should have called first. It's not polite to go to someone's house unannounced, but there wasn't time. We were close by and decided to stop by."

When she arrived at the room, Rúbia greeted them.

"And Bruno, how is he?" Ricardo asked.

"In someone's arms, as usual! He is now in the kitchen with my mother."

"He gives you a hard time?" Eloah asked.

"He has been waking up less at night. That's very good. Every once in a while, he gets cold, but it doesn't take long and he's fine again."

"This is common. It's child's play." Said the other. Then she explained the reason for their visit. "Rúbia, I'm here for the following: Ricardo commented with me about your situation in the company where he works. It seems that you don't want to go there anymore, is that right?"

"That's right. My license is up and I need another job as soon as possible."

"Okay, I'll tell you something. The company where I work is expanding. We need someone with management experience, your area. It's not a great service and it doesn't pay as well." She laughed. "However, it's a start. What do you think?"

"I don't have to find anything!" She smiled with satisfaction. "Do you want me to start tomorrow?" They laughed and Eloah said in a joking tone;

"No. It could be the day after tomorrow." After a moment, she explained; "Things there are being arranged. In about twenty days, we will surely need someone with your profile. I had left a resume with Ricardo. He passed it on to me and I took it to the staff. If you agree, I'll drop everything to go there for an interview and other arrangements. First you will have to cancel your work permit, but we will wait. Maybe you can be fired and receive the rights that belong to you."

"Of course, I agree. Whenever you want, I'll be there. I just finished my maternity leave and I'll be there. Wow! Thank you, Eloah!" She exclaimed, getting up and hugging her.

The other answered happily.

"Well... If you don't mind, I'll leave."

"No! It's early! Let's have a coffee."

"Thank you but I really need to go. I have an appointment this morning. But if Ricardo wants to stay..." Said Eloah.

"Look..." Ricardo laughed. "I'm very expensive and I accept that coffee."

Mrs. Celeste entered the room with Bruno in her lap. Eloah played with the boy, then said goodbye and left. Mrs. Celeste went to the kitchen to prepare coffee and Mr. Salvador hugged his grandson and accompanied her.

In the room, Rúbia said she was still surprised.

"I can't believe what's happening."

467

"As soon as Eloah told me that you could fill the vacancy, I decided to tell you to make it easier. I saw how worried you were about getting another job."

"You can't imagine how much. It's a relief to know that the doors are opening. I have a lot to thank you for."

"Well... you don't have to." He said.

"Changing the subject... How are you, Ricardo? I find you a little quiet, a little sad…"

"The day for Renán to go to the United States with his mother is coming, and that is killing me."

"Jeez...! I'm really sorry."

"I feel terrible."

"I can imagine. If someone took my son away from me, I would die."

"I'm burying myself in work, so I don't think about that. I'm afraid of going back into depression."

"I don't know what to say, but... If you need to talk, let it out... It could help you feel better."

Mr. Salvador entered the room and called them to the coffee that was ready. Ricardo and Rúbia got up and went to the kitchen.

24.– TRUE FRIENDSHIP

AS TIME PASSED, Cláudio, more recovered, prepared to leave Simone's house.

It was a cold morning and they were having breakfast when the friend said;

"You can rest assured. Next semester, you'll be teaching in a much better place. I'm sure you'll like it there. It is logical that there are boring people everywhere. But there, the number of people like that is much less."

They laughed and Simone said;

"Thank you, Cláudio. I don't know how I will ever thank you enough."

"I owe you, my friend. If it weren't for your friendship, your solidarity... I would have many difficulties."

"True friends are like us." He smiled generously. A peaceful smile like no one has seen in a long time. Simone looked better, pinker and healthier. She looked at him with a sweet and beautiful expression. "Many things have happened in my life in the last two years. I was a very different person. I have always found myself practical, objective, direct, modern... However, all the circumstances, all the movements I experienced, changed me profoundly. I was always the kind of person who liked everything under control, so I programmed my life meticulously, until the moment came when I didn't program it and I had to improvise."

"Improvise? I didn't understand, honey."

"I had to improvise to live and survive. I was expecting a child, but I didn't know he was in trouble. I was terrified. When I thought I would get my husband's support, I found myself alone. I had to improvise so I wouldn't fall apart, especially when I caught Samuel with another woman. It was the that I hit rock bottom"

"You got to the bottom of the well, but you didn't stay there waiting for them to throw dirt on you."

"I have strengthened my soul to be stronger than ever and to continue. After Pedro was born, there were worries and concerns…"

"And Cristiano also came at that time." She smiled beautifully and agreed;

"Cris was a blessing in my life. It was that angel sent by God." She sighed, paused briefly and continued; "Today I'm someone else. All that despair, all that anguish made me different. I don't know how to explain... I place much more value on life, on people close to me, on friendships... They were true friends who were by my side supporting me, helping me to get up and go on." After a few seconds she continued. "I learned to live with adversity. I know that the future will be written in the best way if I do my part well. As I have heard: the universe echoes our actions and thoughts. Of course, I will be sad if something bad happens, but I will not lose control, because I learned to have extreme trust in God."

Silence reigned and Cláudio wanted to hear more, but she did not continue.

"How beautiful, my friend, you said something so beautiful! It's beautiful to see someone so wise."

"I believe that when we get along with ourselves, that's the result. Also…" The intercom rang and Simone interrupted what she was saying to respond. It was Samuel waiting at the door. Patient, she walked slowly down the side hallway of the house, reaching the door.

He didn't even say good morning and asked aggressively;

"Why can't I open this door? Why did you change the lock?"

"Good morning, Samuel. I changed the lock so you can learn to call as soon as you arrive. After all, you don't live here anymore."

"I need some things that are in the little house."

Simone opened the door and when he came in, she said;

"It would be nice if you take away everything that belongs to you, don't you think?"

"Don't think you own this place. This house was for your comfort while you were with our son. Now he is gone." When he saw Cláudio looking through the kitchen door, he looked at her and attacked; "I won't be the one to support your laziness! Every day a different man."

"Look, Samuel, take what you need and go. Please." She said in a calm and bored tone. Dismissing him, she went into the kitchen, saying. "When you leave, call me to open the door."

Returning to the table, she poured herself another cup of coffee and waited.

"Simone, how cold!" Cláudio admired her.

"The day is beautiful." She laughed. "I don't want to spoil it."

"Beautiful! A cold and rainy day? Beautiful?"

"Won- der- ful!" She said, laughing again.

"Girl! What did it give you?"

Samuel called her and Simone went to open the door.

They didn't speak or say goodbye. She returned to the house. Upon entering, she announced.

"I'll have to leave this house." She laughed. "If my parents or Cris don't give me a place to live, I'll move into your apartment."

"I will be delighted to welcome you! It will be an honor! However, I doubt that Cris will allow that to happen."

"Sometimes, I feel a little cold in the belly…" She spoke in a sweet and funny way. "I think I'm in love. I feel like a teenager." After a while, she confessed; "I miss Pedro. I miss his smell, picking him up, taking care of him…"

"Have you thought about Pedro's mission in such a short life?"

"I'm sure of one thing: my father. Because of Pedro, he asked about life, about the earthly experience and began to look for answers. He stopped drinking and smoking. He became someone else. He is no longer angry or critical." She laughed. "You know that sometimes I'm waiting for him to come with a complaint and when that doesn't happen it seems strange to me." She laughed again. "In the past it was unbearable."

"It wasn't just your father that Pedro moved. You didn't really know your ex-husband, and you didn't know Cris either."

"And since then, our lives have changed completely. Cris has recovered since we met… We will never be the same again. The other day, Mrs. Janaina said that."

They continued to talk about all the changes that occurred until Cláudio decided to pack up his things. He was determined to return home and wanted his friend to resume her life.

✷ ✷ ✷

That weekend, Simone was alone. She was waiting for her brother to arrive, since he had called to say he would visit her.

In her room, she tidied some things up when she experienced an unexplainable sensation. She could not see which spiritual friends were visiting her.

A wave of longing squeezed her heart while a different joy touched her soul. She sat up in her bed remembering her dear, beloved son.

At that moment, the spirit of Pedro approached her and wrapped her in all tenderness. It was perfect. A tall, handsome boy with considerable light.

"Thank you for everything, my dear mother." She felt emotional. "Thank you for the opportunity of life, for your care, for your love... For the days and nights you were with me, taking care of me. Staying in your arms, receiving your affection made me feel happy, relieved. It ended my fears, my pains. How warm you are, how tender you are, your sweet voice, your tenderness healed me in spirit. You cannot imagine it. It all passed. It was like a dream that ended. Your dedication resulted in an immense feeling of love, strength, growth and evolution for both of us." After a brief moment, he continued; "Mom, I know you didn't have to do everything you did for me. I made many mistakes in the past, but thanks to you I got up, I recovered. Today I know what love and affection is because of you. Now, right now, I know what I must give to others: all the affection, love and care that is within my reach. Before, I didn't know what that was. For that reason, I could not give what I did not have."

Tears ran down Simone's face, but it was not a cry of anguish, there was something different in her feelings that she could not explain.

"Mom, when you have my little brother in your arms, pray with him too, even if he doesn't understand yet. Your prayers led me to tranquility and your generous voice, as you pronounced those sharp words from your generous heart, made blessings of light shine out that you cannot imagine. My recovery, here on the spiritual plane, was easy and quick because of all you did for me. I will always be grateful and do anything for you if you need me. I will always love you. As for my father... Don't hate him. Understand that he has not yet been able to evolve. On the other hand, Cristiano…" The tears ran down his face and he stopped his words for a moment, but continued; "He will have my eternal gratitude and love. I will still pay for everything this wonderful creature did for me. He is an example of unconditional forgiveness: he was touched again."

And truly, Cristiano was a great example of forgiveness and love.

In the distant past, Cristiano and Samuel were brothers and were victims of Pedro, who, with the power offered by the Church, condemned them to terrible tortures in order to confess to witchcraft practices, which were unjustly accused.

Both died under the torturous barbaric tortures imposed by the cardinal of the Inquisition, who was Pedro. Disincarnated, when helped on the spiritual plane by a friendly and prepared group, Cristiano and Samuel met Simone, a friendly spirit from other times.

She cared for them and helped them in their clarification.

A Christian, a more understanding spirit, understood the inferiority and harshness of the cardinal who condemned him and was not offended or indignant. He believed in God and in the necessity of that sad experience.

Samuel, in turn, was hurt, he rebelled, despite the need for that terrible experience. In his heart, he never forgave Pedro, who, because of his cruel practices and persecution of his disincarnated victims, experienced centuries of pain, anguish and indescribable sadness in spirituality.

After a long time, he was helped and assisted by Simone, his dear sister, when he was incarnated.

She offered him the first and most important guide along with other kindly rescue partners.

After so much conscientious suffering, Pedro begged for relief and peace.

To get rid of hundreds of observers and persecutors, he had short reincarnations, in which the pregnancy was short-lived. By reincarnating through criminal abortion, he experienced some of the suffering he offered, especially when he felt every part of her body being torn in the procedure or burned by products intended to terminate the pregnancy.

On the spiritual plane, between one incarnation and another, Simone found him, guided him and helped him as much as she could.

Cristiano and Samuel, familiar spirits, also followed their suffering and painful experiences. But only Cristiano felt compassion and helped him with all his heart. Samuel, more hardened, thought he could forgive him, but that was not the case. He was satisfied with so much suffering.

In planning the reincarnation, Simone decided to welcome Pedro as a beloved son to get rid of the last remains of sad expiations that inhibited his evolution. Her purpose was to offer him love and protection from hardship so that he could learn.

Because of the need for a short experience with Samuel, who had the goal of forgiving and helping, Simone made him understand the benefits of, together, supporting Pedro in a short earthly experience with countless challenges.

It was an opportunity for Samuel to receive him as a son and love him unconditionally. An opportunity that should serve to soften his heart.

But that's not what happened. Samuel rejected his own son as soon as he learned of his difficulties. Now he would be a victim of himself.

Cristiano, in turn, although he did not need to support Pedro, was the one who supported him and loved him as if he were his own son.

Samuel lost the opportunity to learn, but that did not stop Pedro and the others from rising up.

Simone did not know why she felt that sweet longing at that moment. However, she felt good about the healthy energies she received.

Not much time passed and Pedro's spirit said goodbye.

"I leave, but I will always come back to visit you. I have a lot to learn here on the spiritual plane and I may have been here for years. I need guidance, experiences and spiritual knowledge." He smiled. "I intend to prepare myself for a future reincarnation much better than this one. If possible, with you. Who knows…"

After kissing her face for a long time, he said;

"Go with God. May Jesus illuminate your ways."

The spirit of Pedro had gone with the others.

Simone sighed and could not explain the happiness she experienced at that moment. She felt impregnated with something very good.

When Abner arrived with David, they came in and wanted to know how she was.

"I'm fine and I'm still in the reconstruction phase. After Pedro left…" Her voice cracked due to the emotion experienced a little earlier and for which she did not know the reason. She disguised it with a nice smile and then continued. "Despite knowing and preparing for everything that was going to happen to him, it is…" She was at a loss for words. "I miss him. This offers an indescribable emptiness. While Cláudio needed attention and came here, I felt useful again. But after he took off his cast and decided to leave…"

"When we deal with good things, we strive to do good, everything that is bad disappears. Do you remember the depression, the panic syndrome that Cris experienced?" Without waiting for her to respond, David continued. "It disappeared little by little since he met you, because you became interested in his difficulty, helped him… he resumed his life and therefore overcame his fears. Cristiano took care of others and, in fact, took care of himself. Today he does not take any medicine and feels well. It seems that he never lived in that state."

"I'm very grateful to him! You can't imagine."

"And he is grateful to you." Said David.

"I need to tell you something new." He said with a funny smile. "I'm packing my things because I'm moving out."

The brother looked at her in surprise and asked her;

"Are you and Cris going to live together?"

"No. We don't have anything scheduled. In fact, he doesn't even know I'm leaving this place."

"Where are you going?" Abner asked.

"I still don't know." She laughed, again, in a funny way. "I don't want to experience being evicted. That's why I'm leaving before."

"How so?" David was worried.

"Samuel was here and was very unsatisfied, especially when he saw Cláudio early in the kitchen door. Then he said that this house was for my comfort while I took care of Pedro. Since Pedro is no longer here…"

"Oh no! How absurd!" The brother was outraged. "I'll talk to this man and…"

"No, Abner! Please don't do anything." She interrupted.

"How could I not?"

"Please. I'm asking you. To be honest, I don't want to stay here. This house has a whole history between Samuel and me. A story that was good at first, but today it is no longer good. The time to move out, to get out of here is now." After a brief silence, she said. "I have already donated everything I bought for Pedro. Also... Furniture and utensils, I don't want anything. I will not wait for a lawsuit and a fight in court. I want him to sell this house and make the most of it. I don't know what I'm going to do with my share. As soon as possible, I will take my clothes and get out of here. It doesn't matter if I still don't have anywhere to go, if I don't have a car, if I don't have a neat job, if I don't have a house and I'm abandoned with a son my arms. None of that matters. I will find a way. I'm not and never have been a complacent person. I will work and get what I need."

"Wait." Asked David, concatenating his ideas. With delicacy to ask, since he thought she had forgotten about Pedro's death, he asked calmly. "Did you say abandoned with a son? How so?"

Simone laughed heartily and lit up when she said;

"Cris is going to be a father. He doesn't even know it. Nor do I know if he will want to take care of his son."

"Are you pregnant?" Exclaimed the incredulous brother.

"Today, a pharmacy test was positive, but Cris does not suspect. With so much going on, I was careless and... If I'm right, I think that when Pedro left, I was already pregnant and didn't know it."

The brother stood up and hugged her warmly. David did the same.

"Please, I don't want you two to tell anyone." She asked, laughing. "I just told you because I couldn't hold it anymore."

"Simone, what a blessing! Congratulations."

"Thank you, David." There was a brief pause and she joked. "So, people! I'm homeless, jobless, with a baby on the way and I can't even say I have clothes, because in a few months nothing will help. I also can't say if the father will take care of the baby." She laughed.

"You won't stay without a roof. No way!" Decided David, smiling. "By the way... We are very happy, because next month the apartment we bought at the plant will be delivered, remember?"

"Of course! How nice!"

"So... In it, for sure, there will be a very special room for our nephew."

"Thank you. It's good to know that I have so much support."

"You deserve it." Said the brother.

"Oh, guys... I'm kidding... I don't think I'm going to be homeless. Let me tell Cristiano and we'll decide what to do. With the sale of this house, I will get half and that will help. I can't deny that it's good money. Cláudio said it's okay for me to teach next semester at the other university where he teaches, but now, pregnant, I don't know if they will accept me." She laughed again and said; "And I just hope Cris doesn't abandon me."

"I doubt it! I know my brother! He loves you!"

"I know. I'm kidding."

At that moment the intercom rang. Simone got up and went to answer. Then she went to the door and returned with her father.

He had already noticed that Abner and David were there before he came in. But he didn't say anything and went in anyway.

In the living room, to her surprise, he greeted his son and held out his hand. And the same compliment was offered to David.

Seeing this peaceful atmosphere, Simone considered it convenient to leave them at ease so that, by themselves, something would emerge and they would speak again, so she decided;

"I'm going to make some really good coffee for us!" She said excited

"I will help you!" David decided, rising quickly and following her like a shadow. In the kitchen, smiling and shrinking, and holding David's arm, she whispered;

"And now! Either they talk…"

"Or they talk." The other one laughed.

In the living room, Mr. Salvador was embarrassed and Abner, without a theme. It didn't take long and he asked awkwardly;

"What about the apartment you bought? Are you there already?"

"It'll be given next month." He said with relief, noting that his father seemed friendly. "Now comes the nice part, which is the furniture and decoration."

"You like that, don't you?"

"I do like it. I appreciate joyful, life-giving things that offer peace."

"I never had a gift for decoration. I don't even know how to choose my clothes." He laughed. After a few minutes of silence he commented; "You and David also attend that spiritist center, right?"

"Recently, David can't go much because of a course. However, every time we can, we go. I like it there very much."

A little later, he looked up, looked at his son and decided to say.

"Abner, I know I'm a rude, tough man. I have no form with words or people." A long pause was felt. The son waited and the man continued; "I learned a little and I can even say that I improved my way, but I still have a lot to improve."

"What do you mean, dad?" He asked humbly, showing himself to be receptive.

"I mean, I don't approve of the life you lead or your condition, but... Damn it! You're my son! Damn it! I like you even though I think what you do is wrong! I'm proud of you for who you are, for what you do at work..."

"Oh dad!" He got up and went to the man, who also stood up. They hugged for a long time.

They had tears in their eyes and tried to hide their faces when they left the loving hug. The, the man said;

"I don't approve of your behavior because it's strange to me. I just heard that living together ends prejudice, so, if you allow me, I want to participate more in your life."

"Of course, dad! Of course!" In front of him, he confessed; "Today is the happiest day of my life." He got excited and hugged him again.

Meanwhile, Simone and David hugged each other and jumped for joy. When she screamed, he covered her mouth and hugged her laughing.

It was then that he invited his son;

"You and David could go home for lunch today. Your mother won't mind. She asked to take Simone. She doesn't even know I found you here."

"Yes! We'll go! With immense pleasure!"

Without delay, Simone prepared herself. She didn't even serve coffee. And everyone went to Mr. Salvador's house, to the surprise of Mrs. Celeste and Rúbia.

Ricardo was there. He had bought a souvenir for Bruno and went to give it to him. Taking advantage of the occasion, he expressed to Rúbia his bitterness about his son's trip.

It was almost lunchtime and Mrs. Celeste was very satisfied, she recalled;

"Only Cristiano and Janaina are missing. Addressing David, she asked him with love; "Oh, son, call them and invite them…or don't you want to go and look for them?"

"Not me! Call them, they'll come." He laughed, joking. So, it was done and Cristiano and his mother soon arrived. Mr. Salvador experienced satisfaction and joy in his home, having kind and true people around him.

He discovered that prejudice is ignorance. You cannot fight the inevitable. It's easier to understand. You live better and happier with differences.

Early in the evening, after leaving his mother at home, Cristiano went to Simone's house.

When he entered, he prepared a coffee and, while drinking, told what Samuel had said about the house.

"So that was it."

"What about you?" He asked.

"As I said, I'm determined. I don't want anything from here except half the value of this house. And what belongs to me."

"You are absolutely right." Caressing her hair, he proposed. "Come home. I'm sure my mother won't mind. And... That is until we get our situation in order. I have also saved half the value of the property I sold. The other part I gave to Vitória's family. It belonged to her. We can unit what you will have and... - He looked at her with a pleasant smile, observing her reaction."

Smiling sweetly, she asked;

"Is that an application or a proposal?"

"A summons!" He joked, kissing her. "As soon as your divorce comes through, we will definitely get married. For now, we can live together. I see no reason to wait. We're not kids, we know what we want. Do you agree?"

"Of course, I do. I don't want to raise a child without a father." Cristiano stopped for long seconds and concatenated the ideas.

He stared at her, while his face was drawn in a beautiful smile and asked amidst laughter.

"What?!"

"I was suspicious. I did a pharmacy test and it was positive. I made a doctor's appointment next week. However, I have no doubt."

He put his arms around her and kissed her as much as he could. There was so much happiness in that.

✳✳✳

The confirmation of Simone's pregnancy made everyone happy.

She moved into Mrs. Janaina's house; however, she and Cristiano had plans to get a place just for the three of them, although the boy's mother did not like the idea. She wanted them there.

Simone began teaching at the university where Cláudio found her a job. Not long after, Rúbia and Ricardo began to go out and make plans for the future.

Even before Simone and Cristiano's son was born, Rúbia and Ricardo married and moved together.

Only Mr. Salvador and Mrs. Celeste did not like that Bruno had to go with his mother. They were used to their grandson. However, every weekend, they were at their grandparents' house.

The family grew up. Everyone was happy with the arrival of Rafael, son of Simone and Cristiano, who was born perfect and healthy.

While visiting them, Cláudio, the faithful friend, commented;

"He's cute, isn't he? And has the face of Cristiano."

"Beautiful, cute and wonderful! Thank God." Said Simone smiling, looking tenderly at her son.

"You deserve to be happy, my friend."

"To tell you the truth, Cláudio... Deep down, I was afraid that Rafael would be born with some problem."

"God is good for those who are good, my dear. Your son is perfect." After a while, he looked for privacy and said; "Have you heard of Samuel?"

"No. The lawyer approached me and I only got the part that fit the house and... I never saw or heard from him again."

"He was fired from college and couldn't get a job anywhere. I learned from bad tongues that he started drinking and last week he crashed his car. It was ugly. Rosa, a teacher who taught on his blackboard, went to visit him. She said he is unrecognizable. He will be left with severe deformities and paraplegia."

"You're kidding!"

"I wouldn't play with that. You know me." After a moment, he commented; "And... Samuel ran away from work with his own son. Now, I want to see him run away from himself."

"Poor man." Lamented Simone.

Cristiano's approach ended the matter. Much later, when the friend left, Simone told her what had happened.

"Are you planning to visit him or do you want news in some way?"

"No, Cris. My time with him is over. If he comes to me seeking help, it will be different. I will think and want your opinion. Otherwise... I have a lot of work with this big guy here and with you." She laughed.

"Me?" He laughed. "Do I give you any work?"

"A lot! You can't imagine!" She joked, pinching him lightly. The husband kissed her and hugged her tenderly.

Some tests that we experience are really difficult and, at the time we live them, it seems impossible to overcome them. However, we can always do our best under God's blessings and discover that when we have faith, we are stronger than ever.

THE END

Schellida

More from Eliana Machado Coelho and Schellida

Aimless Hearts

The Shines of Truth

The Right to be Happy

The Return

The Silence of Passions

Force to Start Over

The Certainty of Victory

Lessons that Life Provides

Strongest than Ever

Without Rules to Love

A Dairy in Time

A Reason to Live

ELISA MASSELLI

Just Beginning

There is Always a Reason

Encounters with the Truth

Nothing is left without answers

Life is made by decisions

God was with Him

Books by
MÔNICA DE CASTRO & LEONEL

Despite Everything

Love is not to be played with

Head on with the truth

From my all being

Desire

The price of being different

Twins

Giselle, the lover of the Inquisitor

Greta

Till Live do us part

Heart Impulses

The Actress

The Force of Destiny

Secrets of the Soul

Memories that the wind brings

World Spiritist Institute
https://iplogger.org/2R3gV6

Milton Keynes UK
Ingram Content Group UK Ltd.
UKHW010736130823
426785UK00003B/45